Monetary Plurality in Local, Regional and Global Economies

The idea that each country should have one currency is so deeply rooted in people's minds that the possibility of multiple and concurrent currencies seems unthinkable. Monetary systems contribute to problems of high unemployment and social distress during financial and economic crisis, so reforms to increase the responsiveness and flexibility of the monetary system can be part of the solution.

This book discusses 'monetary plurality', which is the circulation of several currencies at the same time and space. It addresses how multiple currency circuits work together and transform socio-economic systems, particularly by supporting economies at the local level of regions and cities. The book shows that monetary plurality has been ubiquitous throughout history and persists at present because the existence of several currency circuits facilitates small-scale production and trade in a way that no single currency can accomplish on its own.

Monetary plurality can improve resilience, access to livelihoods and economic sustainability. At the same time, it introduces new risks in terms of economic governance, so it needs to be properly understood. The book analyses experiences of monetary plurality in Europe, Japan, and North and South America, written by researchers from East and West and from the global North and South. Replete with case studies, this book will prove a valuable addition to any student or practitioner's bookshelf.

Georgina M. Gómez is Associate Professor in Institutions and Local Development at the International Institute of Social Studies of Erasmus University Rotterdam, the Netherlands.

Financial History
Series edited by Farley Grubb and Anne L. Murphy

Reforming the World Monetary System
Fritz Machlup and the Bellagio Group
Carol M. Connell

Debt and Slavery in the Mediterranean and Atlantic Worlds
Edited by Gwyn Campbell and Alessandro Stanziani

Bonded Labour and Debt in the Indian Ocean World
Edited by Gwyn Campbell and Alessandro Stanziani

The Globalization of Merchant Banking before 1850
The case of Huth & Co.
Manuel Llorca-Jaña

Monetary Statecraft in Brazil
1808–2014
Kurt Mettenheim

Banking Modern America
Studies in regulatory history
Edited by Jesse Stiller

Money, Politics and Power
Banking and Public Finance in Wartime England, 1694–96
Richard A. Kleer

Regulation of the London Stock Exchange
Share Trading, Fraud and Reform 1914–1945
Chris Swinson

Monetary Plurality in Local, Regional and Global Economies
Edited by Georgina M. Gómez

For more information about this series, please visit www.routledge.com/series/FINHIS

Monetary Plurality in Local, Regional and Global Economies

Edited by Georgina M. Gómez

Routledge
Taylor & Francis Group
LONDON AND NEW YORK

First published 2019
by Routledge
2 Park Square, Milton Park, Abingdon, Oxon OX14 4RN

and by Routledge
52 Vanderbilt Avenue, New York, NY 10017

First issued in paperback 2020

Routledge is an imprint of the Taylor & Francis Group, an informa business

British Library Cataloguing-in-Publication Data
A catalogue record for this book is available from the British Library

Library of Congress Cataloging-in-Publication Data
Names: Gomez, Georgina, editor.
Title: Monetary plurality in local, regional and global economies / [edited by] Georgina M. Gomez.
Description: 1 Edition. | New York : Taylor and Francis, 2018.
Identifiers: LCCN 2018009213 | ISBN 9781138280281 (hardback)
Subjects: LCSH: Money. | Foreign exchange. | Banks and banking. | Sustainable development. | Monetary policy.
Classification: LCC HG221 .M81414 2018 | DDC 332.4/6—dc23
LC record available at https://lccn.loc.gov/2018009213

ISBN 13: 978-0-367-58759-8 (pbk)
ISBN 13: 978-1-138-28028-1 (hbk)

Typeset in Times New Roman
by Swales & Willis, Exeter, Devon, UK

To the memory of my father

Contents

Figures

Tables

Contributors

Jérôme Blanc is a Professor of Economics at Sciences Po Lyon (France). His works deal with money and the plurality of its forms and practices, mainly analysed through socio-economic lenses and in the history of ideas. In 2015, he co-founded RAMICS (Research Association on Monetary Innovation and Community and Complementary Currency Systems). He is a member of the Editorial board of the *International Journal of Community Currency Research (IJCCR)*. In addition, he has also written about social and solidarity economy and the history of monetary ideas.

Ludovic Desmedt is a Professor in Economics at the University of Burgundy and a member of the Laboratoire d'Economie de Dijon (LEDi). He is co-editor of the *Revue d'histoire de la pensée économique*. His research interests are focused on the history of economic thought and the evolution of banking practices. He has published several chapters and articles on these topics and co-edited two collective books: *Les pensées monétaires dans l'histoire* (with J. Blanc, 2014) and *Théories françaises de la monnaie* (with P. Alary, J. Blanc and B. Théret, 2016).

Marie Fare is an Associate Professor in Economics at the University of Lyon, France, and a researcher at the Triangle Laboratory (UMR 5206). Her research focuses on monetary plurality and more particularly on social and complementary currencies, analysed in relation to sustainable territorial development (potentialities, impacts and prospects). She is the author of a thesis on 'Monetary conditions for sustainable local development: complementary exchange systems for subsidiary currencies', supported in 2011. She co-organised the first 'International Week of Social and Complementary Currencies' in February 2011 in Lyon. She authored the book *Rethinking money, transforming territories, making society* (ECLM, 2016).

Georgina M. Gómez is an Associate Professor in Institutions and Local Development at the International Institute of Social Studies of Erasmus University Rotterdam. She obtained a PhD with distinction with a thesis on 'Community and complementary currency systems in Argentina'. She has published and supervised doctoral candidates on monetary innovation, local economic development in Latin America, social and solidarity economy, and institutional and grassroots economics.

Takashi Hashimoto is a Professor in the School of Knowledge Science, Japan Advanced Institute of Science and Technology. He received his PhD from the Graduate School of Arts and Sciences, University of Tokyo. He studies the origin and evolution of language, the dynamics of communication, and the formation and design of social institutions. He thinks that language and communication are at the core of human nature and that it is essential to design social institutions, including CCs and monetary systems. He has published 'Evolutionary linguistics and evolutionary economics' (*Evolutionary and Institutional Economics Review*, 3: 27, 2006).

Shigeto Kobayashi received his PhD in Knowledge Science from the Japan Advanced Institute of Science and Technology in 2010. He was a visiting fellow at the Department of Economics and Finance, University of Torino, Italy, in 2010. Since 2011, he has been an Assistant Professor at the Japan Advanced Institute of Science and Technology. His research focuses on institutional design in local communities. Two topics in his current research are the study of circulation mechanism of CCs using multi-agent simulation and gaming simulation, and the analysis and design of 'third place' where individual-oriented people co-exist with social-oriented people.

Ken-ichi Kurita has a doctorate in Economics from the Hokkaido University, Japan. He is now a part-time lecturer at Tokyo University Agriculture of Japan. He teaches administrative law and local development. His research is mainly on the community developments using CCs, municipal studies and regional revitalisation.

Akinobu Kuroda is a Professor of East Asian History in the Institute for Advanced Studies on Asia at the University of Tokyo. His interests cover comparative studies of monetary history on East Asia, India, Africa and Europe, as well as specific studies of China's monetary history. The concept of complementarity among monies which he has developed has been influential in monetary study, economic history and anthropology. He has argued that we can determine the characteristics of monetary system according to two binary oppositions: cohesive or anonymous in the relationship between persons making transactions; and fixed or flexible in the conversion between the currency for local transactions and that of inter-regional settlements.

Laurent Le Maux is a Professor in Economics at the University of Brest and researcher at the University of Paris Saint-Denis, France. He is co-editor of the *Cahiers d'Economie Politique* (*Papers in Political Economy*). Research interests include monetary and banking economics, central banking policy, history of monetary analysis, and money and banking in history. On these topics, he has published in the *Annales: Histoire Sciences Sociales*, *Cambridge Journal of Economics*, *History of Political Economy*, *Journal of Economic Surveys* and *Revue Economique*.

Jaime Marques-Pereira is a Professor in Economics at University of Picardie Jules Verne and member of its Centre de Recherche sur l'Industrie, les Institutions et les Systèmes Economiques d'Amiens, France. His current research interests are mainly focused on a policitical economy of monetary sovereignty and on the variety of capitalisms in peripheral economies. His recent contributions in these fields comprise several book chapters published in Latin America or articles in *Revue de la Régulation*, *Revue Tiers Monde* and *Economie et Institutions*.

Masahiro Mikami obtained his doctoral degree in economics in 2012 from Hokkaido University, Japan. He is an Associate Professor at the School of Business Administration, Meiji University, Japan. His main publications include 'Evolutionary aspects of Coasean economics' (*Evolutionary and Institutional Economics Review*, 8(1): 177–187, 2011) and 'Evolutionary foundations of Coasean economics: transforming new institutional economics into evolutionary economics' (*Erasmus Journal for Philosophy and Economics*, 6(1): 161–164, 2013).

Yoshihisa Miyazaki has a doctorate in Economics from Hokkaido University, Japan. He is now an Assistant Professor of Liberal Arts at the National Institute of Technology, Sendai College, Japan. His research interests include history of economic thought on CCs and endogenous development in rural areas.

Makoto Nishibe is a Professor in Evolutionary Economics at Senshu University, Japan, with a doctoral degree in economics from University of Tokyo. He is a professor emeritus of Hokkaido University, the President of the Japan Association for Evolutionary Economics and an executive board member of the Research Association on Monetary Innovation and Community and Complementary Currency Systems. His main publications include 'Theoretical model of institutional ecosystems and its economic implications' (co-authors, *Evolutionary and Institutional Economics Review*, 14(1), 2017), *The enigma of money* (Springer, 2016), *Community currency* (in Japanese, Minerva shobo, 2013), 'Globalisation: evolution of capitalistic market economy through "internalisation" of the market' (*Evolutionary and Institutional Economics Review*, 12(1), 2015) and 'Community currencies as integrative communication media for evolutionist institutional design' (*International Journal of Community Currency Research*, 16(D), 2012).

Pepita Ould-Ahmed is an economist, Research Fellow at the Institute of Research for Development (IRD) and member of CESSMA at the Paris Diderot University, France. She is co-editor of the *Revue de la Régulation*. She specialises in monetary issues involved in development. More specific areas of interest include money issues in a political economy perspective, complementary currency systems, microcredit, rotating saving and credit associations, monetary exclusion and solidarity, and the discourses and practices of debt, with a specific focus on Argentina, Morocco and Russia. She has published seven collections, two special issues and refereed journal articles. Recently, she published with Michel Aglietta and Jean François Ponsot *La monnaie. Entre dettes et souveraineté* (Paris, Odile Jacob, 2016) and *An anthropological economy of debt* with Bernard Hours (New York, Routledge, 2015).

Bruno Théret graduated in Engineering (Paris, 1970) and then received an MA in Economics (Paris Panthéon Sorbonne, 1971), an MA in Sociology (Paris Descartes, 1973) and a PhD in Economics (Paris Panthéon Sorbonne, 1990). He is an associated member of the CEIM, University of Québec at Montréal (UQAM), the CEI, Colegio de Mexico, and Catedra UNESCO sobre las manifestaciones actuales de la cuestion social, Instituto Torcuato di Tella and UNSAM, Buenos Aires. From 1972 to 1987 he worked at the Forecasting Office of the French Economy and Finance Ministry. He has been a member of several editorial and advisory boards of economics, history, sociology and political science journals. He has developed an institutional, historical, comparative and interdisciplinary perspective on relationships between politics and economics, federalism, systems of social protection, financial and monetary systems, and theories of the state and sovereignty. He has published many books and articles in different languages. His last book, co-edited with P. Alary, J. Blanc and L. Desmedt, is *Théories françaises de la monnaie. Une Anthologie* (Paris, PUF, 2016), and he is preparing the edition of *La monnaie contre l'Etat? La souveraineté monétaire en question*.

Wilko von Prittwitz und Gaffron has been Senior Lecturer in Business Studies at the Universidad Nacional de Educación a Distancia in Madrid, Spain since 2004. He received an MA degree from Emory University, Atlanta, USA and an MBA from the International Business School CEREM of the Universidad Rey Juan Carlos I, Spain. He specialises in Spanish local currencies and is a painter and expert on offset, aquatint and other etching techniques. In 2005 he created www.BilletesMunicipales.com, a systematised and unique online catalogue of emergency and other rare currency notes. He researched 'The social help and the role of money: historical, symbolic and social value' at Jaen University, Spain. He has completed his PhD on Sociology and Solidarity Economy at the Autonomous University of Madrid.

Acknowledgements

This book gathers together my thoughts about money and complementary currencies from a period of almost two decades. As such, I kindly remember the many persons that have been part of this journey. I especially wish to mention Professor Emeritus Bert Helmsing, Professor Jérôme Blanc, Professor Akinobu Kuroda and Rolf Schroeder, with whom I framed my thoughts in many engaging and lengthy discussions across several scenarios in the world.

I am indeed grateful to the persons that have collaborated in this project and indebted to their patience because the book publication has taken longer than it should have. I would mainly like to acknowledge the goodwill and positive attitude of the contributors during the production of this book. Working with researchers in three continents could have posed a challenge from the outset, and it was, instead, nothing but a pleasure. I am grateful to the work of the anonymous reviewers that also contributed to this collective project.

I would like to acknowledge the funding of the International Institute of Social Studies of Erasmus University Rotterdam through its Innovation Fund 2013. The grant allowed us to organise the 2nd International Conference on Complementary and Community Currencies: Monies for Development. Some of the papers presented in that event were the basis for chapters included in this volume. A research grant won by Akinobu Kuroda at the University of Tokyo made it possible to organise two other events on De-Teleologising the History of Money and Its Theory, held in Tokyo and Paris in 2014 and 2015, respectively. The series of events facilitated this book as well as the interaction of a network of researchers on monetary plurality and complementary currencies. The configuration of the network also supported the foundation of the Research Association on Monetary Innovation and Complementary and Community Currency Systems (RAMICS).

I especially thank the Civic Innovation Research Initiative, research programme of the International Institute of Social Studies, for stepping in to cover some of the production costs of this book. The grant includes the English proofreading and editing that Soumita Basu has performed with care and professionalism, as always. I wish her good health and, as they say in India, many returns of the day.

I am equally grateful to Paula Sánchez de la Blanca for her thorough and prolonged assistance in the preparation of this manuscript. She is a graduate who makes us proud.

I am indebted to the Routledge team of editors for their patience in the completion of this book through so many obstacles and delays that would be too long to detail.

I most especially thank family, friends and colleagues that fed my will to see it through.

– Georgina M Gómez

1 The monetary system as an evolutionary construct

Georgina M. Gómez

1.1 Introduction

The history of money reflects a story of innovation of several millennia in which agents and societies have experimented with a myriad of money-things and organisational models. A key feature of this long and creative construction relates to the dichotomy between plural and singular money systems. Monetary plurality is defined as the concurrent existence of more than one type of money in a particular space, as opposed to monetary singularity, which addresses a monetary system with one type of money. Monetary plurality may happen at the local, regional or national level, while monetary singularity occurs in the sovereign space of a country or monetary union where a legitimate authority can impose it. Money includes types of paper money as well as metal, commodities, tokens, and electronic and virtual payment systems. This introduction will unpack what we mean when we say 'more than one type of money'.

The issue has been debated for several centuries and it is far from settled. While most people nowadays are used to thinking along the principle of one currency per country, hundreds of agents and networks around the world are presently active in establishing parallel currencies at both the local and global levels. The latest arrival of digital currencies and the contestations of monetary unions like the Eurozone are further evidence that the construction is ongoing. They are indications that we are standing on another spot along the evolutionary path and that the organisation of money continues to be in progress.

This book comes at a timely moment to understand why the issue of monetary plurality versus singularity has not been settled. It aims to disclose how societies have dealt with the organisation of monetary systems along the tension of one versus multiple moneys and what led to their institutional choices and outcomes. It represents a collection from the production of two partially overlapping international research networks on monetary innovation, institutions and complementary currencies. These research groups met in the biennial conference on Complementary Currency Systems at the International Institute of Social Studies of Erasmus University Rotterdam in The Hague and in two workshops on De-Teleologising the History of Money and Its Theory in Tokyo and Paris. One of the prominent characteristics of this book lies in collecting the views of researchers in Europe, Japan and Latin America, and their studies in three continents.

The authors in this volume do not share a common view on monetary plurality per se but share an interest in understanding money as an institution, a product of social, economic and political life that is still in the making. An institution is defined as 'a socially embedded system of rules' and is characterised as the kind of social structure that matters most in the social realm (Hodgson, 2006: 2). Institutions, like all social structures, indicate regularity. They are, however, special social structures because they also signal the socially acceptable actions among several technically possible options. For instance, the institution of money comprises the unit of account that is acceptable to use as a standard of value to measure prices, savings, contracts, and debts. Other rules indicate the acceptable ways to obtain, keep, use, and convert money to other units of account. Monetary institutions also involve organisations that regulate money in the territory where it is valid, who is allowed to make it, what it looks like, and what happens to those that alter its appearance or counterfeit it. In this line, money is the object that binds stable patterns of interaction among social, political and economic agents for the actions mentioned (Gómez, 2009).

In terms of institutionalisation, a single money system is relatively a newcomer in economic history, while monetary plurality is not. Monetary singularity became normal with the consolidation of nation-states around the 19th century. From a political point of view, states considered it a priority to assert their sovereignty in their territory by unifying their money (Gilbert and Helleiner, 1999). It was not before the late 1800s that central banks were concerned with issuing a national currency and enforcing a monopoly on the issuance of money. In the case of Great Britain, the 1820s were occupied with a debate between two main positions, the Currency School and the Banking School (Ingham, 2004; Schwartz, 1989), which discussed monetary singularity against allowing for several issuers and currencies. As a result of these debates, England and Wales started having one currency in circulation issued by the central bank that enforced its monopoly over issuance decisions through the Bank Charter Act of 1844. In practice, however, monetary singularity was contested repeatedly. In the United States monetary plurality continued until later and it was only in 1907 that the Federal Reserve was given the 'mandate of providing a uniform and elastic currency' (Bordo, 2007).

Fractional monetary plurality, in particular, continued to be salient in most countries until the present day. It is known worldwide as the 'problem of small change' (Carothers, 1967) in reference to the small denomination coins and notes which cost more to be produced than their actual face value. The scarcity of small change affects everyday transactions, and especially low income buyers who spend a significant percentage of their income in daily necessities (Baubeau, 2014). It was one of the reasons why until a century ago there were moneys used by the rich and moneys used by the poor (Cohen, 1999), with combinations in between. The scarcity of small change even delayed the adoption of money, because it led to exclusion of segments of the population that could go by without money. They consumed their own production or bartered. The differentiation of uses of money by social strata is an issue still under scrutiny, as is their regional and local differentiation (see Gómez, Chapter 4; Gómez and von Prittwitz, Chapter 7; Fare, Chapter 10, all this volume).

In conceptual terms, monetary theory has been mostly fragmented in explaining monetary singularity and plurality (see Blanc et al., Chapter 2, and Blanc, Chapter 3, both this volume). There are several ways of organising money as Nigel Dodd asserts in his 2014 book, *The Social Life of Money*. One of the ways is to have one type of currency per sovereign country and bank notes issued by the state, normally through the Central Bank. Other agents, namely banks, multiply the monetary base by giving loans according to legal regulations, so that a vast majority of money used by the public is actually being created by the banks through these credit expansion mechanisms. It is a model centred on the principle of scarcity; frugality in issuing money by banks and politicians is celebrated as a virtue (Dodd, 2014).

However, that is not the only way to organise money and that is where monetary plurality comes in, Dodd (ibid.) continues. Complementary currencies may be specifically designed to benefit groups that earn irregular or small amounts of money (see chapter by Kobayashi et al. in this volume) or to empower issuers by taking back power from the central banks and private bankers, so that they can promote local economies and subnational finances, regenerate social ties, or encourage desirable behaviour such as volunteering and environmental sustainability (see chapters by Miyazaki and Kurita in this volume). To pursue these goals, complementary currencies tend to follow the principle of abundance, and issue as much money as needed to support the goals and the aspirations of the agents involved (see chapter by Fare in this volume). Monetary plurality, in general, has multiplied markedly in the last decades (Blanc, 2016). This book discusses monetary plurality in connection to these goals and is conceived as a theoretical and practical toolkit to explore the risks and potentials of monetary plurality.

1.2 Perspectives on the ontology of money

The distinction made by Dodd (2014) between the principles of scarcity and abundance in monetary systems reflects on an ontological issue. This subsection aims at unpacking the meanings of monetary plurality and singularity. It will first discuss the perspectives on the origins and meanings of money to further develop the distinctions between monetary systems with one or several types of money. Considering the diversity of money and that its history is almost as long as the human capacity to calculate and write, there is no simple answer to basic questions such as what money is and how it started (Smithin, 2000). What money is and does also depends on the time and place that we pose the question. Such contextualisation does not mean that we are unable to define it. It is a note of caution that says that the ontology of money requires us to not focus on the money-things but on the stable patterns of social interactions, in which agents measure value, make payments, cancel debts and keep savings. Moreover, not all money has performed these four primary functions at the same time or in the same ways (see chapters by Blanc et al., Gómez, and Kuroda in this volume).

Dodd's distinction of the two main perspectives of money follows, in fact, an original differentiation in Joseph Schumpeter's book *The Theory of Economic Development* (1961 [1934]). Schumpeter distinguished between a metallist and an anti-metallist conception of money. The metallist conception proposes that a commodity of intrinsic value emerged as preferred medium of exchange in barter-based markets. Metals and other goods considered to have intrinsic value had a predetermined limit fixed outside the economic system, so this conception builds on the principle of scarcity. It is the dominant view in economic and policy circles, at least since Menger published *On the Origin of Money* (1892). Instead, the anti-metallist conception emphasises the social production of money as an institution (Bell, 2001; Ingham, 1996; Wray, 1998) and centres on money as a unit of account that is created by credit relations (Ingham, 2004; Keynes, 1976 [1930]; Wray, 1998, 2004). Money created as debt-credit social relations is not limited to a predetermined amount of a money-thing with intrinsic value but is endogenously fixed within the economic system. Its issuance has a limit, of course, but the limit is posed by trust in the social rules and legitimate authority that regulates and sustains the social institution of money. Michel Aglietta (2002) and Charles Goodhart (1998) further develop the distinction as a realist versus an institutionalist approach, respectively. We will now take a closer look into both positions and their relations to the perspectives on the origins and meanings of money.

The dominant view among economists is the commodity theory of money, which has fed the realist or metallist position. It argues that a single money system arose because several money-things competed with each other until the most efficient one in terms of transaction costs eventually displaced the less efficient ones (Menger, 1892). Money changers acted as points of interphase between the single currency of one area and the single currency of other areas. The outcome of one country = one money is hence presented as the winning option after a period of competition in plural money systems. This account attracts and dominates policy circles because, apart from becoming a credible explanation, it justifies a policy option in their hands by securing the monopoly over the issuance of money.

From a historical point of view, there is a broad variety of objects that were used as means of payment in different settings and periods in time, used apparently to facilitate trade. Anthropologists' and historians' studies of 'primitive monies' include the cocoa beans of the Aztecs, the wampum of the North Eastern Mexican Indians, the cowrie shells of the African West Coast, tea blocks in Upper Asia and Siberia, dates in the Sivah-Oasis, wax cakes on the Amazon, cod fish in early Iceland, ivory and glass coral in Portuguese Africa, small strips of cotton and sugar in British West Indies and tobacco in Maryland and Virginia, among others in a very long list (Melitz, 1974). Primitive money, as it is often referred to, was always local, the chosen commodity was contextual, and payments were sometimes effected only once from one person to another for a specific purpose. Einzig (1966) underlined that whatever money-thing was used, its emergence marked a transition from a self-sufficient economy to one based on production for exchange, and later to general trade in markets with a large number of participants. In societies where trade played a major role, a general equivalent often developed spontaneously as means of payment.

According to this perspective, a certain commodity became acceptable as money 'when some alert people realised that they could benefit by holding greater stocks of the most marketable commodities than they had immediate use for' (Glasner, 1989: 6). Thus, the chosen commodity became means of payment and originated money in an attempt to reduce the transaction costs of barter (Menger, 1892), and solve the double coincidence of wants (Jevons, 2001 [1875]). This means that when there are means of payment, the problem of finding an immediate direct buyer and seller for a certain good is solved and the transaction costs of exchanging are minimised, hence making that commodity the most efficient channel to conduct trade. In this way, Melitz (1974: 77) defined money as 'all goods that are held in significant measure in order to economise on transaction costs in the activity of trading a variety of other types of goods'.

Moreover, the chosen money-thing can be hoarded to make payments later, so metals like copper, brass, gold and silver were preferred as common means of exchange. Metals have the key characteristics of durability, divisibility and portability. They were eventually standardised into coins and later industrialised with the appearance of the mint. Their value as means of payment was determined by the amount of the precious metal that they contained and, later on, by the amount that they represented. To economise on the use of metals and to avoid risky transportation, the amounts arose as a symbolic substitute for gold or silver (Wray, 1998). By then, the public had become used to the denominations of the various coins and notes, and these are the origins of fiat money, according to the commodity theory of money. For Hicks, each step represented 'ever more sophisticated ways of reducing transaction costs' (Hicks, 1967), as societies evolved from local tokens and stones to golden coins and then national bank notes to the most recent form of digital cash. From this perspective, money is a creature of the market, an efficient solution to facilitate exchange which is not related to any particular time or place or historical sequence.

This theory on the emergence of monetary singularity has been criticised from both the analytical and empirical angles. Among other arguments, some authors note that it is difficult to see how money could have been unified across civilisations that barely communicated with each other. Moreover, it is counterintuitive to think that this coinage could reduce the transaction costs of bartering (Goodhart, 1998; Wray and Forstater, 2006). Medieval coins were extremely varied in weight, denomination, alloy and fineness; they were chipped and adulterated in various ways, and sometimes they had the same face value but different exchange value. For example, in Merovingian Gaul there were 1200 currencies, most of them issued by private individuals (MacDonald, 1916 quoted in Wray, 1998). Besides, transaction costs could hardly have been the driving force behind creating monetary singularity. There were complex civilisations, advanced in production and trade and with a few million inhabitants like the Incas or the Phoenicians, that managed their economy without any kind of money (Melitz, 1974). John Maynard Keynes, unlike Hicks, considered that commodity money might have functioned as a 'convenient medium of exchange . . . but if this is all, we have scarcely emerged from a state of barter' (Keynes, 1976 [1930]: 3). There is more to the origins of a single money than the preference for a commodity. This explanation on the evolution from gold to scrip is not credible, especially after the abandonment of the gold standard and the dissemination of electronic and digital money.

The alternative draws from sociology and heterodox economics as an institutional theory of money. This version does not dispute that specific commodities have originated as a means of payment throughout history but rejects that these were self-organised choices that resulted from the inherent efficiency of one of these money-things. Instead, Ingham argues that a monetary system is a set of institutions embedded in a society (1996, 2004, 2006). The construction of money follows an evolutionary structuration process along the social, economic and political needs, and possibilities that rose with impersonal exchange (Seyfang and Pearson, 2000). When a community grows, it requires a standard and stable unit of account as reference of value (Aglietta, 2002). The money-thing was present but its transition as unit of account was not spontaneous.

The institutionalist view has several strands because they emphasise different aspects. One strand places the origin of money as credit money and argues that it did not emerge out of barter but out of obligation to cancel debts with various authorities, such as sovereigns or priests to whom religious payments had to be made (Wray, 1998, 2004). These local, religious or community authorities would create a unit of account when they proclaimed that they would accept certain money-things at explicit values to cancel taxes and religious debts. While barter was used for local and small trade, larger transactions such as dowries and inter-regional trade were conducted on the basis of credit (Innes, 1913).

The oldest archaeological findings of money are consistent with this perspective. The tallies were written promises to cancel debts; they were 'sticks of squared hazel wood, notched in a certain manner to indicate the amount of the purchase' found abundantly in old Mesopotamia (Wray, 1998: 40). They were already being used 2000 years before the oldest known coins were minted (Ingham, 2001). They were frequently transferable and negotiable so that clearing between several merchants holding tallies from the same creditor/debtor was possible. When coins were developed, they were renovated versions of the tally: evidences of debt (Wray, 1998) that could be transferred and written off against one another.

Indeed, the next important innovation in the evolution of money was the technique to expand personalised debt relations into anonymous credit money that could circulate and balance out against each other. When trade resumed in the Mediterranean in medieval times, the equivalent of bankers arrived on the scene in northern Italy. These bankers exchanged local coins for those of other cities. Gradually, rather than giving actual coins, they started giving bills of credit and they kept the gold in store. And then they started issuing more bills than the actual coins they had in stock because they could balance the deposits of one client with the payments of another and people were unwilling to carry physical gold. Even if payments continued to be named for much longer, they were transferable, so it was possible to balance them out among customers and bankers. Banks became clearing houses instead of creators of money 'with the stroke of a pen' (Glasner, 1989).

The networks of merchants and bankers met regularly to transfer and cancel debt and credits in several local currencies. A market for bills of exchange emerged, when trade along and beyond Europe became active (Boyer-Xambeu et al., 1994). Bills eventually were detached from any direct relationship to actual commodities and, rather, began to serve as autonomous media of exchange and means of payment. Eventually, credit became detached from both goods and persons, transforming a deferred payment scrip system into money that could circulate anonymously. The value of these liabilities depended on the willingness of people to hold them (Glasner, 1989), and they were specifically designed to scale up credit instruments in larger networks of users (Kim, 2011).

John Maynard Keynes (1976 [1930]) argued that the transition to full transferability of bills of exchange was a major structural innovation in the evolution of money: while barter is bilateral and local, transferable money makes it possible to develop an extensive multilateral decentralised market around the world. This was a plural money system, in which private credit-monies based on bills of credit became integrated with metal coinage minted by kings and authorities at explicit units of account. Monetary plurality hence incorporated public and private monies. Depersonalised, transferable promises of pay were thus woven into deep and complex layers of debt in which the trustworthiest notes were kept as base money to back the rest of the system.

The monetary system continued to evolve when states themselves joined in issuing promises to pay, accompanied with some pressure for their acceptance (Wray, 1998). The Bank of England in 1694 was the benchmark state institution created to organise these layers of credit, although it was not until almost 150 years later that it started imposing the circulation of its own promises of payment to crowd out private golden coins in England and Wales (Ingham, 1999). In the 19th century, states started centralising the monetary system under monopoly control and outlawed third-party issuers and currencies, such that money became a creature of the nation-state at the outset of modernity. The monopoly, however, is still incomplete and contested (see chapters by Théret, Blanc et al., and Kuroda in this volume).

Schumpeter considered that the transformation of long-term debt and other illiquid assets into short-term instruments or money with a set unit of account was the quintessence of capitalist monetary practice (Schumpeter, 1994 [1954]: 613). Third-party debts are cancelled by other third-party debts, although this can be done, at least initially, only within social networks in which there is either minimum trust that credits will be honoured or built in institutions to penalise an untrustworthy payer. It allowed for the expansion of the system and a number of other institutions appeared to support this monetary system. It produced a qualitative transformation in credit-debt relations and in monetary production to dematerialised or abstract money. As Ingham (1999: 80) reminds us, credit money was not only a facilitator of exchange but a 'transformative power'. Monetary plurality is compatible with the credit-money approach and historically, several currencies coexisted. The poor, for instance, used mainly low denomination tokens, mostly privately issued and not easily convertible into the monies of the wealthy (Gilbert and Helleiner, 1999). Money creation is decentralised and expands with the establishment of every new credit-debt relationship.

This endogeneity of monetary creation was already understood by Keynes (1930) and is the foundation of post-Keynesian monetary theory. It is critically at odds with the commodity perspective of money. In *The Philosophy of Money*, Georg Simmel (1982 [1900]) presented a view that resolves the tension between the two perspectives, to some extent. Simmel argued that money is a norm in the sense of an abstract expression of a community that establishes social relations of trade and sets shared mental structures. While trade creates social interaction, money appears as an abstract object out of these interactions and subsequently reinforces trade relations and trust on the unit of account. As it is an intersubjective abstraction to express value, money is based on trust in the community where the units of account originate and which builds 'communities of payments'. This explanation leaves open the possibility of monetary plurality if various communities of payments coexist and trade across them is enabled by stable exchange rates. However, there is still the question of how stable relationships among units of account are reached.

Several authors (for example, Wray, 1998; Ingham, 2004; or Keynes, 1976 [1930]) underscore that the definition of the unit of account by the collective authority was key in the transition to monetary singularity. Tax collection expressed an exchange rate at which different commodities would be accepted for the obligations owed to the state. In times when there were countless types of coins, the authority's measurement was used to value the many forms of commodity money in circulation into a single unit of account. Acceptance by the state also indicated a hierarchy between monies (Bell, 2001) and, in the long run, it would steer the system towards the money accepted by the state. In other words, the actions of the state established a preference for monetary singularity. Later on, the state consolidated the central position of its money by the rule of law, coercion and force (Aglietta and Orlean, 2006), so the state wiped out other units of account and currencies. Still, the principle of abundance was not ruled out; money was primarily a unit of account, so other credit moneys could circulate and were not limited to a fixed amount.

Another strand within the institutional perspective of money offers a different view on the role of the state and monetary singularity. It argues that the role of the authority did not stop at choosing a specific money-thing and guaranteeing the value of the unit of account (Aglietta, 2002; Aglietta and Orlean, 2006; Goodhart, 1998) but includes creating a single acceptable money-thing. The state became the monetary authority and imposed an abstract means of payment that served as symbol of its sovereignty, its capacity to levy taxes and to indicate what currencies were legitimate across its territory (Goodhart, 2006). Once the state decided to declare one type of money as the valuable money-thing (gold or whatever was accepted as payment for taxes), others had to use it. Aglietta (2002: 50) characterises the centralisation process as 'interlocking networks of networks with the central bank at their fulcrum'.

The state centralised the issuance of coins from bullion to standardised stamped coins and later, fiat money. The theory hence receives the name of Cartalist approach, from the Italian 'carta' for paper and was elaborated by Knapp (1973 [1924]). It establishes a division of labour in which there are two types of social actors in a centralised monetary system: those who make money (the state) and the public that uses it (Ingham, 1996). In the 19th century, 'the forging of national, uniformed monetary systems was a central project undertaken by states across the world' (Gilbert and Helleiner, 1999: 4). As central and only issuer, the state could easily decide on the limit of issuance. It could apply the principle of scarcity, consistent with its desire to affirm its control over the economy.

The origin of modern money was thus intimately related to the nation-state (Goodhart, 1998) and modernity. An important critique of the Chartalist approach argues that money existed as a social construction long before the nation-state came to impose the principle of control and scarcity into the system. In rigour, this theory explains the completion of the modern money system based on monetary singularity and it is not incompatible or separate from the credit-debt perspective to the origin of money. There is a historical gap of a few thousand years before the nation-state appeared in the long evolution of money. Several currencies were used in distant trade long before there were official monetary systems, before nation-states used it as a symbol of sovereignty and before rational authorities collected taxes (Seyfang, 2001). However, in present times, modern money is centred on the state which implies that the modern monetary system embeds the many limitations and failures of states (see chapters by Théret in this volume).

Based on these perspectives on what money is and how it developed, we can now unpack the meanings and origins of monetary plurality and singularity (Table 1.1).

1.3 Modern money and monetary singularity

The long and innovative process of organisation of the modern monetary system converges on the principle that one country = one money. The role of the nation-state was critical, but it is not the only factor that supported the social construction of modern money as, primarily, a creature of modernity. Aglietta (2002) identified three parallel processes that led to the institutionalisation of modern money, defined as a depersonalised, dematerialised, abstract, transferable promise to pay (Smithin, 2000). The first force in the construction of modern money is a process of abstraction and consequent separation from persons and physical money-things. In the credit theory of money, credit-debt relations depended on the trustworthiness of the issuers. With the scaling up of the monetary system, money became increasingly dematerialised and abstract, and separated from the issuers. Modern money is anonymous, depersonalised and abstract, hence the perfect foundation for modern rationality, as Max Weber expressed it (1978). Abstract money is compatible with monetary singularity as well as plurality. A second process in the construction of modern money is the social and political control over 'monetary spaces' (Ingham, 2002). Monetary singularity implies that the state concentrates

Table 1.1 What does monetary plurality and singularity mean?

PLURALITY	*SINGULARITY*
Institutionalist approach	Realist approach
Anti-metallist tradition	Metallist tradition
Social production of money: credit relations	Technical production of scarce commodity
Creature of social interaction: issued by collective authority to organise measurement of value (state, banks or other agents)	Creature of market trade: money solves coincidence of wants and transaction costs
Ruled by principle of abundance	Ruled by principle of scarcity
Frugality of issuer may be harmful	Frugality of issuer perceived as a virtue
No physical collateral as intrinsic value	Commodity of intrinsic value
Value determined within the social, political and economic system (limited by trust and authority)	Value determined exogenously (limited to availability of commodity)
Several means of payment perform different functions complementing each other	Several means of payment compete until one is proven to be the most efficient
Marginalised view in policy circles	Dominant view in policy circles
Time and space simultaneity of more than one currency seen as positive for local development. Agents deal with currencies in the same time and space.	Time and space simultaneity of more than one currency seen as temporal anomaly. Money changers as points of intersection between currencies
Normally small-scale circulation, locally or in social networks	Large-scale, national circulation, within and between countries
Associated with primitive and traditional societies	Associated with modernity

Source: Own elaboration

this control. The third dimension of modern monetary systems is its centralised administration around the state and banks as key issuers, as opposed to the decentralised nature of credit relations and concurrent commodity currencies. Different issuers require decentralised information about each other, which is not always as available or easy to get as when information is centralised.

The centralised information typical of monetary singularity systems only reduces uncertainty if states or other central authorities function. In episodes of war and severe distress, monetary singularity is suspended because many other institutions that sustain monetary singularity have fallen apart as well (see Chapter 7 by Gómez and von Prittiwitz in this volume). The failures of states beg us to ask why monetary singularity is so often seen as the superior, and often, the only option. There is a missing link in explaining monetary singularity and modern money as creatures of the state and which is rarely considered in the analysis of money as an institution of modernity.

By definition, institutions are resistant to change and based on habit (Hodgson, 2006, 2007), which is a critical characteristic in stabilising the system. Once economic agents started using a certain unit of account and means of payment in their daily economic life, modern money became a 'habit of thought' (Veblen, 1899). We will explore this concept further. Habits are submerged inventories of possibilities to guide human behavior and they can be retrieved by an appropriate context. Following Veblen, habits are defined as 'a causal mechanism, not merely a set of correlated events' (Hodgson, 2004: 653), so reasoning and beliefs rely on habits of thought with which agents interpret social life. In addition, a hidden and most salient characteristic of institutions is their capacity to shape agents' aspirations. As expressed by Hodgson: 'Because institutions not only depend upon the activities of individuals but also constrain and mould them, this positive feedback gives institutions even stronger self reinforcing and self perpetuating characteristics' (Hodgson, 2004: 656). Monetary singularity for several generations has been the norm and has shaped the interpretations and understandings of what modern money is.

In short, the approach to modern money as an institution implies adopting the non-rational elements of institutional thought and incorporating its habitual component in the analysis (see Kobayashi et al., Chapter 11, and Mikami and Nishibe, Chapter 12 in this volume). Swanke (2004) follows this line in analysing the origins and meanings of money, and asserts that:

> [t]he people who started this habitualised behaviour pattern almost certainly did not plan to create an institution. The institution is created when new people begin to interact with those who act in the habitualised way and the newcomers adopt the habitualised behaviour. The newcomers take the habituated actions as objects that create an institution.
>
> (Swanke, 2004: 87)

The current reappearance of a myriad of complementary currencies and modern versions of monetary plurality (Blanc, 2012) do not happen in an institutional tabula rasa but face the challenge of standing against the habits of over a century of experience in which monetary singularity is apparently the rule (see Kobayashi et al., Chapter 11, and Mikami and Nishibe, Chapter 12, both this volume). Projects of complementary currency hence proclaim a desire to repersonalise money and the economy, decentralise its organisation, and reclaim control over a territory (see Gómez, Chapter 4; Kuroda, Chapter 6; Fare, Chapter 10; and Miyazaki and Kurita, Chapter 9, all this volume). In addition, monetary plurality is endorsed by the power of the nation-state, which is being challenged from a number of different angles by the apparent transition of the human race to postmodernity. It is no wonder that monetary plurality surges in periods of war, socioeconomic demise and political affirmation of non-state agents (see Théret, Chapter 8, and Gómez and von Prittwitz, Chapter 7, both this volume).

A key scholar in the old institutionalist tradition, Veblen (2006 [1914]: 6) claimed in *The Instinct of Workmanship* that:

> [t]he higher the degree of intelligence and the larger the available body of knowledge current in any given community, the more extensive and elaborate will be the logic of ways and means interposed between these impulses

> and their realisation, and the more multifarious and complicated will be the apparatus of expedients and resources employed to compass those ends that are instinctively worthwhile.

This book aims at increasing the available body of knowledge to understand the tension between monetary plurality and singularity with an aim to gain insight in their implications. Thus, it presents a collection of current research on theories and practices from several continents.

1.4 Contributions in this volume

Our first step in the journey to understand and make sense of monetary plurality was to review how monetary theory understands the tension between plurality and singularity. In Chapter 2, Jérôme Blanc, Ludovic Desmedt, Laurent Le Maux, Jaime Marques-Pereira, Pepita Ould-Ahmed and Bruno Théret review a wide canvas of the literature on monetary theory. They organise monetary theories along two key criteria: money neutrality versus their significance in terms of their effects on the rest of the economic system, and plural versus singular monetary systems. The study covers several views on monetary plurality from the New Monetary Economics to the Free Banking model, in addition to different approaches to monetary singularity from the point of view of Walrasian, Chartalist, post Keynesian and Marxist theories. The authors opt to focus their research on the plurality of means of payment and units of account. They find that theories allow for all sorts of combinations of plurality and singularity of these two elements. For example, there are configurations of a single unit of account with several means of payment, or several issuers with one or more units of account. The spectrum of theories hence ranges from strong to weak singularity and from strong to weak plurality depending on the combinations of these two criteria. Looking at the diversity of approaches on the tension between monetary plurality and singularity indicates that the search for a theoretical framework to account for monetary plurality would not come from economics alone.

Jérôme Blanc takes the challenge in Chapter 3 and adopts a multidisciplinary approach to account for monetary plurality. The search for a theoretical framework leads to the instruments developed by Karl Polanyi, namely the distinction between all-purpose money and special-purpose money. Moreover, Polanyi proposed three or four forms of integration of economic activities into socioeconomic systems: exchange, redistribution, reciprocity and, depending on the stage of his analysis, a fourth one called communal sharing. The relation between these institutionalised systems and monies resulted in a rich categorisation with three ideal types: public money, business money and associative money. The analysis facilitates the understanding of real cases, including modern money and other contemporary complementary currencies. At the same time, the framework suggests an inseparable relation between individual activity, monetary plurality and the institutions that bring them together.

The same direction is followed in Chapter 4, where Gómez adopts a Polanyian approach to the economy as instituted process. The chapter conceptualises currency circuits as stable social structures that connect a currency with specific products and categories of agents. Based on the case of Argentina, during the crisis of 1998 to 2005, the author analyses how agents dealt with monetary plurality by matching each currency to the four functions of money: accountancy, exchange, payments and savings. There were five different types of currencies circulating at the same time at the national, regional and community level. The research discloses that households and small businesses can deal with monetary plurality by organising what currencies they use for what purpose, without converting one currency into another. What is more important, having different levels of currencies facilitates access to goods and services for segments of the population that would not have had any money or ways to satisfy their needs at all, which offsets the extra transaction costs involved. Monetary plurality enabled production and the use of skills that were idle, hence showing that several currencies could do more than any one currency.

Bruno Théret reaches a similar conclusion in Chapter 5, also based on the experience with money in Argentina. The chapter develops the concept of monetary federalism with the methodology of grounded theory. That is, exploring the recurrent episodes in which the provincial governments issued currency at the subnational level between 1890 and 2003. Monetary federalism refers to a specific design of monetary systems that accommodate the interests of subnational entities (states, provinces, landers, cantons) that share the decisions over the monetary system. Théret aims at explaining why Argentina presents such a strong inclination towards monetary federalism and what the implications were. Monetary federalism represents a middle way between the prevailing dichotomy between fragmenting the international currency system and allowing for the appropriation of monetary policy in territories that share a single currency and also show significant disparities in their geographic, social, economic and political systems. The author suggests that the experience of Argentina may inspire solutions to monetary unions such as the Eurozone.

The reasons underpinning monetary plurality and its enabling conditions are even broader than the alternative of monetary federalism, as suggested in Chapter 6. The issuance of local currency depends on the preferences and social cohesion of local groups, the roles of local elites and their regional self sufficiency. Akinobu Kuroda adopts a historical perspective with empirical evidence of China and Europe to find out why local currencies have been recurrent despite political pressures towards monetary singularity. The author shows that a certain percentage of currency tends to disappear as it circulates, so currency-dependent societies recurrently suffer its shortages and fall into recession. This phenomenon is called 'famine of cash' in China and causes economic stagnation at the local level. With the aim of escaping such economic downturns, local actors create their own means of exchange to conduct local trade and increase the stability of their local economies. A second pattern is the use of credit, and although at the local level there may be high level of trust, there is also non-performance. That means this alternative of credit instead of local currency is equally problematic, although for different reasons. In a third path, when local elites concentrate a significant proportion of the local trade, they are also able to create local currency circuits. In that case, they would issue tokens that cannot be exchanged for goods from outside the locality, but which are conducive to keeping alive the trade for local necessities. The social structure in each locality defines the transaction and currency solution to avoid local economic crisis.

With evidence from several cases of crisis, Gómez and von Prittwitz in Chapter 7 substantiate that episodes of war and social, economic and political demise have been conducive to the creation of complementary currencies. The pattern has been pervasive for several centuries and establishes a clear link between crisis and monetary plurality, although the authors analyse in depth only the 20th century. The chapter results from an unlikely collaboration between a numismatic amateur and a social scientist, in which the authors followed the money-things and scrip during countless hours of archival work. They study the emergency currencies of the postwar period in Europe, the hyperinflation, the Great Depression and the Spanish Civil War. These were all periods during which unknown money was better than no money at all for most of the local agents. The authors conclude that the emergence of complementary currencies during episodes of severe crisis is not only designed as a temporary solution, but that they sometimes also express the desire to take the crisis as windows of opportunity to pursue structural changes and rebuild the world according to local possibilities and aspirations.

As a further illustration of that conclusion, in Chapter 8 Bruno Théret focuses on one specific case in which the governors, the local business elites and several groups in the population converged on creating and sustaining a subnational currency. The chapter studies the complementary currency issued by the Argentinian province of Tucuman between 1985 and 2003, called Bocade. It examines why it was issued, how it functioned at its outset and how it evolved. Théret corroborates that this experiment was not simply the result of a situation of emergency, as was already hinted by Gómez and von Prittwitz, but had its political and symbolical rationality. The case of Tucuman represents a structural effort to create a longer-term device to gain autonomy, strengthen the provincial fiscal accounts in the long run, increase economic resilience and promote local economic development.

Under different conditions, complementary currencies in some areas in Japan are designed precisely to avoid serious crisis. Monetary plurality appears as an instrument to promote local economic development and environmental sustainability in hilly and mountainous regions that critically depend on engaging volunteers. With aging and shrinking populations in the hilly and mountainous areas in Japan, a shortage of workers has resulted in degraded forests and threatened ecosystems. In Chapter 9, Yoshihisa Miyazaki and Ken-ichi Kurita study how community currencies affect forest and ecosystem sustainability, promote community involvement, and local economic development. They conduct a survey questionnaire of volunteers and non-volunteers and find that community currencies facilitate the regional circulation of labour of forest volunteers, local products and wood, and money, thereby supporting local economic development projects.

Marie Fare follows the thread of local economic development in Chapter 10, from the perspective of sustainable territorial development and monetary subsidiarity. In view of the economic and environmental challenges that many communities around the world are exposed to, community and complementary currencies appear as an option in the inventory to look into. Fare explores the contributions and limitations of complementary currencies by looking into empirical studies of the SOL Alpin in Grenoble, France, and the Accorderie in Quebec, Canada. The author discusses the use of complementary currencies from the principle of monetary subsidiarity. Each currency circulating in complementary mode on a subnational scale is perceived as being developed and issued at the relevant level in relation to the socioeconomic and geographic conditions. Fare concludes that, in the two cases she studied, monetary plurality did not reach the necessary scale to have a significant impact on local economic development. However, the complementary currencies had important effects for the populations involved.

Chapter 11 delves deeper into institutional and evolutionary theory with evidence of several cases of monetary plurality. Shigeto Kobayashi, Takashi Hashimoto, Ken-ichi Kurita and Makoto Nishibe conceive a theoretical framework to explain the micro-meso-macro connection between complementary currencies and individuals' understandings of monetary plurality. Only a few community currencies have achieved high circulation and maintained a certain economic scale over a long period. They draw on conceptual tools of behavioural psychology to show that users of complementary currencies place more importance on monetary plurality and shared notions of fairness than the employees of financial organisations. This characteristic was evident among agents that had a deeper insight into complementary currencies. The authors conclude that the individuals' perceptions of monetary plurality are fundamental in creating and sustaining complementary currencies at the institutional or meso level. In the opposite direction, the direct experience with complementary currencies improves individuals' perceptions, indicating a feedback loop between individual cognition at the micro level and institutional compliance at the meso level.

Chapter 12 presents a game simulation developed in Japan that confirms that complementary currencies change an individual's dispositions and perceptions. Using behavioural analysis of self-versus-community consciousness, Masahiro Mikami and Makoto Nishibe design an experiment based on a mutual credit system with 18 agents. The authors simulate a centrally issued electronic complementary currency to test in what ways its actual use affected the perceptions of the participants. They propose that participants' cognition and behaviour would change as they gained insight into the potential and pitfalls of complementary currencies. They examine the extent to which participants' behaviour patterns changes depending on the transaction costs of the currency, participants' consciousness about self and community, and the availability of aggregate information on the transactions and activities within the community. They find that the most significant factor to support complementary currencies is whether participants prioritise community over self-interest.

References

Aglietta M. 2002. Whence and whither money? In: OECD, ed. *The Future of Money*. Paris: OECD. 31–72.

Aglietta M and Orlean A. 2006. *Money Between Violence and Trust*. Moscow: Publishing House HSE.

Baubeau, P. 2014. L'histoire de France en 'vignettes': deux siècles de circulation fiduciaire. *Revue numismatique* 6(171):631–653.

Bell S. 2001. The role of the state and the hierarchy of money. *Cambridge Journal of Economics* 25(2):149–163.

Blanc J. 2012. Thirty years of community and complementary currencies: a review of impacts, potential and challenges. *International Journal of Community Currency Research* 16(D):1–4.

Blanc, J. 2016. Unpacking monetary complementarity and competition: a conceptual framework. *Cambridge Journal of Economics* 41(1):239–257.

Bordo M. 2007. *A Brief History of Central Banks*. Cleveland, OH: Federal Reserve Bank of Cleveland.

Boyer-Xambeu M-T, Deleplace MG and Gillard L. 1994. *Private Money and Public Currencies: The Sixteenth Century Challenge*. London: Sharpe.

Carothers N. 1967. *Fractional Money: A History of the Small Coins and Fractional Paper Currency of the United States*. New York: AM Kelley.

Cohen BJ. 1999. The new geography of money. In: Gilbert E and Helleiner E, eds. *Nations-States and Money. The Past, Present and Future of National Currencies*. New York and London: Routledge. 121–138.

Dodd N. 2014. *The Social Life of Money*. Princeton, NJ: Princeton University Press.

Einzig P. 1966. *Primitive Money*. London: Pergamon Press.

Gilbert E and Helleiner E, eds. 1999. *Nation-States and Money. The Past, Present and Future of National Currencies*. London, New York: Routledge.

Glasner D. 1989. *Free Banking and Monetary Reform*. Cambridge, UK: Cambridge University Press.

Gómez GM. 2009. *Argentina's Parallel Currency: The Economy of the Poor*. London: Pickering & Chatto.

Goodhart CAE. 1998. The two concepts of money: implications for the analysis of optimal currency areas. *European Journal of Political Economy* 14(3):407–432.

Goodhart CAE. 2006. Monetary and social relationships. In: Wray R and Forstater M, eds. *Money, Financial Instability and Stabilization Policy*. Cheltenham, UK: Edward Elgar. 22–36.

Hicks J. 1967. *Critical Essays in Monetary Theory*. Oxford, UK: Clarendon Press.

Hodgson GM. 2004. Reclaiming habit for institutional economics. *Journal of Economic Psychology* 25:651–660.

Hodgson GM. 2006. What are institutions? *Journal of Economic Issues* 40(1):1–25.

Hodgson GM. 2007. Institutions and individuals: interaction and evolution. *Organization Studies* 28(1):95–111.

Ingham G. 1996. Critical survey: some recent changes in the relationship between economics and sociology. *Cambridge Journal of Economics* 20:243–275.

Ingham G. 1999. Capitalism, money and banking: a critique of recent historical sociology. *British Journal of Sociology* 50(1):76–96.

Ingham G. 2001. Fundamentals of a theory of money: untangling Fine, Lapavitsas and Zelizer. *Economy and Society* 30(3):304–323.

Ingham G. 2002. New monetary spaces? In: OECD, ed. *The Future of Money*. Paris: OECD. 123–45.

Ingham G. 2004. *The Nature of Money*. Cambridge, UK: Polity Press.

Ingham, G. 2006. Further reflections on the ontology of money: responses to Lapavitsas and Dodd. *Economy and Society* 35(2):259–278.

Innes AM. 1913. What is money? *Banking Law Journal*:377–408.

Jevons WS. 2001 [1875]. *Money and the Mechanism of Exchange*. London: Elibron Classics.

Keynes JM. 1976 [1930]. *A Treatise on Money*. New York: Harcourt, Brace and Co.

Kim J. 2011. How modern banking originated: The London goldsmith-bankers' institutionalisation of trust. *Business History* 53(6):939–959.

Knapp GF. 1973 [1924]. *The State Theory of Money*. Clifton, NY: Augustus Kelley.

MacDonald G. 1916. *The Evolution of Coinage*. Cambridge, UK and New York: Cambridge University Press and G.P. Putnam's Sons.

Melitz J. 1974. *Primitive and Modern Money*. Reading, MA: Addison Wesley.

Menger K. 1892. On the origin of money. *Economic Journal* 2(6):239–255.

Schumpeter J. 1994 [1954]. *History of Economic Analysis*. London: Allen & Unwin.

Schumpeter JA. 1961 [1934]. *The Theory of Economic Development: An Inquiry into Profits, Capital, Credit, Interest, and the Business Cycle*. New York: Oxford University Press.

Schwartz AJ. 1989. Banking school, currency school, free banking school. In: Eatwell J, Milgate M and Newman P, eds. *Money*. London and Basingstoke, UK: Palgrave. 41–49.

Seyfang G. 2001. The euro, the pound and the shell in our pockets: rationales for complementary currencies in a global economy. *New Political Economy* 5(2):227–246.

Seyfang G and Pearson R. 2000. Time for change: international experience in community currencies. *Development* 43(4):56–60.

Simmel G. 1982 [1900]. *The Philosophy of Money*. London: Routledge & Kegan Paul.

Smithin J, ed. 2000. *What is Money?* London: Routledge.

Swanke, T. 2004. Understanding the implications of money being a social convention. In: R. Wray and M. Forstater, eds. *Contemporary Post Keynesian Analysis*. Cheltenham, UK: Edward Elgar Publishing. 84–99.

Veblen, T. 2006 [1914]. *The Instinct of Workmanship and the State of the Industrial Arts*. New York: Cosimo Classics.

Veblen T. 1899. *The Theory of the Leisure Class*. Champaign, IL: Project Gutenberg.

Weber M, ed. 1978. *Selections in Translation*. Cambridge, UK: Cambridge University Press.

Wray R. 1998. *Understanding Modern Money: The Key to Full Employment and Price Stability*. Cheltenham, UK: Edward Elgar.

Wray R. 2004. The credit money and state money approaches. In: Wray R, ed. *Credit and State Theories of Money: The Contributions of A. Mitchell Innes*. Cheltenham, UK: Edward Elgar. 79–98.

Wray R and Forstater M, eds. 2006. *Money, Financial Instability and Stabilization Policy*. Cheltenham, UK: Edward Elgar.

2 Monetary plurality in economic theory

Jérôme Blanc, Ludovic Desmedt, Laurent Le Maux, Jaime Marques-Pereira, Pepita Ould-Ahmed and Bruno Théret

2.1 Introduction

Traditionally, economic analysis considers the circulation of multiple currencies under the umbrella of international economics. It assumes that there is a single currency within a country and, thus, excludes the idea that several currencies or moneys might circulate within a national territory. Having several currencies circulating alongside the one with international standing, all in the same country, would seem to indicate that something is wrong with the socio-economic arrangements. Beyond such an interpretation, the spectre of the circulation of several moneys haunts contemporary monetary analysis and remains a problem for monetary theory. Ever since the 1970s, the monetary literature on private monetary systems or competitive payment arrangements has developed substantially whereas mainstream economics had until then taken the uniqueness of money for granted. The purpose of this chapter is to investigate the relations between monetary singularity (defined as the use of a single money or currency) and plurality (defined as the use of more than one money or currency) in the theoretical literature. Any survey of the various theories, whether orthodox or heterodox, static or dynamic, holistic or individualistic, will reveal the surprising amount of attention paid to the problem of monetary singularity and/or plurality. In the monetary literature, the issue may be raised directly or indirectly, may be seen as a result of equilibria or disequilibria and may be interpreted either as a failing to be remedied or an objective to be achieved. Moreover, the reasoning involved may be empirical or hypothetico-deductive, or it may be normative, saying what should be, rather than what is.

By presenting a 'field and method map of monetary economics', Arestis and Mihailov (2011) combine monetary theory, monetary policy and public finance to provide a useful panorama of current debates among monetary theorists. As they argue, 'seeing the big picture and various interrelationships often helps one to better focus on the specific problem in hand' (ibid., p. 791). This chapter focuses on monetary singularity/plurality and its scope is limited to authors or research programs addressing this subject. Monetary plurality may be defined as the use of multiple means of payment and/or units of account. Accordingly, in order to study the diversity of monetary analyses, we suggest a multi-dimensional pattern of monetary plurality and we shall study the plurality of means of payment and units of account. The geographical areas involved in each approach do not necessarily correspond to sovereign territories. They may be merely abstract spaces in which there are market relations among economic agents. The function of store of value cannot be equated with the other two functions inasmuch as many potential instruments may preserve wealth without necessarily becoming money. We envisage the different cases of monetary plurality or singularity based on this multi-dimensional definition (Table 2.1).

The first axis of theorisation contrasts the analyses in terms of general equilibrium, on the one hand, and evolutionary dynamics, disequilibrium and regime crises, on the other. The general equilibrium theories usually assume that money is neutral and even 'super-neutral' in the New Classical Economics (Lucas, 1972) and the New Monetary Economics (Black, 1970; Fama, 1980). In contrast, the other theories see money as an evolutionary process influencing the system of relative prices (Austrian tradition) or impacting the dynamics of production and redistribution (Keynesian and Marxian tradition). So money is not neutral, either in neo-Mengerian and post-Keynesian approaches or neo-Chartalist and neo-Marxist approaches. The neo-classical synthesis and monetarism stand in an intermediate position: even though they come within the analytical framework of general equilibrium, they concede that money does matter in a market economy. The distinction between neutrality and non-neutrality allows us to examine a broad spectrum of monetary theory, whether mainstream or not.

The second axis of theorisation contrasts singularity and plurality – even if, as we shall see, a clear-cut opposition must be amended. Indeed, plurality can encompass singularity and singularity can contain plurality. For instance, although certain theories endeavour to promote forms of monetary plurality, they are still under the influence of the idea that monetary singularity remains the ultimate condition that guarantees the stability of the payment system and the effectiveness of market transactions. The 'plurality' approaches are thus haunted either by the need for a single unit of account (Free Banking Theory) or by the selection of a stable unit of account (New Monetary Economics). Symmetrically, the 'singularity' approaches are troubled by the idea of plurality, incorporating it either positively (case of equilibria involving multiple currencies, in some

Table 2.1 Differentiation criteria

	Approaches giving precedence to plurality	*Approaches giving precedence to singularity*
General equilibrium models: neutrality of money	New Monetary Economics (Section 2.2)	General equilibrium and money (Section 2.4)
Disequilibrium or evolutionary models: non-neutrality of money	Neo-Mengerianism (Section 2.3)	Money and economy of production (Section 2.5)

search models) or negatively (case of pathology involving the circulation of several currencies within a single sovereign territory, in some Chartalist, Marxist or Institutionalist approaches).

With these two perspectives in mind (neutrality/non-neutrality and plurality/singularity), this chapter examines the 'plurality' approaches: the *strong* and the *weak* plurality approaches, which remain troubled by the problem of singularity (Sections 2.2 and 2.3). Hence, it also studies the 'singularity' approaches: the *strong* and the *weak* singularity approaches, which do not entirely dispel the question of plurality (Sections 2.4 and 2.5). Accordingly, Section 2.2 deals with the financial and radical plurality approach developed by New Monetary Economics, which lies within the analytical framework of general equilibrium (Black-Fama-Hall model, Greenfield-Yeager system). Section 2.3 examines the neo-Mengerian or evolutionary plurality approach, which lies outside the framework of general equilibrium (the Free Banking model, the Competitive Private Fiat Money model). Section 2.4 focuses on the micro-foundation of monetary singularity approach within the general equilibrium framework (the overlapping-generations, cash-in-advance, search-theoretic models and monetarism). Section 2.5 deals with the holistic singularity approach that reasons in terms of disequilibrium and antagonistic processes, such as Chartalism, post-Keynesianism and neo-Marxism. Section 2.6 concludes on the surprising oscillation between the postulate of a single money and a logical construction of the monetary plurality.

As we shall see, some approaches such as the New Monetary Economics, Black-Fama-Hall model and Greenfield-Yeager system are governed by *financial* economics, while most other approaches such as Free Banking, search models of money, neo-Chartalism, post-Keynesianism and neo-Marxian analysis are more specifically governed by *monetary* economics. So our survey will give rise to a typology of the forms of monetary singularity and plurality, and the relations between them. Hence this will frame new readings of monetary analyses. Moreover, we shall specifically focus on economic theories of money. Space here is too short to explore socio-economic, sociological, anthropological and historical works on monetary plurality. Moreover, the related empirical observation, methods of theorisation and analytical generalisation remain different to some extent from those prevailing in economics.

2.2 The New Monetary Economics: from a plurality of means of payment to a plurality of units of account

In line with neo-classical financial economics and the financialisation of the market economy over the past forty years, the New Monetary Economics, a name coined by Hall (1982), calls for complete deregulation of the financial intermediation and payment system. As paradoxical as it may appear, the New Monetary Economics argues for an economic system without money, which is, without non-interest-bearing means of payment such as token money issued by the Treasury, monetary base issued by the central banks or demand deposits issued by commercial banks. Previously Black (1970) and later Fama (1980) and Hall (1981) had proposed a payment system without base money seen as a non-interest-bearing government asset. These contributions gained acceptance through the work of Greenfield and Yeager (1983), Yeager (1983), Woolsey (1992), as well as Greenfield, Woolsey and Yeager (1995). Greenfield and Yeager (1983) presented such an alternative payment system based on financial markets as the 'Black-Fama-Hall model', even though McCallum (2010) deems the term 'Greenfield-Yeager system' more appropriate. Moreover, Cowen and Kroszner (1987, 1994) have offered a historical perspective. So the New Monetary Economics comprises a rather broad array of notions that do not limit the question to one of competition between different means of payment, but include the question of the plurality of units of account. Yet whatever the payment system proposed, the main stumbling block with the New Monetary Economics is the mode of stabilising the overall level of prices and the way to anchor the unit of account.

The New Monetary Economics addresses two theoretical concerns stemming from the attempt to separate the circulation of the means of payment and the determination of the unit of account. From an institutional point of view, the separation of the means of payment (real money) and the unit of account (imaginary money) in models built by the proponents of the New Monetary Economics makes them different from the neo-Mengerian approaches in general, and the Free Banking school in particular (White, 1984a; O'Driscoll, 1985) (Section 2.3.2). Given the context of total financial market deregulation, the New Monetary Economics is intrinsically associated with a wager on the efficiency of 'monetary dualism' defined as the separation of the medium of exchange from the medium of account. According to Cowen and Kroszner (1987, p. 569–570), 'money as we know it', that is, the unique entity supporting all monetary functions, has become obsolete inasmuch as it constitutes an inefficient, sub-optimal and 'fundamentally disequilibrating force' that should be dissolved by separating the functions of accounting and payment. Each function should be assigned to a specific support: 'The unit of account might be purely abstract or take a real commodity form' and should exist 'separately from the media of payments', which would 'take the form of real assets claims' (ibid.). The unit of account is defined in terms of a broad basket of goods, which is supposed to reflect the overall level of prices.

On the other hand, from a methodological point of view, the New Monetary Economics adopts an evolutionary approach close to neo-Mengerianism: the invisible hand of competition, technological progress and financial market forces are supposedly evolving towards an economy without money. Three stages of financial evolution are thus distinguished: the early stage (barter), the intermediate stage (money), and the late stage (competitive payment systems without money). 'Although an intermediate stage of financial evolution uses a dominant medium of account, considerable multiplicity prevails in the early and late stages' (Cowen and Kroszner, 1994, p. 38). The separation of the medium of exchange from the medium of account is not merely an abstract notion but is the possible outcome of the historical trend as a part of the evolution of finance. The broad diversification of interest-bearing financial assets is increasingly likely to make them ever more liquid, allowing them to be used as means of payment in lieu of money.

The range of competing monetary systems proposed by the New Monetary Economics stretches from weak plurality – limited to means of payment, to strong plurality – extended to units of account. The Black-Fama-Hall model and the Greenfield-Yeager system do not upset the singularity of the unit of account (Section 2.2.2), while Hall (1997) implicitly, and Cowen and Kroszner (1994) explicitly, contest it (Section 2.2.3). Despite the divergence between weak and strong monetary plurality, all these approaches assume that money is neutral and that it could definitively be neutralised by separating its functions.

2.2.1 Weak monetary plurality: competition in issuing means of payment

Basically, the New Monetary Economics in general, and the Greenfield-Yeager system in particular, advocate the institutional arrangement in which private banks supply financial and payment services simultaneously. Means of payment are shares of money market mutual funds (more generally, shares of portfolios of negotiable securities held by banks) and their value fluctuates daily in the financial markets. Under such an institutional arrangement, banking would no longer be about collecting current accounts and time deposits that are legally convertible at a fixed price into currency issued by the Treasury or base money issued by the central bank. Banking would henceforth supply shares of the assets portfolio and interest-bearing 'deposits', which could be used as means of exchange and payment. The absence of convertibility into base money, and the absence of base money itself, would lead to the end of central banking.

Due to the separation of the accounting and payment functions of money, the overall value of the means of payment varies constantly with the value of the financial assets backing them. In addition, the unit of account can no longer be based on the means of payment and has to be set in some other way, independently of the payment system. The ensuing return to monetary dualism, on the one hand, leads to a plurality of means of payment and, on the other hand, leaves the question of defining one or more units of account open. Initially, most proponents of the New Monetary Economics in general, and the Greenfield-Yeager system in particular, upheld the singularity of the unit of account. In this case, the market value of the competing means of payment is expressed in an abstract unit of account fixed outside the payment system – a *numeraire* (Greenfield and Yeager, 1983). This does not necessarily imply that the unit value of the means of payment (for instance, the value of the shares of money mutual market fund) is variable: the value of each share can be exchanged at par with the unit of account and, in that case, the number of shares vary from day to day with the value of the assets portfolio backing them. In other words, competition among banks and among the means of payment they issue does not affect the exchange rate of units of payment in terms of units of account, but rather the level of returns on shares (which would depend on the quality of assets portfolio management and the level of management fees).

Greenfield and Yeager (1983, p. 308) are well aware that under the institutional arrangement assumed by the New Monetary Economics, the absence of 'base money' (the government-issued fiat money or the monetary stock of a particular commodity) raises the crucial question of the settlement of inter-bank debts. In their system, under the auspices of the clearinghouses, banks are supposed to agree on the financial assets that can be accepted as means of settlement of inter-bank debts. When there is indirect convertibility of the means of exchange into the unit of account, the convertibility is guaranteed only for specific means of redemption (such as gold or actively traded securities), which are used for inter-bank settlements. As noted by Scialom (1995), the search for a liquid inter-bank means of payment, implying a hierarchical dimension within the banking system, contradicts the 'overall project' of the New Monetary Economics. Actually, two kinds of arrangements can be distinguished: one is the system built by Greenfield and Yeager and the other is the Optimal Fiduciary Monetary System constructed by Hall. Yeager (1994, 1997, 1999) is rather sympathetic to the project in favour of competitive private fiat money (see Section 2.3.1). Hall (1981) mentions the role of the State defining the unit of account and monetary rules that automatically stabilise the unit of account in terms of purchasing power. Moreover, Hall (1983) sees as optimal an institutional arrangement by which the government issues reserve certificates that function not only as a medium of account, but also as a store of value and a means of inter-bank settlement. Hall (1992) also comes closer to the Free Banking system advocated by White (1984a, 1989) (see Section 2.3.2).

2.2.2 Stabilisation of the unit of account: the compensated dollar plan

Despite their different preferences as to the optimal type of standard, the proponents of the New Monetary Economics share the same concern – stabilisation of the purchasing power of the unit of account. This reveals the recognition of the non-neutrality of money (Austrian aspect) combined with the objective of neutralising money as far as possible (neo-classical aspect). For the New Monetary Economics, instability of the overall level of prices is the main obstacle to making competitive payment systems really practicable (Black, 1981; Fama, 1983; Greenfield and Yeager, 1983; Sumner, 1990; Cowen and Kroszner, 1994). On this question, Yeager (2010, p. 434) deems that 'further thought is (still) needed'. Many arrangements have been suggested to solve the problem.

For instance, Black (1978) first evoked fiat money backed internationally against other national currencies within a 'global monetarism' before proposing (Black, 1981) a 'flexible commodity money standard' in the form of a 'gold standard with double feedback and near zero reserves', something 'almost identical to Fisher's compensated dollar plan' (Sumner, 1990, p. 115). Like Fama (1980), Black (1981) envisages a simple system with commodity money used as a reference (a barrel of crude oil, a spaceship permit, etc). Fama (1983) considers that a State-issued money would play only a marginal role and could continue to function as cash: it would be used only for retail trade payments and by people who do not have access to the financial system. On the other hand, Fama (1983, p. 19) holds that 'either the monopoly fiduciary currency approach' that he prefers, 'or the flexible commodity standards of Fisher (1920) and Black (1981) could be used to control the price level'. Hence, Fama (1983) broadens the idea of Fisher's (1920) compensated dollar plan and also refers to the Chilean monetary system, which introduced an 'imaginary' unit of account (the *Unidad de Fomento*) in 1976, that was supposed to be stabilised in terms of purchasing power and linked to the consumer price index expressed in pesos (the 'real' unit of account associated with the currency used for current transactions). The Chilean monetary system, it is argued, proved its stability during the financial crisis in 1981 and allegedly enabled the country to face dollarisation. For Hall (1997) and Shiller (2002), the *Unidad de Fomento* system was close to the compensated dollar plan applied to the fiat money system.

Finally, Hall (1983, 1992, 1997) recommends a system of fiat money with a dual unit of account: the nominal current account, based on the national currency and used for short-term contracts and another unit of account with fixed purchasing power used for long-term contracts. In a way, the New Monetary Economics in general, and Hall's recommendations in particular, reveal the effective duality of units of account in present day financial economies, even though they seem highly normative.

2.2.3 Plurality extended to units of account

The major feature of the New Monetary Economics is not merely its stability but also the singularity of the unit of account. To solve the problem of stability of the overall price level, the proponents of the New Monetary Economics are led either to imagine systems that they themselves deem inoperative and/or unviable (Schnadt and Whittaker, 1993; Cowen and Kroszner, 1994) or to return to government monetary regulation. The New Monetary Economics is torn between the plurality endogenously fulfilled by private issuers of means of payment, and the singularity of the unit of account exogenously organised by the government. Moreover, the viability of competing systems of payment, which theoretically no longer require base money, depends paradoxically on maintaining money that does not bear interest and is based on a stabilised unit of account. Cowen and Kroszner (1994, p. 100) thus conclude their comparative study of the different monetary systems imagined within the New Monetary Economics by opining that, 'the scenario with financial assets (as medium of exchange) and currency (as medium of exchange and unit of account) is the most likely to evolve from a deregulation of today's financial institutions'.

In fact, Cowen and Kroszner explicitly acknowledge the unsustainable nature of the principle of a unique unit of account and endorse a strong plurality approach. They do not hesitate to recommend a return to the Middle Ages during which there was a proliferation of moneys of account and of payments, making an argument that new technologies of information and communication would subsequently make this possible. Even if Hall (1997) evokes the plurality of monetised indexed units of account, Cowen and Kroszner (1994, pp. 38–39) are the only declared proponents of the New Monetary Economics who stress that:

> [t]he possible proliferation and co-existence of different currencies of account at advanced stages of financial evolution. (. . .) In an unregulated environment, the evolution of multiple media of account follows a path similar to exchange media and settlement evolution. (. . .) Even if consumer convenience dictates a common medium of account for most retail transactions, we still expect medium of account proliferation for large wholesale and financial transactions.

So banks would competitively provide several units of account and each of them would correspond to different baskets of commodities selected to represent the differing costs of living of social groups or consumers.

> The value of a bank account, for instance, can be linked to the value of a chosen medium of account (. . .). In effect, the depositor is a creditor of the bank and returns are denominated in terms of chosen accounting media. Accounts linked to the value of regional or personal consumption baskets would give rise to multiple mediums of account in this context.
>
> (ibid)

Cowen and Kroszner's analysis of the plurality of the unit of account may be interpreted as a thought experiment attempting to enlighten the inconsistency of the plurality of the means of payment with a unique unit of account. Hayek had previously opened such a thought experiment in a different way (see Section 2.3.1). Moreover, Cowen and Kroszner's transposition of Mundell's idea of an optimal monetary zone, which is a justification for the unification of units of account extended on ever broader scales, enables us to interpret their position as tending towards such a unification in homogeneous monetary spaces, with only the spatial or social scales being variable. Cowen and Kroszner do refer to regional and sectorial fractioning of optimal currency zones and, thereby, raise the whole problem of the fractioning of spheres of exchange.

So a two-fold question remains. First, how do markets set the exchange rates between different moneys? Second, what is the cost of information in such a system? The routine solution suggested by Yeager (2010) consists of simply aligning the unit of account with that used by government in its operations and fiscal policies. In line with the general equilibrium framework or the Austrian Free Banking approach, the singularity of the unit of account in a given space is almost considered to be an inescapable economic requisite such that it makes transaction costs and exchange rate risks lower than in a system with multiple units of account.

2.3 Neo-Mengerian approaches to money: between plurality and singularity of the unit of account

Even if the New Monetary Economics (particularly in the works of Yeager, Cowen and Kroszner) has been influenced by the Austrian school, it should be clearly distinguished from the neo-Mengerian approaches which conceive payment systems with money and mainly suggest two kinds of payment systems. One corresponds to the competitive model with private fiat moneys as developed by Klein and Hayek (Section 2.3.1) while the other corresponds to the Free Banking tradition as renewed by Selgin and White (Section 2.3.2). These evolutionary approaches accept monetary plurality (in its strong and medium form respectively) and rather reject the assumption that money is neutral.

2.3.1 Competitive private fiat money and denationalisation of money: absolute plurality

Klein (1974, 1976) and Hayek (1978, 1979) develop the idea of monetary competition applied to instruments of payment and units of account. Hayek claimed to have reached exactly the same conclusion as Klein without any knowledge of his writings (Vaubel, 1986). The competitive fiat money model formulated by Klein and Hayek can be distinguished from the New Monetary Economics by the fact that it does not preclude money in general. On the other hand, it can be distinguished from the Free Banking system, in which banks issue inside money convertible at par and on demand into outside money (for instance, metallic money) selected by the system of payment itself. The Klein-Hayek model amounts to transposing competition between currencies in the international context to competition between fiat moneys within a national territory. The distinction between the different competitive fiat moneys also enables the Klein-Hayek model to avoid criticism based on Gresham's Law according to which bad money drives out good money. This principle initially applied to coinage of the same metal and involved two factors: (i) the clipping, wear-and-tear of coins, or debasement and (ii) the maintenance of fixed legal parity between moneys. The Klein-Hayek model is different for two reasons: (i) banks issue competitive fiat money without intrinsic value, and (ii) there is a flexible exchange rate between moneys. So flexible exchange rates, despite their drawbacks, are thus essential for the viability of the competitive fiat money model and for the mechanism ensuring that stable money drives out depreciated money.

Under the competitive fiat money system each bank has its own distinguishing mark (the unit of account), which it uses to denominate its own money (the means of payment). There is not a priori a common unit of account (as is the case under the Free Banking or the central banking system) so that each money fluctuates against the others. Agents are able to differentiate between moneys, thanks to their fluctuating exchange rates and thus bear the exchange rate risk. They are free to choose the money according to its stability in terms of purchasing power and banks can rely on or even construct a price index to help agents monitor the stability of the money selected. The basic idea is that monetary regulation is determined by the quantity of money put into circulation by the issuing bank; it is no longer determined by the issuing bank's ability to reimburse its issues on demand and at a fixed price into an outside money (the metallic money or base money). So, Hayek (1978, p. 42) supposes that the issuing bank will announce its 'intention to regulate the quantity of [its money] so as to keep [its] (precisely defined) purchasing power as nearly as possible constant'.

While the quantitative regulation of competitive fiat moneys constitutes the mechanism determining their purchasing power and exchange rate, competition between banks sets an 'effective limit' to these issues (Hayek, 1978, p. 44; Hayek 1979, p. 4). Monetary plurality is hence appreciated essentially from the viewpoint of competition and market discipline; money also draws its legitimacy essentially from the stability of its purchasing power. In a competitive environment, an issuing bank can therefore decide whether or not to increase its money supply. If its money appreciates, the bank can issue new means of payment and/or buy rival moneys according to its consumers' demands. If its money depreciates, the supply of its money exceeding public demand, it stops roll-over credit and/or sells off its reserves of rival moneys. Thus, in formulating the competitive fiat money model, Hayek (1978, p. 55) feels that he has found a way of regulating and constraining the banking system to offer only short-term loans:

> In order to retain control over its outstanding circulation, (the issuing bank) will on the whole have to confine its lending to relatively short-time contracts so that, by reducing or temporarily stopping new lending, current repayments of outstanding loans would bring about a rapid reduction of its total issue.

To designate the unit of account specific to each bank, Klein (1974) uses the term 'trademark' or 'brand name' and applies the concept of property rights to each monetary brand name, however only to banknotes. Similarly, Hayek (1979) uses the term 'distinctly named money'. Hence, counterfeiting would apply only to banknotes and could be defined as the illegal printing of banknotes using not only the name of the issuing bank, but also its unit of account. Thus, counterfeiting corresponds to an infringement of the issuing bank's property rights. It corresponds to an overissue not desired by the bank, leading to a depreciation of its money and loss of agents' confidence, damaging its reputation and the value of its trademark. This being said, Klein and Hayek take only the quantity of banknotes into account and their analysis of the issuing bank's trademark and property rights remains too restrictive. Indeed, deposits should not be overlooked. The property rights should be protected by banking laws and applied to private banknotes as well as deposits. In this respect, the experiment of the Euro-dollar market gives us a better grasp of the problems raised here and also of the difficulties implicit in the protection of property rights to the monetary trademark. In other words, the monetary plurality envisaged by Hayek appears far more difficult to put into operation than Hayek himself supposes. The central banking system and even the Free Banking system do not entail difficulties of this sort: the unit of account is unique and it is a public good that issuing banks can use.

2.3.2 *Free Banking as a return to monetary singularity*

Unlike the competitive fiat money model, the Free Banking system corresponds to a theoretical and historical tradition (White, 1984b; Selgin, 1988; Dowd, 1992; Selgin and White, 1994). Banks are free to issue inside money in the form of banknotes and deposits that are convertible at a one-to-one ratio into outside money (metallic currency or even frozen fiat money). A recurrent misunderstanding of the Free Banking system stems from the fact that convertible banknotes have always been associated with inconvertible paper money. So, the Free Banking system is often erroneously seen as a system in which moneys issued by banks fluctuate in relation to one another (for instance in Baye, De Grauwe, and De Vries, 1993). During the early days of the Free Banking system, banknotes could actually be changed at a discount, especially if brokers organised the exchange of banknotes. The rate of discount depended on the costs of transport and authentication and also on the risk of bank default. The discount setting, however, did not last. There is an incentive for banks themselves to organise a clearing system of compensations – initially bilateral, then multilateral – that enables them to reduce and finally to annul the rate of discount (Selgin and White, 1987). Then, the routine and mutual exchange at par of banknotes and checks within a clearing system reinforces their acceptability among rival banks and the public.

The Free Banking system thus stands at the intersection of monetary singularity and banking plurality. The singularity of the unit of account is preserved, for instance, when the State defines the country's unit of account in terms of the weight of precious metal it contains. Then, the Mint coins specie (and competition between different mints is even envisaged to improve the quality of coins). To some extent, the Free Banking system can be compared to the central banking system, inasmuch as there is a unique unit of account and as the banks issue demand debts that are convertible into an ultimate money: specie in one case and central bank money in the other. The difference lies in the fact that under the Free Banking system (*i*) the ultimate money is outside the banking system and monetary authorities, and (*ii*) the degree of bank regulation is limited. The Free Banking theory entails neither abandoning the centralisation of money reserves and inter-bank clearing operations nor abandoning a unique unit of account. It sets up a high degree of deregulation of banking and tends towards an abolition of the lender of last resort so as to address moral hazard and reinforce market discipline.

Competition is thus limited to the different issuers of inside money, that is, demand debts issued by banks in the form of banknotes or deposits. The outside money, which preserves the regulation of the system, is not strictly involved in competition. This is the last component of monetary policy still retained, though admittedly in atrophied form, by the Free Banking theory. Moreover, money is first and foremost treated as a commodity endowed with qualities that lend themselves to its use as money (Menger, 1892). If fiat money emerges and is accepted at face value, according to the regression theorem, no matter how far one goes back in time, it must initially have been linked to the metallic currency by virtue of its convertibility (Mises, 1949). Conversely, Selgin (2003) investigates the hypothesis of adaptive learning in order to show the transition from the metallic standard to the fiat money standard – and the quantity of fiat money under the Free Banking system should hence be frozen.

To sum up, under the competitive payment system designed by the New Monetary Economics, the unit of account is separated from the means of payment and agents bear the risks that burden assets. In the Klein-Hayek model of competitive fiat money, agents bear exchange rate risks. Under the Free Banking system, the unit of account is a public good and agents bear the liquidity risks entailed in the issuing of demand debts. The Klein-Hayek model and, to some extent, the New Monetary Economics, would seem to be much more radical than the Free Banking system. Hayek's normative construction is similar to the New Monetary Economics as both propose a strong, if not radical, degree of plurality while the Free Banking theory rather proposes a medium degree of plurality and is closer to the Mengerian methodological approach in considering the payment system as an evolutionary process.

2.4 Integrating money into the general equilibrium theory

A vast swathe of economic theory deals with the conditions governing the integration of money into the framework of the general equilibrium theory that was previously developed without taking money into account. Trying to solve the omission of money raises two questions, especially with regard to fiat money which is neither produced nor consumed. The first is the Hicks problem (Hicks, 1935): why does an agent hold money in an economy in which there are liquid financial assets bearing interest? The second is the Hahn problem (Hahn, 1965): how can fiat money have a positive value in exchange, when it has no intrinsic utility? In a Walrasian perspective, Patinkin (1956) opened up one line of reflexion by making money part of the utility function of agents. The trouble with 'monetary Walrasianism' (Mehrling, 1998) is that it has never been possible to show how money appears with a positive price. This problem inherent in monetary Walrasianism leads the neo-classical paradigm to relax the assumption of the centralised economy *à la* Arrow-Debreu model. In this perspective, Ostroy and Starr (1974) open another line of reflexion by assuming a decentralised economy with no coordination process a priori. Hence, the entire research program has been based not only on neutrality (money has no effect on relative prices), but also on essentiality (money is essential in a decentralised economy). As we shall see, the overlapping-generations models focus almost exclusively on the function of the reserve of value (Section 2.4.1), while the cash-in-advance model (Section 2.4.2) and the search-theoretic model (Section 2.4.3) focus on the function of the medium of exchange. On the other hand, within the neo-classical paradigm, monetarism and especially the Chicago plan propose a highly normative construction that emphasises the need for pure centralisation and strict monopolisation of money issuance (Section 2.4.4).

2.4.1 The overlapping-generations models

Models of overlapping-generations are first and foremost analytical tools with a broad field of application since Samuelson's (1958) seminal paper, which has been completed by Diamond (1965) among others. Monetary theory is not the main topic of the overlapping-generations models and monetary theory does not use them extensively. These theoretical models suppose an economy as being set up by two successive generations of agents, one young and active and the other older and inactive, over a non-finite series of periods. The tradable goods are perishable from one period to the next, making it problematic to transfer wealth from one generation to the next. Samuelson (1958) shows that without money no trading of goods or transfer of wealth can take place. The general characteristic of overlapping-generations models is that the general equilibrium can be sub-optimal without money. Hence, money is seen as a 'social contrivance' or a 'social compact' (Samuelson, 1958, pp. 481–482), which enhances the utility of all agents involved in trade. From the late 1970s some models have been calibrated specifically to integrate money into general equilibrium theory. With the work of Wallace (1977) and Kareken and Wallace (1980), overlapping-generations models deal with the money demand function in an economy with frictions (and thus different from the economy supposed by the general equilibrium theory) so that the existence of money is also explained by its usefulness as a 'lubricant'.

In the overlapping-generations models, money can have a positive price if the number of generations involved in trade is non-finite, that is, if there is no last generation: what matters for the young agents is that money should still be acceptable when they grow old; otherwise, they would not accept and demand money and its price would be nil. Compared with monetary Walrasianism, the overlapping-generations models show that money has utility because exchange cannot take place without money, and that it thus circulates at a positive price. Money is used in trade as a tool for the inter-temporal allocation of resources and it is first and foremost a perfect arrangement for conserving wealth through its function of reserve of value. However, nothing is said about its role as a medium of exchange, and even less about its use as a unit of account (not observable in these models apart from assumptions about the price level). The absence of the medium of exchange function has consequently been strongly criticised (as shown in the special issue edited by Kareken and Wallace (1980), and in McCallum's (1983) comment). So the research program has converged toward the search model of money since the late 1980s (see Section 2.4.3).

With regard to the question of plurality of means of payment, Wallace (1980) examines the problem raised by the co-existence of fiat money and financial assets with a positive yield and shows that fiat money has a positive price in an economy with financial assets if money has a particular utility of its own. Wallace (1983) concludes that legal restrictions alone make perfect substitution difficult between financial assets for money. While the overlapping-generations models endeavour to show the positive price of money, such a conclusion paradoxically opens the door of the legal-restriction theory of money and the New Monetary Economics (seen in Section 2.2.1). Another way to grasp monetary plurality may be found in Kareken and Wallace (1981) and Chang (1994), who drop the hypothesis that residents of a given country seek to hold only the country's currency. Their objective here is to explain phenomena of currency substitution that were drawing increasing attention because of the high inflation in Latin America. They built a model with two fiat moneys in circulation in the same country and with an internal exchange rate that could vary – a situation interpreted as a *laissez-faire* regime.

In summary, the overlapping-generations models lead to envisaging monetary plurality as the co-existence, within the same territory, of either a fiat money and financial assets held by agents and liable to be used as means of payment or several fiat moneys. In both cases, monetary plurality is conceived as competition either between assets and moneys or between moneys, both being seen as mutually substitutable. As an extreme result, only legal restrictions prevent fiat money from disappearing.

2.4.2 Cash-in-advance models

Clower (1967, p. 5) attempts to establish the utility of money on its function as a medium of exchange, taking as a basic principle that 'money buys goods and goods buy money, but goods do not buy goods.' Clower assumes that fiat money is exogenous from the supply side and that there is a given cash-in-advance constraint from the demand side: in each period individual spending cannot exceed the amount of money already held. The cash-in-advance constraint stems from costs of transactions of exchange with money being less costly than with barter especially because of the durability, divisibility and portability of money. In general, cash-in-advance models maintain a distinction between financial assets and fiat money, and their reasoning assumes the circulation of a single money. Though they make it possible to formulate a function of demand for money (Lucas and Stokey, 1983), they do not however explain why exactly money exists (Duca and Van Hoose, 2004). Thus, for Kiyotaki and Wright (1989, p. 928), they 'have no hope of explaining endogenously either the nature of money or the development of monetary exchange'.

Despite these limits, monetary plurality can be envisioned within the cash-in-advance models. For instance, Uribe (1997) refers to currency substitution processes and Sturzenegger (1992) to the high inflation in Argentinian and Brazilian experiences. Considering an inflationary process and the ensuing formation of two 'currency circuits', Sturzenegger (1992, pp. 4, 23) studies the effects of adapting agents' behaviour to the dual circulation: one circulation concerns payments with the domestic currency, the other payments with an alternative 'inflation proof technology' (namely, dollarisation, interest-bearing accounts, or alternative money commodities). The co-existence of two forms of money depends on technological restrictions implying transaction costs, such as costs of changing money and of access to technology enabling agents to use forms of indexation. The sum of these costs prevents the national currency from being completely replaced by alternative means of payment. Monetary plurality is seen as a consequence of imperfect substitutability of moneys related to costs of various transactions associated with each of them. To sum up, the cash-in-advance model regards money as a medium of exchange and envisions the substitution between several currencies, not just between barter and money. The cash-in-advance constraint remains exogenous and has been challenged by the search models of money.

2.4.3 Search models of money

Several developments in monetary theory have analysed the barter/money alternative from the perspective of both Menger's problem of the emergence of money (Menger, 1892) and Jevons' problem of the double coincidence of needs (Jevons, 1875). To address these problems within the neo-classical corpus, search models of money first assume a decentralised economy. Starting with the idea that medium of exchange rather than store of value is the main function of money, they seek the endogenous causes of the selection of one money by agents, attempting to go beyond the ad hoc cash-in-advance assumption of the existence of a means of exchange (Kiyotaki and Wright, 1989). The search models assume that agents can choose between two modes of transacting, namely, barter or money. Once all the agents involved in trade have selected money, they must hold some before any transaction can take place.

The model of Kiyotaki and Wright (1989) envisages two possible cases in a decentralised market economy that requires a means of exchange in order to realise random bilateral exchanges. The first case explores the possible emergence of money on the basis of selection of one commodity amongst others, which rests on a combination of properties of the goods in question and beliefs concerning these properties. In the second case, fiat money is introduced and it finally contributes to increased well-being. On the other hand, Iwai (1988, 1996) formalises the selection of money as a 'bootstrap mechanism' and attempts to solve the non-determination of equilibrium (due to the absence of elements determining either money equilibrium or barter equilibrium). It hypothesises a small group of agents who begin to choose a medium of exchange and, once such an initial choice takes place, the other agents soon follow it. The increasing returns stemming from the use of the means of payment initially selected explain the generalisation of its use: as a result, 'money is money simply because it is used as money' (Iwai, 1996, p. 452). The 'speculation' strategy among agents about what is used as money and the ensuing monetary equilibrium thus entail absolute monetary singularity.

Most search models commonly deduce two kinds of equilibrium: one is equilibrium in a barter economy; the other is the equilibrium with money. Although monetary plurality is not usually a subject these search models deal with, Kiyotaki and Wright (1991, 1993) mention the possibility of accounting for the existence of monetary equilibria involving several fiat moneys. Within the assumptions of the plurality of fiat moneys, these authors present a model with two fiat moneys and a real commodity. This model reveals the variable articulations between these means of exchange according to their yield levels and their partial or universal acceptability. It opens up the possibility of simultaneous circulation of two currencies, even if one dominates the other in terms of yields or acceptability.

Even so, monetary plurality does not constitute the main theoretical topic of the search models or the overlapping-generations models. Kocherlakota and Krueger (1999, p. 243) undermine this weakness: 'Even the "deepest" models of international currencies do not give rise to a motivation for having different currencies'. They construct a signalling model of individual preferences in commodities on the basis of a random matching model in the territory of a country. Agents are presumed to be sensitive to the national origin of the commodities in question but this origin remains private information. Agents' preference for one money over another thus serves to reveal their preferences as regards commodities according to their country of origin. Money here is a medium of information between supply and demand. The model thus applies to multiple currencies (national and foreign currency), with a fixed rate of exchange, between which the agents can choose prior to the matching process. It is assumed that the agents have a preference for their own country's products but that the sellers are neither opposed to the use of foreign money nor are the buyers opposed to the purchase of a foreign commodity. Kocherlakota and Krueger (1999, p. 243) then conclude that 'multiple national currencies may play an essential role in achieving an optimal allocation of resources'.

In the neo-classical models presented here, money is treated as an asset without intrinsic utility and does not bear interest. There are consequently two series of possible choices: one of them is between money and goods endowed with intrinsic utility; and the other is between money and interest-bearing assets. All in all, monetary singularity is rather absolute. Money facilitates trade and enhances well-being. Monetary plurality is presented as a range of options for agents with different nationality and fiat money is used as means of payment. As the function of unit of account is missing from the search models, it remains difficult, if not impossible, to place this conception of plurality in our scale of configurations running from weak to strong plurality. In addition, a noteworthy feature is the absence of regulation and homogenisation of the different types of money through the guarantee of convertibility and parity supervised by an overseeing authority.

2.4.4 Monetarism

Monetarism fits into the neo-classical paradigm and is featured by the normative emphasis it places on monetary singularity. The particularity of the quantity theory is not only its postulate of a proportional causality from the variation in the exogenous money supply to the variation in the overall price level, but also its application of this postulate to *all* forms of money, whether metallic currency, fiat money or convertible bank issues. The quantity theory thus sees the money question as that of a homogeneous mass of means of payment that agents consider to be immediately available, an aggregate of means of payment to be measured and controlled. Furthermore, the homogeneous mass has no effect on real variables and on the system of relative prices in the long term (and even in the short term) – this makes it neutral (or super-neutral). If money is neutral in theory, it should also be neutral in practice. In addition, private institutions such as commercial banks should not be authorised to produce any kind of money, hand-to-hand currency or demand deposits. In Friedman's (1959, p. 7) words, 'The production of a fiduciary currency is, as it were, a technical monopoly'.

The stumbling block facing the quantity theory has always been the construction of the monetary aggregate, which is perpetually destabilised by the plurality of monetary practices. Moreover, the very action of the central bank in attempting to control the aggregate leads to destabilisation of the aggregate itself. Among the quantity theorists, Allais (1975) concludes that in a credit system in which commercial banks 'create money', the quantity of money is essentially a 'subjective' variable, depending on agents' practices in spending and saving. This being the case, what has to be done is to establish a regulatory framework applied to banking and financial institutions so as to set up once and for all an 'objective' definition of the quantity of money, over which the authorities can then exercise sovereign control. The reformulations of the idea of a government monopoly on the issuing of money is found in the writings of Simons (1934) and Fisher (1935), who formulated the Chicago plan. The principle of government monopoly of the issuing of paper money and demand deposits was adopted by Soddy (1926), Fisher (1935), Allais (1947, 1975) and Friedman (1959), and more recently by Benes and Kumhof (2012) and Dyson, Hodgson and Jackson (2013).

From an institutional point of view, the idea of the Chicago plan is that government should exercise its sovereign rights in full to control money both as a unit of account and means of payment. In other words, the unit of account is the monetary brand name of the State, which should have the exclusive right to use it. Thanks to these powers, the government can effectively pursue a policy aimed at securing complete control of the monetary aggregate and thus stabilise the purchasing power of money. In a situation of *laissez-faire*, however, practices in the private sphere, and particularly in that of banking, can lead to infringement of the government's sovereign right. Banks that issue monetary signs are thus freely engaging in what amounts to 'counterfeiting', which should be forbidden with respect to both banknotes and bank deposits. Thus the Chicago plan requires banks to hold 100% of their reserves, that is, to back all their demand liabilities by the central bank money in reserve. Consequently, it deprives banks of all monetary initiative.

From both positive and normative points of view, the Chicago plan is no doubt the most extreme assertion of monetary singularity within a sovereign territory in which the State guarantees centralisation, monopolisation and control of the supply of money. Monetary plurality is seen as counterfeiting, a violation of sovereign rights. Finally, of all approaches to money, that of the Chicago plan asserts most forcefully the principle that *money is State*.

2.5 Chartalist, Keynesian and Marxist approaches to money

Most of the approaches described in this section are based on the monetary theories of Marx or Keynes and share the theoretical principle that money is *a sine qua non* condition for an economy of production. According to Hein (2004, pp. 8–9), 'An understanding of money as socially accepted token of value in Marx's monetary theory of value is perfectly compatible with the post-Keynesian view of a modern credit money system'. The theoretical framework that goes from neo-Chartalist and post-Keynesian to contemporary Marxist approaches shares the idea that monetary plurality is hardly conceivable other than as a pathology at worst, and as an expression of the difference of quality and acceptability of the means of payment at best. On the one hand, these theoretical views regarding monetary plurality as a problem to be faced are then opposed to the New Monetary Economics that regards monetary plurality as a solution, as an expression of competition between private issuers. On the other hand, they also show concern for the monetary impact of the plurality of debts and financial derivatives and they are, to some extent, drawn towards financial economics. Ultimately they endorse a strong singularity approach and consider that far from being neutral, money is the institution echoing conflicts and disequilibrium.

2.5.1 Chartalism: plurality as a symbol of 'imperfect sovereignty'

For most neo-Chartalists and post-Keynesians, Knapp and Keynes respectively provide the essential analytical components used to construct a coherent monetary theory according to which the separation of the monetary from the real sphere is irrelevant. According to Knapp (1924), if the monetary singularity in a political territory is a fact beyond doubt, in contrast, payments can be distinguished from one another by taking into account the parties involved. While Keynes (1930, p. 4) in his *Treatise* claims to be a follower of Knapp, he subsequently tends to neglect the concept of State money and to focus above all on bank money and what he terms 'financial circulation'. So, in the work after the *Treatise* and related to the 'finance motive', Keynes (1936, 1937) focuses his analysis on the monetary economies of production (capitalist market economies).

Similarly, neo-Chartalistism and post-Keynesianism share many views but, as Goodhart (2005, p. 817) points out, 'not all Chartalists are post-Keynesians, and not all post-Keynesians are necessarily Chartalists, though the overlap is admittedly large'. Whereas the neo-Chartalists focus on the creation of State money, and particularly on the way in which monetary singularity is established within a territory, post-Keynesians are mainly interested in bank money and plurality of debts. Hence, neo-Chartalism endorses an absolute monetary singularity approach, while post-Keynesianism examines weak plurality of debts inasmuch as there are several banks. A stronger plurality may be conceived if both State money and bank money are taken into account.

Lerner (1947) and, more recently, Wray (1998, 2003) have revived Knapp's view of money as a creation of the State: 'At the present time, in a normally well-working economy, money is a creature of the State. Its general acceptability, which is its all-important attribute, stands or falls by its acceptability by the State' (Lerner, 1947, p. 313). Fiat or State money is 'the money used as the link between the public and the private pay communities. It is the money that sits at the top of the debt pyramid (or hierarchy), or the "definitive" and "valuta" money' (Wray, 1998, p. 77). Neo-Chartalism rejects the use of the term money in its fullest sense when applied to any instrument of payment that is not official. Despite a multitude of historical examples that weaken this position, it is asserted that the principle of 'One nation, one money' is logically indisputable. Fiscal systems can rely on currencies other than the central money, but these are merely examples of imperfect sovereignty given that 'sovereignty can be defined as the ability to impose tax liabilities' (Wray, 2003, p. 90).

2.5.2 Post-Keynesianism: monetary singularity and plurality of debts

The Radcliffe Report (1959), Kaldor (1960) and Rousseas (1960) all maintained that the money supply was 'credit-driven' (Niggle, 1991). In line with this research program, Davidson (1978), Kaldor (1982) and Moore (1988) analyse the mechanisms of the demand for credit instead of reasoning in terms of the exogenous stock of money. The money supply is perfectly elastic and endogenous to demand: in a credit economy the money supply is necessarily endogenous (Kaldor, 1982), whereas Friedman and Lucas construct that money supply is exogenous in the sense that the central bank can fully determine the money supply (Minsky, 1986). The post-Keynesians explain the endogenous nature of money creation, which characterises modern economic systems:

> [m]oney 'comes into existence along with debts' – in other words, the supply of money is related to contracts and the debts they necessitate. Money does not enter the system like manna from heaven – nor from the sky via Friedman's helicopter.
>
> (Moore, 1988, p. 374)

There is general agreement among the post-Keynesians that (*i*) the banking system responds to demand by distributing loans, and (*ii*) its hierarchical organisation guarantees compensation and homogeneity of credit money. Though all post-Keynesians share the hypothesis of the endogenous nature of money, it is not always analysed in the same way when the curve linking money supply to interest rate is flat and also when it gradually rises (Moore, 1988; Goodhart, 1989; Dow, 1996): the endogenous nature is complete for the 'horizontalists' (Kaldor, Moore, Lavoie) and only partial for the 'verticalists' (Dow, Goodhart). In addition, within the horizontalist view, two groups may be distinguished: the 'Americans' who tend to privilege the view that money is a stock and the 'Europeans' who see it as a flow that is required to finance spending (Wray, 2003).

As previously emphasised, monetary analysis in Keynes's *Treatise* is ambivalent: Keynes views State money as 'money proper', but subsequently proceeds as if only 'bank money' were worthy of interest. The distinction between the two types of money determines the divergence between neo-Chartalists and post-Keynesians. Post-Keynesian horizontalists consider that the State cannot be seen as the initiator of money creation (Mehrling, 2000; Gnos and Rochon, 2002), while Wray (2003, p. 91) argues that money is driven by taxes given that the State is 'the monopoly supplier of currency' and that is more relevant to 'consolidate the central bank and the treasury, calling the conglomerate "the State"'. Asserting that State money is exogenously imposed by the government in accordance with a fiscal logic, neo-Chartalists contradict the notion that modern banking money is endogenously supplied in a capitalist economy. However, Bell (2001) overcomes the contradiction and re-examines the different types of debt. In a modern banking system, debts are superimposed one upon the other and the 'debt pyramid' is composed of several steps, differentiated by the degree of acceptability of the instruments: households issue debts that are less liquid than those issued by enterprises, which in turn are less liquid than money issued by banks, which in turn is less liquid than the ultimate money issued by the State. There is thus a plurality of debts and their homogenisation is ensured by the hierarchical nature of the banking system.

In summary, the tricky articulation of private debts and public money, and the complex relationships between them determine the debate between neo-Chartalists and post-Keynesians. The emergence of parallel instruments of payment is mentioned but it is mainly seen as a process of substitution taking place between financial assets. Monetary plurality is related to the plurality of the sources and timeframes of debts, and remains merely implicit. Basically, the banking practices fit into the singularity of the unit of account. In other words, neo-Chartalists and post-Keynesians are not concerned by the deepening of an analysis of monetary plurality, except when it appears as a factor of the payment system crisis (for instance, the European crisis of the national public debts is related to the tax-driven-money and its relationship to financial distrust regarding the homogenisation of the territorial plurality of debts issued in euros).

2.5.3 Marx and beyond: the tension between singularity and plurality as pathology

The analyses start out from Marx's conceptualisation of the social function of money as a general equivalent, that is, the unit of account of the general form of value. Marx (1857 [1973], p. 191) defines trade as a social relationship that is the foundation of the existence and role of money: 'Money does not arise by convention, any more than the state does'. The genesis of money stems from a process that excludes one commodity among others and hence provides social measurement of their value. Though money is defined as the general equivalent providing a common language, the forms it takes in circulation of goods are multiple. Money as a measure of values can have substitutes as an instrument of trade, such as banknotes or any other material assets used as a symbol of value to fulfil its function (Marx, 1867 [2011]). It must, however, be present in its material or metal form as the real equivalent of goods, or as a commodity money itself, in order to fulfil its function as a reserve of value and means of payment and also as universal equivalent. All monetary forms are backed by the general equivalent which ensures the convertibility of credit money. Thus, in Marx's analysis, there is a priori no possibility of opposition between the plurality of means of payment and the singularity of the unit of account because the functional forms of money are all interdependent. Money is indeed a social recognition of the unit of account that is expressed in its function as a reserve of value, by means of which its social power becomes the private power of individuals. Even so, the relation between monetary singularity and plurality is obvious in recent studies, setting the theoretical model on the general equivalent against empirical observation of the plurality of units of account among financial assets and more so among means of payment.

Within the contemporary Marxist school, three types of analysis can be distinguished according to their mode of analysing the link between the existence of a plurality of forms of money and the postulate of a unique measure of value. Different approaches may be discerned. First, Bryan and Rafferty (2006, 2007), based on the analysis of plurality of units of account characteristic of the globalised financial system, show that the singularity of general equivalent appears merely as a contingent historical development and is currently confronted with the monetary aspects of financial derivatives. Second, Saad-Filho and Mollo (2002) restate the anchoring of the general equivalent in the labour theory of value and interpret the resultant plurality of units of account as a pathological fragmentation of the monetary system. Finally, Aglietta and Orléan (1982) also consider the emergence of the plurality of units of account as a monetary pathology and monetary fragmentation. Nonetheless, they depart from the Marxist concept of money as the expression of the substantial value of commodities and redefine the general equivalent as the result of 'election' of one money among several embryonic moneys reappearing in severe monetary crises (see Section 2.5.4).

Bryan and Rafferty (2007, p. 153) hypothesise that financial derivatives constitute a new form of global money not driven by state decree but by competitive forces: 'Their specific capacity as commodity money is to be self-transmutable, for this is the basis of (competitive) commensuration. In this sense, they have a universal as well as self-referential dimension'. This feature gives financial derivatives a monetary character: 'Derivatives, through options and futures, establish pricing relationships that "bind" the future to the present and one place to another. (. . .) Derivatives, especially through swaps, establish pricing relationships that readily convert between ("commensurate") different forms of asset' (*ibid.*, p. 140). These empirical observations call for renewal of monetary theory so as to take account of this monetary function that the dynamics of capitalism have conferred on financial derivatives. The attempt to theorise the function of commensurability of different types of capital, which is fulfilled by financial derivatives, implies however a generic concept of money that encompasses the multiplicity of moneys of account. This, in turn, entails abandoning the principle of the singularity of a general equivalent of value.

If the historical evolution of the monetary abstraction previously goes from metallic money to fiat money, the development of financial derivatives is another step in such an evolution. For Bryan and Rafferty (2007, p. 152), they reveal an increase in the degree of abstraction of the intrinsic value of the monetary material compared with its exchange value: 'Derivatives (. . .), being derived but separated from the ownership of the underlying assets, are systematically abstracted from "particular commodities". They have the attributes Marx saw as integral to the essence of money'. In other words, they constitute a new form of money by means of which capital takes on the attributes of money, and money, the attributes of capital. Its new capacity for abstraction renders values commensurable over and above the differences in space and time (synthesised concretely by differences in interest rates between spot and forward exchange rates). In Bryan and Rafferty's conception of money, the singularity of the unit of account is merely historically contingent. The competition between units of account for fixing capital value characterises the new phase in the evolution of the money-capital relationship implied by the derivatives' innovations.

These recent revisions of the concept of general equivalent reveal the relation between monetary singularity and plurality. Bryan and Rafferty (2007, p. 153) show how the financial derivatives play the role of a 'concrete universal equivalent form of monetary value'. Even so, as financial derivatives constitute a form of money whose stability is in question, their study explicitly does not take up the question of the future of financial derivatives. Anyhow, the idea of a new kind of general equivalent that would lead to plurality seems paradoxical. Such an oxymoron hides the tension between monetary singularity and plurality. Also, the relationship between market and monetary expression of value as in Bryan and Rafferty's analysis appears to be symmetrically opposite to those postulated by the Klein-Hayek model or the New Monetary Economics. However, the necessity for a unique unit of account of value involves the intervention of the State (supposing that the financial derivatives are a contingent non-sustainable monetary form) inasmuch as the social recognition of the unit constitutes a proper monetary solution to the distributive conflict. Only Aglietta and Orléan's analysis recognises this explicitly (see Section 2.5.4).

The influence of Marx's definition of the general equivalent may be found in a different way in the work of Saad-Filho and Mollo (2002), who analyse hyperinflation in Latin America as an expression of a distributive conflict. High inflation has been previously conceptualised as the result of an extra money issue, validating prices that are higher than exchange value (de Brunhoff, 1978; de Brunhoff and Cartelier, 1979; De Vroey, 1984; Itoh and Lapavitzas, 1999). Saad-Filho and Mollo show that mark-up price behaviour and anticipations are related to the extra issue of quantity of money, which in turn is linked to the rise in base rates of interest entailed by the institutionalisation of the indexation of monetary assets. The restrictive effect of the interest rate is neutralised by the monetary swaps of compulsory reserves in Treasury bills, which enables banks to index their interest rates on high current account holdings. The cumulative effect of inflation entails the destruction of the functions of the national currency and the function of reserve value is ensured by an equivalent index in dollars. The index in dollars is subsequently recognised as the unit of account for durable goods and Treasury bills. The national currency ends up by losing its ability to fulfil its function as a means of circulation, which undermines its social recognition as a general equivalent. Distortions of relative prices impede the process of accumulation, and primarily the level of interest rates guaranteeing the liquidity of the internal debt, to the detriment of investment, just as the international function of the currency was being undermined.

This analysis follows Marx's conception of money and also converges with Aglietta and Orléan's theory of rivalry about the 'election' of the unit of account. Monetary authority can face competitive indexations so that the monetary crisis is more specifically a crisis of the singularity of unit of account. Although this analysis of hyperinflation affirms the need for the singularity of the unit of account and the convertibility at par of the various means of payment, for Bryan and Rafferty, on the contrary, this condition no longer holds with the development of derivatives. Starting with a revision of the Marxian concept of the general equivalent, Aglietta and Orléan give a new view of the plurality of units of account as a pathology, which remains a threat to contemporary monetary systems. The singularity of the unit of account gives money, considered as an institution, its sovereignty.

2.5.4 An institutionalist revision of Marx

Aglietta and Orléan (1982, 2002) reject the hypothesis that a substantial value in terms of utility or labour exists prior to market relationships. The genesis of money is the result of a mimetic rivalry among agents leading to intrinsic violence within market relationships: the 'election' of a general equivalent corresponds to the unanimously accepted symbol of wealth. The mimetic process selecting the symbol of wealth and the measure of value is not seen as the result of trade or exchange but rather as a construction of social cohesion. Money is then raised to a position of sovereignty within the market sphere. With the capitalist production of commodities, the sovereignty of money takes the form of authority of the Mints in a metallic regime or of the central bank in the modern payment system. The central bank rests on the foundation of a hierarchical monetary system and brings into play conflicting logics, either of centralisation by ensuring the convertibility of debt commitments into the base money or of fractioning this convertibility on financial markets. The predominance of one or the other of these logics formats differing growth models by means of norms that regulate the development of private assets, 'by fostering the development of certain assets while forcibly constraining others' (Aglietta and Orléan, 1982, p. 86). Unanimity about the unit of account is not always assured and implies arbitration by the monetary authority which can favour debtors, by opting for centralisation in applying an accommodating policy about the funding of private liabilities (debt-led system), or favour creditors, allowing the fractioning of the payment system to take its course by granting creditors direct control over the financial markets (finance-led system).

The plurality of issuers and the recognition of liquidity as the undisputed representation of wealth are both crucial points as unanimity is not always guaranteed by the debt-led or finance-led system. The value of claims is potentially under threat (and consequently the source of a possible monetary crisis) either by inflation, when the predominant logic is that of centralisation, or by asphyxiating debtors, when there is no longer an automatic guarantee inherent in the logic of fractioning. The tension between monetary singularity and plurality is located at the very heart of the conception of money that sees money as a mediator between different types of debt. It is expressed in two particular forms – through banking or finance – according to the type of hierarchy of the monetary initiative. When the banking configuration is predominant, the tension is incorporated into financial innovations which make it possible to circumvent limitations of the power of banking institutions issuing liabilities convertible at par with the central money.

When the finance configuration is dominant, the tension comes out in the mimetic logic and speculation process in financial markets, which leads to the sovereign decision of the lender of last resort ensuring the liquidity of private assets and the sustainability of their evaluation. In both configurations, the singularity of the unit of account is essential and its social acceptance is not only a logical concern, but also the result of political arbitration (which remains temporary) of the trial of strength between debtors and creditors and, more generally, between different social classes.

2.6 Conclusion: a typology of combinations of monetary singularity and plurality

From a multi-dimensional pattern of monetary plurality defined as the use of diverse means of payment and/or of units of account, this chapter has set out to examine each theoretical approach in its appropriate analytical context. Our examination of contemporary theories of money has revealed a variety of situations involving singularity and plurality so that a typology can be suggested. Figure 2.1 presents an overview of possible configurations associating units of account and means of payment, positioning the economic theories in their treatment of monetary singularity and plurality. As the economic theory is constructed on the basis of the two functions of account and payment, monetary singularity and plurality should not be diametrically opposed and, in particular, a plurality of means of payment is not incompatible with a unique unit of account.

Indeed, the present day national monetary systems articulate the link between the singularity of the unit of account (the State establishes its sovereignty in the monetary realm by setting the unit of account used by public and private economic agents) and the plurality of means of payment (the State authorises not only the issuing of external money by the central bank, but also the issuing of different types of internal money by commercial banks). The plurality of means of payment is organised centrally through the convertibility at par of internal moneys in relation to one another and into external money. The guarantee of convertibility is so strong through the deposit insurance or the lender of last resort that economic agents tend to see no difference between the forms of money concerned (the only differences that may crop up between the several issuers concern the interest rates at which they borrow funds in the money market). We call this canonical configuration *weak* plurality: the system is unified, homogenised and hierarchical but it is built on a plurality of means of payment. On the other hand, when there is no such guarantee of convertibility at par, premiums and discounts can be set by economic agents in accordance with their perception of the risks involved and of the cost of logistics. In the case of the Greenfield and Yeager model and that of the Free Banking system, the plurality of means of payment is made commensurable by using a common unit of account, which does not however involve all means of payment being equivalent. Indeed, issuers do not enjoy the same degree of solvability and are not protected by any public agency such as deposit insurance or a lender of last resort. We call this configuration *medium* plurality.

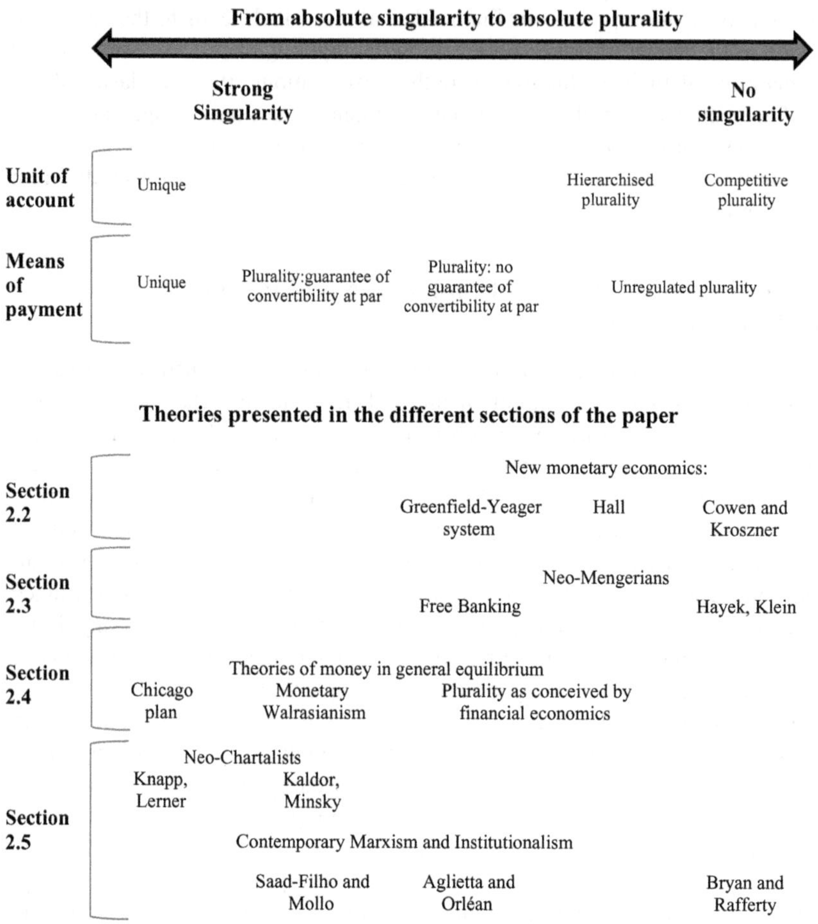

Figure 2.1 Range of configurations of singularity and plurality

There is thus a whole series of possible configurations. The gradation runs from *no* plurality to *strong* plurality with *weak* and *medium* plurality in between. At one extreme of the spectrum, no plurality corresponds to a system with a unique issuer as designed by the Chicago plan or analysed by post-Walrasian models. At the other extreme, strong plurality corresponds to a system with several unregulated issuers together with a plurality of units of account as imagined by Cowen and Krozsner. In between, there are intermediate forms with weak plurality (contemporary national monetary systems) and medium plurality (means of payment not guaranteed by convertibility at par into the unit of account).

Though singularity is not the exact reverse image of plurality, an additional gradation should be used in order to take account of the strength of the singularity of the unit of account. The criterion here is the degree of unification of units of account. But such a degree also depends on the way in which the plurality of means of payment is articulated with the unit of account and homogenised by this relationship. In economic analysis, the *numéraire* is unique in the model and postulated by the theorist. In monetary practice, the unit of account is unique in each contemporary national territory and defined by the sovereign power. So plurality of units of account is by no means self-evident. The gradation runs from *no* singularity to *strong* singularity with *weak* singularity in between. At one extreme, the singularity is nil when there is an unorganised set of competing units of account as supposed by Hayek in his monetary denationalisation program. Almost at the other extreme, singularity is *strong* when plurality is confined to issuers of means of payment or when there is only one. A *weak* form of singularity may cover those theories that conceive an organised or hierarchical plurality of units of account.

References

Aglietta, M. and Orléan, A. 1982. *La violence de la monnaie*. Paris: Presses Universitaires de France.

Aglietta, M. and Orléan, A. 2002. *La monnaie entre violence et confiance*. Paris: Odile Jacob.

Allais, M. 1947. *Economie et intérêt*. Paris, Imprimerie Nationale et Librairie des Publications Officielles.

Allais, M. 1975. 'Le concept de monnaie, la création de monnaie et de pouvoir d'achat par le mécanisme de crédit et ses implications', in *Essais en l'honneur de Jean Marchal*, edited by P. Coulbois (106–145). Paris: Cujas.

Arestis, P. and Mihailov, A. 2011. 'Classifying monetary economics: fields and methods from past to future', *Journal of Economic Surveys* 25(4): 769–800.

Baye, M. R., De Grauwe, P. and De Vries, C. G. 1993. 'An oligopoly model of free banking: theory and tests', *De Economist* 141(4): 497–514.

Bell, S. 2001. 'The role of the state and the hierarchy of money', *Cambridge Journal of Economics* 25(2):149–163.

Benes, J. and Kumhof, M. 2012. 'The Chicago Plan revisited', *International Monetary Fund*. Working Paper, No. 12/202.

Black, F. 1970. 'Banking and the interest rates in a world without money', *Journal of Bank Research* 1(Autumn): 9–20.

Black, F. 1978. 'Global monetarism in a world of national currencies', *Columbia Journal of World Business* 51(Spring): 27–32.

Black, F. 1981. 'A gold standard with double feedback and near-zero reserves', reprinted in *Business Cycles and Equilibrium*, in F. Black (115–120). Oxford, UK: Basil Blackwell Press, 1987.

Bryan, D. and Rafferty, M. 2006. *Capitalism with Derivatives: A Political Economy of Financial Derivatives, Capital and Class*. London: Palgrave.

Bryan, D. and Rafferty, M. 2007. 'Financial derivatives and the theory of money', *Economy and Society* 36(1): 134–158.

Chang, R. 1994. 'Endogenous currency substitution, inflationary finance, and welfare', *Journal of Money, Credit and Banking* 26(4): 903–916.

Clower, R. 1967. 'A reconsideration of the microfoundations of monetary theory', *Western Economic Journal* 6(4): 1–8.

Cowen, T. and Kroszner, R. 1987. 'The development of the New Monetary Economics', *Journal of Political Economy* 95(3): 567–590.

Cowen, T. and Kroszner, R. 1994. *Explorations in the New Monetary Economics*. Oxford, UK: Blackwell.

Davidson, P. 1978. *Money and the Real World*, 2nd edition. London: Macmillan.

De Brunhoff, S. 1978. *The State, Capital and Economic Policy*. London: Pluto Press.

De Brunhoff, S. and Cartelier, J. 1979. 'Une analyse marxiste de l'inflation', in *Les rapports d'argent*, edited by de S. de Brunhoff (119–135). Grenoble, France: Presses Universitaires de Grenoble.

De Vroey, M. 1984. 'Inflation: a non-monetarist monetary interpretation', *Cambridge Journal of Economics* 8(4): 381–399.

Diamond, P. A. 1965. 'National debt in a neoclassical growth model', *American Economic Review* 55(5): 1126–1150.

Dow, S. 1996. 'Horizontalism: a critique', *Cambridge Journal of Economics* 20(4): 497–508.

Dowd, K. (ed.) 1992. *The Experience of Free Banking*. London: Routledge.

Duca, J. V. and Van Hoose, D. D. (2004) 'Recent developments in understanding the demand for money', *Journal of Economics and Business* 56(4): 247–272.

Fama, E. F. 1980. 'Banking in the theory of finance', *Journal of Monetary Economics* 6(1): 39–57.

Fama, E. F. 1983. 'Financial intermediation and price level control', *Journal of Monetary Economics* 12(1): 7–28.

Fisher, I. 1920. *Stabilizing the Dollar*. New York: Macmillan.

Fisher, I. 1935. *100% Money*. New York: Adelphi Publications.

Friedman, M. 1959. *A Program for Monetary Stability*. New York: Fordham University Press.

Gnos, C. and Rochon, L.-P. 2002. 'Money creation and the State: a critical assessment of Chartalism', *International Journal of Political Economy* 32(3): 41–57.

Goodhart, C. A. E. 1989. 'Has Moore become too horizontal?' *Journal of Post Keynesian Economics* 12(1): 29–34.

Goodhart, C. A. E. 2005. 'What is the essence of money?' *Cambridge Journal of Economics* 29(5): 817–825.

Greenfield, R. L. and Yeager, L. B. 1983. 'A laisser-faire approach to monetary stability', *Journal of Money, Credit and Banking* 15(3): 302–315.

Greenfield, R. L., Woolsey, W. W. and Yeager, L. B. 1995. 'Is indirect convertibility impossible? Comment', *Journal of Money, Credit and Banking* 27(1): 293–297.

Hahn, F. M. 1965. 'On some problems of proving the existence of an equilibrium in a monetary economy', in *The Theory of Interest Rates*, edited by F. H. Hahn and F. Brechling (126–135). London: Macmillan.

Hall, R. E. 1981. 'The government and the monetary unit', *NBER*, Working Paper 159.

Hall, R. E. 1982. 'Monetary trends in the United States and the United Kingdom: a review from the perspective of new developments in monetary economics', *Journal of Economic Literature* 20(4): 1552–1556.

Hall, R. E. 1983. 'Optimal fiduciary monetary systems', *Journal of Monetary Economics* 12(1): 33–50.

Hall, R. E. 1992. 'A free-market policy to stabilise the purchasing power of the dollar', in *Money in Crisis. The Federal Reserve, the Economy, and Monetary Reform*, edited by B. N. Siegel (303–321). Cambridge, MA: Harper and Row Pub.

Hall, R. E. 1997. 'Irving Fisher's self-stabilizing money', *American Economic Review* 87(2): 436–438.

Hayek, F. 1978. *Denationalisation of Money. The Argument Refined*. London: IEA.

Hayek, F. 1979. 'Toward a free market monetary system', *Journal of Libertarian Studies* 3(1): 1–8.
Hein, E. 2004. 'Money, credit and the interest rate in Marx's economic. On the similarities of Marx's monetary analysis to post-Keynesian economics', *International Papers in Political Economy* 11(2): 1–43.
Hicks, J. 1935. 'A suggestion for simplifying the theory of money', *Economica* 2(5): 1–19.
Itoh, M. and Lapavitzas, C. 1999. *Political Economy of Money and Finance*. London: Macmillan.
Iwai, K. 1988. 'The evolution of money – A search-theoretic foundation of monetary economics', CARESS Working Paper 88–03, University of Pennsylvania.
Iwai, K. 1996. 'The boostrap theory of money: a search-theoretic foundation of monetary economics', *Structural Change and Economic Dynamics* 7(4): 451–477.
Jackson, A., Dyson, B. and Hodgson, G. 2013. *The Positive Money Proposal*. London, PositiveMoney.
Jevons, W. S. 1875. *Money and the Mechanism of Exchange*. London: H. S. King.
Kaldor, N. 1960, 'The Radcliffe report', *Review of Economics and Statistics* 42(1): 14–19.
Kaldor, N. 1982. *The Scourge of Monetarism*. New York: Oxford University Press.
Kareken, J. and Wallace, N. (eds) 1980. *Models of Monetary Economies*. Minneapolis, MN: Federal Reserve Bank of Minneapolis.
Kareken, J. and Wallace, N. 1981. 'On the indeterminacy of equilibrium exchange rates', *Quarterly Journal of Economics* 96(2): 207–222.
Keynes, J. M. 1930. 'A treatise on money: the pure theory of money', in *The Collected Writings of John Maynard Keynes*. London: MacMillan, 1971.
Keynes, J. M. 1936. 'The general theory of employment, interest and money', in *The Collected Writings of John Maynard Keynes*, Vol. 7, edited by E. Johnson and D. Moggridge. Cambridge, UK: Macmillan, 1973.
Keynes, J. M. 1937 'Alternative theories of the rate of interest', *Economic Journal* 14: 201–215.
Kiyotaki, N. and Wright, R. 1989. 'On money as a medium of exchange', *Journal of Political Economy* 97(4): 927–954.
Kiyotaki, N. and Wright, R. 1991. 'A contribution to the pure theory of money', *Journal of Economic Theory* 53: 215–235.
Kiyotaki, N. and Wright, R. 1993. 'A search-theoretic approach to monetary economics', *American Economic Review* 83(1): 63–77.
Klein, B. 1974. 'The competitive supply of money', *Journal of Money, Credit and Banking* 6(4): 423–453.
Klein, B. 1976. 'Competing monies: a comment', *Journal of Money, Credit and Banking* 8(4): 513–519.
Knapp, G. F. 1924. *The State Theory of Money*. London: Macmillan.
Kocherlakota, N. and Krueger, T. 1999. 'A signaling model of multiple currencies', *Review of Economic Dynamics* 2(1): 231–244.
Lerner, A. P. 1947. 'Money as a creature of the state', *American Economic Review* 37(2): 312–317.
Lucas, R. E. 1972. 'Expectations and the neutrality of money', *Journal of Economic Theory* 4(2): 103–124.
Lucas, R. E. and Stokey, N. L. 1983. 'Optimal fiscal and monetary policy in an economy without capital', *Journal of Monetary Economics* 12(1): 55–93.
Marx, K. 1973 [1857]. *Grundrisse – Foundations of the Critique of Political Economy*. London: Penguin Classics.

Marx, K. 2011 [1867]. *Capital. A Critique of Political Economy (Volume 1)*. New York: Dover Publications.
McCallum, B. T. 1983. 'The role of overlapping-generations models in monetary economics', *Carnegie-Rochester Conference Series on Public Policy* 18: 9–44.
McCallum, B. T. 2010. 'Issues concerning nonpecuniary yield of money', *Cato Journal* 30(3): 439–449.
Mehrling, P. 1998. 'The money muddle: the transformation of American monetary thought, 1920–1970', in *From Interwar Pluralism to Postwar Neoclassicism*, edited by M. S. Morgan and M. Rutherford (293–306). Durham, NC: Duke University Press.
Mehrling, P. 2000. 'Understanding Fisher Black', Barnard College, Columbia University, manuscript.
Menger, K. 1892. 'On the origin of money', *Economic Journal* 2(6): 239–255.
Minsky, H. P. 1986. *Stabilizing an Unstable Economy*. New Haven, CT: Yale University Press.
Mises, L. 1949. *Human Action*. London: William Hodge.
Moore, B. J. 1988. *Horizontalists and Verticalists: The Macro-economics of Credit Money*. Cambridge, UK: Cambridge University Press.
Niggle, C. J. 1991. 'The endogenous money supply theory: an institutionalist appraisal', *Journal of Economic Issues* 25(1): 137–151.
O'Driscoll, G. P. 1985. 'Money: Menger's evolutionary theory', Research Paper 8508, Federal Reserve Bank of Dallas.
Ostroy, J. M. and Starr, R. M. 1974 'Money and the decentralisation of exchange', *Econometrica* 42(6): 1093–1113.
Patinkin, D. 1956. *Money, Interest and Prices*. Evanston, IL: Rown Peterson.
Radcliffe Report 1959. *The Report of the Committee on the Working of the Monetary System*. London: Committee on the Working of the Monetary System.
Rousseas, S. W. 1960. 'Velocity changes and the effectiveness of monetary policy', *Review of Economics and Statistics* 42(1): 27–36.
Saad-Filho, A. and Mollo, R. 2002. 'Inflation and stabilisation in Brazil: a political economy analysis', *Review of Radical Political Economics* 34(2): 109–135.
Samuelson, P. A. 1958. 'An exact consumption-loan model of interest with or without the social contrivance of money', *Journal of Political Economy* 66(6): 467–482.
Schnadt, N., and Whittaker, J. 1993. 'Inflation-proof currency? The feasibility of variable commodity standards', *Journal of Money, Credit, and Banking* 25(2): 214–221.
Scialom, L. 1995. 'Les modèles de paiement concurrentiels. Éléments d'analyse critique', *Revue économique* 46(1): 35–55.
Selgin, G. A. 1988. *The Theory of Free Banking: Money Supply Under Competitive Note Issue*. Totowa, NJ: Rowman & Littlefield.
Selgin, G. A. 2003. 'Adaptive learning and the transition to fiat money', *Economic Journal* 113(484): 147–165.
Selgin, G. A. and White, L. H. 1987. 'The evolution of a free banking system', *Economic Inquiry* 25(3): 439–457.
Selgin, G. A. and White, L. H. 1994. 'How would the invisible hand handle money?' *Journal of Economic Literature* 32(4): 1718–1749.
Shiller, R. J. 2002. 'Indexed units of account: theory and assessment of historical experience', *Indexation, Inflation and Monetary Policy*, edited by F. Lefort and K. Schmidt-Hebbel (105–134). Santiago, Chile: Central Bank of Chile.
Simons, H. C. 1934. 'A positive program for laisser-faire', in *Economic Policy for a Free Society*. Chicago, IL: University of Chicago Press, 1948.

Soddy F. 1926. *Wealth, Virtual Wealth, and Debt*. London: George Allen and Unwin.

Sturzenegger, F. N. 1992. 'Inflation and social welfare in a model with endogenous financial adaptation', *UCLA* Working Papers 658.

Sumner, S. 1990. 'The forerunners of "New Monetary Economics": proposals to stabilise the unit of account: note', *Journal of Money, Credit and Banking* 22(1): 109–118.

Uribe, M. 1997. 'Hysteresis in a simple model of currency substitution', *Journal of Monetary Economics* 40(1): 185–202.

Vaubel, R. 1986. 'Currency competition versus governmental money monopolies', *Cato Journal* 5(3): 927–942.

Wallace, N. 1977. 'Why the Fed should consider holding M0 constant', *Federal Reserve Bank of Minneapolis Quarterly Review* 1(1): 2–10.

Wallace, N. 1980. 'The overlapping generations model of fiat money', in *Models of Monetary Economics*, edited by J. Kareken and N. Wallace (49–82). Minneapolis, MN: Federal Reserve Bank of Mineapolis.

Wallace, N. 1983. 'A legal restrictions theory of the demand for 'money' and the role of monetary policy', *Federal Reserve Bank of Mineapolis Quaterly Review* 7(1): 1–7.

White, L. H. 1984a. 'Competitive payments systems and the unit of account', *American Economic Review* 74(4): 699–712.

White, L. H. 1984b. *Free Banking in Britain: Theory, Experience and Debate, 1800–1845*. Cambridge, UK: Cambridge University Press.

White, L. H. 1989. *Competition and Currency*. New York: New York University Press.

Woolsey, W. W. 1992. 'The search for macroeconomic stability: comment on Sumner', *Cato Journal* 12(2): 475–485.

Wray, R. 1998. *Understanding Modern Money: The Key to Full Employment and Price Stability*. Cheltenham, UK: Edward Elgar.

Wray, R. 2003. 'L'approche post-keynésienne de la monnaie', in *Théories monétaires post keynésiennes*, edited by P. Piégay and L. P. Rochon (52–65). Paris: Economica.

Yeager, L. B. 1983. 'Stable money and free-market currencies', *Cato Journal* 3(1): 305–326.

Yeager, L. B. 1994. 'Mises and Hayek on calculation and knowledge', *Review of Austrian Economics* 7(2): 93–109.

Yeager L. B. 1997. 'Austrian economics, neoclassicism, and the market test', *Journal of Economic Perspectives* 11(4): 153–165.

Yeager L. B. 1999. 'Should Austrians scorn general-equilibrium theory?' *Review of Austrian Economics* 11(1–2): 19–30.

Yeager, L. B. 2010. 'Privatizing money', *Cato Journal* 30(3): 417–438.

3 Making sense of the plurality of money

A Polanyian attempt

Jérôme Blanc[1]

3.1 Introduction

This chapter aims at accounting for the dramatic plurality of money through the discussion of a conceptual framework built on Polanyian writings. Indeed, a multiplicity of moneys has emerged in the last 30 years that are not national currencies. These moneys include systems set up by community groups, local authorities or even by private businesses for their own interests. They come in various shapes and sizes, ranging from electronic moneys on smart cards to systems for debt settlement by multilateral clearing arrangements via more or less sophisticated notes or vouchers. The space in which they circulate extends from small communal groups to politically borderless cyberspace. They are created to secure customer loyalty, to revitalise an area's economy, to give impetus to social policies, to act as incentives to virtuous behaviour and for many other purposes.

Although the rapid emergence of these new schemes requires a theoretical framework within which they can be accounted for, little has been done so far to produce one. The only journal on forms of money characterised as 'complementary currencies' or 'community currencies', the *International Journal of Community Currency Research* (*IJCCR*), has so far published monographs for the most part, with a few exceptions like Blanc (2011) and Martignoni (2012) that deal with typologies. The multiplicity of money in its theoretical dimension is seldom addressed as such, aside from mainly Austrian approaches such as Hayek, as well as New Monetary Economics or Free Banking, all of which consider competition as the standard interaction mode between moneys.[2] Conversely, to speak of 'complementary currencies', as frequently done in studies on LETS (local exchange and trading systems), local currencies, etc., does not contribute substantially to our understanding of the issue, because the concept of complementarity is only one of the criteria for an in-depth analysis of relations among all forms of money (on this matter, Blanc, 2017). Moreover, attempts to construct typologies and proposals for naming moneys have generally proven to be disappointingly incoherent or unsystematic, as if the subject of analysis itself were not amenable to any stringent form of classification.

A major difficulty facing observers is the obsolescence of previously established typologies because of the pace of innovation and the removal of boundaries that previously seemed unlikely to be crossed. Since the 1980s, LETS and time-based schemes mixed social innovation with the principle of mutual credit accounted with an internal currency. Offline softwares and then online platforms were developed to provide the infrastructure of such schemes, like Cyclos or CES, allowing the creation of new communities with their moneys in a simple way, locally or remotely. Since the 1990s, the internet has thus made it possible to create communities that are not confined within any political borders. With different goals to those of LETS and time-based schemes, the metaverse Second Life implemented its own money, the Linden dollar (Hueber, 2011). New forms of local currencies have emerged in North America in the 1990s, followed by South America and Europe in the 2000s. In the specific case of France, where the local implementation of LETS from 1994 was barely considered monetary schemes by their founders and users (Servet, ed. 1999), any fear of illegality seems to have vanished by the late 2000s. More than 40 local currencies were created between 2010 and 2016 which were also made convertible into euros. There was also a surge in the number of projects in this domain. Again, in France, the possibilities of compiling various items of information and keeping simultaneous but separate accounts on smart cards has been an important line of thought for what has become SOL money (Fare, 2011). SOL was also a project that brought together the private sector (above all social and solidarity economy organisations), local authorities and community groups around a number of objectives: retail trade, non-market services, welfare support and payment for commitment to work among associations. With the spread of participatory instruments of web 2.0, there has been a rise in initiatives promising to establish reputational currencies – by which web users reward other deserving web users in a decentralised and voluntary way, or attention currencies – which reward those who read e-mails, visit internet pages, etc. Eventually, in 2009 Bitcoin opened a new phase in monetary experiences with blockchain technology, which allowed keeping the memory of transactions and establishing confidence into the money by way of a distributed ledger (Maurer, 2016). Hundreds of such crypto-currencies flourished in the following years. A growing number of activist associations, corporate strategic-watch managers, developers and futurologists are taking up the monetary terminology that seemed to be confined formerly to bankers and monetary authorities. Banks themselves are increasingly considering the disruptive capacity of these innovations while monetary authorities are trying to understand and regulate this wave. A whole array of technological, legal, political and ideological boundaries have thus been and are continuing to be pushed back, making it difficult to construct any typology.

At the very least, a working definition of money must be given to provide a basis on which to examine this plurality: in agreement with a range of institutionalist and socio-economic works, money here shall be considered to be an institutionalised 'principle' for debt settlement, thus requiring its minting and its use as a unit of account and a means of payment (Alary et al., 2016). The argument made here is that the instruments developed by Karl Polanyi are decisive for framing and thinking about this multi-dimensional and changing whole.

Section 3.2 briefly discusses the requirements for a relevant typology, followed by Polanyi's distinction between all-purpose money and special-purpose money. The proposed re-evaluation recognises modern forms of special-purpose money, even if they do not relate to the same sociological and anthropological functions as in exotic societies.[3] Three ideal types of moneys are then outlined: public, business and associative moneys, depending on the nature of their issuer: political entities, companies or associations. In Section 3.3, the conceptual framework is deepened in order to add analytical complexity to the ideal types. Polanyi's discussion of the forms of economic integration brings out the major criteria for understanding money systems in their complexity and hybridisation. In Section 3.4, the three ideal types are used in the light of this conceptual framework so as to take into account a variety of cases within the contemporary multiplicity of moneys.

3.2 Outline of a typology of money

3.2.1 Conditions for, and difficulties with, a relevant typology

Meaningful discussion on the classification of money among contemporary economists often stops with exchange rate regimes, since national currencies pertain to State sovereignty while providing the essential vehicle for transactions as measured by the classical indicators of wealth production. This leads to focus on either sovereign moneys or credit moneys, or both. When presented, new forms of money are often reduced to their most dramatic features, without any attempt to conceive a general typology. Benjamin Cohen (2004), for example, builds a 'currency pyramid' with seven categories of national currencies depending on their autonomy and power, and dedicates the last chapter of his book, *The Future of Money*, to 'new frontiers' in which he develops 'local money' and 'electronic money'. Historical and anthropological work, when confronted with a different viewpoint, can more readily relativise the obvious facts about modern moneys. The scientific outlook does not only focus on the phenomena because of their magnitude, but also because of what their specific features signify. In the same way, paying attention to the burgeoning of non-bank and non-State moneys since the 1980s does not involve addressing the large-scale phenomena (since for the most part they are still not quantitatively widespread) but in identifying schemes whose features raise questions about the social representation of money today and even about learned considerations on money. Examination of these moneys raises the need for categorisation so that some things can be distinguished and others put together. This is an especially active approach for scholars interested in the dynamics of monetary innovation over the past 30 years and also for the actors directly involved, who also need these insights.

Drawing on the attempts to categorise complementary and community currencies that have developed since the 1990s, one can keep a few requirements in mind (DeMeleunaere and Blanc, 2007). First of all, with respect to community or complementary currencies, a distinction must be made between typology of items and typology of systems. The latter consists of identifying coherent systems combining a series of elementary items. Secondly, a general typology of monetary systems should be established prior to any specific typology of community or complementary currencies. Thirdly, the relevant typology must be flexible enough to have scope for innovation through the development of new systems.

In previous works, I have tried to go beyond items and focus on possible organisational choices in community or complementary currencies (Blanc, 2009a). This led me to identify a set of five coherent schemes defined in terms of the compatibility of their organisational choices and their objectives. This attempt did not result in the definition of any rigorous criteria for a general typology. Polanyi's approach seems to be a heuristic one as it enables us to move beyond these difficulties (Blanc, 2011, 2013).

It is a call for the construction of ideal types, in the way Weber uses the term as an abstract, utopian and exemplary construction designed to bring together, in some coherent form, a set of features that are not necessarily observed as such in the real world. These ideal types are then mobilised to make the real world more intelligible and enable in-depth studies of variations, changes, contradictions and so on. That is the direction taken in this chapter, by connecting the ideal type with the underlying projects of the monetary systems and with Polanyi's forms of integration.

A preliminary step, though, is to return to the distinction Karl Polanyi drew between all-purpose money and special-purpose money (Polanyi, 1957, 1968, 1977). This contributed greatly in challenging the idea that the distinguishing feature of primitive or even archaic societies was their use of barter; on the contrary, what supposedly characterised them was their use of special-purpose money, in forms other than those found in modern societies.

3.2.2 All-purpose versus special-purpose money

To understand this, we have to return to the foundations of Polanyi's approach: a work on the uses of money in the context of what he calls substantive conception of economics, where the central feature is 'the interchange with his natural and social environment' and where no assumptions are made about behaviours with respect to individual choices and their rational character (Polanyi, 1957, p. 243). Polanyi reasons on the basis of 'quantifiable objects' (Polanyi, 1957, p. 264), which may be employed for three main uses: 'payment use', 'standard or accounting use' and 'exchange use'. Elsewhere, he also introduces the use of storing wealth, which clearly does not rank as highly as the first three; his emphasis on this use is related to his examination of the role of treasure in exotic societies (Polanyi, 1968, pp. 183–188 and 1977, p. 97 sq.; Servet, 1993).

On this basis, Polanyi makes an intuitively sharp distinction between moneys in modern societies and what now appear as moneys of exotic societies, which were long considered to be forms outside of money. 'Early money is [. . .] special-purpose money. Different kinds of objects are employed in the different money uses; moreover, the uses are instituted independently of one another' (Polanyi, 1957, p. 266). All-purpose money is a feature of modern societies, where the market dominates. In this case, the primary use of money, above its payment use (in the sense of settlement of taxes, rents and tributes) and its accounting use, is a means of exchange. This use ranks above the other two and gives rise to them (Polanyi, 1957, p. 264).

Polanyi's distinction, and more generally his entire analysis, has two major points of interest that have been largely underscored: for one, they lead to a clear distinction between money and the market; for another, they lead to a rejection of the 'barter fable' (Servet, 1988) and even to an assertion of the universality of money as an institution (Polanyi, 1977; Servet, 1993). In this, a sharp demarcation line is drawn between what are plainly very different forms of money.

Conversely, Polanyi's conception does not lead us to break from some key features of the classical conception of money: for one thing, the idea that money takes on all the functions of money simultaneously (even if he thinks in terms of uses rather than functions and does not consider a reserve use); and for another the idea that money provides access to all available goods and services, with the corollary principle that money is fungible.[4] Consequently, it leads to the view that modern societies do not have any special-purpose money. The classical conception of money in modern societies remains largely free from criticism.

The observation of money uses, and more specifically of those 'quantifiable objects' that are used as money, takes us beyond the scope that Polanyi imparts to this distinction. It brings out the fragmentary character of money and no longer its supposedly full or unified character: money is dispersed into an array of varied instruments. Money is unitary as a system but fragmentary as an instrument. As a system, Polanyi's second proposition (that modern money assumes the three money uses of means of payment, instrument of exchange and unit of account) is a truism: it cannot be otherwise. However, in terms of monetary instruments, no single instrument of those that compose the 'modern money' system can claim to cover all of the uses of money by itself: Polanyi's second proposition seems absurd in this respect.

3.2.3 Thinking about modern special-purpose moneys

There is a multiplicity of money instruments in modern societies, not just in crisis situations but also in economically, politically and financially stable societies (Blanc, 2000). This plurality is first of all the plural character of what is called national currency. Far from being a perfectly homogenous and indistinguishable set of instruments, national currency is made up of means of payment that differs in terms of their issuers (a variable number of commercial banks issue scriptural money, while banknotes and coinage are generally issued by the central bank), their possible uses (their use is not universal in the sense that none of these instruments alone can cover all possible money uses; only a combination of these means of payment can provide access to everything that requires money), and their social meanings (such as the social distinction in the use of certain top-end bank cards or co-branded cards). This plurality of national currency, which is generally brushed over, reveals itself in times of crisis (fractionated or centralised system as Aglietta and Orléan, 2002 put it; Grahl, 2000; Théret, ed., 2007). It is the central bank that nowadays makes a coherent whole by ensuring the mutual convertibility of these forms of money and their convertibility into central money around a single unit of account.

The concept of plurality relates also to other monetary forms that we encounter, here again very vividly in crisis situations, but that can nevertheless be observed in quiet times too. Extensive research into money uses worldwide over the period 1988–1999 threw up a wide variety of units of account and means of payment used by populations both in situations of crisis and in what were considered normal situations in the industrialised world and in the global South (Blanc, 2000). A little over 500 examples of practices relating to monetary instruments that were distinct from the national currency were identified, revealing an astonishing diversity of forms of money. Upon first examination, some forms of money are designed as all-purpose money such that there are no limits in principle on their validity, while others, on the contrary, can be viewed as special-purpose money because of the limits imposed on their use (by law or by rules laid down by the issuer).

The upshot of this line of thought is that modern money is not all one and the same, even if its plural character is the subject of attempts to homogenise and unify it that are probably unprecedented in history. Moreover, modern money brings together schemes that differ considerably in their logic and their terms of validity.

First of all, modern societies have special-purpose moneys. To understand them, it can be posited that the validity of moneys is modulated by five criteria: temporal (the time horizon for use of an instrument), territorial (spatial limits of its use), economic (the range of things paid or accounted for by the instrument, which does not presuppose any market transaction), social (the group of people using the instrument) and legal (the regulatory restrictions on use of the instrument, which potentially cross-cut the previous four criteria but also extend beyond them, for example by setting limits to the use of coins or banknotes as legal tender). Any instrument has a monetary quality to a degree that is dependent on these restrictions. The special purpose of Polanyi's exotic moneys may be re-interpreted here by a combination of criteria of economic and social validity, since they define who can use the money and what for. The modern equivalent of exotic special-purpose moneys is not necessarily related to community reproduction but rather to the organisation of procedures for accounting and payment in a circuit combining an identified group of users and a set of things covered by the money use. This is the way in which we can understand schemes such as community or complementary currencies or vouchers such as meal tickets. The possible restrictions in terms of time horizon, territorial area and regulation are not enough to define these modern special-purpose moneys by themselves, but they do modulate their uses.

Secondly, as a consequence, it seems that the monetary quality of an instrument is not related so much to the universality of its use as to the socialisation of the practices of accounting or payment conducted by means of it within a given social group. There is no single money that has a universal or unlimited character. However, there are a host of instruments whose monetary quality is constrained by various boundaries on their validity. This leads to a reformulation of Polanyi's idea of all-purpose money: money of the kind that relates to monetary instruments which can be used for payment or accounting of a large number of things (but not all), among the commensurable things of a society (of which an important part is also alienable). Only the combined use of these instruments affords access to the largest possible number of economic operations and to the largest possible number of potential users. Moreover, modern societies confine money to uses within certain moral boundaries, although these may change, whether they are market uses or not. Historical debates on slavery and slave trade (leading to their formal prohibition), as well as contemporary debates on implementing markets for organs, display cases of contested moral limits on money uses. The bounds of all-purpose money are very broad but are not indefinite. As Warnier (2018) emphasises when discussing Annette Weiner, some goods are inalienable and cannot move other than through non-monetary and non-horizontal forms of transmission: 'whatever is too valuable to be sacrificed in a transaction without causing a scandal: ancestors, a name, family heirlooms, a native land, convictions, gods possibly'; for Godelier, 'religion and whatever is sacred'; but 'one might just as well say "whatever is sovereign" or even "life"' (Warnier, 2018).

Thirdly, the co-existence of more than one monetary instrument appears to be normal and lasting, even in modern and politically, economically, financially and monetarily stable societies – unless one begins with a political definition of normality that excludes this type of practice *de facto*. This conclusion relates to two foundational assumptions that break away from common opinion about the general fungibility of moneys in modern societies. First, an epistemological, if not an ontological, distinction must be made between political sovereignty and monetary sovereignty. In addition, the scope must be broadened by including a set of money uses (that is, uses which articulate accounting and payment) that cannot be channelled through the usual money instruments.

3.2.4 Three ideal types of moneys: public, business and associative

On this basis, initially and starting first from an idea of the multiplicity of issuers of moneys today and of their rationales, three major ideal types can be developed: public money, business money and associative money. We start with a short presentation of these ideal types before detailing the argument in Sections 3.3 and 3.4.

The type 'public money' relates to the logic of authority and sovereignty via a fiscal circuit in which the treasury historically has pride of place. Public money comes from political entities with rationales of political control. Sovereign domination makes it possible to capture resources, in the form of seigniorage and, more importantly, of tax collection as far as this public money is required for tax payment. Being the product of sovereign power, public money is all-purpose, in a sense close to Polanyi's ideal: a money that can be used for all things commensurable and alienable in a society delimited by geographical space.

The type 'business money' relates to the logic of resource seeking by business organisations. Currency issuance and management are the ways they capture resources. Resources may be obtained in various methods: seigniorage, interest rate on credit, levies on transactions or orientation of transactions to their benefit. Business money can be all-purpose or special-purpose, depending on the boundaries defined by their convertibility rules and, thus, the spheres of users and the uses they give access to.

The type 'associative money' relates to the construction of schemes by groups of people who voluntarily associate for the purpose of collective utility. The focus is put on the particular way these moneys are designed and implemented: the association is considered here as a general way of assembling people around common projects, distinct from resource-seeking motives of business money or instituted political control of public money. Consequently, associative money may be special-purpose money such that its validity can be limited, as a matter of principle, to a very specific set of actors and, above all, goods and services.

3.3 Forms of integration and money

Applied to modern societies, the distinction between all-purpose and special-purpose money is translated into a continuum of situations in which the restriction of validity in social and economic spaces brings about a qualitative leap. It is nevertheless Polanyi's analysis of the forms of economic integration that provides the main keys for deepening our typology of moneys.

Polanyi distinguishes several 'principles of behavior' which, resting upon 'institutional patterns' (Polanyi, 1944, pp. 49–51), he calls 'forms of integration' in *Trade and Market*. These forms are 'instituted processes' that confer 'unity and stability' on economic processes (Polanyi, 1957, p. 250; see also Polanyi, 1977, p. 39). These forms 'thus designate the institutionalized movements through which the elements of the economic process – from material resources and labour to transportation, storage, and distribution of goods – are connected' (Polanyi, 1977, p. 39). The 'main' forms are reciprocity, redistribution and exchange. Providing a critical re-reading of Polanyi's forms of integration and their actual use by scholars, Servet (2013) establishes that one should not focus on Polanyi's approach as related to circulation alone. Polanyi indeed analyses instituted principles that ensure 'production and distribution'. This is a condition for refusing a dichotomous approach separating money from so-called real activities. It is also an argument for considering a fourth principle that Polanyi was apt to overlook after 1944: householding.

Each of these terms should be clarified so as to bring them closer to the question of money. When Polanyi addressed money and economic integration together, he began by rejecting the catallactic definition of money whereby 'all money uses are dependent upon the existence of markets' (Polanyi, 1957, p. 264). He then settled for examining the close relationship of each of the three uses identified (payment, account and exchange) with three societies (primitive, archaic and modern respectively), each dominated by a specific form of integration that did not, however, exclude any articulation with other forms (reciprocity, redistribution and exchange respectively) (Polanyi, 1957, p. 264–266).

3.3.1 Exchange

Exchange 'refers here to vice-versa movements taking place *as* between "hands" under a market system' (Polanyi, 1957, p. 250 – emphasis added); it is 'the mutual appropriative movement of goods between hands' (*ibid.*, p. 266). Exchange may be organised through a self-regulating system of markets, that is, 'an economy directed by market prices and nothing but market prices', market prices being self-regulated prices (Polanyi, 1944, p. 45). But exchange may also relate to non-market forms. Thus trade is a kind of exchange that is long-distance and not necessarily market-based. In the case of what he calls 'administered trade', it is politically regulated and 'prices' are actually fixed equivalents existing before the exchange.

Beyond Polanyi's characterisation of market and trade, the important thing here is that exchange and market must be distinguished in the substantive economy Polanyi constructs: not all exchanges stem from price-forming markets, that is, markets where prices, which are flexible by definition, arise from the confrontation of supply and demand in such a way that their quantities balance out.

This point enables us to understand that some monetary systems are built around the will to promote forms of exchange that stand at varying degrees from self-regulating market. This is the case of some private special-purpose monetary arrangements within the national monetary system that fall into the 'business money' ideal type previously outlined. Some are designed to activate a customer relationship, that is, lasting exchange relations based on loyalty among partners (Blanc, 2009b), which breaks from the anonymity, theoretical equality and lack of memory that characterise the market transaction. Likewise, the idea of fair trade relates to a form of exchange in which prices and the terms of transaction result from a redefinition of market conditions passed through the screen of commutative justice. This redefinition ranges from a blunt rejection of market terms to a problematic involvement in market order. Many cases of 'associative money' also promote a kind of fair trade within local territories, for example with the promotion of community-based agriculture and short commercial circuits (Blanc and Fare, 2016).

3.3.2 Redistribution

Redistribution 'designates appropriational movements toward a center and out of it again' (Polanyi, 1957, p. 250). It is 'apt to integrate groups at all levels and all degrees of permanence from the state itself to units of a transitory character' (*ibid.*, p. 254). It refers to 'collecting and redistributing from a center' (Polanyi, 1977, p. 41).

The necessary centrality may be interpreted as the outcome or institutionalisation of political power over the group, which may be reflected by not only a form of protection, but also of domination. In this way, collection and redistribution may be associated with a form of 'unreleasable debt' that recurring payments may only appease, contrary to debts arising from exchange that are released by the transfer of money (Commons, 1990; for a widened view of unreleasable debt, see Saiag, 2014). Redistribution relates especially to the structuring and control of a territory by a politically legitimated institution: from the central or federated State to the lowest tiers of public authority. The important point here is the idea of political control to which individuals and groups are subjected and that requires mandatory payments towards the centre and is reflected by payments out. The exercise by the State of this movement of collection and redistribution is just one specific instance that is historically and politically situated. Eventually, allowance must also be made for non-State or non-public organisations such as foundations, which exert a form of power over their beneficiaries by establishing vertical forms of circulation of wealth through redistribution.

'Public money' that has been outlined above is historically linked to sovereign domination. It is based on the same institutional pattern as redistribution because of the centrality of the sovereign power. Collecting and redistributing behave as tools for political control over the territory and its population. Money issuance may be a major vector for such movements, as with metallic currencies whose issuance require first the collection of precious metals by the Mints, and whose issues, after a period of circulation, flow back to the sovereign power through tax collection.

3.3.3 Reciprocity

Reciprocity 'denotes movements between correlative points of symmetrical groupings' (Polanyi, 1957, p. 250). These are flows among symmetrically ordered individuals or social groups, around the three-way obligations to give, receive and return. Polanyi includes the idea that

> [k]inship, neighbourhood, or totem belong to the more permanent and comprehensive groupings; within their compass voluntary and semi-voluntary associations of a military, vocational, religious or social character create situations in which . . . there would form symmetrical groupings the members of which practice some sort of mutuality.
>
> (*ibid.*, p. 253)

Reciprocity is marked by the indefinite time of reciprocal actions (unlike exchange) and by the capacity to construct reciprocal actions involving more than two individuals or groups: reciprocity is then multilateral. It should be noticed then, contrary to the argument generally employed by theoreticians of solidarity-based economy, that reciprocity cannot be reduced to a non-monetary exchange; apart from the reasons above, primitive moneys, as contemplated by

Polanyi, circulate precisely according to the principle of reciprocity. In this context, money may be a vehicle for community reproduction by being at the heart of reciprocal circulations.[5]

It is not possible to link reciprocity to only one of the three ideal types of money outlined. However, reciprocity is at the core of a specific mode of debt settlement, which is sometimes called 'mutual credit'. Mutual credit systems rely on closed groups of actors whose transactions are recorded and settled in accounts without prior monetary issuance: they are credit-clearing systems. Mutual credit requires precise symmetry between the (ever-evolving) groups of debtors and creditors. Public, business and associative moneys may be built on this principle, as shown respectively by Keynes' Bancor project (public money at an international level), so-called 'barter' systems (business money), LETS and time banks (associative money), as will be seen later. In a reciprocity-based money system, money is defined and legitimised within a community, which the circulation of money circumscribes, identifies, binds and reproduces in constructing standings within the community that are equal but in which differences are also recognised.

3.3.4 Communal sharing

In *The Great Transformation*, Polanyi also contemplates the principle of householding. It consists of 'producing and storing for the satisfaction of the wants of the members of the group' in a self-sufficient manner, and for a group whose nature may be 'the patriarchal family, locality as with the village settlement, or political power as with the seigneurial manor'; and whose 'internal organization' can be despotic as well as democratic (Polanyi, 1944, p. 56). It is not the place here to present the debates that took place after Polanyi's own renunciation of the specificity of householding (1957). However, drawing on Hillenkamp's (2013) critical reassessment of householding, on Servet's (2013) advocacy for separating 'sharing' from 'gifting' within reciprocity, we propose here reconsideration of this fourth principle as 'communal sharing', as named by Fiske (1992). 'Communal sharing' would then refer to more open and evolving groups than households (as Polanyi's definition already suggests). It would be characterised by sharing activities by giving access to members of the community, and by the possible voluntary nature of belonging to this community. It is important to stress that the action of sharing does not necessarily lead to debt relations (contrary to reciprocity).

The blockchain technology takes communal sharing to monetary relations, similarly to mutual credit with reciprocity. The blockchain is 'the database that makes the Bitcoin system run . . . a digital ledger that exists on all nodes in the Bitcoin network or the network of a similarly structured digital currency system' (Maurer, 2016). Being distributed throughout the network of users, the information on transactions becomes trustworthy without the requirement of a third party. The blockchain must be considered a technology whose first major historical use was that of Bitcoin, but that can be applied to different sorts of moneys. As such, the blockchain may be used for public, business and associative moneys as well. It has then the capacity to place a degree of communal sharing, through peer-to-peer relations, at the heart of any sort of money systems.

3.4 Deepening the ideal types: sub-types and hybrids

The four forms of integration as considered after Polanyi thus lead to deepening the typology initially built in Section 3.2 on the simple criterion of issuers. We will now confront the four forms of integration with real cases and, accordingly, identify hybrids.

3.4.1 State and sub-State public money

At first, one should refine the 'public money' ideal type by making a distinction between 'State money' and 'sub-State money'. They do not differ in terms of the form of integration they activate as a priority (redistribution through centrality), but in terms of the relationship to sovereignty and territory and to the issuer. State public money is related to the highest sovereignty, whereas sub-State public money, typically that of a federated State, is related to a possible level of power delegation to create money.

In the case of co-existence of State money and several sub-State moneys (such as the moneys of the Argentinian provinces in 1984–2003, see Théret and Zanabria, 2007, and Théret in this volume), monetary space is united through the unit of account, which remains defined by the highest sovereign level (that of the sovereign authority, like the Argentine *nación*); and the sub-State moneys' validity is limited to the corresponding territory. Another difference, consequently, is that State public money is defined by what it is measured in: it is measured against other State public moneys, thus making it a currency, whereas the sub-State moneys are measured against that currency, being subordinate to it.

3.4.2 Contemporary ordinary money as a hybrid of public money and business money

While early modern monetary systems were mostly built around all-purpose State public money (metallic money being issued by Mints out of any debt relationship), from the 17th and 18th centuries a new form of money developed with banks as issuers. This credit-based money was at first special-purpose, since it circulated within a small network of important users. It was essentially related to market activities. Its development allowed a financial and monetary revolution that enabled the financing of the burgeoning industrial activities. The issuance of smaller denominations and the extension of its use made them all-purpose. Controversial at the beginning, the credit money issued by banks later became mainstream.

The combination of public money and this business money issued by banks produced the money of industrial societies. It mixes sovereignty and market resource-capture motives. Thus, behind the deceptively generic term of 'national currency' are diverse agents through whom a public good (money) is essentially created and managed by private agents for their own self-interest (commercial banks).

Since the 1980s, the role of treasuries in creating money has admittedly been abolished for the benefit of independent central banks in several western countries, which is what Théret (2011) calls 'monetary repression'. The fiscal circuit of money is nonetheless a reality in many countries and remains a potentiality in those countries where it has been abolished. In the latter case, the central bank alone issues public money in the form of manual currency (coin and notes) through interest-bearing credit. Beyond the principle of redistribution, public money, which is all-purpose, is also to be used in market transactions as well as reciprocity relations and communal sharing. It therefore connects the fiscal circuit (where there is one) with other circuits, and public policies often promote such connections, for example, by offering tax deductions on donations.

3.4.3 Various cases of business money, depending on their convertibility

At least two major sub-types of business money can be distinguished, depending on the ability to convert them. A generalised and unconditional convertibility turn them all-purpose, while constraints over their convertibility turn them special-purpose, by raising boundaries that define specific spheres of circulation. This allows separating bank moneys from other sorts of business moneys when confronting this typology with contemporary cases.

Convertible business money is issued by banking organisations. It is intended to circulate among the many actors in the market sphere. Market exchange is therefore the form of integration allowing resources to be captured. This capture is achieved by the quantity of the monetary issue, interest rate on credits at the source of money creation and the various management costs charged to customers by banks. Commercial banks serve their customers using their own bank money which can be converted into any other bank money or external money, that is, the ordinary money as presented above. In contemporary banking systems, a public guarantee ensures formal parity among bank moneys subjected to the State public money, so much so that the conversion from one to the other is transparent (but potentially costly for customers, depending on various factors like the fees charged on withdrawals at ATMs). The success and the continuation of horizontal market exchange driven by bank money are therefore subject to the redistribution principle, a dependency that is forgotten in times of growth and even of periodic downturn, but becomes obvious when systemic banking crises occur, as illustrated by the international banking crisis that began in 2007. Convertible business moneys are all-purpose as the scope of their use covers different spheres since it irrigates not just the market sphere, but also the sphere of redistribution through taxation and borrowing, as well as the spheres of reciprocity and communal sharing.

Other forms of business money are built on the principle of inconvertibility, which formally defines a closed circuit and makes money special-purpose.

So-called 'barter' companies act as clearing houses for the reciprocal credits and debts of their customers, who are themselves firms. When debts and credits are accounted in a specific unit of account and when lines of credit are provided by the 'barter' company in this money, the scheme is built as inconvertible business money (e.g. Stodder, 1998 and Young, 2012). The capture of resources for the benefit of the 'barter' company is not in contradiction with the principle of horizontal solidarity among member firms. The latter obtain non-negligible financial advantages from their membership such as cash-flow savings and, often, lower interest rates. In the case of the cooperative Swiss bank WIR, emphasis is on the small and medium sized member firms whose belonging to a community is most directly expressed in the name of the bank and the money (WIR means 'we' in German). This organic market solidarity through market transactions is based on the mutual credit principle which, as presented earlier, conveys reciprocal relationships.

While 'barter' companies manage the horizontal transactions of their customers, other inconvertible business moneys circulate vertically and are issued by and for the direct benefit of the issuing centre. This centre exerts a form of domination that can mask various strategies. This is special-purpose money since it is confined to a user group defined by its subordinate relation to the organiser and which accedes in this way to a given set of goods and services. This capture reverses the redistribution logic as it assumes that resources are injected and then pumped out. An example is the colonial companies, mining companies or large landowners notably in Latin America that paid their employees with tokens that could be used only in their own warehouses or in affiliated shops (Rulau, 2000). A second, contemporary example is the implementation of customer loyalty schemes. They distribute benefits to their loyal customers in the form of internal purchase points that can be accumulated but cannot be converted into other forms of money. This purchasing power cannot be used unless it is converted into goods provided by the issuing firm. Customer transactions are thus directed entirely by the organising firm, without any decentralised transactions, and the firm captures the purchasing power through their conversion into goods.

3.4.4 Associative moneys outside market determination

What makes the type 'associative money' specific is the association of persons around the takeover of money as a possible tool for an active and empowered community. Nothing is said on the nature of this community (does it exist prior to the introduction of this money?), nor on the nature of the association (what form does it take?). Moreover, associative money can be built with or without connections with the authorities; it may or may not be convertible into and even commensurable with ordinary money; it may or may not be used along with it. Eventually, contrary to bank money, there is no such thing as a generalised and unconditional convertibility at par. This is why the major distinctive feature between associative moneys is the way their value is defined rather than their convertibility. Three cases may thus be distinguished: when the value of the associative money is defined by market exchanges; when it is fixed to the public money; and when it is defined independently.

The value of the contemporary cases of associative money that spread out after 1983 with LETS, time banks and local currencies, and which led to the creation of the *IJCCR* in 1997 are not defined by any direct market process. They are often characterised as local, complementary or community currencies. However, as stated above, 'complementarity' is a very misleading term since it may be falsely considered as the opposite of competition (Blanc, 2017), and since 'complementary currencies' have sometimes been used indiscriminately to refer to sub-State money (like the Argentinian provincial currencies), to business money (like the WIR) as well as to associative money (like local currencies).

In any case, these contemporary associative moneys highlight either reciprocity or exchange as the promoted form of integration, and sometimes combine both. The transactional space is marked by a strong identity structured by values manifested in charters, articles of association or internal rules and regulations. The purpose of solidarity within the community may lead to earmarking resources for funding community projects: in this way, the principle of communal sharing is made concrete through a monetary scheme that conveys different forms of integration.

From this general presentation, it is possible to discuss the way in which the value of associative moneys is defined when it is not market-based.

What are generally called community currencies in English (*monnaie sociale* in French and *moneda comunitaria* or *moneda social* in Spanish) mostly activate the principle of reciprocity in a closed system without convertibility and sometimes even without commensurability with public money by setting up a system of reciprocal exchange marked apart by the use of a money, distancing its conditions for circulating from those of market exchange. Time banks are typically community currencies, being established by associations in accordance with rules they lay down themselves. They can be used for swapping services among members of the community, with the view to build social cohesion via the principle of time-accounting regardless of the services provided (Seyfang, 2004). Moreover, as seen above, the principle of mutual credit conveys reciprocal relations. Eventually, a fair part of time banking schemes are supported (if not set up) by local authorities and by non-profit organisations such as foundations, which makes them interesting hybrids: associative monetary schemes that promote reciprocity and whose resources are of redistributive nature.

LETS-type systems are much more ambiguous since some of them establish a unit of account at par with the national currency, include professional providers and authorise the simultaneous use of both currencies, so as to let the professional providers pay for their related taxes and for their inputs with ordinary money. Yet there is no convertibility between them. In such cases, that can be found especially in Anglo-Saxon countries, LETS systems combine the reciprocity conveyed by mutual credit systems with various forms of exchange in which the market is fully present.

Contrary to them, local currency schemes like the Brazilian Palmas, the various German 'regios', the local currencies of 'transition towns' in the United Kingdom or the '*monnaies locales complémentaires*' in France, do not rely on mutual credit but on paper (and sometimes digital) money issuance, based on the conversion of inflowing ordinary money. Local currencies have economic objectives in the sense of stimulating a specific set of activities for the production and provision of goods and services by actors who are collectively organised to this end. The promoted form of exchange is therefore a professional one and the local currency is not only commensurable with public money but is also convertible into it (though outflows may entail costs). Conversely, their relationship with market rules may be complex, since they select the professional users, depending on the moral values attendant upon the creation of this money. While they are a kind of associative monetary scheme, they also rely on the local community and should strengthen social cohesion, and also require funding that can be provided by local governments and various partners.

3.4.5 New libertarian associative moneys: market value and data communal sharing

Eventually Bitcoin was created as an associative money of a libertarian nature. It is based on the blockchain technology which has been said to be applicable elsewhere. As a specific currency, Bitcoin emerged from a voluntary gathering of geeks around a new kind of project: the peer-to-peer form of association. There is no business or political authority that issues Bitcoins (though many businesses developed around Bitcoin and created an ecosystem specific to it) since the Bitcoin creation (called 'mining') is distributed throughout the network of miners, in proportion to their computational power – which gives rise to major inequalities. However, whereas the peer-to-peer blockchain technology (and thus a form of communal data sharing) is at the heart of mining and payment processes, Bitcoin is anchored in market relations. Above all, its value is neither completely autonomous and non-commensurable with other moneys, nor fixed to any specific money. Its value changes permanently, depending on market balances between supply and demand.

3.5 Conclusion

The analysis thus provides three ideal types and seven sub-types, as summarised in Table 3.1. Money as we use it ordinarily is a combination of two sub-types: State

Table 3.1 Ideal types and real cases

Ideal types	*Subtypes*	*Cases*	
Public money	Sub-State public money	Argentinian provincial currencies (1984–2003)	
	State public money	National currencies	Contemporary ordinary money
Business money	Convertible business money	Bank money	
	Inconvertible business money	WIR, Sardex; tokens of colonial landowners; purchase points of loyalty schemes	
Associative money	Market-value associative moneys	Bitcoin	
	Fixed-value associative money	Local currencies (e.g. Chiemgauer), Anglo-Saxon LETS	
	Non-commensurable associative money	Time banks and some LETS-type systems	

public money and convertible business money, thus combining redistribution (as political control exerted from centrality and permanently re-affirmed by taxation) and market exchange (bank money being issued as market relation between banks and borrowers, and ordinarily used for market exchange). But the contemporary plurality of money goes far beyond this ordinary gathering of market and redistribution conveyed by all-purpose money. It also implies special-purpose money, as well as reciprocity and communal sharing, in a series of other moneys whose nature may be public, business or even associative.

Notes

1 This chapter is an extension and refinement of earlier work on Karl Polanyi's contribution to the conceptions of money and to a typology of 'complementary currencies' (Blanc, 2006, 2009a, 2009b, 2011, 2013). I am grateful to the many commentators on preliminary versions, especially Marie Fare, James Stodder and Georgina Gómez, and to Isabelle Hillenkamp, Jean-Louis Laville and Jean-Michel Servet for their thought-provoking observations.
2 For a critical review of economic theory on the plurality of moneys, see Chapter 2 by Blanc et al., this volume.
3 In this text, 'modern money' shall mean money in modern societies, that is, societies where a market principle of circulation of wealth dominates, as opposed to 'exotic societies', meaning ancient, archaic or primitive societies.
4 Fungibility appears as an element for defining money within a substantive approach. Polanyi characterises the quantifiable objects that constitute money as 'fungibles' (Polanyi, 1977, p. 102). For primitive and archaic societies, it must be understood that this consubstantial fungibility of money is confined to a given class of quantifiable objects whose uses are compartmentalised and are not all purpose.
5 For a critical analysis of the idea of reciprocity, especially in the way it is often likened to the Maussian gift, see Servet (2007, 2013).

References

Aglietta, M and Orléan, A. 2002. *La monnaie entre violence et confiance*. Paris: Odile Jacob.

Alary, P, Blanc, J, Desmedt, L and Théret, B. eds. 2016. *Théories françaises de la monnaie: une anthologie*. Paris: PUF.

Blanc, J. 2000. *Les monnaies parallèles: unité et diversité du fait monétaire*. Logiques économiques. Paris: L'Harmattan.

Blanc, J. 2006. 'Karl Polanyi et les monnaies modernes: un réexamen'. In *Contributions à une sociologie des conduites économiques*, edited by Gilles Lazuech and Pascale Moulévrier, 51–66. Paris: L'Harmattan.

Blanc, J. 2009a. 'Contraintes et choix organisationnels dans les dispositifs de monnaies sociales'. *Annals of Public and Cooperative Economics* 80 (4): 547–77.

Blanc, J. 2009b. 'Usages de L'argent et Pratiques Monétaires'. In *Traité de sociologie économique*, edited by Philippe Steiner and François Vatin, 649–88. Quadrige. Paris: PUF.

Blanc, J. 2011. 'Classifying "CCs": community, complementary and local currencies' types and generations'. *International Journal of Community Currency Research* 15 (D): 4–10.

Blanc, J. 2013. 'Penser la pluralité des monnaies à partir de Polanyi: un essai de typologie'. In *Socioéconomie et démocratie: l'actualité de Karl Polanyi*, edited by Isabelle Hillenkamp and Jean-Louis Laville, 241–69. Toulouse, France: Érès.

Blanc, J. 2017. 'Unpacking monetary complementarity and competition: a conceptual framework'. *Cambridge Journal of Economics* 41 (1): 239–57.

Blanc, J and Fare, M. 2016. 'Turning values concrete: the role and ways of business selection in local currency schemes'. *Review of Social Economy* 74 (3): 298–319.

Cohen, B J. 2004. *The future of money*. Princeton, NJ: Princeton University Press.

Commons, J R. 1990. *Institutional economics: its place in political economy*. 2 vols. New Brunswick, NJ: Transaction Publishers.

DeMeleunaere, S and Blanc, J. 2007. 'Systems – mechanisms'. In *Social Money Workshop. Facilitation Committee Report, 2006–2007*, edited by Stephen DeMeleunaere. Paris: Fondation pour le Progrès de l'homme.

Fare, M. 2011. 'The SOL: a complementary currency for the social economy and sustainable development'. *International Journal of Community Currency Research* 15: D57–60.

Fiske, A P. 1992. 'The four elementary forms of sociality: framework for a unified theory of social relations'. *Psychological Review* 99 (4): 689–723.

Grahl, J. 2000. 'Money as sovereignty: the economics of Michel Aglietta'. *New Political Economy* 5 (2): 291–316.

Hillenkamp, I. 2013. 'Le principe de householding aujourd'hui. discussion théorique et approche empirique par l'économie populaire'. In *Socioéconomie et Démocratie: l'actualité de Karl Polanyi*, edited by Isabelle Hillenkamp and Jean Louis Laville, 215–39. Toulouse, France: Erès.

Hueber, O. 2011. 'Innovation in virtual social networks: the widespread of new electronic currencies and the emergence of a new category of entrepreneurs'. *International Journal of Transitions and Innovation Systems* 1 (2): 163–74.

Martignoni, J. 2012. 'A new approach to a typology of complementary currencies', *International Journal of Community Currency Research* 16: A1–17.

Maurer, B. 2016. 'Re-risking in realtime. on possible futures for finance after the blockchain'. *Behemoth: A Journal on Civilisation* 9 (2): 82–96.

Polanyi, K. 1944. *The great transformation: the political and economic origins of our time*. Boston, MA: Beacon Press.

Polanyi, K. 1957. 'The economy as instituted process'. In *Trade and market in the early empires. Economies in history and theory*, edited by Karl Polanyi, Conrad M. Arensberg, and Harry W. Pearson, 243–70. New York, London: The Free Press, Collier-Macmillan Ltd.

Polanyi, K. 1968. *Primitive, archaic, and modern economies: essays*. Edited by George Dalton. Garden City, NY: Anchor Books.

Polanyi, K. 1977. *The livelihood of man*, Edited by Harry W. Pearson. New York, San Francisco, London: Academic Press.

Rulau, R. 2000. *Latin American tokens: an illustrated, priced catalog of the unofficial coinage of Latin America – used in plantation, mine, mill, and dock – from 1700 to the 20th century*. Iola, WI: Krause Publications.

Saiag, H. 2014. 'Towards a neo-Polanyian approach to money: integrating the concept of debt'. *Economy and Society* 43 (4): 559–81.

Servet, J M. 1988. 'La monnaie contre l'état ou la fable du troc'. In *Droit et monnaie. États et espace monétaire transnational*, edited by Philippe Kahn, 14: 49–62. Cahier Du Credimi. Paris: Litec.

Servet, J M. 1993. 'L'institution monétaire de la société selon Karl Polanyi'. *Revue Économique* 44 (6): 1127–50.

Servet, J M. ed. 1999. *Une économie sans argent: les systèmes d'échange local*. 1 vol. Paris: Seuil.

Servet, J M. 2007. 'Le principe de réciprocité chez Karl Polanyi, contribution à une définition de l'économie solidaire'. *Revue Tiers Monde* 190 (2): 255–73.

Servet, J M. 2013. 'Le principe de réciprocité. un concept Polanyien pour comprendre et construire l'économie solidaire'. In *Socioéconomie et démocratie: l'actualité de Karl Polanyi*, edited by Isabelle Hillenkamp and Jean Louis Laville, 187–213. Toulouse, France: Erès.

Seyfang, G. 2004. 'Time banks: rewarding community self-help in the inner city?' *Community Development Journal* 39 (1): 62–71.

Stodder, J. 1998. 'Corporate barter and economic stabilisation'. *International Journal of Community Currency Research* 2: 1–11.

Théret, B and Zanabria, M. 2007. 'Sur la pluralité des monnaies publiques dans les fédérations. Une approche de ses conditions de viabilité à partir de l'expérience Argentine récente'. *Economie et Institutions* 10–11: 9–66.

Théret, B. ed. 2007. *La monnaie dévoilée par ses crises*. Paris: Éditions de l'École des hautes études en sciences sociales.

Théret, B. 2011. 'Du keynésianisme au libertarianisme. La place de la monnaie dans les transformations du savoir économique autorisé'. *Revue de la régulation*. Capitalisme, institutions, pouvoirs 10.

Warnier, J P. 2018. 'Biens aliénables, biens inaliénables et dette de vie. Autour de Annette Weiner'. In *La souveraineté monétaire et la souveraineté politique en idées et en pratiques: identité, concurrence, hiérarchie, corrélation?* edited by Marie Cuillerai and Bruno Théret. Forthcoming.

Young, M. 2012. 'A two-marketplace and two-currency system: a view on business-to-business barter exchange'. *International Journal of Community Currency Research* 16: D146–55.

4 How does monetary plurality work at the local level?

The division of labour among currencies in Argentina (1998–2005)

Georgina M. Gómez

4.1 Introduction

The concept of monetary plurality addresses the existence of more than one kind of money – defined in the widest sense as a unit of account – in a territory, which implies that there are separate monetary spheres. Each monetary sphere is defined by one currency, a circulating monetary instrument, that binds uses of money with agents. The keywords in the definition are 'uses of money' and this chapter approaches monetary plurality from the point of view of the agents and the uses they make of various moneys. For simplicity, monetary uses are grouped into the four main functions that money performs: definition of value for accountancy purposes, intermediation of exchanges, payments for debts and credits, and storage of wealth for later use.

The definition of monetary plurality in the previous paragraph assumes that each currency can perform some of the four monetary functions. All combinations are possible, so agents may use one currency to cancel payments, for example, and another currency to reserve value. It is also possible that two or more currencies can perform any one function, so agents could indistinctly choose a currency to buy product A or another currency to buy product A. Another possible combination is using one currency to buy a product from one vendor and another currency to buy the same product from another vendor, which makes sense if vendors are also the issuers of the paper money at hand. There is ample historical evidence of episodes of monetary plurality in which all of these combinations of currencies, products and agents have occurred (for example, Engdahl and Ögren, 2008; Kuroda, 2007; Wolters, 2008; as well as Kuroda, Chapter 6, this volume).

Combinations of currencies, products and agents are diverse but tend to be notably stable. Based on research of the 18th to early 20th centuries in China and India, Kuroda underlines the characteristics of that stability, and uses the term 'currency circuit' to address the steady 'coupling of a particular money and a particular trade' and which are concurrent in time and space but operate autonomously from each other and only occasionally with stable exchange rates (Kuroda, 2008a, p. 21). The concept of currency circuit facilitates a discussion on the organisation of monetary plurality in stable relations of trade and money. The stability of the combinations that constitute currency circuits is consistent with the Polanyian view of the economy as an instituted process (Polanyi, 1992). Institutions structure, organise and sustain economic processes so that they become stable. Monetary plurality is one of such processes and the agents that participate in each circuit are stable as the combinations of currency and trade.

An examination of the ways in which agents use money under conditions of monetary plurality is still pending, probably out of the absence of current viable examples to conduct such a study. This chapter seeks to understand the ways agents combine currencies to use them for accountancy, exchange, payments and savings. In what ways do agents choose which currencies to use for what purposes? Alternatively, agents may incur extra costs to exchange the currency they have for another currency they need or prefer. Unless currency circuits are completely autonomous, any two currency circuits intersect each other at points such as money changers who will use an exchange rate to pass from one currency to the other. These are points of intersection between any two currency circuits and they are also structured by institutions like exchange rates and exchange costs. Under what conditions do agents change currencies to pass from one currency circuit to another?

The proposition in this chapter is that monetary plurality can exist without exchange institutions that bridge currency circuits as long as a stable division of labour between currencies emerges. In other words, categories of agents design and sustain specific combinations of currencies and trade without incurring additional exchange costs to pass from one currency circuit to another. The implication is that monetary plurality need not be significantly costlier than a single money system. The final question that guides this chapter is, in what ways do currency circuits become institutionalised as stable relations binding agents, currencies and trade.

This study is based on the case of Argentina between 1998 and 2005, when economic agents dealt with several currencies to make their payments and perform other monetary functions. The research sought to establish which currencies were used by agents for what purposes and on what grounds these choices were made. Data was collected on the monetary practices of households and small businesses that participated in the community currency circuit, the *Redes de Trueque*, because these households would also use national and provincial currencies. The opposite does not stand: some households used only national currency, namely households where the breadwinners had formal and well-paid jobs. The use of private currencies such as business vouchers was restricted to a minority of households with formal jobs, so they were excluded from the analysis. The data used in this research belongs to a larger and ongoing research project on the *Redes de Trueque* that includes participant observation and a survey of 386 households with a semi-structured questionnaire which was administered face to face in marketplaces where the participants had goods on sale. The initiators of the *Redes de Trueque* were interviewed repeatedly in order to reconstruct the evolution of the scheme based on oral history. Extensive interviews were conducted also with various experts and academic researchers. A desk study of other research and journalistic reports on the topic is ongoing.

4.2 Dealing with monetary plurality

Periods of monetary plurality have been ubiquitous throughout history in both the Eastern and Western hemispheres. This is hardly news (see Gómez and von Prittwitz, Chapter 7, and Kuroda, Chapter 6, this volume). However, patterns or the ways in which agents have combined currencies for different purposes is not a well-researched aspect of monetary plurality. The assumption behind this is, perhaps, that agents would change the currencies they had at hand for a 'better' currency. The belief that there is a clear hierarchy among currencies veils the significance of binding them to agents and uses in stable relations. This has also limited the analysis of currency circuits.

One of the few attempts to look into the organisation of monetary plurality is an article by Jerome Blanc (2016), 'Unpacking monetary complementarity and competition: a conceptual framework'. The study offers mainly a theoretical conceptualisation of how several currencies relate to each other. Currencies stand in relations of competition or complementarity with other currencies. Depending on whether they can be used to price goods interchangeably, they can be converted into one another by means of exchange rates, they can be used together, and they can be used in the same or similar monetary spheres. The different combinations of these four dimensions allow for more possibilities than simply stating that monies compete or complement each other. Blanc's work does not centre on the choices or uses decided by agents in contexts of monetary plurality but how currencies stand in relation to one another, leaving agents and dynamics out of the analysis. With a static approach, Blanc argues that currencies can be substitutes (only one currency can be used at a time in a given territory), simultaneous (several currencies can be used at a time in a given territory but conversion may add costs), supplements (one currency does what another currency does not, so several currencies are needed at a time in a given territory to cover all the possible uses of money) or autonomous (they are independent in time and territories). A graphic interpretation of these relations is shown in Figure 4.1. In this way, Blanc (2016) contributes an analysis of monetary plurality that admits several relations between currencies, and while some currencies compete with each other, other currencies complement one another. The question is whether one currency will end up dominating a territory and push all others to disappear. Blanc hints that the answer is no, as long as there is no Polanyian all-purpose money that can perform all the functions, always and everywhere. In other words, as long as currencies complement each other, monetary plurality would expand the universe of production and exchange from a substantive economy approach.

Kuroda (2008a, 2008b) asserted that no money does all the functions that economic agents need it to perform. His views emphasise supplementarity and add that, in most cases, monetary plurality was not incidental but conducive to the functioning of the economy. Kuroda argues specifically that, 'one money could do what another money could not, and vice versa. In other words, an assortment of monies could do what any single money could not, and supply what the market required' (Kuroda, 2008b, p. 7). The implication of this reasoning is that in

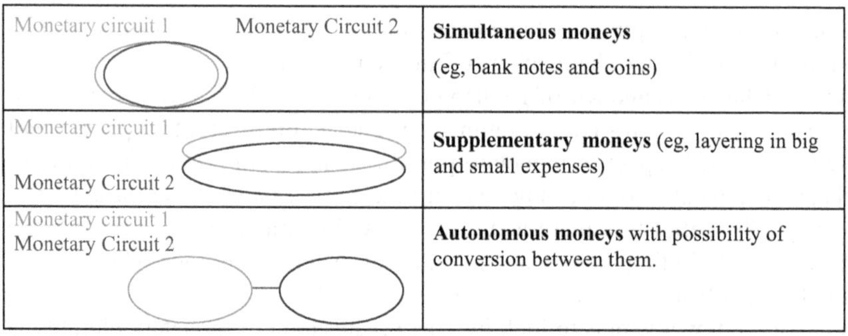

Figure 4.1 Articulation between complementary monetary circuits
Source: Own interpretation of Blanc (2016).

contexts of monetary plurality, a division of labour among currencies must exist. Agents hence use one currency for one purpose and another currency for another purpose. The institutionalisation of currency circuits reflects on particular properties of each currency to function in the medium term, so that some agents give it and other agents accept it in exchange for goods or other currencies.

Kuroda's notion of currency circuits emphasises the stability that binds agents, uses and products. Stability is the key characteristic of institutionalised economic processes. Hodgson's (2006, p. 2) established definition of institutions conceptualises them as 'systems of established and prevalent social rules that structure social interaction'. These dispositions refer to socially accepted courses of action for various situations. According to Hodgson's account (Hodgson, 2003; Hodgson and Knudsen, 2004), institutions are formed in processes of reconstitutive upward causation, by which agents' repeated actions structure new institutions that become stable and achieve ontological existence at a social level. Under conditions of monetary plurality, institutions indicate that for each purpose of trade, savings and payments, there is a particular currency that is acceptable in the local context. The notion that economic interactions among agents are structured extends to the repeated and preferred use of a specific currency per vendor or product.

The second aspect of the organisation of monetary plurality in distinctive and stable currency circuits regards their articulation. If currencies partially share spaces, as Blanc suggested, then there must be points of intersection linking the various currency circuits such as legal regulations, exchange rates, exchange banks, money changers, and other institutions that structure the interaction of agents across currency circuits (Boyer-Xambeu, Deleplace and Gillard, 1994; Kuroda, 2007). In the next section we will explore how monetary plurality was organised in distinct but concurrent circuits in the Argentine case and the ways in which division of labour emerged.

4.3 Inflation and bimonetarism in Argentina

In contrast to most countries, in Argentina the concept of money is seen as a social construction that governments mould to their policy objectives. A broad menu of failed anti-inflationary policies has been tried since 1930s, including four changes in the national currency that scrapped digits and sought to add credibility to policy efforts to curb monthly average two-digit inflation rates. There were other equally desperate efforts to control monetary supply seen as responsible for the inflation. For instance, in the winter of 1962, the government paid civil servants their wages in bonds instead of official money. The fiscal accounts were then seriously distressed, and the government wanted to avoid the inflationary effects of issuing money to cover its deficit (Cortes Conde, 2005). These bonds were accepted by most shops and firms, and public servants spent them as soon as they could. Later, in the 1980s, provincial money was issued in two provinces that could not pay wages to their public employees and printed small amounts of provincial bonds to cover the expense. They were accepted reluctantly in their territories and the holders spent them as quickly as possible (Schvarzer and Finkelstein, 2003). Shopkeepers referred to provincial money as 'hot bread', a reference to the desire to get rid of it quickly. Banks and the entire financial system were also affected. For instance, in 1989 bank deposits were confiscated and exchanged for government bonds. The tradition of inflation, coupled with monetary and financial manipulation, generated the curious understanding that what is socially accepted as money has been as much a matter of social judgement as of political decision.

Argentines rarely regard their national money as an untouchable institution that the state commits to ensure. A long-term search for a harder currency gradually led agents to adopt the US dollar as a second currency. Initially, it was only a reserve of value, but the dollar was gradually institutionalised as unit of account for pricing most goods and services, and to use as means of payment. In the second stage, the dollar was used to express the prices of larger goods such as houses and cars, and to stabilise the value of contracts. In the third stage, the dollar was also preferred as means of payment to buy those larger goods and services. The inflationary problem kept aggravating and reached a peak with three hyperinflations between May 1989 and the end of 1990, a period of less than two years. It then became common practice to pay for all goods and services in pesos calculated at the hourly advertised exchange rate of the price in dollars. It was the fourth stage in which the dollar became means of payment accepted by most private actors.

After three hyperinflations, the top policy priority in 1990 was to 'reconstruct' the institutions regulating the relationship between the population and money, the monetary system, and monetary-defined property rights (Cavallo, 1999). Domingo Cavallo, the Economy Minister, contested the monetarist view that the source of inflation was the quantity of money in an economy and was instead inspired by Friedrich Hayek (1976) in the view that it was the quality of money that determined agents' monetary preferences. Cavallo (1999) describes the monetarist theory of inflation as incomplete because it does not pay attention to the institutional aspects of money. Full dollarisation at the macro level was discussed within policy circles but the idea did not gain ground because it was seen as politically inviable (Fanelli and Heymann, 2002). Instead, the government opted for a consolidation of the two-currency monetary system captured in the Convertibility Plan.

In March 1991, the Congress approved a law transforming the Central Bank into a currency board, pegging the Argentine currency to the US dollar at a rate of one to one and allowing all transactions to be performed in any currency of choice (Fernandez and Schumacher, 1998). The law forbade indexation in contracts but protected the option of denominating prices in dollars. This also applied to bank deposits over any term. It gave the Central Bank autonomy and specified the level of foreign currency reserves it would have to maintain, while it determined that the Central Bank would no longer act as lender of last resort to the banking system (no other institution was designated for that function). In practice, this ensured that money would be issued endogenously in alignment with inflows of foreign currency. In January 1992, the national currency would be the peso, at par with the dollar. It was a shortcut for the recovery of the institution of money, and the combined M3 increased to 20 percent of GDP by 1994 (Fanelli and Heymann, 2002). Convertibility allowed agents to choose, at any point in their economic activity, which currency they wanted to use for what purposes. Instead of fighting it, the Convertibility Plan built upon the practice of monetary plurality and achieved what no other stabilisation plan could in the past in Argentina: inflation disappeared for a decade and the credibility of the peso was restored.

The Convertibility Plan formalised a monetary system composed of two currency circuits with significant overlap, which was termed bimonetarism. The origin is to be found in the long-term experience with inflation and the failure of indexation to adjust quantities properly: price indexes tell a story of past price increases while the exchange rate reflects the increases currently going on (Heymann, 2000). The substitution of a bad currency (peso) for a good currency (dollar) was termed 'reverse Gresham's Law' in Argentina (Guidotti and Rodríguez, 1992). When inflation started rising, agents would flee to good currencies such as the dollar to protect the value of their payments, goods for sale and savings. Uncertainty over the future purchasing values in pesos prevented agents from seeing the peso as the 'natural' unit of account and would only have good currencies in circulation. The 'natural' unit of account then became the currency that could effectively guarantee purchasing power in the future (the dollar).

Back to the articulation of currency circuits, this section has shown that inflation created the conditions for a second currency circuit to emerge, which was complementary to the official Argentine currency and centred on the use of the US dollar for specific types of payments and savings. The formalisation of this dual monetary system came with the Convertibility Plan, which extended the scope of the second currency circuit to bank deposits and tax payments. The relationship between the two currencies evolved into one of simultaneous complementarity, in Blanc's typology, because any payment could be made with the combination of pesos and dollars, in the same manner as coins and bank notes can be combined.

However, the two currencies could not be used for all the same purposes and there were conversion costs between the currencies.

4.4 Structural adjustment and non-state monetary circuits

The formalisation of a bimonetary system was only one of the components of the Convertibility Plan. Monetary reform was implemented together with one of the most ambitious and swift privatisation programmes in Latin America, involving almost all state-owned enterprises, public utilities, the pension system, and much of the healthcare and banking sectors (Kosacoff, 1993). Markets were opened to trade, the regulations on foreign investment were relaxed, and several other sectors were deregulated. The structural reforms triggered a significant growth rate of eight percent a year from 1990 to 1994. GDP increased by 27 percent between 1991 and 1994 but with a marked heterogeneity between sectors: while the industrial GDP hardly grew, services bloomed and with it, part of the middle class (Kosacoff and Heymann, 2000). At the same time, regional economies based on agriculture and small enterprises were particularly hit.

In 1995, a major economic crisis hit the 'modernised' Argentina of the Neoliberal experiment. It caused major disruptions in the balance of payments and the peg of the peso to the dollar almost collapsed but was saved at the cost of a recession that skimmed five percent off the national product in 1995. The financial crisis also introduced many Argentines to the traumatic novelty of not having a job. The unemployment rate had stayed around 5 percent in the 1980s but it was rising due to the changes in the industrial sector, the retreat of the state, and privatisations. In 1995, Argentina had a record unemployment rate of 18.8 percent and the term 'hyper-unemployment' was coined. Real wages in 1995 fell to 68 percent of its 1986 level and 62 percent of its 1975 level. The social costs of the structural reforms were beginning to be reported by the media, which revealed pools of poverty that had never been seen before. The crisis induced a moment of awareness. It was then that the public realised that the institutions regulating economic activity and the relationships between the private sector, the state and civil society had changed permanently.

On the upside, part of the Argentine society bloomed with the opening of markets and the arrival of a myriad of transnational corporations in the service sector that introduced a private type of money. These were vouchers issued by private businesses and sold to employers, who gave them to their workers as part of or in addition to their wages. These vouchers allowed employees to buy meals in restaurants and, later on, food in supermarkets and oil in most gas stations. They were not considered part of the salary according to the labour laws, so they became a cheaper option for employers to reward their workers with than regular money. Private vouchers hence overlapped with pesos for purchasing those basic necessities, but rarely overlapped with dollars. There was no segment of the market for which it was the main money.

On the downside, poverty grew dramatically. Argentina had been used to pockets of poverty for decades, but what was striking in the 1990s was that the poverty extended to a larger segment of the population and was much more visible. An early study of the social consequences of the structural reforms coined the term 'new poor' to describe households that had recently fallen under the poverty line in a country where about 70 percent of the population had declared itself as middle class (Minujin, 1993). They were shopkeepers, public servants, skilled workers, graduates, blue collar workers, bank clerks, teachers and small firm owners. Many of the sectors in which the middle class worked were targets of the reform policies and were thus overwhelmed by their disenfranchisement. Scholars define the new poor as those whose situation depends on their previous status, educational attainment, availability of savings, and assets, such as their house, personal capabilities and social network (Lvovich, 2000; Minujin, 1993; Minujin and Kessler, 1995; Murmis and Feldman, 1993). Their structural basic needs were covered, but with the drastic reduction in their income, they could no longer afford their lifestyle. Their network of contacts was crucial in delaying the decline, but they no longer felt a sense of belonging with them. They understood the world differently from the structural poor and were demanding of society and the state. They were the poor with a voice.

Collective actors set to reorganise social life independently from the state, ensuring representation through new channels and promoting alternative income generation schemes. Among these were the *Redes de Trueque*, the brainchild of two grassroots groups that organised a local exchange network where participants would buy and sell goods and services from each other by using a money they had created themselves. They were launched at a local level with 25 members on 1 May 1995, but their replication in other locations was extremely fast. The initial success and the potential of the scheme to alleviate the economic problems of the disenfranchised middle class neighbours made the organisers 'want to spread it everywhere' (Interview with national leader in Bernal, Buenos Aires, on 4 August 2004). In the beginning, each local exchange centre had its own community currency, which was not convertible to pesos outside it, but after a while the currencies were accepted in other local centres. Eventually, a number of systems of complementary currency centres (nodes) emerged at the local, regional and national levels with abstract means of payment, depersonalised, dematerialised, and transferable money created by civil society organisations. The *créditos* was the only currency that circulated in the *Redes de Trueque*, although some accepted their combination with pesos to cover raw materials and inputs.

It was clear from the start that the *Trueque* had a strong gender bias and at least 70 percent of the participants were women. As observed by other researchers (González Bombal, Leoni and Luzzi, 2002; Parysow and Bogani, 2002), middle class women were the most affected by the slide into poverty, as it deprived them of access to the public spaces they were used to visiting, and they quickly accepted the proposal of the *Trueque*. Used to unpaid work, women were the first to understand that the *Trueque* offered satisfaction of needs without the mediation of regular money. The *Trueque* linked directly to the reproduction of life: it 'fills the fridge, paints the home, gets you a plumber to fix the pipes', one participant said (Interview with RT participant, Billinghurst, Buenos Aires, 9 November 2004).

At first sight, it seems to be a major innovation for a civil society group to print its own money, but in Argentina, it was not. The creation of the *crédito*, the name the community currency was usually referred to as, represents a small innovation on the institutionalised practice in Argentina of using several currencies at the same time. For decades, the country had a bimonetary system in which both pesos and dollars circulated together. The *créditos* were added as a new currency created by a grassroots organisation to circulate within its social network. They were just an extra option in a list of means of payment at hand. The creation of a currency parallel to the official one would have been illegal or bluntly rejected in other countries, but in the Argentine case, it was within the acceptable responses. People were used to living with two or three currencies, so why not four or five? As Swanke (2004) expresses it, once an institution is in place, the actors simply forget how it was created and adopt it for their use.

In terms of monetary circuits, the *Trueque* added a currency and with it, a new stable relation was born between specific community currencies, their participants (agents willing to trade their goods and services for *créditos*), and their products. Most products on sale proceeded from the resale of stocks such as second-hand goods or bought within the formal currency circuit in pesos, or home production with small scale technologies). The community currencies were a supplementary currency circuit because they were used for additional products or trade that would not have had any value in pesos or would not have occurred if everyone had a strong preference for pesos.

4.5 Subnational state currency circuits in Argentina

The moment of truth for Argentina's neoliberal development model came at the end of the 1990s. Community currencies were well established and growing by the time the country suffered a new and more severe crisis. In 1999, the GDP dropped by 3.4 percent and the recession was met with more deregulation and structural reforms. A new government, formed by the opposition party, took office in December 1999 with its entire campaign based on reassuring the public that it would maintain the peso's peg to the dollar and continue implementing the Convertibility Plan. Unfortunately, it was able to do little to spur economic growth and one of its first measures was to raise taxes to correct the fiscal deficit. Tax increases delivered the Argentine economy directly into a recessionary trap with higher budget deficits and further cuts in government spending (Harman, 2002). It was the beginning of the longest and deepest productive retraction in Argentine history. The economic demise of four years skimmed 20 percent of the GDP between 1998 and 2002 (Gerchunoff and Llach, 2005).

The fiscal cuts applied to the provinces, some of which historically had high public employment, and protests started there (Pastor Jr and Wise, 1999). The combination of provincial deficits and the refusal of the central government to cover their deficits brought several subnational governments to the brink of default on their debt and in arrears with suppliers. The province of Buenos Aires was the first one to issue an Emergency Provincial Bond to avoid a general default on its payments, and soon used them to partially cover the payments of wages. The experience was successful to increase the liquidity and reactivate the depressed local economy of the province, which encouraged other provinces to replicate the issuing of their own subnational currencies.

Argentine provinces had already issued subnational bills in the 1980s and some provinces had never stopped using them, such as Tucuman (see chapters by Théret in this volume). The 2001 generation of subnational currencies was slightly different because they were meant to circulate as almost compulsory debt. The bills created a provincial unit of account in which their value was denominated. At the same time, they served as a reserve of value because they paid an interest when they matured, and as means of payment to cancel debts with suppliers and utility companies in their territories. They also circulated as a medium of exchange because public servants used them to buy from shops and supermarkets, for example, which in turn used them to pay local taxes and their workers' wages, among other costs.

The provincial bills were generically called 'quasi-currencies' and were institutionalised already by the end of 2001 (Schvarzer and Finkelstein, 2003). According to Alvarez et al. (2011), the issuance of subnational currencies reached a peak in September 2002, when they represented 51.32 percent of the monetary base. Alvarez et al. (2011) consider subnational currencies as an 'unheard of' measure because the provincial bonds formed locally restricted monetary circuits of a scale that exceeded the value of the transfers from national tax revenues. The reason behind these proportions was related to the severity of the crisis: there was not enough national currency to perform the basic functions of money as media of exchange and means of payment. Some sources, hence, consider that the provincial currencies had clear reactivating effects in the local economies (Schvarzer and Finkelstein, 2003; Théret and Zanabria, 2009), because they activated production and trade that would otherwise have remained idle with the scarcely available national money.

At the same time, provincial currencies were restricted to the provincial territories, so agents that needed to make payments outside the province would have to convert them to pesos or dollars. Many economic agents would hence try to spend their quasi-currencies to cancel taxes first, wages second, other costs third, and what was left was converted to pesos or dollars. A supermarket manager noted that:

> [a]ll in all, we noticed that a very large proportion of our costs are local. Moreover, when we realised the provincial currency was not circulating fast enough, we would stop accepting it. But there was not much choice because customers did not always have anything else to pay with.
>
> (Interview with Supermarket Manager in San Martin, Buenos Aires, 4 December 2004)

As their circulation became more common, provincial currencies established a new stable relation between themselves, agents and products. The products were those that were produced and consumed locally, which explains why local currencies are seen by some authors as having supported economic recovery in the middle of the economic demise. The agents were initially public servants and public sector suppliers, but later it was any business that had them as clients and managed to make payments with provincial currencies. They were a supplementary currency circuit, in Blanc's typology, because they sustained the local economy throughout the crisis, keeping workers in waged employment and businesses afloat that, perhaps, otherwise would not have been possible.

4.6 Matching money and transactions

By the turn of the millennium, many Argentine households were using up to five currencies – pesos, US dollars, provincial quasi-currencies, private vouchers and *créditos*. The phenomenon fits Kuroda's (2008a) analysis, that different currencies fulfil the four main functions of money to different degrees, in different spaces and for different groups of agents. Each type of money did something that the others did not, so it took several currencies together to satisfy the various needs to pay for all the transactions that a household or small business needed.

In line with Blanc's (2016) definition of complementarity, dollars and pesos circulated together and could be combined at the same time, so they were complementary instead of competitive. For savings and larger payments like capital goods and housing, the dollar was the preferred currency. The peso was the only currency used to pay taxes and debts with the state. Basic necessities could be bought with private vouchers or pesos in supermarkets and regular shops, with provincial currencies if the recipients could recirculate them to other agents or pay their taxes, with community currency if they were obtained in the *Redes de Trueque* or with a combination of *créditos* and pesos when the exchanges were made with small shops that accepted *créditos*. So, under conditions of monetary plurality, different currencies circulated in different spaces where different agents participated.

If currencies are arranged in a hierarchy based on the level of stability perceived by the public, dollars would be at the top because they were also used as reserve of value, which was a function that many community currency *créditos* would perform poorly. While dollars are issued by the government of the largest economy in the world, the *créditos* were issued by local civil society organisations without any real or legal guarantee. In the middle, the pesos were issued by the Argentine government and protected by the constitution, regardless of how contested the state was at that time. The provincial notes were printed by subnational governments and could also claim legality by the provincial constitutions and were to some extent backed up by the transfers of the central to the provincial governments. The private vouchers were distributed by large transnational corporations and had a validity of less than one year, a period during which the issuers were considered reliable. However, the hierarchy of money in terms of its reliability was not an issue for the vast majority of Argentines that did not have the choice to compare currencies and decide which one they wanted to use. Any currency was better than no currency at all, so the place of each currency in a hierarchy of money was secondary to their availability for different agents. For the poor and unemployed who could only generate income in complementary currencies, the reliability of the dollar as the hardest currency was of no significance.

The fieldwork surveyed households and small businesses that participated in the *Redes de Trueque* in order to obtain a full range of uses of the different monies available. A summary of what exchange each household would use to pay for what goods and services is shown in Table 4.1. The ideal currency to use as reserve of value was the dollar, which was also the hardest to obtain, but that functionality was not perceived as crucial because most of the households interviewed did not save any income at all. That means that a vast number of households did not save and barely had access to dollars, so they did not belong to the dollar currency circuit.

In contrast, community currencies were the money that poor households could access the easiest. Although *créditos* sustained the smallest currency circuit in terms of geographic and temporal scope, because they were limited to one or a small number of exchange centres, they were also the easiest to obtain. In addition, users' preference for them was related to their consumption needs. A very large percentage of the daily necessities of low-income households could be met in *créditos*. So, they participated strongly in the circuits of the community currencies. These circuits were hence inclusive of segments of the population that, in their absence, would have remained excluded from the economic activities of production and trade.

Table 4.1 Households: which money for what?

	Monetary circuits	*Dollars*	*Pesos*	*Treasury/ provincial*	*Private vouchers*	*Créditos*
1	Savings	√	√			
2	Taxes		√	√ Local tax		
3	Public services (electricity, water, transportation)		√	√ Locally		
4	Large purchases (houses, cars, electronics, machines)	√	√			
5	Petrol	√	√	√ Locally	√	
6	Other non-food purchases (clothes, shoes, toys, school articles)	√	√	√ Locally	√	√ (in RT)
7	Personal services (health care, home maintenance, personal care)	√	√ some	√ Locally		√ (in RT)
8	Every day food necessities	√ some	√ some	√ Locally	√	√ (in RT)
9	Inter-household informal trade					√ (in RT)

Households assessed the various currencies based on the entire flow of money and contrasted the use of the various currencies with their own accessibility to them and compared the suitability of currencies to their needs and expenses. The articulation of each currency to the other types of money would have been significant if households could choose in which currency circuits they wanted to participate, but that was not the case. The dimension of accessibility to various currencies in conditions of monetary plurality is a key factor for assessing the quality of money.

The Argentine experience provides evidence to Kuroda's analysis that none of the monies available in Argentina was capable of satisfying all the needs of all the households. Each one of them was acceptable towards paying for goods and services that other currencies could not, although there were clear overlaps. Even the money with the widest acceptance, the dollar, was not valid for paying taxes and other transfers to the public sector, and payments in dollars for small expenses faced problems of conversion of the change that had to be given back. There was no small change in dollars, so fractionary money was always in currencies other than the dollar.

A similar analysis for small shops and businesses is shown in Table 4.2. Like with households, saving was not a concern that many of these shops could attend to in the middle of a severe crisis.

Monetary plurality in Argentina was not a matter of choice but a response to a deep crisis that undermined economic activity and the legitimacy of the state and monetary institutions at the same time. Different actors then created means of payment for different groups of agents and for different purposes. The outcome was a fragmented market with various types of currency circuits and groups of agents.

Table 4.2 Small businesses and shops: which money for what?

	Monetary circuits	*Dollars*	*Pesos*	*Treasury/ provincial*	*Private vouchers*	*Créditos*
1	Savings	√	√			
2	Taxes and rent	some	√	√ Locally		
3	Public services (electricity, water, transportation)		√	√ Locally		
4	Large purchases (houses, cars, electronics, machines)	√	√			
5	Petrol	√	√		√	
6	Wages		√	√ Locally	√	
7	Suppliers		√	√ Locally		√ (in RT)
8	Daily business services (cleaning, small maintenance)		√	√ Locally		√ (in RT)
9	Sale of leftover, second class or expired stocks					√

At the same time, it was a larger market than what the use of only one type of currency could have sustained, had monetary plurality not existed. Especially for the groups of the population who had problems of access to money, the existence of complementary currencies supported their survival. A large number of households and small businesses were able to get by during the worst crisis in Argentine history precisely because they had access to various currencies which allowed them to participate in several monetary circuits at the same time. Monetary plurality therefore implied that households and small businesses had to find the best match between currency and purpose.

4.7 Conclusion

This chapter seeks to understand in what ways agents combine currencies to use them for accountancy, exchange, payments and savings. Moreover, it traces the origin and reasons behind the institutionalisation of currency circuits as stable relations that bind agents, currencies and trade. Following Blanc's argumentation beyond the competition approach to money (2016), the Argentine case suggests that competition is only evident when money is assessed in terms of all its four functions together (definition of value for accountancy purposes, intermediation of exchanges, payments of debts and credits, and storage of wealth for later use). When these four functions are looked at one by one, it becomes evident that agents chose different currencies for different uses. A further breakdown of these four functions shows that a division of labour arose as stable combinations of purposes and social strata of the agents, as shown in Tables 4.1 and 4.2.

Agents become included in the currency circuits that are more accessible to them. So, while agents of higher socioeconomic conditions may have a choice in which currency they use for what purpose, agents of lower economic strata do not have such a choice. Currency circuits do not only represent pairs of trade and currencies, as theorised by Kuroda (2007, 2008a, 2008b) but trios of trade, currencies, and the social strata of the agents that receive and spend a specific currency. There is a logical preference for the type of money that does all or most of the four basic functions of money, including the denomination of savings or large investments (reserve of value). For social strata that do not save, money becomes primarily means of payment and medium of exchange for daily necessities, and these households use the currency they can obtain through the easiest way – or perhaps the only way – in currency circuits that rank lower in the monetary hierarchy. In other words, money is layered along social lines which dominate the inclusion in currency circuits.

Lower level currency circuits relate the closest to everyday consumption needs. For households that use most or all of their income in daily necessities, complementary currencies are adequate to sustain their survival. These currencies procure most of the goods and services in their household consumption baskets. For households that consume other goods, the inclusion of a currency of lower level represents a loss of welfare. Instead, households that consume mostly basic necessities (items 6 to 9 in Table 4.1) use lower level currencies.

The account of monetary plurality presented in this chapter supports Kuroda's reasoning (ibid.) that the coexistence of currency circuits enables more trade and more production than would have otherwise been possible with only one currency. Moreover, the analysis of the evidence suggests that monetary plurality can have a positive effect in terms of social inclusion, because lower level users can have access to income generation and make payments in a lower level currency. Clearly, their choice is restricted to goods produced and traded in these lower level circuits, but the alternative is not having any money at all and, consequently, no chances of accessing those goods or any others. While the regular economic system excludes the lower socioeconomic strata of the society, lower level currency circuits appear as a 'better-than-nothing' option to sustain life during a deep economic demise. If complementary currencies had been forbidden, it would have been damaging for the poor. We reached a similar conclusion in Gómez and Von Prittwitz, Chapter 7, this volume.

The emergence of a division of labour among currencies adds another dimension to the statement that currency circuits supplement each other within a relationship of complementarity, as argued by Blanc (2016). Simultaneous complementarity is about choosing to use a harder currency as reserve of value, while supplementarity relates to need. It appears as a defense mechanism against exclusion that enables different conditions of inclusion. It suggests that passing from one currency circuit to another is not only costly, but also generally unnecessary. Households participate in several currency circuits at the same time and combine each currency with a particular purpose, meaning that they make payments in the same currency in which they obtain their income. In other words, circuits intersect within the households and shops that use them, and they do not exchange one for the other. The users can and will avoid incurring extra costs to move between currencies. They do not convert currencies to buy a specific good but match the currency in their hands with the goods on offer in that currency.

The conclusions presented here are using a circular argument: different level currencies emerge because they include users that can access them and use them to procure most of the goods and services in their household baskets. The more these agents use supplementary currencies, the more these currencies sustain their lives, so agents use them more. Circular argumentations like this resonate with most accounts of institutionalisation and structuration processes. The concept of reconstitutive upward causation (Hodgson 2003; Hodgson and Knudsen 2004) argues that repetitive usage and convenience can reconcile agents with options that were new for them at an earlier point, so that they reproduce actions and support their dissemination to other agents. Currency circuits follow a pattern of emergence, usage, and dissemination around an episode of economic crisis. They present the institutionalisation of links between the users of a currency, the purpose, and access to it. Institutionalisation suggests that the rules of inclusion and engagement in each currency circuit are clear, as well as their limits and potentials. This may be relevant for the subsequent stability of the currency circuits and their reemergence in other periods of crisis.

References

Alvarez C, Manes M, Paredes P and Ivani C. 2011. El acceso al crédito de los gobiernos subnacionales. El caso de las provincias y municipios de la República Argentina. *Jornadas Internacionales de Finanzas Públicas*, Facultad de Ciencias Económicas, Universidad Nacional de Córdoba. Córdoba, Argentina.

Blanc J. 2016. Unpacking monetary complementarity and competition: a conceptual framework. *Cambridge Journal of Economics* 41(1):239–257.

Boyer-Xambeu MT, Deleplace MG and Gillard L. 1994. *Private money and public currencies: the sixteenth century challenge*. London: Sharpe.

Cavallo D. 1999. 'The quality of money'. Document prepared for the Award Ceremony of the Doctorate Honoris Causa University of Paris 1-Pantheon Sorbonne, published in *ASAP* (Asociación Argentina de Presupuesto y Administración Financiera Pública) No. 33, Buenos Aires, *junio 1999 and Économie Internationale – La revue du CEPII, La qualité de la monnaie*, 80, 4, Trimestre, Paris.

Cortes Conde R. 2005. *La economía política de la Argentina en el siglo XX*. Buenos Aires: Edhasa.

Engdahl T and Ögren AO. 2008. Multiple paper monies in Sweden 1789–1903: substitution or complementarity? *Financial History Review* 15(1):73–91.

Fanelli JM and Heymann D. 2002. Dilemas monetarios en Argentina. *Desarrollo Económico (Buenos Aires)* 42(165):3–24.

Fernandez RB and Schumacher L. 1998. The Argentine banking panic after the 'Tequila' shock: did 'convertibility' help or hurt? In: Rehman SS, ed. *Financial crisis management in regional blocs*. Dordrecht, Netherlands: Springer. 183–208.

Gerchunoff G and Llach L. 2005. *El ciclo de la ilusión y el desencanto; un siglo de políticas económicas argentinas*. Buenos Aires: Ariel.

González Bombal I., Leoni F. and Luzzi M. 2002. Nuevas redes sociales: los clubes de trueque. *Conference Proceedings: Respuestas de la Sociedad Civil a la Emergencia Social: Brasil y Argentina Comparten Experiencias,* Facultade de Economia, Administração e Contabilidade, University of São Paulo, Brasil, November 4. Buenos Aires: CEDES–UNGS.

Guidotti P and Rodríguez C. 1992. Dollarization in Latin America: Gresham's Law in reverse? *IMF Staff Papers* 239:518–544.

Harman C. 2002. Argentina: rebellion at the sharp end of the world crisis. *International Socialism* 94:3–48.

Hayek FA. 1976. *Denationalization of money*. London: Institute of Economic Affairs.

Heymann D. 2000. Políticas de reforma y comportamiento macroeconómico. In: Kosacoff B and Heymann D, eds. *La Argentina de los noventa. Desempeño económico en un contexto de reformas*. Buenos Aires: EUDEBA and CEPAL Naciones Unidas.

Hodgson G. 2003. The hidden persuaders: institutions and individuals in economic theory. *Cambridge Journal of Economics* 27:159–175.

Hodgson G. 2006. What are institutions? *Journal of Economic Issues* 40(1):1–25.

Hodgson G and Knudsen T. 2004. The complex evolution of a simple traffic convention: the functions and implications of habit. *Journal of Economic Behavior and Organization* 54(1):19–47.

Kosacoff B. 1993. *El desafío de la competitividad*. Buenos Aires: CEPAL-Alianza.

Kosacoff B and Heymann D. 2000. *La Argentina de los noventa*. Buenos Aires: EUDEBA and CEPAL Naciones Unidas.

Kuroda A. 2007. The Maria Theresa dollar in the early twentieth-century Red Sea region: a complementary interface between multiple markets. *Financial History Review* 14(1):89–110.

Kuroda A. 2008a. Concurrent but non-integrable currency circuits: complementary relationships among monies in modern China and other regions. *Financial History Review* 15(1):17–36.

Kuroda A. 2008b. What is the complementarity among monies? An introductory note. *Financial History Review* 15(1):7–15.

Lvovich, D. 2000. Colgados De la soga. La experiencia del tránsito desde la clase media a la nueva pobreza en la ciudad de Buenos Aires. In M. Svampa ed. *Desde Abajo. La Transformación De Las Identidades Sociales*. Buenos Aires: UNGS and Biblos. 51–80.

Minujin A, ed. 1993. *Cuesta abajo. Los nuevos pobres: efectos de la crisis en la sociedad argentina*. 2nd ed. Buenos Aires: Losada and Unicef.

Minujín, A. and Kessler G. 1995. *La nueva pobreza en Argentina*. Buenos Aires: Planeta.

Murmis, M. and Feldman S. 1993. La heterogeneidad social de las pobrezas. In A. Minujin ed. *Cuesta Abajo. Los Nuevos Pobres: Efectos De La Crisis En La Sociedad Argentina*. Buenos Aires: Losada and UNICEF. 45–92.

Parysow, J. and Bogani E. 2002. Perspectivas de desarrollo económico y social para las mujeres pobres y empobrecidas en los clubes del trueque. Estudio De Caso: La Bernalesa. *Seminario Las Caras de la Pobreza*. Buenos Aires: Universidad Católica Argentina. 215–230.

Pastor Jr M and Wise C. 1999. Stabilization and its discontents: Argentina's economic restructuring in the 1990s. *World Development* 27(3):477–503.

Polanyi K. 1992. The economy as instituted process. In: Granovetter M and Swedberg R, eds. *The Sociology of Economic Life*. Boulder, CO: Westview Press. 29–52.

Schvarzer J and Finkelstein H. 2003. *Análisis – Bonos, cuasi monedas y política económica*. Revista Realidad Económica, IADE, Buenos Aires. 193.

Swanke T. 2004. Understanding the implications of money being a social convention. In: Wray R and Forstater M, eds. *Contemporary Post Keynesian Analysis*. Cheltenham, UK: Edward Elgar Publishing. 84–99.

Théret B and Zanabria M. 2009. On the viability of monetary complementarity in federations: the case of fiscal provincial monies in 2001–2003 Argentina's crisis. *XV World Economic History Congress*. Utrecht, The Netherlands.

Wolters W. 2008. Heavy and light money in the Netherlands Indies and the Dutch Republic: dilemmas of monetary management with unit of account systems. *Financial History Review* 15:37–53.

5 Monetary federalism as a concept and its empirical underpinnings in Argentina's monetary history

Bruno Théret[1]

> 'Monetary federalism', unlike fiscal federalism, is still a theory in its embryonic stage and this is undoubtedly due to the fact that there is no substantial difference between the monetary organisations of existing federal and non-federal states. . . . But asking whether federalism can make an original contribution in the monetary field is no longer an idle question. The struggle to provide Europe with a common currency requires that at least the federalists are capable of reflecting on these topics without being hidebound by the monetary organisation model that has characterised centralised national states.
>
> (Jozzo 1985, 185 and 201).

5.1 Introduction

This chapter develops the concept of monetary federalism by drawing from both theory and history. The theory includes the concept of federalism in philosophical and political thought, while the history mainly concerns monetary experiments in Argentina. The chapter is divided into three sections. The first section presents the general principles and several historical underpinnings of the application of federalism to monetary systems. The second section presents one of the clearest historical manifestations of monetary federalism, namely the recurrent waves of issuances of provincial fiscal complementary currencies (CC) in Argentina between 1890 and 2003. The third section looks at why this country has exhibited such a noteworthy case of monetary federalism, even if a repressed one. In conclusion, we suggest an Argentinian scenario of monetary federalism for the eurozone that would allow a breakthrough in the monetary crisis of the European Union without falling into the deadlocks of either the present generalised austerity policies, or breakdown of the monetary union.

While it is common to speak of political federalism and fiscal federalism, and less frequently of economic federalism, the expression 'monetary federalism' is extremely rare. Google searches in English and French lead to fewer than ten occurrences of it, and show that, like 'federalism' and 'federalist', its usage has contradictory meanings. While in the tradition of the *Federalist Papers*, to be a federalist is to be partisan of the federal State, politicians and economists equate monetary federalism with a single money managed by a Federal Central Bank (Wyplosz 1999; Grégoriadis 2007). Thus, it concerns neither an organisational structure nor a specific institutional regime of distribution of monetary powers within a federation.

On the contrary, according to a philosophical view of federalism, to be a federalist is to respect the federal principle of balancing unity and plurality, and monetary federalism refers to a specific design of monetary systems where interests of federated entities (states, provinces, landers, cantons) are taken into account, and where the sharing of monetary competencies is stressed upon (Jozzo 1985; Théret and Zanabria 2007; Arnsperger 2011; Théret and Kalinowski 2012; Saiag 2013). The concept of monetary federalism developed in this chapter belongs to this second stream of thought within which monetary plurality is recognised as empirical evidence and theorised as more efficient and resilient than monetary singularity.

The current crisis of the euro is an outcome of a single monetary policy for economically and culturally diverse heterogeneous territories and prompts us to rethink such a monetary policy and its theoretical underpinnings. Many historical experiments of monetary plurality, especially in political contexts of federal polities, indicate that we should not think of money as singular or plural, but as simultaneously singular and plural. That is, we should not consider monetary plurality as an expression of competition between monies but of complementarity among them (Kuroda 2008a, 2008b). In fact, in our view, the concept of monetary federalism, as a form of federalism complementing fiscal and political federalism, is a theoretical way to design this complementarity among monies caused by locality. It refers to territoriality as an extrinsic dimension of money.

However, monetary federalism cannot be reduced to this territorial dimension for two reasons. Firstly, like political federalism in general, monetary federalism has both territorial and functional dimensions: it balances political relations among territorial interests (due to the spatial division of a country into different tiers of government), as well as 'functional' interests (entrenched in the social division of labour). It regulates the interactions between both types of societal relations (Sbragia 1993). Secondly, monetary federalism also refers to the intrinsic federal structure of modern (capitalist-statist) money which combines singularity (of the system-unit of account) and plurality (of the means of payment).

Eventually, a hypothesis of institutional complementarity considers that the principles of organisation of a monetary system have to fit, in one way or another, with those of the political organisation of the society within which the monetary system functions. Therefore, if the intrinsic federal structure of modern money does not appear clearly in the monetary institutions of most of the existing federations, it means that monetary federalism is politically repressed. As empirical evidence from many federations shows, such repression can cause monetary and/or political instabilities that may destroy the federation either by splitting it into many independent states, or by transforming it into a unitary state through violence.[2]

Therefore, when federated public powers issue fiscal tender CCs circulating at parity with the federal legal tender currency used as the unit of account, one can conceptualise this fact as 'monetary federalism'. But, why should we conceptualise recurrent social facts, if not to transform them from particular cases into more general categories that are useful to widen our understanding of collective action. Thus, our interest in the concept of monetary federalism resides in its capacity to design an issue to the current European Union's political and economic crisis in line with the original purposes of the Union.

From this perspective, even if innovative federal monetary experiments have been overlooked because most economists and politicians view them only as emergency devices, not susceptible to produce efficient and permanent institutions, they must be considered as crucial material of scientific knowledge. They are indeed part of the 'buried knowledges' praised by Michel Foucault, and whose failure to survive was not the outcome of their economic inefficiency, but of political defeats of the social forces that were promoting them. We have to uncover these experiments not only for the beauty of scientific work aiming at historical truth, but also as genuine and original social innovations enlightening the design of new federal political and monetary institutional arrangements. Let's keep in mind that purely fiat paper currencies were considered only as an emergency form of money and discredited as counterfeit money by mainstream economists and politicians until the 1930s when they became the standard form of money.

5.2 Principles and historicity of monetary federalism

Federalism is a political set of normative principles whose purpose is to accommodate unity within diversity, without sacrificing one or the other. Thus, it is no surprise that, albeit non-pluralist views on money can prevail even there, social scientists may find empirical evidence of monetary plurality and complementarity in federal polities. In mainstream economics and political science where rational choice theory dominates, federalism is conceived as a 'market-preserving' device, and no attention is paid to principles of human action other than competition (Weingast 1995; McKinnon 1997). But this view does not fit with the empirical evidence of many federations whose purpose is mainly 'peace-keeping', and which are based on cooperation and complementarity more than economic competition between the different territorial tiers of the government (Théret 2015). Then, if federalism refers to an institutional way of combining unity and diversity without destroying either, it is possible to consider that its general principles apply to the modern capitalist-statist money. In most federations this federalist structure of money, with its territorial and functional dimensions, is not recognised and is not reported by 'normal' scientific knowledge, but it nonetheless surfaces recurrently in critical periods and can be studied. I will draw on new empirical evidence from three cases: the United States in the ten years separating the Articles of Confederation and the Federal Constitution, again the United States in the 1930s, and Argentina in the 1990s. We argue that the issuance of a plurality of municipal and provincial fiscal CCs is not a simple outcome of emergency conditions, but is a structural manifestation of monetary federalism.

5.2.1 From political federalism to monetary federalism

Federalism can be defined as a way to shape a political order on the basis of a hierarchy of values and not of a hierarchy of powers (with concentration of power at the top), as usual in a unitary State (Théret 1999, 2002, 2004, 2015). The federal tier of government is not more powerful than the federated governments, for it does not have the monopoly over political competencies. In the domains where they are sovereign, federated entities are superior in power to the federal government, but the latter is in charge of competencies which are greater in value because they form the federation as a whole, for instance by ensuring internal peace between member-states, and acting on their behalf in the external world. Therefore, in a federal polity, there is an overlapping hierarchy of powers and no sovereign power in the strict classical meaning of the word. Sovereignty becomes the attribute of an authority separated from any executive power, and whose decisions are enforceable only if federal and federated powers recognise it as a sovereign authority to whom they submit themselves; if not, the federation is on the way towards dissolution. This authority, whose might is purely symbolic, is a third party placed in the position of sovereignty above any political power, either federal or federated. It usually takes the material and institutional forms of a constitutional text and special judicial power – the Supreme or Constitutional Court – which has the necessary authority to settle the conflicts of powers between or within the tiers of governments of a federative political order.

Now this general structure of federalism as a hierarchy of values also makes sense for the monetary order of the modern state-and-market societies where economy is differentiated from the political, the religious and the domestic orders. Decreeing the system and unit of account and maintaining its uniqueness are competencies of the federal tier, as notably stated by Hawtrey (*Currency and Credit*, 1919, cited in Commons 1934, 472 and 477) or Keynes (*A Treatise on Money*, 1930, cited by Ingham 2004, and Wray 2014, 15). They are of greater social value than the powers to issue and circulate means of payments. The latter powers can be shared, decentralised and even decentered. In order to allow monetary transactions, they are usually distributed to different agents and organisations acting at different territorial scales and with different purposes. Monies of payment – currencies – circulate in multiple spheres of transactions and users' networks (public or private, market or non-market, small or large, local, regional or national); they take different material forms, are not *a priori* 'all purpose money', and most often have to be 'earmarked' to be accepted in transactions (Zelizer 1994; Blanc 2006). For them to form a payment community despite the fact that they cannot be unified, they must be federated, allowing them to circulate in more extended and impersonal networks as well as across *a priori* heterogeneous transaction spheres by the mediation of a common federal unit of account.

Therefore, in a society symbolised by a common system and unit of account, the power to issue monies of payment can be distributed functionally and territorially among different issuers (banks, private companies, States, cities, local exchange trading systems, associations, etc.) without necessarily being a danger for the unity and cohesion of the society. On the contrary, the competence of issuing instruments of debt settlement appears to structurally pertain to the domain of decentralised or federated economic and political powers. But for unification to be effective without centralisation the various means of payment have to be denominated at least in a common unit of account (or convertible at a stable value) and the parity between units of payment and the unit of account has to be maintained.

As for the third party that would represent the federal sovereign monetary authority, it can be neither the federal power that decrees and maintains the unit and the system of account, nor the federated powers that issue means of payment. History shows that the true sovereign in monetary matters is the People who are the users of money and who decide the future of any money, imaginary or real, in accepting or refusing its use in the internal multi-lateral transactions (Wennerlind 2011). The People can delegate its authority through a monetary constitution to an institution independent of the monetary powers (public and private) and give it the power of interpreting this constitution in order to settle conflicts between issuers of currencies, and to maintain the commonality of the system and unit of account.

From this perspective, such a monetary authority should not be confused with any central bank which is not independent from issuers of currencies, and is, most often than not, only a police and executive power, part of the federal tier of government. Central banks have powers that have to be legitimised, which means that they *a priori* are deprived of the ethical authority residing in the values and social norms constituting a population of money users as a social whole. In order to legitimise their monetary policies, central banks need an ethical backing in the values sustaining the political community, either unitary or federal. Surely, the Federal Reserve Board of the US Federal Reserve Bank System, in its design at least, is the closest institution of such an ideal-type monetary authority. Its presence could explain why in the US, despite the tremendous monetary power of its private financial industry, monetary repression of non-commercial bank issuances of monies is presently one of the weakest in the world.

Why does this intrinsic federal structure of modern money not appear clearly in the monetary institutions of most of the existing federations? Why are complementarities between monetary and political institutions not realised or, at least, taken into consideration by social sciences? Why are the relationships between the political organisation of a society and the organisation of its monetary system so little investigated and taken into account, even when falling into deep crisis? There is no room in this chapter to answer such questions, answers which would involve an examination of the strong links existing between standard monetary theories prevailing in a historical period, and monetary institutions and policies (Théret 2011). Let's focus on monetary experiments which unveil the effective presence of federalist monetary arrangements in some federations.

5.2.2 Emergency monies or repressed monetary federalism

In general, and even in federations, the importance taken in various historical periods by federated states' issuances of 'quasi-monies' under the form of tax anticipation scrips and small denomination bonds or warrants is under-investigated.

Nevertheless, three cases are well documented: the United States during the colonial and postcolonial periods before the Philadelphia Convention (Ferguson 1969, 1983; Schweitzer 1989; Grubb 2003, 2005, 2012), the United States during the crisis of the 1930s (Elvins 2010; Gatch 2012), and Argentina during the convertibility crisis of the dollarised peso from 2001 to 2003 (Argañaraz *et al.* 2003; Chelala 2003; DNCP 2003; Licari *et al.* 2003; Schvarzer and Finkelstein 2003; Feliz 2004; Sbatella 2004; Colliac 2005; Douthwaite 2005; Théret and Zanabria 2007). In the USA, the usual practice of issuance of IOUs in order to finance their unbalanced budget by some US federated States, like California, cannot be considered as a monetary practice since these IOUs do not circulate as paper money. In Argentina, to the contrary, issuances of quasi-monies were not the only seen in 2001–2003 but have been recurrent since the fall of the last military dictatorship in 1984.

Nevertheless, issuances of provincial fiscal paper monies in Argentina in the form of tax anticipation scrips (generally called bonds or letters of debt settlement), are noticed by economists only in times of intense social stress and political crises, and, most of the time, these quasi-monies are considered exclusively as emergency monies and not further investigated. This supposed emergency character is nothing but the outcome of a normative prejudice regarding what constitutes a 'normal' state of monetary order, which implies that the federal State (or an independent central monetary power) has to be fully sovereign in public monetary matters, even if the polity is officially organised in accordance with federalist principles (Helleiner 2003). So provincial States' currencies are mostly visible to official actors only during periods of emergency, and, as soon as crises are overcome, they are outlawed and/or forgotten. When they appear to be significant for the macroeconomy, they are eliminated or redeemed by the central power in search of 'return to normality'.

Consequently, they are thought to be politically unacceptable and the empirical evidence that under certain conditions they have been (and therefore could be) successful in resolving the issues of balancing public finance and promoting local economic development is not taken into account and integrated into monetary theory. Thus, what Loren Gatch writes about the US municipal tax anticipation scrips of the 1930s, holds for the provincial monies of Argentina:

> If the money-sovereignty nexus is constitutive of 'monetary space', then the implied lessons of the historical experience with tax anticipation scrip will come from answers to political questions about the powers and autonomy of local governments, and not to economic questions about the putative benefits of local currencies . . . For us to take cognizance of the significance of local currency, and to revive public consciousness of its potential in our present day, requires us to appreciate those historical moments when local currency, despite its success, disappeared as an expression of local power. (. . .) From the broader perspective of American monetary history, the proliferation of local currencies during the 1930s appears as an anomalous development in the progressive centralisation of monetary power and authority in Washington D.C.
>
> (Gatch 2012, 33).

Farley Grubb (2003, 2005, 2012), following Lester (1970 [1939]), Ferguson (1956, 1983) and Schweitzer (1989), draws similar conclusions in his works on fiscal monies of the North American Colonies and then States after the 'Articles of Confederation'. Monetary systems backed by public taxing powers have not been recurrently outlawed because they are economically inefficient but because their supporters have been regularly defeated in the political arena by coalitions between (and sometimes merging of) private financial interests and politically dominant ruling classes (Beard 1913; Ferguson 1969; Holton 2005). In fact, economic arguments legitimising the political devaluation of tax backed monies in favour of private fractional reserve credit money issued by commercial banks are, as stated by Richard Lester, nothing more than 'economic theology' that we need to overcome:

> 'Above all, today we need some of the intelligent scepticism that our colonial forefathers had towards the financial dogma of the day. They did not hesitate to challenge the existing economic theology or to engage in intelligent experimentation'
>
> (Lester 1939–1970, 307).

Economic theology indeed is not limited to the United States; it is also reigning in Argentina as an internal report of the Argentinian Ministry of Economy and Finance (DNCP, 2003) testifies. This report referred to the 2003 federal redemption of the provincial quasi-monies issued by about 16 provinces in the period 1999–2002 and admitted that complementarity between public monies – national and provincial – was perfectly viable, since they had distinct spatial spheres of circulation. Nevertheless, the authors considered that it was not 'optimal', since optimality required the union of the monetary power in order to resolve the two problems of monetary plurality: externality and uncertainty. But this reference to optimality is purely theological; it is sustained neither by general empirical evidence (*Financial History Review* 2008) nor by evidence in this particular case.[3] For, if provincial monies expanded in 2001, as we shall see below, it was in fact because the federal monetary policy had produced strong negative externalities and increased uncertainty to the point of destroying confidence and trust in the whole monetary system, and therefore, the credibility of the centralised monetary power. Moreover, provincial monies had produced positive externalities and reduced uncertainty when they were successfully managed, as has been the case in many provinces and for the largest amount of money issued (Greco 2001; Théret and Zanabria 2007, 2009).

In this context, the issuance by the province of Tucuman of quasi-money called *bocade* that lasted over 17 years (1985–2003) is important. Although it concerns a small North Western peripheral province of Argentina, this 'experiment' proves two main things: that provincial tax anticipation small denomination bonds are not necessarily of an emergency nature, and that they do not compete with national money but are complementary to it.

The Tucuman CC has been ironically called 'funny tucuman dollar' by the *Financial Times* (Pilling 1996), maintaining the view that provincial currencies were only answers to crises. In a 'normal' state of affairs the Argentinian monetary system shows long-term unresolved contradictions that render it structurally unstable. That would mean that the Argentinian 'standard state' of centralisation and commodification of money issuance is not an optimal steady state. Moreover, unlike the cases of late-comers in provincial CCs issuances such as Buenos Aires (*patacon*) and Entre Rios (*federal*), it is possible to assume that the 2001 crisis of the convertibility regime had not given life but death to the Tucuman currency. The federal government and most of provincial governments themselves, under the pressure of the IMF, took advantage of the failure of some of these CCs, due to over-issuance and of the common view of their emergency character, to redeem them all together and to re-centralise the whole system in Buenos Aires. Thus, it is more accurate to say that during the convertible peso's crisis (2001–2003), the Tucuman *bocade* which was circulating as a CC for 16 years had been constrained to become a substitute to the peso that was scarce at the national and provincial levels. Therefore, it was over-issued and lost a part of the trust put in it due to growing difficulties to ensure its convertibility at par with the national legal tender that was in short supply. That did not imply that the *bocade* was condemned to disappear. As shown in Chapter 8 in this volume, it had already successfully overcome the confrontation of deep crises of the national monetary system, notably hyper-inflation. Moreover, if the *bocade*'s exchange rate in pesos deteriorated in the market during the crisis, it nevertheless was maintained under control, as shown in Figure 5.1 where the *bocade* appears as good money as the *lecor*, issued by the province of Cordoba, usually considered a successful experiment (Luzzi 2012).

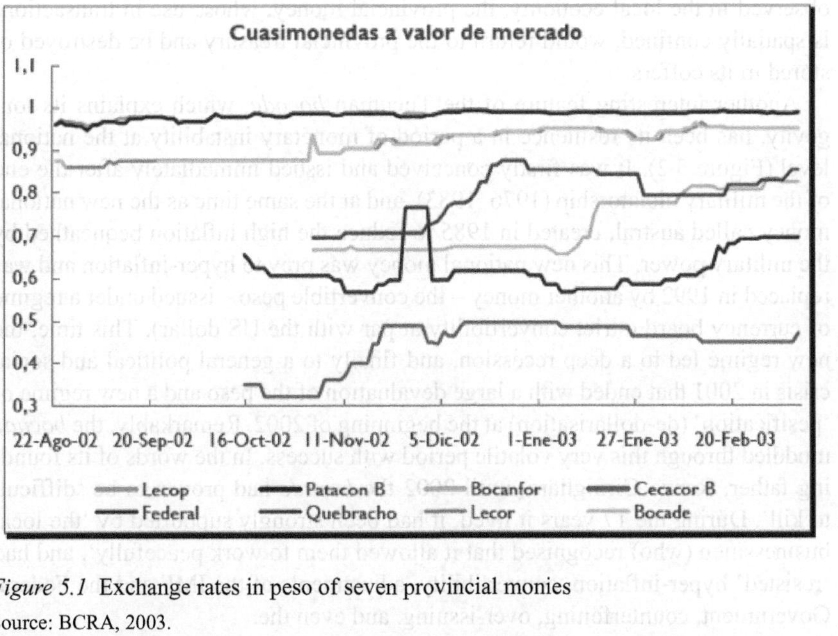

Figure 5.1 Exchange rates in peso of seven provincial monies

Source: BCRA, 2003.

Finally, if the *bocade* disappeared in 2003, it was not an outcome of its endogenous economic functioning, but because it did not benefit anymore from the benign neglect of the central and international financial powers, and became, with the whole set of 'quasi-monies', a stake in the negotiation between the federal Government and the IMF which was now pre-occupied by them:

> Quasi-money issuance by provincial governments in 2002 amounted to Arg$ 3.2 billion . . . and should be compensated by orderly financing as provided in the 2002 bilateral agreements. The main drawbacks of quasi-monies are: they erode the ability of the central bank to conduct monetary policy . . . they complicate the commitment to fiscal management and do not alter the budget constraint; they contribute to the growth of the informal economy and to tax evasion . . . they have an adverse effect on inter-provincial trade . . . [since] they generate important trade diversion flows, promoting regional inefficiencies and tend to regionalise provincial economies at the expense of efficiency-enhancing nationwide integration.
>
> (IMF 2003, 34)

Issuance of provincial quasi-monies can be an efficient response to provincial structural problems of shortage of national currency and credit money, which are the outcomes of centralised fiscal and monetary federal institutions and policies. It also clearly shows that provincial CCs are not competing and driving the national legal tender out of circulation as a media of payment; they complement them within the limits of the provincial economic spaces where they are accepted as means of redemption of taxes and as such they are a clear expression of an efficient monetary federalism. If a surplus of national legal tender currency is observed in the local economy, the provincial money, whose use in transactions is spatially confined, would return to the provincial treasury and be destroyed or stored in its coffers.

Another interesting feature of the Tucuman *bocade*, which explains its longevity, has been its resilience in a period of monetary instability at the national level (Figure 5.2). It was firstly conceived and issued immediately after the end of the military dictatorship (1976–1983), and at the same time as the new national money called austral, created in 1985 to reduce the high inflation bequeathed by the military power. This new national money was prey to hyper-inflation and was replaced in 1992 by another money – the convertible peso – issued under a regime of currency board (strict convertibility at par with the US dollar). This time, the new regime led to a deep recession, and finally to a general political and social crisis in 2001 that ended with a large devaluation of the peso and a new regime of 'pesification' (de-dollarisation) at the beginning of 2002. Remarkably, the *bocade* muddled through this very volatile period with success. In the words of its founding father, Renzo Cirnigliaro, until 2002 the *bocade* had proven to be 'difficult to kill'. During the 17 years it lived, it had been strongly supported by 'the local businessmen (who) recognised that it allowed them to work peacefully', and had 'resisted' hyper-inflation, convertibility, adjustments of the IMF and the Federal Government, counterfeiting, over-issuing, and even the:

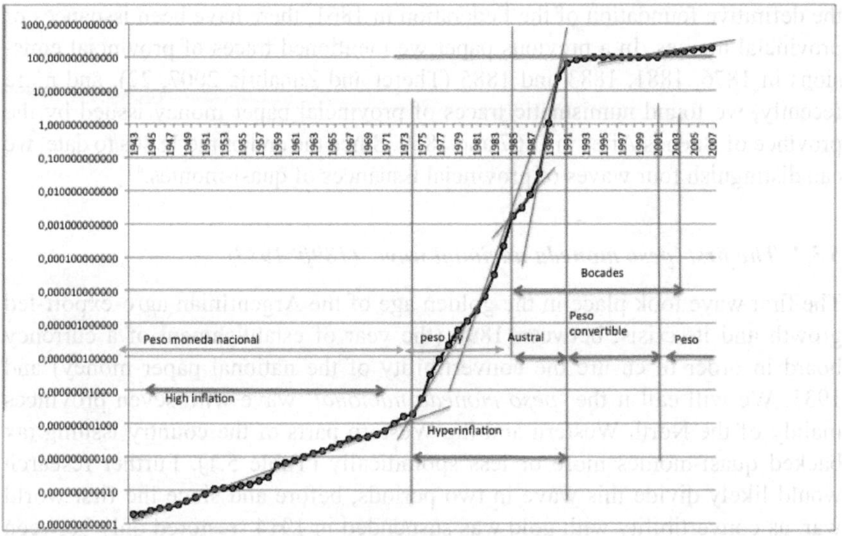

Figure 5.2 Argentinian consumer price index (1943 to 2008)
Source: Vitelli, 1986.

> [a]ttack that changed a credit without interest from the people into a credit at high rates from the banks and the markets. And finally, it twisted the governments' arms, since after 16 years of critics towards provincial monies, it had to issue a younger sister of them, the lecop.
>
> (Cirnigliaro 2004, 125)

This resilience at the provincial level compared with the recurrent monetary chaos at the national level is paradoxical. On one side, the *bocade* found its viability and efficiency upon strict convertibility with the national money. On the other side, it was an autonomous device since it had a peripheral character vis-à-vis the central monetary system to which it could freely adapt. Its autonomy was therefore independence within inter-dependence, a good definition for complementarity. Since independence within inter-dependence is also at the core of the concept of federalism, it justifies tackling complementarity caused by locality in terms of monetary federalism.

Let's now examine this point more precisely by adopting a long run perspective and recalling the importance, recurrence and causes of provincial fiscal monies issuance in the history of Argentina as an independent federal Republic.

5.3 The four waves of issuance of provincial CCs in Argentina since 1890

Since the origin of Argentina as an independent country in 1810, monetary plurality, tax-based money and problems of convertibility of paper money have marked its history (Grinfeld 1910; Bordo and Vegh 2002; Irigoin 2000, 2003). Even after the definitive foundation of the Federation in 1861, there have been issuances of provincial monies. In a previous paper we mentioned traces of provincial emissions in 1876, 1881, 1883 and 1885 (Theret and Zanabria 2007, 22), and more recently, we found numismatic traces of provincial paper money issued by the province of Buenos Aires in 1867 and 1869. Since the end of the 1880s to date, we can distinguish four waves of provincial issuances of quasi-monies.[4]

5.3.1 The first 'peso moneda nacional wave' (1890–1933)

The first wave took place in the golden age of the Argentinian agro-export-led growth and its crisis, between 1890 (the year of establishment of a currency board in order to ensure the convertibility of the national paper money) and 1933. We will call it the '*peso moneda nacional*' wave with seven provinces mainly of the North Western and the Western parts of the country issuing tax backed quasi-monies more or less sporadically (Table 5.1). Further research would likely divide this wave in two periods, before and since the first world war, as convertibility with gold was suspended in 1914 (restored only between 1927 and 1929) (Bordo and Vegh 2002). Nonetheless, this wave holds its unity from the fact that issuances of provincial monies were made on the same peso (m$n) standard.

As displayed in Table 5.1, the North Western provinces (Jujuy, Salta and Tucuman) were more active (Figure 5.3). These provinces were also at the forefront in the second and third waves. But between 1934 and 1984, 50 years of military and/or authoritarian rule, and import-substitution-led growth regime associated with a central bank (created in 1935) 'absolutely centralised' (Olivera 1992), we find no trace of any issuance of provincial money other than one of certificates of debt settlement by the province of Tucuman in 1965–1966, which were not anonymous and looked as transferable checks.

Table 5.1 Issuances of provincial quasi-monies between 1890 and 1933

Unit of account	*peso moneda nacional m$n (1881–1969)*
Provinces concerned	Years of issue of provincial monies
Corrientes	1891
Jujuy	1903 – 1905 – 1928 – 1932
Mendoza	1892 – 1908
Salta	1891 – 1916 – 1921 – 1927 – 1932 – 1933
San Juan	1894 – 1896 – 1899 – 1909 – 1923 (4% interest)
Santa Fé	1890
Santiago del Estero	1891
Tucuman	1900 – 1915 – 1917

Figure 5.3 One example from Jujuy (1932)

5.3.2 The second 'austral wave' (1984–1991)

Only around the end of the last military dictatorship in 1984 were there new issuances in four North Western provinces, starting with Salta in 1984, La Rioja and Tucuman in 1985, and Jujuy in 1986. In the World Bank Report of 1990 on Provincial Government Finance, five (including Catamarca) and not four provinces are named issuing money in this period (World Bank 1990, 77). Oppenheimer (1985) and Cirnigliaro (2004, 126) also mention Catamarca as one of the North Western provinces having a possible monetary regional space where quasi-monies from every province could have circulated at par. But we have found no numismatic traces of issuance in Catamarca before 1993.

This second wave that lasted until 1991 will be called the 'austral wave' since it coincides with the replacement of the peso in 1985 by the austral in which the quasi-monies were convertible at par, thanks to the institution of currency boards managed by the public banks of each province. Only the first issue of the *bocade* of Salta preceded the 'austral plan' and was initially denominated in peso argentino (1000 $A = 1 austral), and the first bills had to be surcharged by a stamp to circulate on the basis of the austral standard (Figure 5.4).

The monies issued during these years, called *bocade* in Salta, Tucuman and La Rioja, and *titulo publico al portador*, usually called *publico* in Jujuy (and Catamarca in 1993) (Figure 5.5), were very similar in the four provinces. They followed the Salta model, especially the Tucuman bond which was originally a copy of the Salta one (Del Rey and Orive 1986; Cerro 1988).

This speaks of a particularly resilient North Western sub-type of Argentinian provincial bonds. The first striking difference is that *bocades*, as well as *publicos*, were the only quasi-monies emerging and maintaining themselves in the austral period of high and then hyper-inflation. Another peculiarity is that while *patacones, lecors, cecacors, federales*, and other more recent bonds bore interest, the 1980s generation of bonds were non-interest-bearing assets although, at least in the case of Tucuman, an interest rate was considered in their legal origin but was

Figure 5.4 The Salta's *bocade* issued in 1984 in 'peso argentino'

Figure 5.5 The *publico* of Jujuy issued in 1986

never implemented. Like the federal *lecop* issued in 2001, they were pure fiscal tender currencies anchored in the national money. It is no coincidence that these North Western provinces represent the older part of Argentina where provincial belonging is an important part of individual identity. It reveals the outstanding political nature of the region's CCs: financial market incentives for building trust and confidence in them were excluded since the beginning. These incentives were to be found in lotteries, a traditional fiscal instrument of states.

Finally, another possible important specificity of these CCs is the political fact that their convertibility at par, which was not easy to maintain especially in time of high inflation, was *de facto* and sometimes explicitly defended by the local business community even when the local political ruling classes were in a hurry to come back to 'normality'.

5.3.3 The third 'dollarised peso wave' (1992–2000) and the fourth 'convertibility crisis and de-dollarised peso wave' (2001–2003)

After the 'convertibility plan' by which the country moved out of hyper-inflation in 1992, it is usually considered that there were no more quasi-monies issued by provincial governments. Researchers and the general public only remember the successful issue of the *cecor* by the government of the Cordoba province in 1995 and link it to the 'Tequila' crisis. However, while Salta stopped its issuance of provincial money, Tucuman (continuously), Jujuy (with an interruption between 1992 and 1995), and La Rioja (with an interruption between 1997 and 2001) carried on issuing *bocade* or *publico* throughout the decade.

Moreover, other provinces entered the game: Catamarca in 1993 (Figure 5.6); Cordoba (*lecor*), Formosa (*boncafor*), Mendoza (*petrobono/petrom*), Rio Negro (*cedern*) (Figure 5.7), and San Juan (*crefi/huarpes*) (Figure 5.8) in 1995, Missiones (*cemis*) in 1996, and Corrientes (*cecacor*) in 1999. Thus 11 provinces had already started to issue small denomination bonds in convertible peso before 2001 and the great crisis of the national currency board regime. Thus, it is necessary to distinguish between a third wave of provincial issuance between 1992 and 2000 and a fourth wave starting in 2001.

We name the third wave of 11 provinces, forgotten by both the scientific and journalistic literature, the 'dollarised peso' wave. The fourth and last wave starting in 2001 concerns four more provinces that were new-comers in the movement: Buenos Aires (with the *patacon*), Chaco (with the *quebracho*) (Figure 5.9) and Entre Rios (with the *federal*) in 2001, and San Luis (with the *sanluis*) in 2002.

Figure 5.6 The *publico* of Catamarca issued in 1993

Figure 5.7 The *cedern* of Rio Negro issued in 1995

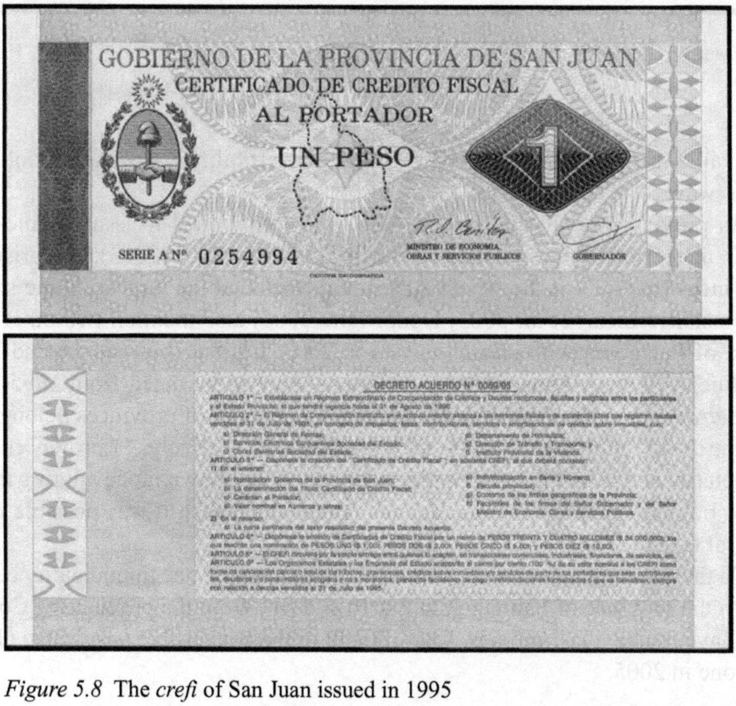

Figure 5.8 The *crefi* of San Juan issued in 1995

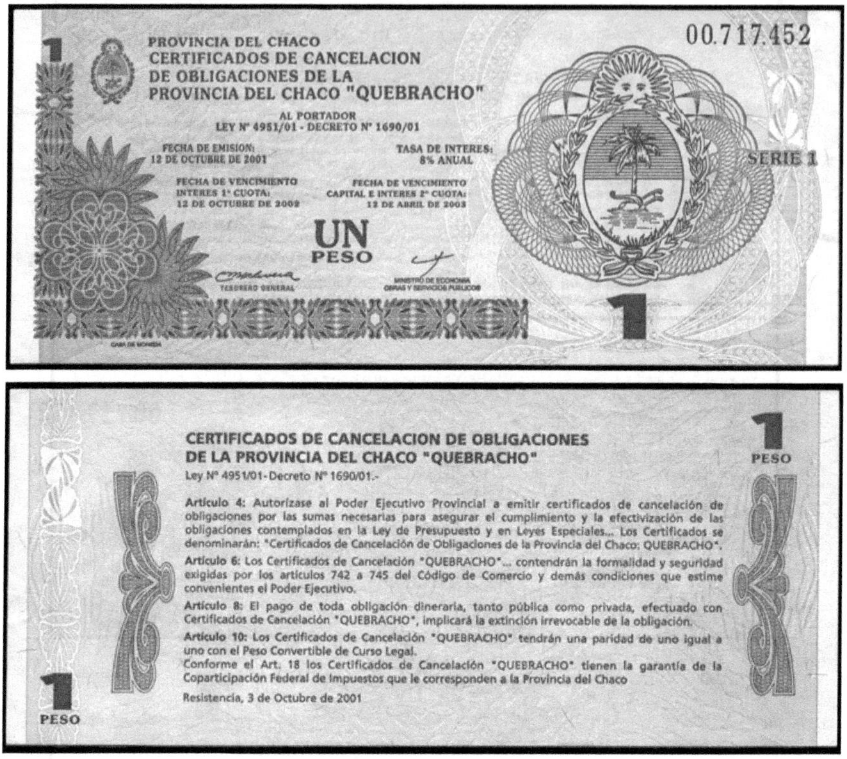

Figure 5.9 The *quebracho* of Chaco issued in 2001

We name this last wave (2001–2003) the 'convertibility crisis and de-dollarised peso' wave.

As provinces of the 'dollarised peso' wave continued to issue monies until 2003, the period of the so-called convertibility crisis (2001–2003), comprising 15 provinces (over 23 of the whole Argentina), included the largest. Some sources (for instance Licari *et al.* 2003; Douthwaite 2005) also mention two other provinces of Patagonia with *cuasimonedas* in 2003: Chubut (*petrobono*) and Tierra del Fuego (*letras*). Thus, if these emissions were to be dated from 1995 as for the *petrobono* of Rio Negro, it would push the number of provinces belonging to the third and fourth waves to 13 and 6 provinces respectively, 17 provinces being monetarily active in 2002–2003 (Jujuy did not issue its own money during the last wave but used *patacones* from Buenos Aires with which it was possible to pay federal taxes).

To these provincial monies, we must still add at least one municipality belonging to the province of Santiago del Estero and five from the province of Cordoba that have issued quasi-monies, four of them in the convertible peso wave (1995), and one in 2005.

Eventually, in 2001 the federal government itself started to issue a large amount of quasi-money, called *lecop* (Figure 5.10). The *lecop* was inter-provincial money (not convertible to dollars) that was put into circulation through the system of federal fiscal transfers to provinces and municipalities and was a legal tender for payment of federal taxes.

The total issuance of provincial and inter-provincial small denomination bonds in 2002 was nearly 50% of the monetary base (Douthwaite 2005; Théret and Zanabria 2007, 28). That year the central bank used a new enlarged concept of the monetary base to include them (BCRA 2002, 39). But standing back from this short period of open crisis and taking into account the previous waves, provincial issuances of tax anticipation small denomination currencies cannot be reduced to this episode.

Another important characteristic of these monetary experiments is their diversity. There have been a wide variety of devices associated with the diversity of political and economic situations in the provinces. Some provinces mobilised local currency boards to keep their CCs at parity (Cordoba, Entre Rios, Tucuman), while others did not. Some benefited from larger tax base than others (especially when the CCs could be used in payment of national taxes and were circulating in the equalisation transfers circuit like the *patacon* of Buenos Aires). Some could

Figure 5.10 The federal interprovincial quasi-money

use special public resources to back their bonds (oil royalties in Mendoza, Chubut and Rio Negro) (Figure 5.11), and one (the *san* luis, issued at the end of 2002) was indexed to a basket of five national currencies (Argentinian peso, Brazilian real, Chilean peso, US dollar and the euro) (Boletín Oficial 2002).

Political strategies for building trust, confidence and credibility were also idiosyncratic. Some succeeded and some failed (Théret and Zanabria 2007 and 2009; Figure 5.12). Few things are known in detail on most of these experiments since historians were not interested in recording these histories until now. Nevertheless, we have sufficient data to understand and explain why issuances of provincial small denomination bonds have been so recurrent in Argentina.

5.4 Why such a historical recurrence? Argentinian fiscal federalism and shortages of currency and credit at the provincial level

In our view, this historical recurrence can be explained by the specific federalist structure of the Argentinian political and fiscal systems. Three elements of this structure must be outlined: first, the form of fiscal federalism; second, the monetary regime; and, third, the constitutional regime.

Figure 5.11 The *petrom* issued in Mendoza in 2002

Figure 5.12 The *san luis* issued in 2002

5.4.1 Fiscal federalism and currency shortage

As it has been recognised by the World Bank, 'understanding the transfers from the national to the provincial governments is key to understanding provincial finance in Argentina' (World Bank 1990, vol. 1, 13). The country is characterised by strong dependence of provincial budgets on federal transfers coupled with a large federal discretion in the distribution of funds.

Argentinian provinces, with the exception of the Autonomous City of Buenos Aires (the national), depend hugely on federal transfers, with variations across time and space. The federal government collects around 85% of all taxes (including social contributions), while spending is decentralised (the provincial and municipal levels are responsible for around 45% of public expenses). The large and wealthiest provinces of Buenos Aires, Santa Fé, Cordoba and Mendoza are less dependent (their own revenues representing around 30–35% of their total revenues) than the poorer and peripheral ones (for instance, autonomous revenues are worth less than 20% in the North Western provinces of Jujuy, Salta, and Tucuman, and 10% in Catamarca and La Rioja) (Saiegh and Tommasi 2000, 69).

This large vertical deficit in the tax primary distribution is structural; it has existed since the outset of the Republic, for Buenos Aires has always benefited from a monopoly on customs duties that were the main source of the tax revenues backing its fiat money issuances (Irigoin 2003). These duties are still outside the revenue-sharing scheme. Moreover, as illustrated in Figure 5.13 for Tucuman, the vertical deficit has been reinforced in the 1970s and 1980s by unilateral devolutions of social expenses without transfers of the corresponding revenues, a policy initiated by the last military dictatorship but carried on until 1993 (Eaton 2001; Falletti 2010; Théret 2015).

In most federations federal tax transfers are of three kinds: general revenue sharing, earmarked transfers and purely discretionary grants. In Argentina the boundaries between these categories are blurred. Even when rules of automatic revenue sharing and/or earmarking are fixed, these are either renegotiated or bypassed through bilateral negotiations between the federal President and provincial governors. Before the updated institutionalisation of revenue-sharing in the Act of *Co-participacion* of 1988, bypassing federal rules was dominant; afterwards, these rules were renegotiated (Bonvecchi 2005).

For these reasons, provinces suffer great instability and uncertainty concerning the true amount of federal money that they are going to receive annually, monthly or daily. Permanent discussions about the effective amounts of federal engagements are coupled with federal discretion related to the agenda of payments, since fund distribution is often conditioned to political support to the President's initiatives in Congress (Bernadou 2009). This uncertainty increases when the federal government is itself prey to a fiscal crisis.

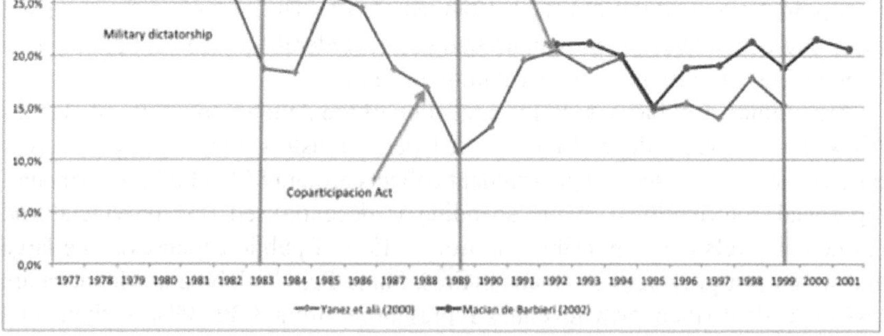

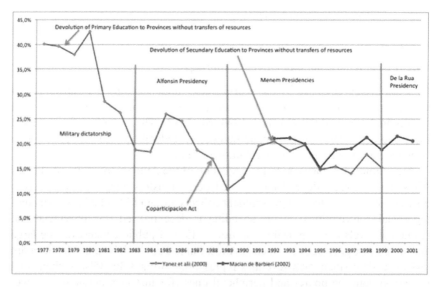

Figure 5.13 Share of provincial autonomous revenues in Tucuman total spending

Sources: Yanez et al. (2000), Macian de Barbieri et al. (1990 and 2002).

Moreover, money shortage is a daily problem for provinces since transfer payments tend to feed provincial treasuries at irregular pace. In fact, federal transfers and devolution of public expenses to provinces are often the primary objects of budget cuts. The Argentinian economy knows a high degree of volatility and strong dependence vis-à-vis external shocks, so federal and then provincial fiscal crises are expected to recur and always feared. It is no surprise to see payments of wages to public employees and/or debts vis-à-vis small suppliers delayed by months in Argentina. It is also not surprising to see these waiting periods correlate with social unrest and emergency situations where provincial governments have to borrow money from banks and/or financial markets, in order to finance current expenses. The dependence of provincial governments on federal resources explains that their public debt is primarily a floating debt funded at high cost.

5.4.2 *'Absolute centralisation' of the monetary system, shortage and high cost of credit*

Another element in the conundrum of provincial public finance is the shortage and correlated high cost of credit for poor, peripheral or impoverished provinces. Their economic dependence towards the federal government is not limited to fiscal transfers, but is extended to federal monetary policy. The monetary policy is hyper-centralised, and the monetary regime is managed exclusively in relation to the exchange rate regime and macro-economic stability, so the economic interests of the peripheral provinces are not taken into account. This exogenous constraint on provincial finance and local economic development varies and depends on the type of management of monetary policy and the institutional design of the financial system. In the austral period, provinces were assisted by a provincial public bank through which they could have access to short-term credit that these banks could rediscount at the central bank. Through this kind of financing, governments were transferring their structural problem of liquidity to their banks, and the consolidated accounts of the provincial public sector were not improved. So the device only allowed for a better short-term smoothing of public debt payments.

In the dollarised peso period, the central bank (BCRA) was transformed into a kind of currency board and forbidden to issue credit money. Moreover, after 1995, most of the provincial banks were privatised and not inclined anymore to directly finance provincial deficits at low cost, and hard budget constraints were put in place. Provinces had to go to more costly financial markets and, for that, could not do anything apart from backing their loans on their revenue-sharing resources. Provincial debt burden thus climbed faster than ever, and their capacity to pay for current expenses declined. This occurred in Tucuman between 1996 and 1999 when the governor wanted to get rid of the *bocade* (see Chapter 8).

Shortage and high cost of credit also have a second impact on provincial finance, one related to the difficulty of funding local economic development and, consequently, the enlargement of the provincial tax base. Julio Olivera (1992) links this problem to the 'absolute centralisation' of the BCRA in Argentina. For Olivera, an economist internationally known for the distinction between active and passive money, on the 'active' side of monetary supply, the 'monetary base multiplier' changes according to the provinces because the growth of the monetary base is unequally distributed among them, an inequality reinforced by the diversity of the economic situations of the provinces. Thus, depending on a province's situation of unemployment or full employment, growth of the monetary supply would stimulate either production or inflation. Moreover, depending on the presence or absence of regional, active and wide monetary and financial markets, the mechanisms of monetary transmission will either stimulate the productive economy or be limited to the financial sector. On the 'passive' side of the monetary demand stimulated by changes in prices and wages, Olivera argues that there is also, even if employment rates are equal, a regional differentiation of the capacity of monetary institutions to respond to demand if they are spatially unequally distributed. Therefore, 'a rational monetary policy must take into account regional differences', and 'the best way to do so is to decentralise the Central Bank', given that 'the optimal degree of decentralisation of the Central Bank is not the same for all countries and depends on the size of the territory, of the regional diversity, of the financial organisation, and of the types of monetary policies implemented (Olivera, 1992, 9).

After examination of different actual types of central banks, Olivera states that the Argentinian one 'functions as a totally centralised organism' despite its federal juridical statute that should constrain it to take a decentralised form (ibid., 14). Thus, instead of its 'absolute centralisation' that is at odds with the federal constitution of the country, the BCRA should be administratively decentralised, according to 'the size of the country and the magnitude of its inter-regional differences' (ibid.).

From this analysis, it can be deducted that Argentinian peripheral provinces are structurally confronted by monetary policies and geographical distribution of monetary institutions that do not fit their economic needs and the stabilisation of their public finance. We better understand why local business groups have been generally supportive of 'currency finance' (Ferguson 1956) that provincial governments in great shortage of national currency and credit have regularly relied on.

5.4.3 States of political emergency and provincial states' initiative to issue local currencies

There is a broad set of factors that compose the structural conundrum that is susceptible to develop in a vicious circle of cumulative and unsustainable provincial indebtedness and bankruptcy, and that motivate the issuance of tax anticipation bonds of small denominations circulating as paper money. These factors include the shortage of national money from above, shortage of market money from below, public expenses composed of inelastic social expenses (education, health, security), uncertainty and discretion of the federal delivery of tax transfers, autonomous tax revenues difficult to expand due to weak domestic markets and production deprived of an adequate access to credit money and investment.

How do provincial governments issue paper money despite perceptions that it is forbidden by the federal constitution (Gallo 1988)? Why do such paper monies persist during long periods without decisions of the federal Supreme Court or modifications of the constitution? Even federal syndicates (interventores) designated by the federal executive to substitute temporarily failing or corrupt governors did not stop these monetary experiments of provincial state money when they were in office (Théret and Zanabria 2007). The usual answer to these questions is that it was tolerated because it concerned small amounts of money. This argument can make sense to economists and international monetary authorities like IMF and World Bank (World Bank 1990, 77–78; 1996, i, 2, 8, 11) but does not fit with the fact that the federal state was actively participating in the issuances at the provincial level and at the national level during the crisis of the dollarised peso: it doesn't explain why the quasi-money *lecop* was issued by the federal Finance Minister, Domingo Cavallo, initiator of the 1992 convertibility plan and back in office in 2001 after having urged the governor of the province of Buenos Aires to issue the *patacon*.

Thus, it seems more accurate to take into consideration three other arguments. Firstly, as soon as it was supported by the provincial legislative and juridical (Supreme Court) powers, the power of the provincial executives to infringe upon a federal constitution that required the authorisation of the national Congress to issue money was legitimised by the character of emergency and urgency of the situations in which the quasi-monies emerged.

Secondly, the constitution contemplates only two forms of money, coins and paper banknotes. Direct printing by the Treasury of paper money backed by taxes is not explicitly considered. Thus, the interpretation of provincial currencies as money that is not legally legitimate is not as straight forward as it seems *a priori*.

The third argument assumes that the federal behaviour of benign neglect or active complicity can be understood more easily if we take into account that the provincial quasi-monies are not in competition with the national money but complementary to it. As soon as we consider that provincial issuances of small denomination bonds do not 'restrict' the circulation of federal currency but rather complement it in politically delimited spaces, they can be perceived positively by federal executives whose monetary policy is therefore not threatened but rather improved. That's precisely what occurred when 'the money supply in pesos dropped from $15,056 million to $10,960 million during 2001', and 'the total issue of quasi currencies, $2,900 million, replaced over half the loss of the money supply in the latter part of the year' (Douthwaite 2005, 21).

The situation is different with issuances of credit money by provincial states through their banks that may be partly re-discounted at the central bank. In that case, the money issued is of the same nature as federal money and may circulate in the whole territory of the federation. Generally, there is confusion between both forms of money, but the federal tolerance of provincial scrips seems to express that federal politicians are conscious of the difference between the two instruments. The federal attitude means that the *bocade, publico, federal, patacon* and other provincial scrips were testimony of a need for monetary plurality and complementarity due to the overlapping geographical tiers of public payments circuits.

5.5 Conclusion

The Argentinian experiences of monetary federalism related above display a complementarity between a federal legal tender and provincial scrip. Richard Douthwaite, in his report for the Club of Vienna in 2005, already had the intuition that these experiments were a source of inspiration in tackling the issue of the current eurozone crisis, since they point out a way towards a monetary system that would overcome this crisis without falling into the deadlocks of either the present generalised austerity policies or breakdown of the monetary union (Théret and Kalinowski 2012; Théret 2013a, 2013b; Théret, Coutrot and Kalinowski 2015). Such a federal monetary system should combine an all-purpose federal currency and unit of account – the current euro, circulating across the whole European Union and abroad – and the member-states-issued CCs backed by their own fiscal resources and denominated in euros as the federal unit of account and exclusive legal tender.

Monetary federalism is thus designing a way out of the prevailing dichotomic debate between carrying on with a single monetary policy combined with fiscal austerity policies or coming back to single national monies combined with competitive devaluations, both like-minded 'single currency'. Promoting monetary federalism in the EU, inspired by the most recent Argentinian experiences, and also by the successful tax anticipation scrips of the US cities at the start of the 1930s, as well as by the currency finance of the American colonies and confederated states, would allow the preservation of the euro as a common currency and unit of account without depriving member states of issuing fiscal CCs circulating within their borders and maintained at par with the euro. It would be both a logical and historically founded way of 'reinventing monies in Europe' (Dodd 2005).

A truly federal monetary system would be efficient and resilient, if national governments can build trust and confidence in their CCs. This is shown in Chapter 8 where we come back with more details of the case of the Tucuman *bocade*. By examining precisely how it functioned and evolved, we demonstrate that this CC has been useful and successful at both reducing the province's public debt and pushing its economic growth contra-cyclically without creating structural inflation and/or the CC's depreciation. Moreover, this outcome was obtained despite unfavourable fiscal conditions to sustain the CC's parity vis-à-vis federal money which was either unstable or extremely rigid. Thus, if plunged by its creditors into a desperate austerity policy that is supposed to reduce its public debt but is in fact increasing it, an EU member-state would engage in a Tucuman type of strategy, it would have easier conditions than Tucuman to succeed, since it would have the full control of its fiscal policy and would suffer a softened convertibility constraint on the CC. Moreover, to give legitimacy to what could be a unilateral innovation for improving the living conditions of its population, the member-state could mobilise the principles of subsidiarity and variable geometry which are still at the core of the EU constitution.

Notes

1 This research was developed in the framework of international programmes on complementarity among monies (2009–2013). The author thanks Akinobu Kuroda (University of Tokyo) for the strong incentives that resulted from his invitation to participate in these programmes. He thanks also Miguel Zanabria (National University of Quilmes) and José Alberto Sbatella (National University of La Plata) for having introduced him in 2001 to the Argentinian field of territorial CCs, and for further collaborations between 2001 and 2009. Thanks also to participants in the two International Workshops De-teleologising History of Money and its Theory in Ecole Normale Supérieure, Paris, December 2010, and University of Tokyo, February 2012, and Conferences at University of Paris Pantheon-Sorbonne, July 2012, Yale University, September 2012, City University of London, February 2013, and Erasmus University, The Hague, June 2013, where previous drafts of this chapter were presented.

2 It can also mean that, due to an ideological ostracism characteristic of unitary countries as France (Beaud 1999), federalism is taboo, and thus scholars lack the concept to analyse what is in fact a form of federalism, as it is the case for the current hierarchical banking systems.

3 In fact, this conception of optimality is also controversial from a standard economic point of view, since if Argentina, like the EU, is considered as a non optimal currency area, the optimality resides in the plurality of provincial monies. 'If creating money would be an essentially technical decision, linked to the optimality of market's adjustments, it would be possible on the basis of the theory of Optimal Currency Areas to maintain that creating multiple currencies in the Argentinean territory is preferable' (Feliz 2004, 114). But OCA theory excludes the possibility of two currencies on one and a same territory. Therefore, unlike monetary federalism, it 'offers no elements for understanding the actual dynamics of monetary plurality' (ibid., 115).

4 Our main source (http://numismondo/pm/arg/) may contain some mistakes and is incomplete. Other numismatic and economic sources are Del Rey and Orive 1986; Greco 2001 (quoting José Reissig 1990, 'Bonds that brought a boom', *New Economics* 20, Winter); Schvarzer and Finkelstein 2003; Colantonio 2010. For complementary sources, see Théret and Zanabria 2007, and Chapter 8 of this book. National and provincial newspapers have also been consulted and interviews made in the City of Buenos Aires, the provinces of Buenos Aires, Entre Rios, Cordoba, Mendoza and Tucuman from 2001 to 2013.

References

Argañaraz, N., Capello, M. and Garzon, J. 2003. 'Cuasi-monedas provinciales: un análisis de su existencla y actual rescate'. *Documentos de Trabajo, Serie Politica Fiscal.* Cordoba, Argentina: IERAL, Fundação Mediteranea, June.

Arnsperger, C. 2011. 'Monetary federalism and the recovery of Swiss sovereignty: enhancing Switzerland's financial autonomy through a cantonal system of complementary currencies'. Paper presented at the ECSA-Switzerland Conference, 'Aspekteder Souveränitätinden Beziehungender Schweizzur Europäischen Union', Basel, Switzerland, December 9.

BCRA. 2002. *Boletin monetario y financiero.* Edicion anual. Buenos Aires: Banco Central de la Republica Argentina.

BCRA. 2003. *Informe monetario mensual.* Buenos Aires: Banco Central de la Republica Argentina. Febrero.

Beard, C. A. 1913–1921. *An Economic Interpretation of the Constitution of the United States*. New York: MacMillan.

Beaud, O. 1999. *Fédéralisme et fédération en France. Histoire d'un concept impossible*. Strasbourg: Presses Universitaires de Strasbourg.

Bernadou, V. 2009. 'Nestor Kirchner: du président 'sans pouvoirs' au 'chef hégémonique', *Critique internationale* 43: 89–107.

Blanc, J. 2006. 'Karl Polanyi et les monnaies modernes: un réexamen'. In *Contributions à une sociologie des conduites économiques*, edited by Gilles Lazuech and Pascale Moulévrier, 51–66. Paris: L'Harmattan.

Boletín Oficial (9 de Octubre de 2002), *Autorizase al poder ejecutivo la emisión de títulos convertibles al portador en la provincia de San Luis*. www.saij.gob.ar/legislacion/ley-san_luis-5338-autorizase_al_poder_ejecutivo.htm

Bonvecchi, A. 2005. 'Les aspects politiques du fédéralisme budgétaire argentin à l'aune des négociations fiscales fédérales', *Problèmes d'Amérique latine* 56: 129–152.

Bordo, M., and Vegh, C. 2002. 'What if Alexander Hamilton had been Argentinian? A comparison of the early monetary experiences of Argentina and the United States', *Journal of Monetary Economics* 49(3): 459–494.

Cerro, E. R. 1988. 'Estudio Financiero del bono emitido por el Gobierno de la Provincia de Tucuman', in *Anales de la Asociacion de Economia Politica*, XXIII Reunion Anual, La Plata.

Chelala, S. 2003. 'La utilizacion de terceras monedas. El caso argentino'. April 9. www.nodo50.org/cubasigloXXI/congreso/chelala_10abr03.pdf

Cirnigliaro, R. 2004. *Tucuman – Argentina. El festin de los caranchos*. San Miguel de Tucuman, Argentina: Editorial Kerigma.

Colantonio, E. 2010. *Bonos de emergencia de Argentina. 1985–2002*. Buenos Aires: Eduardo Colantonio Editor.

Colliac, S. 2005. 'Monnaies parallèles provinciales et fédéralisme budgétaire en Argentine', *Revue d'économie financière* 81(4): 251–269.

Commons, J. R. 1934. *Institutional Economics*. New York: MacMillan.

Del Rey, E. C. and Orive, G. A. 1986. 'Los bonos de cancelacion de deudas de la provincia de Salta'. Published in *1989 in Finanzas Publicas y Desarollo Regional – Ensayos en Honor de Horacio N. Miñana*, edited by Luis Di Marco. Cordoba, Argentina: Universidad Nacional de Córdoba, Dirección General de Publicaciones.

DNCP (Direccion Nacional de Coordination con las Provincias) – Grupo Deuda. 2003. *Cuasimonedas*. Buenos Aires: Ministerio de Economia y Finanzas.

Dodd, N. 2005. 'Reinventing monies in Europe', *Economy and Society* 34(4): 558–583.

Douthwaite, R. 2005. 'Why Europe needs regional currencies'. *Report to the Club of Vienna*, March. www.feasta.org/documents/.../Austria_intro_cut.pdf.

Eaton, K. 2001. 'Decentralisation and liberalisation: the history of revenue sharing in Argentina, 1934–1999', *Journal of Latin American Studies* 33(1): 1–28.

Elvins, S. 2010. 'Scrip, stores, and cash-strapped cities', *Journal of Historical Research in Marketing* 2(1): 86–107.

Falletti, T. 2010. Decentralization and Subnational Politics in Latin America. New York: Cambridge UP.

Feliz, M. 2004. 'Teoria y practica de la pluralidad monetaria. Algunos elementos para el analisis de la experiencia argentina reciente', *Economia, Teoria y Practica* 21: 107–133.

Ferguson, E. J. 1956. 'Currency finance: an interpretation of colonial monetary practices', *The William and Mary Quaterly* 10(2): 153–180.

Ferguson, E. J. 1969. 'The nationalists of 1781–1783 and the economic interpretation of the constitution', *The Journal of American History* 56(2): 241–261.

Ferguson, E. J. 1983. 'Political economy, public liberty, and the formation of the constitution', *The William and Mary Quaterly* 40(3): 389–412.

Financial History Review. 2008. Special Issue on Complementarity among monies. 15(1): 7–91.

Gallo, R. 1988. 'Serios problemas legales con las monedas norteñas.' *La Prensa*, April 19.

Gatch, L. 2012. 'Tax anticipation scrip as a form of local currency in the USA during the 1930s', *International Journal of Community Currency Research* 16: 22–35.

Greco, T. H., Jr. 2001. *Money. Understanding and Creating Alternatives to Legal Tender*. White River, VT: Chelsea Green Publishing Company.

Grégoriadis, N. 2007. 'Un modèle simple de fédéralisme monétaire.' *Document du LEO*, January. Université d'Orléan.

Grinfeld, I. 1910. 'Monetary experiences of the Argentine Republic', *Political Science Quarterly* 25(1): 103–122.

Grubb, F. 2003. 'Creating the U.S. dollar currency union, 1748–1811: a quest for monetary stability or a usurpation of state sovereignty for personal gain?' *American Economic Review* 93(5): 1778–1798.

Grubb, F. 2005. 'The U.S. Constitution and monetary powers: an analysis of the 1787 constitutional convention and how a constitutional transformation of the nation's monetary system emerged', NBER Working Paper 11783. www.nber.org/papers/w11783.pdf

Grubb, F. 2012. 'Is paper money just paper money? Experimentation and local variation in the fiat paper monies issued by the colonial governments of British North America, 1690–1775', NBER Working Paper 17997. www.nber.org/papers/w17997.pdf

Helleiner, E. 2003. The Making of National Money. Territorial Currencies in Historical Perspective. Ithaca, NY: Cornell University Press.

Holton, W. 2005. 'Did democray cause the depression that led to the Constitution?' *Journal of American History* 92(2): 442–469.

IMF. 2003. 'Argentina: 2002 Article IV consultation – staff report; staff supplement; public information notice on the executive board discussion; and statement by the authorities of Argentina', IMF Country Report 03/226. Washington, DC: IMF.

Ingham, G. K. 2004. *The Nature of Money*. Cambridge, UK: Polity Press.

Irigoin, M. A. 2000. 'Inconvertible paper money, inflation and economic performance in early nineteenth century Argentina', *Journal of Latin American Studies* 32: 333–359.

Irigoin, M. A. 2003. 'La fabricacion de moneda en Buenos Aires y Potosi y la transformacion de la economia colonial en el Rio de la Plata (1820 y 1860)'. In *La desintegracion de la economia colonial. Comercio y moneda en el interior del espacio colonial. (1800–1860)*, edited by M. A. Irigoin and Roberto Schmit, 57–92. Buenos Aires: Editorial Biblos.

Jozzo, A. 1985. 'Towards a federal European economy: pre-federal monetary union', *The Federalist* 37(3): 195–201.

Kuroda, A. 2008a. 'What is the complementarity among monies? An introductory note', *Financial History Review* 15(1): 7–15.

Kuroda, A. 2008b. 'Concurrent but non-integrable currency circuits: complementary relationships among monies in modern China and other regions', *Financial History Review* 15(1): 17–36.

Lester, R. A. 1970 [1939]. *Monetary Experiments. Early American and Recent Scandinavian*. New York: Augustus M. Kelley Publishers.

Licari, J. M., Calgagno, J. C., Oviedo, J. M. and Pellegrini, S. 2003. 'Cuasimonedas provinciales. Medición absoluta y comparada', Documento del Observatorio de la Economia. Cordoba, Argentina: Universidad Nacional de Córdoba.

Luzzi, M. 2012. La monnaie en question. Pratiques et conflits à propos de l'argent lors de la crise de 2001 en Argentine, PhD. diss., Paris: Ecole des Hautes études en sciences sociales.

McKinnon, R. I. 1997. 'Monetary regimes, government borrowing constraints, and market-preserving federalism: implications for EMU'. In *The Nation State in a Global / Information Era: Policy Challenges*, edited by T. J. Courchene, 101–142. Kingston, ON: Queen's University.

Olivera, J. 1992. 'Banca central, federalismo economico y constitucion monetaria', Opening Keynote Speech, XXVI Reunion Anual de la Asociacion Argentina de Economia Politica, 6 de noviembre 1991. Published in *Nuevas Respuestas, Revista de la Universidad Catolica de Santiago del Estero Junio* 7–17.

Oppenheimer, A. 1985. 'Cash-starved argentine provinces turning out their own money', *The Charlotte Observer* November 28.

Pilling, D. 1996. 'Funny money fills argentine pockets', *Financial Times* February 13.

Saiag, H. 2013. 'Le trueque argentin ou la question du fédéralisme monétaire (1995–2002)', *Revue Française de Socio-Économie* 12 (2): 69–89.

Saiegh, S. and Tommasi, M. 2000. 'Le labyrinthe fiscal de l'Argentine et la théorie des coûts de trasnaction en politique', *Problèmes d'Amérique latine* 37: 63–90.

Sbatella, J. A. 2004. 'Crisis fiscal y rol de moneda. La experiencia argentina de la década de 1990'. In *La economia argentina y su crisis (1976–2001): visiones institucionalistas y regulacionistas*, edited by Robert Boyer et Julio Neffa, 507–17. Buenos Aires: Ceil-Piette – Miño y Davila.

Sbragia, A. M. 1993. 'The European community: a balancing act', *Publius* 23: 23–38.

Schvarzer, J. and Finkelstein, H. 2003. 'Bonos, cuasi monedas y política económica', *Realidad Económica* 193: 79–95.

Schweitzer, M. M. 1989. 'State-issued currency and the ratification of the U.S. Constitution', *Journal of Economic History* 49(2): 311–322.

Théret, B. 1999. 'Federalism and regionalism: a comparative analysis of the regulation of economic tensions between regions by intergovernmental transfers programs in Canada and the USA', *International Journal of Urban and Regional Research* 23(3): 479–512.

Théret, B. 2002. *Protection sociale et Fédéralisme. L'Europe dans le miroir de l'Amérique du Nord*. Brusells, Belgium and Montreal, QC: PIE – Peter Lang and PUM.

Théret, B. 2004. 'Del principio federal a una tipologia de las federaciones: algunas propuestas', *Foro Internacional* 175: 29–65.

Théret, B. 2011. 'Du keynésianisme au libertarianisme. La place de la monnaie dans les transformations du savoir économique autorisé', *Revue de la regulation* [online], 10, second semester. http://regulation.revues.org/9529.

Théret, B. 2013a. 'Salida del dilema de la crisis de la eurozona: una respuesta en terminos de federalismo monetario'. In *Capitalismos volatiles, trabajadores precarios. Crisis financiera global y cuestion social*, edited by Guillermo Perez-Sosto, 203–250. Buenos Aires: Instituto di Tella.

Théret, B. 2013b. 'Dettes et crise de confiance dans l'euro: analyse et voies possibles de sortie par le haut', *Revue française de socio-économie* 12: 91–124.

Théret, B. 2015. 'La Diversidad de los Federalismos en América Latina: Argentina, Brasil, Mexico'. In V*ariedades de Capitalismo en América. Los casos de Mexico, Brasil, Argentina y Chile*, edited by I. Bizberg, 147–281. Mexico City: Ediciones del Colegio de Mexico.

Théret, B., Coutrot, T. and Kalinowski, W. 2015. 'The Euro-Drachma, a monetary lifeline for Greece', March 16, www.veblen-institute.org/The-Euro-Drachma-a-Monetary-Lifeline-for-Greece.html.

Théret, B. and Kalinowski, W. 2012. 'The Euro as common money, not a single currency. A plea for a European monetary federalism'. *Notes of the Veblen Institute for Economic Reforms September*. Paris: Fondation pour le Progrès de l'Homme.

Théret, B. and Zanabria, M. 2007. 'Sur la pluralité des monnaies publiques dans les fédérations. Une approche de ses conditions de viabilité à partir de l'expérience argentine récente', *Economie et Institutions* 10–11: 9–65.

Théret, B. and Zanabria, M. 2009. 'On the viability of monetary complementarity in federations: the case of fiscal provincial monies in 2001–2003 Argentina's crisis'. Paper presented at the XVth World Economic History Congress. Utrecht, Netherlands: August 3–7.

Vitelli, G. 1986. *Cuarenta años de inflacion en la Argentina: 1945–1985*. Buenos Aires: Editorial Legasa.

Weingast, B. 1995. 'The economic role of political institutions: market-preserving federalism and economic development', *The Journal of Law, Economics, and Organisations* 11(1): 1–31.

Wennerlind, C. 2011. *Casualties of Credit. The English Financial Revolution, 1620–1720*. Cambridge, MA: Harvard University Press.

World Bank. 1990. 'Argentina. Provincial government finance study, Latin America and the Caribbean region. Country Department IV'. Report 8176-AR, 2 vol. Washington, DC: World Bank.

World Bank. 1996. 'Argentina. Finanzas Provinciales: Temas sobre Federalismo Fiscal'. Informe del Departamento I 15437. Washington, DC: Oficina Regional de America Latina y el Caribe.

Wray, L. R. 2014. 'From the state theory of money to modern money theory: an alternative to economic orthodoxy', Working Paper No. 792, Levy Economics Institute of Bard College.

Wyplosz, C. 1999. 'Towards a more perfect EMU'. CEPR Discussion Paper No. 2252. London: CEPR, October.

Zelizer, V. 1994. *The Social Meaning of Money*. Princeton, NJ: Princeton University Press.

6 Famine of cash

Why have local monies remained popular throughout human history?

Akinobu Kuroda

6.1 'Free banking system' without banks

Throughout human history currency shortages have frequently hampered local transactions. Unable to wait for authorities to resolve these shortages, those in need of currency often did not hesitate to generate local payment devices by themselves (see chapter by Gómez and von Prittwitz in this volume). Although these makeshift forms of currency may look mysterious to those accustomed to the idea that money should be backed by either authority or its material contents, these forms of payment proved useful in their localities.

In 1929, Xianrendu, in Laohekou County, Hubei—a town in the middle reaches of the Yangtze River—suffered a serious currency shortage. Soon after, notes issued by 36 different shops began to circulate in the town, even though the area comprised only around 300 households. The stores that issued the notes included 13 grocers, nine grain dealers, two seed oil mills, two medicine dealers, three liquor shops, two tea houses, a wholesale trader, a tofu shop, a rice cake shop, a silver dealer and a butcher (Chen X., 2012, p.116). It seems that all kinds of shops in the town issued their own notes, and that the issuers included no proper financiers. In other words, any type of shop functioned or could function as an issuer of currency.

Xianrendu was not an isolated case. In 1936, native notes issued by 13 shops were in circulation in a rural town in Julu County, Hebei, which had around 400 households. Of the 26 shops in the town, 13—including an inn, grocer, grain dealer and wheat cake shop—issued their own notes. At first only merchants with relatively large assets, such as grain dealers, issued currency notes. However, given the profitability of note issuance, many small-scale merchants soon followed. Even a wheat cake baker, with assets of just 200 yuan, issued notes whose value amounted to 500 yuan (Chen T., 1936).

Most locally issued notes signified that they could be converted into metal currencies. However, contemporary observers have commented that when a bearer requested the conversion, the issuer simply exchanged the note for another one issued by a different shop. In some cases, the issuers would only convert notes into coins on the days of the Five-Day market (which was held every five days). On other days, they would exchange one note for another at the demand of the bearer. Whether the issuers observed the rule or not, the convertibility of the notes was actually rather limited (Dai and Chen, 2011).

Why did people accept local currency despite its limited convertibility? To answer this question it is important to consider the regional situation. Notes available in one five-day market were rarely accepted at other markets. In the case of the unnamed town in Julu County mentioned above, the reporter estimated the total value of native notes to lie somewhere between 8000 and 9000 yuan (Chen T., 1937). If we assume that 400 households likely used 100 yuan in cash each year, native notes totalling 8000 yuan must have circulated through the town five times. The estimated 100 yuan in household expenditure was slightly more than the 83 yuan income of the average peasant household in a village in Taigu County, Shanxi Province (Wu, 1935), but less than half the average household income of a village in Hengshan County, Hunan Province (Wang, 1937). Therefore, the issuance of 8000 yuan in notes does not appear to have been excessive. An account of the situation in Julu County, published in a contemporary journal, indicates that even these locally issued notes could not meet the area's currency demand. Banknotes were also in circulation, but they only accounted for 50 percent of circulating currencies. The remaining 50 percent was made up of locally issued notes. Although it was difficult to tell forged notes from genuine ones and despite their limited convertibility, these notes helped sustain exchange within the region.

Currency shortages forced locals in early 20th-century China to accept inconvertible notes, even those suspected of being forged. Insufficient currency supplies frequently caused transactions in the marketplace to decline, a situation Chinese traditionally called *qianhuang*: the famine of cash. The question then arises as to why serious cash shortages occurred so frequently.

6.2 Currencies stagnate rather than circulate

Table 6.1 shows the distribution of copper coins of different eras excavated from two places in China. Both hoards of coins appear to have been buried around 1270, but the majority of coins date from the 11th century. Although a large amount of paper money, some silver ingots and silk functioned as currency during the Song

Table 6.1 Distribution of copper cash with era names from Chinese excavation

Last year of period	*Yankeshan*	*Wenqiaoyidui*
618	27	—
907	866	57
960	12	3
1004	472	32
1054	2,706	213
1101	7,156	277
1126	2,018	95
1201	212	45
1260	—	4
Total	13,469	726
Latest era	1131–63	1260–65

Source: Miyake, 2005, pp.104–105.

Dynasty (960–1279), copper coins were used for daily transactions. The contents of excavated currency hoards reveal that coin transactions in late 13th-century China involved coins issued two centuries earlier.

The size of the hoard found at Yankeshan is large enough for us to assume that its contents were intentional savings, while the size of the hoard at Wenqiaoyidui is so small that we may consider it a cluster of stray coins rather than savings. In both cases, regardless of the size of the hoard or whether it represented savings, the era names are distributed in almost the same proportion. Besides the propensity of holders to save, this indicates the possibility of a currency tending towards stagnation.

With regard to this point, an investigation of coins collected from bank branches across the UK in 1968 provides some important information. Before the introduction of decimal denominations in 1971, the Royal Mint, in cooperation with major banks such as Barclays, surveyed how many coins of each denomination crossed the counters of banks in one day and tallied the distribution of the dates of issuance of those coins. This allowed the Mint to gauge how many coins should be supplied under the new denomination system. Since the Mint had data on the quantities of minted coins of each denomination for each year, they could estimate how long a coin had circulated outside the banks. The assumption was that the older the coin, the less likely it would be returned from the holders to the bank but the question remained: to what extent?

The survey revealed that aside from those coins disposed of due to physical damage (which accounted for just 0.1 percent of the total), two out of every 100 coins failed to reach the bank counters every year. In other words, those coins became 'economically inactive'. This meant that half of all coins minted in a given period would disappear from circulation within 33 years. The wastage rate of coins varied by denomination, as Table 6.2 shows that nearly 4 out of every 100 'half pence coins' went missing annually. This rate was far higher than that of larger denominations (De Glanville, 1970). An investigation of coins sampled from bank branches across the USA in 1962 showed similar results. The average waste rate was 2 percent; however, the wastage rate of the 10 cent coin, the smallest denomination in the sample investigation, was the highest among all denominations (Patterson, 1972).

Table 6.2 Wastage rates of coins in the UK 1968 (percentages)

Half d coins (half pence coins)	*3.7*
1 d	2.2
3 d	1.7
6 d	2.1
1/-	0.4
2/-	1.2
2/6 d	0.9

Source: Public Record Office, Kew, Mint 20/3965.

People are not likely to save cheap, bulky coins as assets; we can therefore assume that nobody held such coins for any particular purpose. In other words, though some coins are intentionally hoarded, a large amount of coins also becomes inactive unintentionally.

The wastage rates mentioned above were determined by tallying coins passing over the bank counters. Banking systems work to collect currencies once distributed among numerous end users. Even in the UK and the USA, which had the world's most dense banking systems in the 1960s, 2 out of every 100 coins disappeared from circulation every year. It is quite easy to imagine what happened to the circulation of currencies before the establishment of banking systems. Large portions of currency must have been taken out of circulation every year, remaining in the hands of end users.

During the Great Depression in the 1930s, John Hicks sought to understand why people would keep currency that gave no return when they could instead purchase bonds that earned interest (Hicks, 1935). Since he only considered the intentional saving of currency, he overlooked that currency sometimes unintentionally goes out of circulation. Mainstream social sciences have been blind to the stagnant nature of currency. Currency is easy to distribute but difficult to gather on demand; this is the flip side of currency 'acceptability'—its capacity to anonymously circulate.

6.3 Invisible agreements on local currencies

Besides the locally issued notes mentioned above, the regional organisation of currency supplies has occurred in various forms. In 1606, Quanzhou, the largest port city in Southern China, faced a famine due to poor harvest and the increased circulation of illegal coinages. In order to stabilise the local market, the city's magistrate tried to set a maximum price for grains to make it easier for locals to buy them. He also prohibited the use of unofficial coins. Though his actions may seem appropriate from a modern viewpoint, to his contemporaries he appeared to be blind to reality. The traders at the port protested against the price controls and the prohibition of private coinage and went on strike, causing the market to close.

Those in opposition to the magistrate's rules insisted that price control discouraged maritime traders from importing grains and that the private coins would disappear as soon as they became unnecessary. The magistrate lifted the regulations, which encouraged traders to import larger amounts of grains, causing market prices to decrease to a normal level, whereupon private coins disappeared (Chen, n.d.). This process indicates that increasing the amount of privately made coins allowed prices to raise high enough to absorb grains from other regions. When facing famine, in addition to securing actual food supplies, it is also important to avoid disturbing food distribution. In the case of Quanzhou, the local market generated sufficient liquidity to import grains from outside the city. The magistrate failed to notice that the system worked locally and also could not distinguish stability from formality.

China is not the only example of such locally organised currencies: societies already dependent on modern banking systems, such as the US, have seen similar occurrences. On December 7, 1931, the only bank in Tenino, Washington State, the Tenino Citizen Bank, closed its teller, paralysing the town's entire business sector. This was not an isolated case: In the last quarter of that year, 1,055 banks across the USA suspended their services against the backdrop of the Great Depression. However, the emergency measure adopted by the Tenino Chamber of Commerce to counteract the bank's closure was an uncommon one. It issued certificates in an amount equivalent to 25 percent of the bank's total deposit value. These certificates had a face value of 25 cents and were printed on wooden tablets. This wooden money went into circulation, though only within the town. Needless to say, its function as a currency ended once the formal currency system was revived (Preston, 1933).

The Chamber of Commerce took the initiative in the case of Tenino and the acceptance of wooden currency was not backed by any regulations. There was therefore still a possibility that the bank deposits would become non-performing debts. Thus, it was neither official support nor the intrinsic value of the tablets, but a loose agreement among locals that sustained the acceptability of the wooden currency.

Such informal agreements have emerged around the world in various forms throughout history. Local economies have often encountered problems with small denomination currencies in particular, rather than currency in general, due to the former's tendency to experience shortages. Since the majority of exchanges in the local market places are wage-goods-level transactions, small denomination currencies have naturally been in greater demand.

Some native notes in early 20th-century China were printed with a description of the background of issuance. For example, a note with a face value of 100 *wen* issued in 1916 by a shop at Junxian, Hubei Province, featured the following description on the back: 'Copper coins recently disappeared and silver subsidiaries were in short supply. Subsequently, trade stagnated and traders have suffered losses. Thus, we issue these small notes to circulate in the market in order to facilitate the supply of small change. (Shi, 2002, p.503)

Heterogeneous demand and rigid supply have often caused small currencies to circulate independently from the currencies flowing beyond local marketplaces, as have occurred across the world, such as in late medieval Europe (Spufford, 1999) and the Red Sea region in the early 20th century (Kuroda, 2007).

6.4 Credits substitute currencies locally

If a currency tends to be stagnant in nature and people consequently suffer shortages, then it follows that people would seek another device with which to mediate exchanges. History shows that people have indeed sought out such devices. For example, in early modern England a large number of litigation records in local courts of law offer snapshots of the kinds of social devices that were used in transactions.

Litigation records in local market towns and manors show how the ordinary person strongly depends on credit transactions in daily life. Most credit took the form of unsecured small debts and consisted mostly of sales credit, wages, rent, taxes and other payments. Some of these transactions might have been recorded in an account book, a diary, or on a loose slip of paper, but most transactions were undoubtedly only agreed upon orally. Usually ordinary people had debts of less than £1. In other words, credit transactions were used frequently enough to render cash transactions rare. Indeed, in contrast with credit which depends on named relationship, coins were used for small transactions between strangers as well (Muldrew, 1998, p.101).

It cannot have been mere coincidence that most lawsuits were brought by people against members of their own community, in both urban and rural settings. When a villager made an agreement to sell his produce at a local marketplace, he tended to call upon some member of his village community to witness the agreement (Moore, 1981, p.288), a phenomenon that indicates the importance of the community in credit transactions.

The number of suits brought to local courts appears to have peaked in the latter half of the 17th century. In the town of Kings Lynn, each household filed suits nearly three times a year on average. However, it seems to have been the relation between credit and community, rather than a fear of punishment, that effectively led locals to honour their debts. A person had to avoid any conduct that might disconnect them from the community (Everitt, 1967, p.567).

We have no data on the proportion of credit to cash transactions among ordinary people, but anecdotal evidence gives the impression that the usage of currency was very rare. In this sense, the inheritance system of England, which required people to leave an inventory of their possessions, provides us with clear information about their assets. Notably, credit in various forms (such as bonds, bills obligatory and book credit) was predominant, and, in contrast, only modest amounts appear in inventories. According to Kerridge, who mainly studied inventories from Liverpool, 'in the period 1538–1660 the ratio of coins to debts by bond, bill of obligatory and book was on average 1 to 9' (Kerridge, 1988, p.98). A sample of inventories of London merchants and the trading elite shows that the ratio of trade credit, loans, and other investments to cash was 15 to 1 (Muldrew, 1998, p.100).

Of course, the ratio between credit and cash varied by class, occupation and geographical location. The cases mentioned above mainly reflect the patterns of urban merchants. In addition, forms of assets do not always correspond to forms of settlement. Nevertheless, it is safe to say that in early modern England transactions depended heavily on credit supported by communal trust. Named connections, instead of anonymous relationships, supported transactions in early modern England.

Early modern Japan was similar to England in several regards, including the disappearance of local markets; an increasing dependence on named credit (or independence from currency) in transactions and the accumulation of assets; and a general preference for repeating transactions with trusted customers as opposed to one-time transactions with strangers. These features stand in stark contrast to the situation in China (Kuroda, 2013).

6.5 Commercial oligarchies monopolising currencies

There are other ways to reduce the local circulation of currencies than making mutual credit. Cotton plantations in 19th-century Louisiana, USA, present a clear example. The shops in the cotton plantations, which were mostly run by plantation owners, bought raw cotton from share-croppers in exchange for necessities such as dry goods and clothes. Unlike share-cropping practices in the Netherlands, which allowed peasants to sell their products to other merchants, share-croppers in US plantations had no other choice but to make deals with the plantation shops. In order to reduce their debt to the plantation shops, share-croppers paid not only in cotton, but also in other products such as corn. The shop owners would often issue tokens but these could not be easily redeemed for cash. Some tokens could only be used for particular goods sold in the shops, such as bread, meat or flour (Lurvink, 2014). Though most transactions involved cash payments, there was almost none of the currency circulation that might have enabled share-croppers to have more options and choose more freely.

Plantation owners or merchants running the plantation shops, on the other hand, conducted their business via distant exchange through currencies that were available for settling long-distance trade. In the case of China outlined above, long-distance trade used silver, while local exchanges depended on native notes or copper coinages. With a fluctuating exchange ratio reflecting variations in supply and demand, inter-regional and local currencies functioned in a complementary relationship (Kuroda, 2008). In the case of the Louisiana plantations, there was no autonomous currency circulation within the district mentioned.

Agricultural labourers hired on a temporary basis by plantations seemed to be inclined to engage more deeply in monetary transactions than share-croppers, since the labourers were paid in cash monthly or annually, instead of being awarded in kind after the harvest, as was the case for share-croppers. However, the receipt of remuneration in the form of cash does not always mean that the labourer has significant spending possibilities. In the sugar plantations of the Island of Negro in the Philippines, sought after commodities such as liquor, clothes and tobacco were provided only by certain agents who were in close relationship with plantation owners. Labourers used to spend their wages soon after payday. In addition, gambling places owned by plantation owners often baited labourers to immediately spend their remaining salaries (Echaúz, 1978). Thus, under such an inside-market structure, agricultural labourers had little possibility to choose where to buy commodities. Money served as a unit of account, but no negotiation existed between sellers and buyers. The Island of Negro appeared to have no circulation of tokens like in Louisiana, but the structures of exchange in both regions do bear some resemblances.

6.6 Bond between money and society

It is easy for the issuer of currencies to widely distribute them, but difficult to assemble them on demand and subsequently unable to keep their issuances. That is why people often made currencies locally to meet demand adequately. However, making a local currency is not the only solution to chronic liquidity shortages. There are two other solutions: one is to defer payments on a basis of mutual trust among inhabitants, another is for oligarchies to monopolise local exchanges. These two patterns usually need no currency and money serves only as a unit of account.

Importantly, sharing a condition of no oligarchical dominance, the first two solutions—issuing currencies and making mutual credits—can replace each other (Kuroda, 2013). As commercial activities increase, a community has to choose whether to increase the issuance of currency or to strengthen mutual credit, which depends on cohesive relationships. The former device is tangible, while the latter is intangible. The tangible way enables locals to make anonymous transactions, while the intangible method hinges on limited access among well-acquainted or trusted customers. Currency-oriented trade can increase the degree of freedom in choosing who to enter into a relationship with in subsequent transactions but often suffers from currency stagnation. Credit-oriented trade can avoid difficulties caused by currency shortages, but often suffers from accumulating non-performance.

A subsequent story of local money movement in contemporary Buenos Aires interestingly showed that there was clearly a boundary between the stage of keeping records among a small number of the well-acquainted and another stage of issuing tangible devices for circulation among a large number of participants (Gomez, 2009).

A preference for one-time transactions (currency transaction) or for subsequent transactions (credit transaction) indicates whether people emphasise freedom or certainty. However, in both cases of local currency and mutual credit there is no oligarchy monopolising local exchanges like we saw in the previous section. In this sense, the development of exchanges among proximate inhabitants depended on the degree of freedom of those carrying out transactions. Wherever oligarchies dominate transactions there is little space for people to create a currency or a mutual credit system. Thus, two institutional variables determine what kind of monetary system a society forms, and these respond to what extent people can independently exchange and to what extent people prefer freedom over certainty,

It is crucial to note that transaction methods depend on social relationships. We should avoid being trapped in a dichotomy between money and society, a mistake made by a number of egalitarian movements in history.

References

Chen, M. n.d. 'Quannan Zazhi', in *Siku quanshu cunmu congshu, shi*, vol. 247, Jinan, China: Jilushushe, p.859.

Chen, T. 1936. 'Xiangjuriji (Diary during Rural Stay)', in *Zhongguo nongcun miaoxie* (Descriptions of Chinese Villages).

Chen, T. 1937. 'Shixingfabihou de Julunongcun (Julu Villages after the Monetary Reform)', *Dongfang Zazhi* (Eastern Magazine), pp.33–36.

Chen, X. 2012. *Minguo xiaoqu liutong huobi yanjiu* (Study of small regional currencies in the Republican China), Beijing: Zhongguo shehui kexue chubanshe.

Dai, J. and Chen, X. 2011. '20 shiji 20, 30 niandai beifang nongcun qianpiao fanlan de kaocha (Study of excessive circulation of native notes in the 1920–30s northern villages)', *Zhonguo Jingjishi Lundan* (China's Economic History Forum).

De Glanville, R. G. 1970. 'The numbers of coins in circulation in the United Kingdom', *Studies in Official Statistics*, Research Series 2.

Echaúz, R. 1978. *Sketches of the island of Negros, translated and annotated by Donn V. Hart; with an historical introduction by John A. Larkin*, Athens, OH: Ohio University Center for International Studies.

Everitt, 1967. 'The marketing of agricultural produce' in Thirsk, J. (ed.) *The Agrarian History of England and Wales*, vol. 4, Cambridge, UK: Cambridge University Press, pp.466–592.

Gomez, G. M. 2009. *Argentina's Parallel Currency: The Economy of the Poor*, London: Pickering & Chatto.

Hicks, J. R. 1935. 'A suggestion for simplifying the theory of money', *Economica New Series*, 5.

Kerridge, E. 1988. *Trade and Banking in Early Modern England*, Manchester, UK: Manchester University Press.

Kuroda, A. 2007. 'The Maria Theresa Dollar in the early twentieth-century Red Sea region: a complementary interface between multiple markets', *Financial History Review* 14(1), 89–110.

Kuroda, A. 2008. 'What is the complementarity among monies? An introductory note', *Financial History Review* 15(1), 7–15.

Kuroda, A. 2013. 'Anonymous currencies or named debts? Comparison of currencies, local credits and units of account between China, Japan and England in the pre-industrial era', *Socio Economic Review* 11(1), 57–80.

Lurvink, K. 2014. 'Strapped for cash: non-cash payments on Louisiana cotton plantations, 1865–1908', *Tijdschriftvoor Sociale en Economische Geschiedenis* 11(4), 123–152.

Miyake, T. 2005. *Chugoku no umerareta senka* (Chinese copper cashes earthed), Tokyo: Doseisha.

Moore. 1981.'Medieval English fairs: evidence from Winchester and St. Ives', in Raftis, J. A. (ed.) *Pathways to Medieval Peasants*, Toronto, ON: Pontifical Institute of Medieval Studies, pp.283–299.

Muldrew, C. 1998. *The Economy of Obligation*, London: Macmillan.

Patterson, C. C. 1972. 'Silver stocks and losses in ancient and medieval times', *Economic History Review* 2, 25–2.

Preston, H. H. 1933. 'The wooden money of Tenino', *Quarterly Journal of Economics*, 47(2), 343–348.

Shi, C. 2002. *Mingguo difang qianpiao tulu* (catalogue of local copper coin notes in Republican China), Beijing: Zhonghua shuju.

Spufford, P. 1999. 'Local coins, foreign coins in late medieval europe: summing up', in Travaini, L. ed. *Local Coins, Foreign Coins: Italy and Europe 11th-15th Centuries*, Milan, Italy: Estratto.

Wang, D. 1937. 'Hengshanxian Shiguxiang shehui gaikuang diaocha (entire survey of the Shiguxiang village, Hengshan county)' in Li Wenhai ed. *Minguo shiqi shehui diao-cha congbian 2bian xiangcun shehui quan* (Collection of social investigation in the Republican China, second series, volume for rural society), Fuzhou, China: Fujian jiaoyu chubanshe, 2009.

Wu, S. 1935. 'Taiguxian Guanjiabaocun diaocha baogao (Report of the investigation of the Guanjiabao village, Taigu county)' in Li Wenhai ed. *Minguo shiqi shehui diao-cha congbian 2bian xiangcun shehui quan* (Collection of social investigation in the Republican China, second series, volume for rural society), Fuzhou, China: Fujian jiaoyu chubanshe, 2009.

7 The pervasiveness of monetary plurality in economic crisis and wars

Georgina M. Gómez and Wilko von Prittwitz und Gaffron

7.1 Currencies found and currencies made?

During periods of economic, social and political demise, history shows a recurrent pattern of monetary plurality. Of course, not every crisis in the history of human kind has triggered the diversification of means of payment, but the link between chaotic socio-economic contexts and monetary plurality needs further scrutiny around the question of who creates means of payment and how a particular thing becomes acceptable as money. What is the relationship between money and crisis? To what extent is this connection indissoluble?

This chapter explores the relationship between contexts of socio-economic demise and the experimentation with monetary plurality. Our motivation behind these questions relates to the incredible diversity of means of payment, the actors that launch them, and the ways in which they started and ended. The currencies are probably as varied as the crisis that embedded these episodes of monetary plurality. We propose that the emergence of means of payment during episodes of severe crisis cannot be understood only as devices to solve temporary emergencies. Instead, we contend that they sometimes represent attempts to re-build the world and introduce changes that could live beyond the crisis, in line with the aspirations and ideals for a different future. While the emergence of means of payment, most of the time at the local level, tends to be the consequence of severe distress, on some occasions they have also represented attempts to re-organise political, social and economic life in a different direction (Cohen, 1999; Gilbert and Helleiner, 1999). The chaotic socio-economic backgrounds hence provide a 'window of opportunity' in a political sense (Kingdon, 2003) for experiments that propose longer time-horizons.

We review a handful of cases in which the proliferation of complementary currencies emerged bottom upwards in contexts of severe distress. This chapter results from the collaboration with a numismatic amateur that spent hundreds of hours doing archival work and analysing the artistic and symbolical features of currency. Moreover, it represents an effort to approach money from the material reality of currencies, as objects that structured the interactions of humans in chaotic periods even when their entire worlds seemed unstructured. We seek to connect the physical objects, namely local notes and means of payment, with the contexts in which they were issued and the agents that may have used them.

We present monetary plurality as a temporary but ubiquitous solution in the context of war, hyperinflation and depression. In other cases, however, the context supported the experimentation with alternative monetary conceptions and had longer time-horizons. We depart from the basic principle that unknown money was better than no money at all, which meant that socio-economic demise supported the exceptional dissemination of monetary innovations that in normal circumstances would attract just a faithful few. The need for means of payment triggered social experimentation with currencies at the local level and, most importantly, expanded their public acceptance and circulation. Some historical currency circuits reviewed in this chapter were extremely vulnerable in terms of their legality and acceptability, while others evolved within institutional sophistication and lasted in time.

7.2 Historical emergencies and money

The historical experience of the last century offers a broad variety of periods in which local or complementary currencies were used, normally in situations of economic collapse or financial scarcity (Schuldt, 1997; Greco, 2001; Kuroda, 2007). Complementary currencies are created contingently by communities in an effort to facilitate exchange and income generation based on local identity. Their purpose is normally not to disconnect from the national monetary system, but to complement it, adjust it or adapt it (Boyer-Xambeu et al., 1994; Leyshon and Thrift, 1996; Ingham, 2002, 2004). A severe disruption of the national monetary system, however, disputes the notions of mere adaptation and complementation because in such cases actors may become bolder and dare into deep re-invention of money to re-establish a chain of payments or to protect local identity, or a combination of both.

Across history, we find a myriad of episodes in which emergency situations have created windows of opportunity to pursue adaptation and invention at the same time. Critical contexts seem to have weakened the limits between what was strictly allowed or tolerated by nation states and their sovereign monetary systems, which have sometimes allowed complementary currencies to emerge (Greco, 2001; Blanc, 2012). Economic agents turned to more reliable, more accessible or more abundant monies, whether foreign, privately issued or local.

The tradition of monetary plurality has a long history, as evidenced by plenty of examples in which monetary plurality raised or resurged in episodes of severe crisis that provided these windows of opportunities. In Medieval Europe, 'siege certificates' (Pick, 1978: 41) are one of the oldest surviving samples of 'emergency money' in modern Europe and were issued by town hall councils in Europe as needed (for example, Figures 7.1 and 7.2). During the siege of cities, metallic money supply was often impossible to sustain, so the local authorities along with municipal authorities of the city administration and, more frequently, the respective military commanders would issue siege certificates. Spanish siege certificates circulated as currency during the siege of the Spanish fortress of Granada's Alhambra by the Moors in 1483, for example. In 1574, Leyden (currently Leiden, the Netherlands) was besieged by the Spaniards, and coins were stamped on cardboard (the covers of Catholic Church books) instead of precious metal, which was unavailable, and thereby creating 'siege money' embedded in the political sentiment of the event.

Figure 7.1 Note of the siege of Lyon, France (16th century)

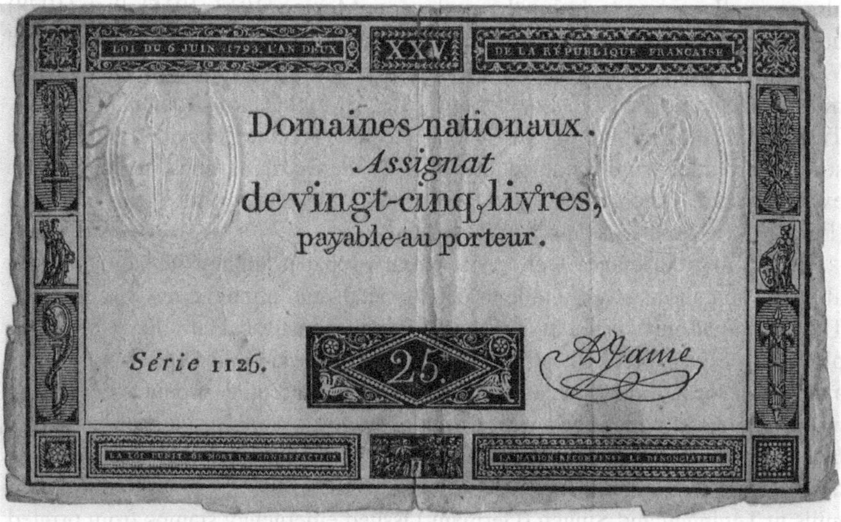

Figure 7.2 Note of the siege of Breda, the Netherlands (16th century)

Other examples of complementary currencies issued during conflicts other than sieges were in Spain by the Catalan villains during the war of the reapers (1640–1652), or the 'Billets de confiance' issued in France (1791–1793) during the French Revolution. There are also some surviving examples of notes issued during the French–German War of 1879–1871, Russian pieces printed on leather in Dorpat (1814, 1818 and 1831) and emergency money (Notgeld) issued in Austria (1848–49 and 1859 to 1869), Poland (1848–49 and 1860–1865), and Germany (for instance, in Kaiserslauten in 1870–71). Italy (1866–1875) had such large amounts of emergency currencies that, according to Pick (1978), 'they are not completely catalogued'. They also existed in the Americas, for example in Brazil (1895–1896), where the communal and private emergency issues were meant to alleviate the shortage of small change. Pick (1978) maintains that there were up to 500 different Brazilian types of emergency currencies, some with positive interest rates. During the civil war in the United States, the Southern States issued the so-called 'Broken Bank Bills' (1861–1865). The issuance of complementary currencies in emergency situations was quite common and Pick's work (1978) shows us a myriad of similar examples of currencies during wars and other catastrophes.

With the development of the capitalist system, monetary transactions became more widespread and paper money became more important, so gradually more central banks were set up around the world. Central banks were one of the strongest institutions to pursue the unification of currencies per country in the 20th century. However, monetary plurality did not end with the dissemination of central banks. In times of economic demise, cash often became scarce and the amounts and varieties of emergency currencies continued to grow, as evidenced by the First and the Second World Wars. In the First one, we can not only find large amounts of emergency currencies in Germany (1914–1923), Austria (1914–1921), but also in smaller amounts during the civil war in Mexico (1913–1915). Pick (1978) has documented approximately 120 Dutch emergency notes from the First World War that may have inspired other countries to issue small amounts of emergency money, including Finland, Luxembourg, Italy, Montenegro, Rumania, Sweden, Turkey and Hungary. During the Second World War, emergency currencies were strictly forbidden in all occupied territories by the German troops, and only some extremely rare Dutch, Norwegian, Polish and Yugoslavian notes can be found (Pick, 1978). We discuss more of these below.

Emergency currencies were mostly fiat or paper money with no backup, although some issuers were able to obtain metals and minted coins as collateral. They were not only issued in domestic, foreign or historical currency (for example Peseta Silver Certificates (Figure 7.3), Gold Mark, Gold Dollar) but also as a claim for local goods such as grain, sugar, wood and other products depending on the region in which they were issued. In addition, materials such as porcelain, cardboard, leather, pressed carbon, wood, velvet or linen were used as more durable substitutes than paper. In 1923, for example, the newly built aluminium mills in Teningen and Singen (Germany) issued emergency stamps from printed aluminium foil (Pick, 1978). It would be too long to detail all complementary currencies that circulated during emergencies and research on many of these experiences is still pending. The examples given so far suffice to substantiate that when societies face crisis and war, emergency currencies have been ubiquitous and often more trusted than official money managed elsewhere by authorities that appeared too remote and aloof from the alarming daily realities on the ground.

Historical complementary currencies were used in extreme emergency situations as means of payment and mediums of exchange, and sometimes as units of account. Other materials were used as reserve of value because metals and other reliable currencies were kept for hoarding and, hence, disappeared from the system. In all the cases of social and economic emergencies described in this chapter, the

Figure 7.3a and 7.3b (continued)

(continued)

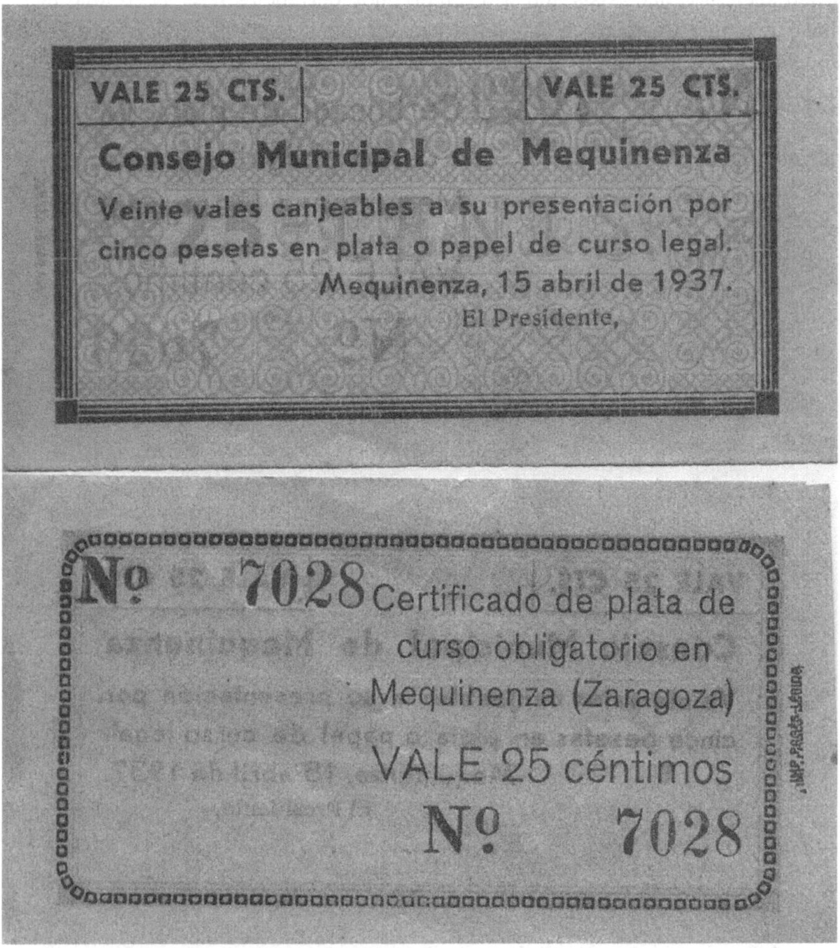

Figure 7.3a and 7.3b Peseta silver certificate

mechanism of allocating the different functions of money to different currencies is recurrent, and confirms that the four inseparable functions that define money, at least in theory, have been repeatedly separated in practice.

7.3 Emergency currencies and the World Wars

The two World Wars in the 20th century provided the crisis context for emergency monetary plurality. The terms emergency currencies, emergency script, crisis money, Notgeld (currency of need in German), municipal notes, emergency script, military and obsidional coins and paper money in besieged locations denote that these are temporary currencies that circulate during a social, political and economic demise. In general, emergency currencies take the functions of national currencies temporarily.

After the First World War, several localities and private issuers in Germany, Switzerland and Austria coined emergency currencies to ameliorate the effects of the economic crisis caused by the conflict and hyperinflation, although they were never formally authorised by the government or the national banks. During the conflict, the central empires had issued great amounts of paper money without collateral in bullion to cover the costs of the war, which was a cause of the hyperinflation. Municipal authorities decided to promote bartering in small localities to facilitate trade, and some gradually issued vouchers that could be used as means of payment. They had a fixed face value in regular money and they were meant to replace within their localities the hyperinflationary national notes that were not performing the function as means of payment. The local alternative notes became known as Notgeld and circulated in low amounts within restricted geographical areas. Most of the metals normally used for minting, such as silver, bronze and copper, were required in the war effort, so coins were missing. Moreover, people kept these metals as reserve of value, which aggravated their scarcity for currency.

While some emergency currencies were simple papers that circulated as small means of payment, other notes had colourful and elaborate designs in an effort to increase the appeal and acceptability of these currencies. Some included expiry dates, details of the territory in which they were valid or the types of payments for which they were acceptable, such as public utilities. The emergency currencies were guaranteed by the local governments or the local savings banks, so their circulation was restricted to the city where they were issued. Many of these notes, in fact, bear the warning that they are only valid within the limits of the district and for transactions with the local government.

The first post-war economic demise severely affected businesses. Several retailers and industries also issued their own emergency currencies that circulated as internal means of payment within a particular sector or client network. The notes were guaranteed by their own capital funds, in a context in which regular money was scarce and lost value rapidly due to hyperinflation (Diessner, 2012). Commercial banks issued low denomination notes, too.

As hyperinflation in Germany worsened, an unthinkable proliferation of complementary currencies followed. Although such currencies were tolerated, they were not formally authorised by the central banks. They circulated because the public accepted them in practice despite their lack of formal legality (for example, Figure 7.4). These papers multiplied not only in number but in purpose and coverage as well. The denominations of the emergency currency notes increased and passed the hundred, thousand, million and eventually billion marks. At the same time, the quality of the scrip paper decreased in order to save on its production costs. In the beginning of 1923, hyperinflation in Germany was out of control and some emergency notes abandoned the mark as unit of account. They were denominated instead in specific goods such as a certain amount of wheat, barley, wood, sugar, or coal; these were called Wertbeständige in German, which translates as ‘fix value notes’.

The emergency currencies were generally conceived as surrogates for the regular money for a temporary period. Towards the end of 1923, inflation was curbed and a new national currency was introduced, so the usage of emergency

Figure 7.4a and 7.4b Goldmark Freistaat Preussen 1.05 = 1/dollar USA

currencies was gradually abandoned or the public stopped accepting them. Diessner (2012) estimated that emergency currencies were definitely withdrawn by 1924. Notgeld was associated with hunger and calamity, so these notes were not popular among the general public. Eventually they were left as toys for children to play with because they had no real value. Others were burnt by the thousands, as colourful but worthless paper. Notgeld was precisely what its literal translation indicates: the money of an emergency situation. It appeared in a vacuum of monetary regulation in which local agents resorted to extraordinary measures to support their daily livelihoods and the local economy, until the economic and social system could recover. Today, however, Notgeld has gained both commercial and academic interest, since the demand for local paper money has increased enormously not only by collectors and for academic research, but also by curators who purchase them for museums worldwide.

Notgeld could, of course, also be military money, for example, the sadly famous Concentration Camp Notes (Lagergeld), and the military banknotes. Pick (1978) mentions issues in Germany, France, Japan and Austria, for example, those of the Allied forces in Germany (Aliierte Militärbehörde 1945–1948), which were put into circulation by the allied military authorities of the occupied territories for the civil populations (Figure 7.5). They were made by the USA in collaboration with private printing houses like Forbes Boston and the Bureau of Engraving and Printing.

The 20th century offers an enormous amount of complementary emergency currencies and other forms of money such as International Military Payment Certificates, Obsidional and Military Banknotes, Banker´s Drafts, Liberty Bonds, Exchequers in the UK or US Treasury Bonds, and the Schatzanweisungen (in German), known also as War Bonds (Kriegsanleihen), which still have to be classified. As in Germany, emergency currencies were prohibited in countries like Holland by the occupying troops but Pick (1978) mentions around 500 different Dutch currencies, which 'were withdrawn and are extremely rare today'. We can find similar amounts of emergency currencies in Norway issued from April to October 1940, as well as in Poland and Yugoslavia. The merchants in Denmark avoided the prohibition issuing notes called 'Frimaerkepenge which were small printed cartons', according to Pick (ibid.).

Apart from these emergency currencies, there were other international paper monies issued and it may be difficult to clearly determine which of these could be considered emergency currencies. Pick (1978) also notes that after 1911 a vast amount of banknotes of communal and military origin circulated in China. Decades later, when Japan declared war in the Pacific, Americans were forced to leave the Philippines and took with them large amounts of cash, so the population was forced to issue emergency currencies to maintain all payment transactions (Figure 7.6). Following a quote by Pick (1978), we have found a rare catalogue by Neil Shafer (1974), 'Philippine emergency and guerrilla currency of World War II', in which Shafer stated that,

Figure 7.5 Allied military bond

> [a]s a result of the war, in 1941 currency from the United States for the Philippines has basically disappeared. The Philippines was a U.S. territorial possession. In dire need for a circulating currency, Philippines President Quezon decided the establishment of emergency currency boards in the provinces to print notes, with most of the currency being produced while the Philippines was under Japanese occupation. These notes served as tangible symbols of resistance and eventual victory. They were really necessary as a currency and most were legally issued by the currency boards. Yet, there were perils in circulating the notes, as the Japanese sometimes tortured and killed those caught with such notes in their possession.

After the Second World War from 1945–1955, and as a consequence of political as well as economic developments, many more countries issued emergency currencies. Pick (1978) mentions Indonesia, Israel, Italy and Hungary. The banknotes of Italian Banks from 1975–1976 (Assegni Circolari and Assegni Bancarie) still circulate today and show that even in more recent times emergency currencies circulate.

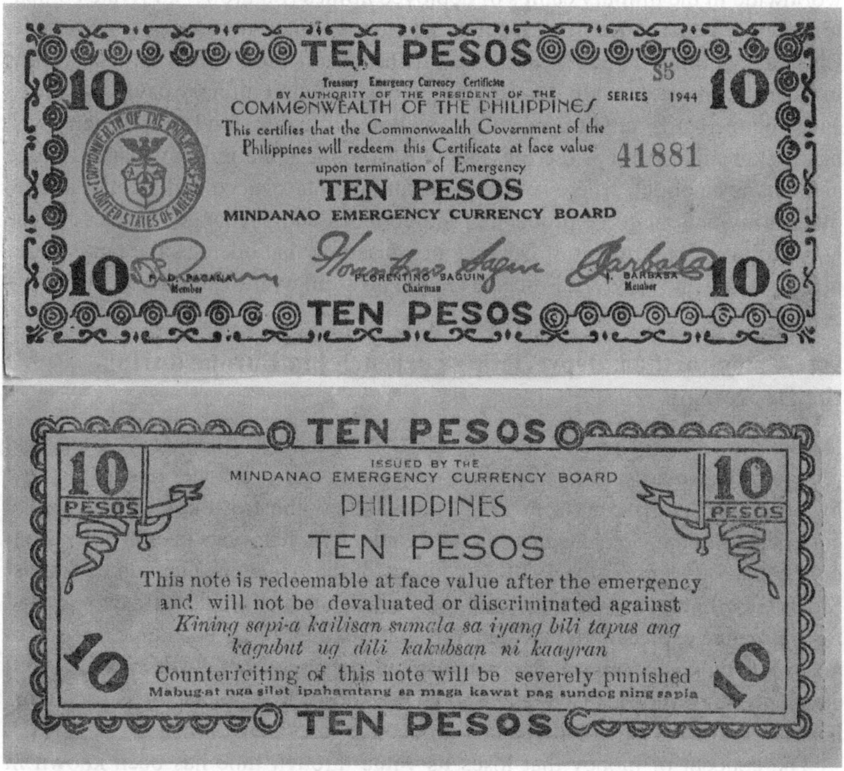

Figure 7.6 Mindanao Emergency Currency Board (USA)

Figure 7.7 Military payment certificate

Other forms of military and emergency currencies and coupons are still used worldwide in the military camps of deployed armies (Figure 7.7). Private companies supply paper money and local people are recruited for labour, for example, Bosnians working in the PX in EUFOR (European Union Force) military camps in Bosnia-Herzegovina. In our research, we have found military payment certificates, phone cards, credit products, as well as gift cards, food coupons and web based exchange. Perhaps the most famous of them is the military star exchange and clearance outlet, where we can also find petrol, tobacco and alcohol among other army and air force products, food coupons and exchange services for the United States Department of Defence organisation, that operates the retail stores at U.S. Army and U.S. Air Force bases and posts all over the world.

7.4 A step further: depreciating currencies in Europe during the Depression

During the inter-war period, the emergency situation lasted longer than the term 'emergency' would suggest. The German government eventually managed to get hyperinflation under control in 1923 and withdrew most of the local emergency currencies, but the Great Depression hit the country a few years later and the economy collapsed again in the 1930s. The ideas of the Argentine-German economist Silvio Gesell attracted the attention of a number of intellectuals as they searched for alternative explanations and solutions to the extraordinary economic demise. In relation to monetary innovation, in a posthumously published book, Gesell (1958) developed the principle that money should be exposed to depreciation to discourage hoarding and what he considered non-productive generation of income.

The concept of money that loses its value through time has been known in French as demurrage, in German as Schwund- or Schrumpfgeld and in English as shrinking or depreciating money. The application of a negative interest rate, as Keynes (1976 [1930]) called it, represented a penalty on its hoarding. In other words, if people decided to retain the currency instead of using it for subsequent payments, they would suffer a loss of value equal to a negative interest rate and eventually the complete loss of its value on the date announced on the scrip itself. The intention behind the principle of shrinking money is to increase its circulation velocity to feed the chain of payments of goods and services, in order to stimulate production and exchange in the local economy. The idea of depreciating money was that the currency runs to the next transaction. This type of money is at odds with saving but during the Depression the priority of economic agents was to enable consumption and, as a result, production and employment. Gesell conceived depreciation of money as a means to discourage its hoarding outside the circular flow of goods and services. He was convinced that one of the main causes of economic crises was the withdrawal of money from the economic circuit due to speculation or what John Maynard Keynes would later refer to the problem of 'liquidity preference'. Gesell believed that people would be pressed to spend shrinking money as means of payment because if they hoarded it, they would have to pay for its depreciation.

The French economist Pierre-Joseph Proudhon (1840) made a somewhat different argument a few decades earlier. Proudhon objected that products like meat, fish or fruit perish in time, while currency does not. The difference in perishability between food and money, Proudhon argued, gave money holders an 'unfair' advantage over producers of food, and this difference led to exploitation because producers may have been obliged to reduce the prices of their perishable goods in order to obtain money that maintained its value through time.

Fisher (1934) attributed the concept of shrinking money to Gesell and investigated its early experimentation around the time Gesell died in 1936. Two friends of his, Hans Timm and Helmut Rödiger, decided to implement the system in Erfurt, Germany, in October 1929 and launched the Wära Exchange Society, a name that combines the German word for 'commodity' (ware) and 'durable' or 'resistant', also used as 'unit of value' (Währung). The Wära Exchange Society expanded across the country and after a while it had offices in all the main cities including Berlin, Bonn, Hamburg, and Cologne. The society issued vouchers to be used as means of payment among the members of the exchange group (Tauschgesellschaft) and the currency included the names of its directors, Timm and Rödiger, as responsible signatories of the notes (Lindman, 2011). At the back, the vouchers had a table with 24 spaces where users were required to stick a stamp at the beginning of each fortnight. Keeping the scrip at the end of the fortnight meant having to add a stamp, so hoarding it worked as a penalty on the person that prevented the voucher from 'running to the next transaction', and at the same time it worked as an incentive to keep money demand at the minimum. Stamps costed 0.5 percent of the value of the voucher, so the notes would depreciate at a rate of 12 percent a year. If members failed to pay the stamp, the vouchers were simply not accepted in exchange for goods and services. The Wära vouchers were redeemable for Reichsmarks at any time, but with a charge of 2 percent of the value. This implied that the group had to keep a permanent reserve fund of Reichsmarks to face claims, but it increased the stability of the vouchers.

By 1931 the Wära vouchers were accepted in about a thousand shops and small businesses across the country. Members included, for example, dairy producers, bakeries, print shops, barbers, small restaurants, and shops selling furniture, flowers, books and bikes. Joining the society may not have been their first choice, but they were persuaded by the scarcity of the national money. They gradually formed an economic circuit in which money would flow along the circuit rapidly, including workers that received the vouchers as partial payment for their work. While the notes served the purpose of facilitating local production and trade, the Wära notes were never endorsed by the Central Bank of Germany, like it had happened before with the first post-war local emergency currencies.

The experiment with the Wära got significant public attention, later enhanced by the economic recovery of Schwanenkirchen, a small town in Bayern (Schuldt, 1997). A mining engineer bought the local bankrupt coal mine in an auction and found it impossible to raise the working capital to set it to work again. He then contacted the Wära Society which lent him 50,000 units of complementary currency. The engineer hired 60 workers willing to accept the complementary currency for up to 90 percent of their wages. Local shops were reluctant at first to accept the rather unknown currency but eventually they consented because they were severely affected by the recession at the time – local money was better than no money at all, they reasoned. Their suppliers and producers accepted them too, and eventually the vouchers circulated back to the engineer and coal mine owner in exchange for coal. The circuit was hence completed. All members tried to buy goods with the Wära as quickly as possible in order to avoid paying the stamp for the scrip.

Werner Onken (1983: 68, quoted in Schuldt, 1997: 36) described Schwanenkirchen as an 'island of prosperity in the Bavarian woods'. The monetary innovation and a full account of the Wära appeared in several national newspapers. The idea of shrinking money was not well known at that time and few people actually understood it. It ran contrary to the deflationary policies that the government implemented to curb hyperinflation (Cohrssen, 1932). Irving Fisher claimed that 20,000 Wära circulated in Germany between 1930 and 1931 and 2.5 million members used them, an estimation that the author considered rather exaggerated (Fisher, 1934: 22). However, not everyone was so positive about the Wära and in October 1931, the Central Bank prohibited the issuance and circulation of any means of payment that were not official, on the argument that these complementary currencies would cause inflation. In accordance with the new regulation, the Wära scrip stopped circulating immediately, the coal mine closed and Schwanenkirchen fell back into recession.

Experimentation with money, however, did not end with the prohibition of the German Central Bank. The Depression was not finished and other villages were ready to design similar bottom-up monetary institutions in an attempt to recover their local economies. The owner of the coal mine in Schwanenkirchen had a fluent correspondence with a friend in Austria, who became the major of the village of Wörgl, Austria, and started another experiment with a complementary currency. In 1932, the mayor of the Austrian town of Wörgl, Michael Unterguggenberger, was inspired by the Wära and decided to use it in a modified way: a public works programme funded by complementary currency. Unterguggenberger observed that with the Depression, local unemployment was soaring and the municipality was almost bankrupt and heavily indebted to a bank in Innsbruck. With the support of the constituency and the local council, the major of Wörgl launched a plan of public works that was financed with the complementary currency issued by the local government.

The currency circulated as scrip and had a stamp of 1 percent of the value of the voucher that had to be paid at the beginning of each month (Figure 7.8). The aim of the stamp was to encourage users to spend the notes rapidly instead of storing them, following the idea of the circular flow. The Wörgl money was also redeemable for the official schillings at a discount of 2 percent. Public servants received half of their wages in complementary currency which was later increased to 75 percent. Shops and local firms accepted it because they believed it increased their turnover (von Muralt, 1934) and the city government also received them as payment for local taxes. Businesses were naturally not thrilled at the prospect of losing 1 percent of their income at the end of the month or 2 percent if they wanted to redeem it for official money, but the emergency money was better than facing the Depression. Von Muralt (1934: 51) reports that businesses were appreciative of the scheme in the context they were facing in 1932.

With the plan, the financial situation of the local government in Wörgl recovered significantly as income generation through taxation increased with the depreciation of the currency, and the payment of arrears was allowed with the complementary currency because the inhabitants became eager to get rid of it by paying taxes. Unemployment fell at the same time as it was increasing in the rest of Austria; more inhabitants accepted getting part of their wages in complementary currency. Their labour was used to improve local infrastructure, such as the sewage system.

The notes carried a 1932 Wörgl 'manifesto' written on the back, significantly titled 'An Alle' (to all, in German). The translation of the text in the notes reads as follows,

> Slowly circulating money has caused unprecedented needs among millions of workers around the world. The end of the economy has begun. It is time to act with determination and prevent wreckage, so the economy can be saved and humanity can avoid brutal conflicts and wars. Humanity lives on the exchange of goods and services. Sluggishness in the circulation of money hinders such trade, causing millions of persons of working age to lose their jobs and their livelihoods. Circulation must be re-established to safeguard the livelihood of humanity. That is the aim of the currency of the market town of Wörgl. It reduces need, supports work and gives bread!'
>
> (Punctuation marks in original; translation by the authors.)

Several towns in the region around Wörgl, such as Kirchbichel, imitated the experiment or expressed their intentions to follow (Figure 7.9; Schwarz, 2006). The complementary currencies of Wörgl and Kirchbichel were accepted on equal

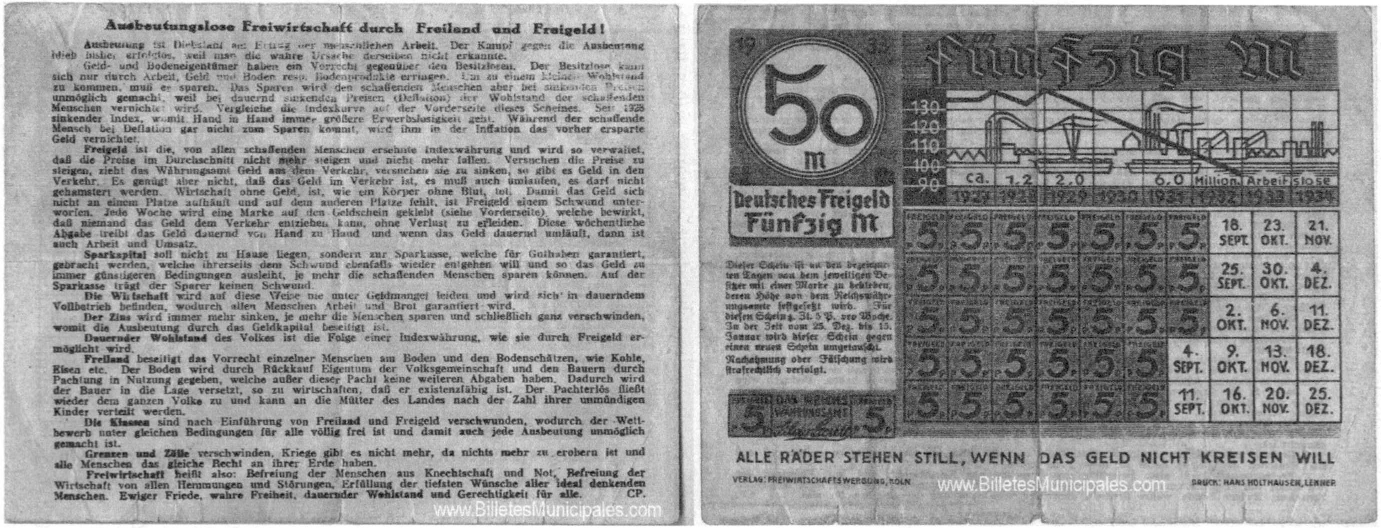

Figure 7.8 ‘Free money’ note with stamps

terms in both towns, with the aim of increasing the economic impact. The schemes attracted considerable international interest, including that from Irving Fisher, as will be explained in the next section. There were many objections to the replication of the scheme across Tirol and a number of issues to reflect on, such as the increase in risk for retailers accepting the stamp scrip for their sales while having to pay for supplies in regular currency. The scheme also met strong opposition from the Central Bank of Austria, which feared that it would lose control over the national monetary system if complementary currencies grew. The bank subsequently prohibited the issuance and circulation of any currency in Austria, other than its own.

The kind of monetary innovation of the Wära Society across Germany and the Wörgl in Austria speaks of different intentions and aspirations to those that sustained the Notgeld or emergency money after the post First World War period. While the Notgeld appeared as an extraordinary and temporary measure in the context of demise of the socio-economic system after a major war, the experiments with shrinking money stem from a desire to implement and further develop the theoretical elaborations of Gesell among a number of idealists that believed in reforming the monetary and economic system. In these last cases, the social actors implemented a scheme at the collective local level that entailed a process of joint reflection and setting of rules within their networks or localities (Offe and Heinze, 1992). Examples of these include the decisions on the amount of interest towards depreciation, the ways to communicate them to outsiders, the agreements on the percentages of the wages that would be accepted, and so on. In that sense, the shrinking money experiments are expressions of efforts to institutionalise solutions at the local level that involve a large number of

Figure 7.9 Free money in 1933

agreements, negotiations, rules and mechanisms to enforce them. It seems the aim was to reform the monetary system beyond the duration of the crisis, although that context was used as a window of political opportunity (Tarrow, 1998; Kingdon, 2003) to test these alternative currencies.

7.5 Stamp scrip in the USA during the Depression

The American economist, Irving Fisher, knew of the experiment in Wörgl and actually asked one of his collaborators in Geneva to visit the town and gather information on the scheme at the site (von Muralt, 1934). Irving Fisher referred to those first experiences as 'stamp scrip' because currency notes were stamped and each stamp reduced its value as time went by (Fisher, 1933; Fisher, 1934). Gatch (2009) claims that the use of stamping for savings was relatively familiar to Americans and offers the examples of the Liberty Bond subscriptions in the First World War and savings cards.

Stamp scrip was first introduced in the USA by a Dutch follower of Gesell, Charles Zylstra, in the small town of Hawarden, Iowa. Due to the Depression and the decrease of means of payment, the general public preferred to keep the currency they could access as reserve of value. The result was the scarcity of means of payment to support the exchange of daily necessities. With the support of the local chamber of commerce, Zylstra convinced the city council of Hawarden to issue complementary currency to finance public works in October of 1932. The model of complementary currency chosen was that of stamp scrip with depreciation, applied through a stamp per transaction. Each time a one-dollar-voucher was used, the buyer had to stick a stamp of three cents as a kind of 'sales tax'. The stamps were on sale in the city hall and the revenues of their sale constituted a reserve fund in dollars with which the issuers guaranteed the convertibility of the local currency into the official national dollars. Each voucher could be used up to 36 times after which the last user could claim one dollar in official money. The remaining eight cents financed the administrative costs of the scheme.

The experience in Hawarden was described in an article in the New York Herald Tribune titled, 'Stamped Money called success in Iowa Town', published on 15 January, 1933 (cited in Schuldt, 1997: 46). According to that source, businesses saw an increase of 50 percent in their revenues, which was partly explained by the fact that the smallest note was of one dollar, so clients could not buy anything of a lower value and preferred to increase their consumption instead of keeping the currency. The currency was used to partially cover the labour to build a local road.

At that time, Fisher had a young German assistant, Hans Cohrssen, who had written about the Wära, and together they worked on the implementation and dissemination of the stamp scrip (Fisher, 1933). Fisher visited Hawarden shortly after the experiment began and his endorsement attracted the attention of other cities across the country (Gatch, 2009: 129). The Hawarden experiment was later imitated by other cities across several states. The maximum amount of exchanges and the value of the stamps varied, as did their taxation. The issuers were not always the local governments but also local chambers of commerce (as in Evanston, Illinois) and churches (as in Sioux City). A renowned case was the Larkin & Co. in Buffalo, New York, a retail store chain that issued 36,000 dollars of Larkin Merchandise bonds. It used the vouchers to partially pay the wages to its employees and accepted them in any of its stores. Other businesses and clients gradually started to accept them too. When the shortage of regular dollars eased, Larkin slowly withdrew the scrip from circulation. The original 36,000 dollars circulated back as payments worth 250,000 dollars of extra sales.

Fisher criticised the Hawarden depreciation mechanism based on transactions instead of one based on the course of time on the grounds that it missed the goal of discouraging the storage of money: 'It costs three cents to transfer the scrip instead of costing three cents not to transfer it' (Fisher, 1934: 31). He also warned that using a stamp each time the note changed hands invited opportunistic behaviour because there was no way to check that the stamp was either bought or stuck as required. Fisher hence advised against the stamp mechanisms of depreciating the currency per transaction and favoured the dated system. He concluded that, 'from a correspondence with four or five hundred communities in every state of the Union, and from other sources of information, I gather that there is now a definite turn toward the Wörgl or dated type of Stamp Scrimp' (1934: 41).

Whether these critiques proved problematic in practice or were Fisher's own elaboration is unknown. Still, stamp scrip became widespread across the country, as Fisher's correspondence seemed to suggest (for example, Figure 7.10). Other sources estimated that one million people, almost 1 percent of the U.S. population at that time, depended on the 200 to 400 self-help and barter groups that existed in the United States from 1930–1936. Eventually, Fisher (1934: 163) proposed, in reference to regular money, a

> [n]ation-wide application of Stamp Scrip – still in quantities as small, proportionately to the size of the nation, as it is in the localities now using it; and still to function only as an emergency supply – substituting for other circulation which has deserted – withdrawing when the deserter returns to service.

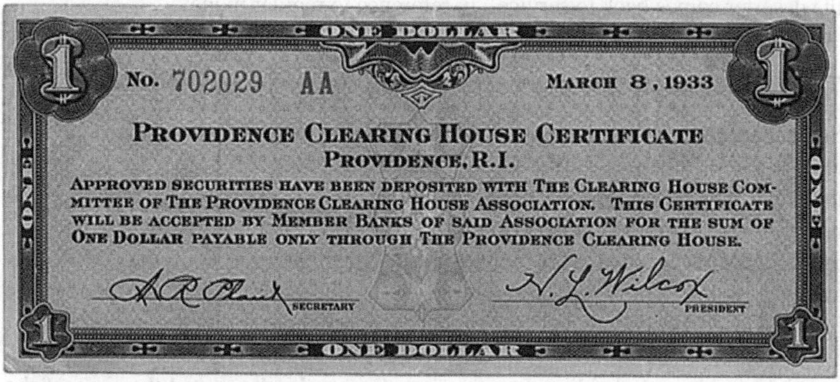

Figure 7.10 Providence stamp scrip

As in post-war and hyperinflationary Germany, the United States also witnessed an unthinkable proliferation of complementary currencies during the Great Depression.

Initially, the U.S. government did not take measures for or against stamp scrip, probably believing that stamp scrip was a creature of the crisis that would fade as employment recovered. Gatch (2009) further reports a wide number of practical problems that undermined the reality in which stamp scrip was supposed to work, such as shirking in the use of stamps, slow circulation, and refusals to accept the currency. The author reports that no fewer than half a million families were active in 600 organisations by the end of 1938, but were replaced as co-operatives and companies settled payments among private individuals using accounts in 'points' or 'certificates' as means of payment, instead of scrip, because those mechanisms apparently worked better. Moreover, in March 1933, President Franklin Roosevelt banned further scrip issue on the grounds that the national government was losing control of the monetary system. The subsequent abandonment of the golden standard gave the country the opportunity to implement a monetary policy that would further support economic recovery. Fisher stopped promoting the idea after 1934, Zylstra moved away from Hawarden, and only Cohrssen continued to advocate Gesell's idea of demurrage.

Stamp scrips, in general, came to be seen as an instrument of economic rehabilitation, creatures of an emergency situation with minimal chances of surviving in better times. In the short run, they helped their members survive the Great Depression but did not constitute a durable solution because they did not support an autonomous flow of currency to support a circuit of exchange. The stamp scrip was dependent on regular money to afford many supplies and was plagued with problems of low managerial capacity and poor accountancy in the exchange systems. In addition, there is no indication that any of its proponents actually conceived of shrinking currencies as part of a trajectory to restructure economic relations after the crisis. That is, as an institution beyond the contingency of a temporary economic demise. As Fisher (1934: 163) presented it, complementary currencies were an appropriate mechanism to support livelihoods and incomes in specific circumstances and 'until the deserter comes back to service', in reference to regular money.

7.6 Municipal emergency currencies in the Spanish Civil War

Spain had an enormous diversity and amount of local notes and currencies of all types and functions during the Civil War (Graeber, 1978). Moreover, before the war started each Spanish town hall had its own currency or was planning to have a local complementary currency. In general, they are barely studied and many hours of archival work fed partial publications (von Prittwitz, 2014) that allowed us to identify monetary forms as varied as currencies with negative interest rates, vouchers issued specifically for social aid, refugees and victims of the heavy bombardments, Catalonian co-operative notes, military money, commercial money and obsidional currencies of many kinds around the time of the Spanish Civil War.

Paper money was virtually unknown in Spain until the middle of the 1800s and the first note issued by the Bank of Spain appeared in 1874. It was meant as a reserve of value, so its denomination of 25 pesetas was high in relation to the prices of common necessities. Daily transactions were traded with metallic coins of smaller values. During the first decades of the 20th century, the denominations of the notes decreased to amounts required for their daily use as medium of exchange (Tortella Casares, 2008). The use of paper money of smaller denominations expanded slowly and was not yet completely widespread when the Spanish crown fell in 1931. In the politically unstable months before the beginning of the Spanish Civil War in 1936, Spanish metal coins gradually disappeared from circulation because they were kept in hoards as reserve of value in anticipation of worse times. The scarcity of Spanish coins worsened and re-appeared very slowly, and the notes and coins issued by Alfonso XII were still circulating, at the end of the war in 1939.

In a nutshell, the war was unleashed after the partial failure of a coup on July 17 and 18, 1936. The parties that faced the conflict were denominated republican, on one side, and rebellious or national, on the other. The republican side was led by the Spanish Popular Front based out of the Government of Spain that was elected democratically before Franco took over the government. It is estimated that Franco's armed forces were composed during the war by almost one million men, including the Falanges, an extreme nationalist political group influenced by Italian fascism. The Falanges issued a manifesto of 27 points repudiating the republican constitution, party politics, capitalism, Marxism and clericalism, and proclaiming the necessity for a national-corporatist state, strong government and Spanish Imperialist expansion. On the opposite side was the Popular Front, an electoral coalition formed in January, 1936 by the main parties of the Spanish Left. On 16 February, 1936 the Popular Front managed to win the last elections during the Second Republic and was followed by a coup that would lead to the Spanish Civil War. A coalition of working-class and middle social strata united for the defence of the democratic government against the forced Franquist government. The war was driven by social, political, religious and military considerations that eventually caused an unprecedented economic collapse. It ended on 1 April, 1939 when Francisco Franco declared his victory and established a dictatorship that lasted until his death in 1975.

As it occurred during other episodes of economic demise, the Civil War in Spain enabled the proliferation of local complementary currencies or 'municipal notes'. Moreover, the war between the two fronts was also fought around money issuance. During the conflict there were two 'official' currencies in parallel to the traditional Spanish peseta: the republican and the national peseta, even though only the republican peseta could claim officialdom since it was the currency of the democratically elected government during the Second Spanish Republic. For example, there were a total of six different types of notes of five and ten pesetas, issued by the Bank of Spain in Burgos, the Bank of Spain in Madrid, vouchers of its subsidiaries in Gijon, Santander and Bilbao, and treasury bills launched by the Catalonian and Asturian governments that claimed economic independence during the conflict (Figures 7.11 and 7.12) (Turró, 1982; López and Lluch, 1983). The Bank of Spain was officially resettled in Burgos in September 1936, after a period in which its subsidiaries opened and operated under the commands of the various groups that ruled the country (Sánchez Asiaín, 2013). It started issuing paper money again but the gold and silver reserves, if there were any left, were kept in vaults in Madrid, so the newly issued currency lacked collateral. Moreover, the Bank of Spain in Burgos over-stamped notes issued before the conflict, in order to reassure that those bills were valid as means of payment. In reality, only silver and other metal

Figure 7.11 Catalonyan peseta

coins were accepted across the entire country during the war, but the public tried to keep metal coins as reserve of value, which subsequently dried out the system of means of payment.

Municipal notes appeared around 1936 and had a relatively stable value, although they were temporary, local, and restricted to specific areas and uses. Approximately 2,000 localities issued about 20,000 notes of various denominations and duration. There are currencies issued by municipal authorities that could still claim legitimacy during the conflict, along with others issued by the fighting armies, rural co-operatives, and local businesses, which were intended mainly to enable the trade of food and agricultural products during the conflict. Some of the city councils were aware that they were introducing a new monetary form and searched for a new name for their currency. Their zeal to reform the socio-economic aspects of money was so great that they avoided the words 'money', 'banknote' or denominations of the units of account such as the peseta. They introduced denominations like degrees and units. Other municipal currencies avoided religious connotations and issued notes that eradicated the existing religious symbolism.

The Popular Front also created a number of complementary currencies for different purposes, mainly in defence of their local municipal finances and organisations. In many cases these currency notes and coins carried the motto of the republic: peace and work. The currencies related the value of labour to products, wages and other payments made with them within the territories of the municipalities and in mandatory admission for all transactions. Social aid for refugees, the unemployed and the poor contributed to palliate the negative effects of the war. Some banknotes were coined for the sole reason of helping refugees and the civil populations, while other banknotes were made specifically for the victims of bombardments. As the war lasted longer than initially expected, it originated a great variety of complementary currencies during the period (1936–1939), and their exact origins are difficult to establish. It was not always clear to which of the two governments each currency corresponded. Although they all bore the nominal value of the 'Spanish peseta' some would be labelled with added stamps or superscripts of the nationalists or the republican parties respectively. Each army considered that the currencies issued by the adversary were the 'money of the enemy', and its use would be punished even with death.

Small change to pay for daily necessities was equally scarce, as it had been in Germany during the post First World War period, so vouchers kept multiplying and were circulated at the same time as the municipal currencies. The vouchers that were issued as small denomination currency were called 'fractionary' in relation to other notes (Carothers, 1930). The list of issuers included the many groups that participated in the conflict, such as communists, socialists, trade union fighters, anarchists, republicans, fascists and the international brigades. These vouchers were sometimes handwritten papers given by a local bakery. There were also handwritten notes stating that a fighting group in either army received a product, usually food, on a certain date and place and promised to pay back the appropriate amount at the end of the conflict. These also circulated as means of payment. Some notes

Figure 7.12 Pesetas of Gijon

even skipped mentioning the value, which was basically unknown in the middle of the conflict, and mentioned only the date when the goods changed hands, the recipient and the products given, in the assumption that these would be redeemed at whatever prices resulted for those products when the war ended. The name of the issuer and the organisation he or she served was also mentioned, which gave the vouchers the appearance of legitimacy. Many of the notes subsequently circulated as currency within the area, reflecting the fact that any means of payment was perceived as better than none at all, and that complementary currencies could be handwritten small papers, made in situ and accepted in trade in the demise of the entire political, economic and social system (Figure 7.13).

In the proliferation of notes, there were some depreciating currencies as well. The notes of the Constitutional City of Montoro were perhaps the first depreciating money in Spain (Figure 7.14). In August 1936, the local council printed a series of bills of five pesetas with a depreciation table on the back in which the value of the bill was decreasing weekly. A bill was worth five pesetas on 24th August, for example, but 4.50 on 2nd November. After twelve weeks, the bill was partially redeemable only in the town hall. The municipality paid civil servants their wages with this shrinking currency and workers tried to spend them immediately to pay for their immediate needs, or deposited them in local banks as soon as possible. A monthly wage for a municipal employee was about 20 pesetas, so a note of five pesetas represented a significant amount of money for a municipal employee in 1936. After seven days the currency would start losing value, so the instrument was aimed at speeding circulation and cash deposits in the banks, which were subsequently able to offer credit for production. It was not possible to establish a direct link between the Spanish shrinking currencies and Gesell's ideas, but considering the large number of anarchists and brigadists

Figure 7.13 Different pesetas, some censored

from Germany fighting in Spain, it is possible that the Spanish municipal banknotes could have been inspired by the German experiences. It is possible that the council of Montoro would have heard of the cases of Wära and Wörgl and aimed at promoting local trade and production using a similar mechanism. This type of monetary experimentation also took place in other locations in Spain, such as the Andalusian villages of Porcuna and others ruled by the Popular Front in the province of Córdoba, where depreciating municipal currencies were introduced in 1936 and 1937.

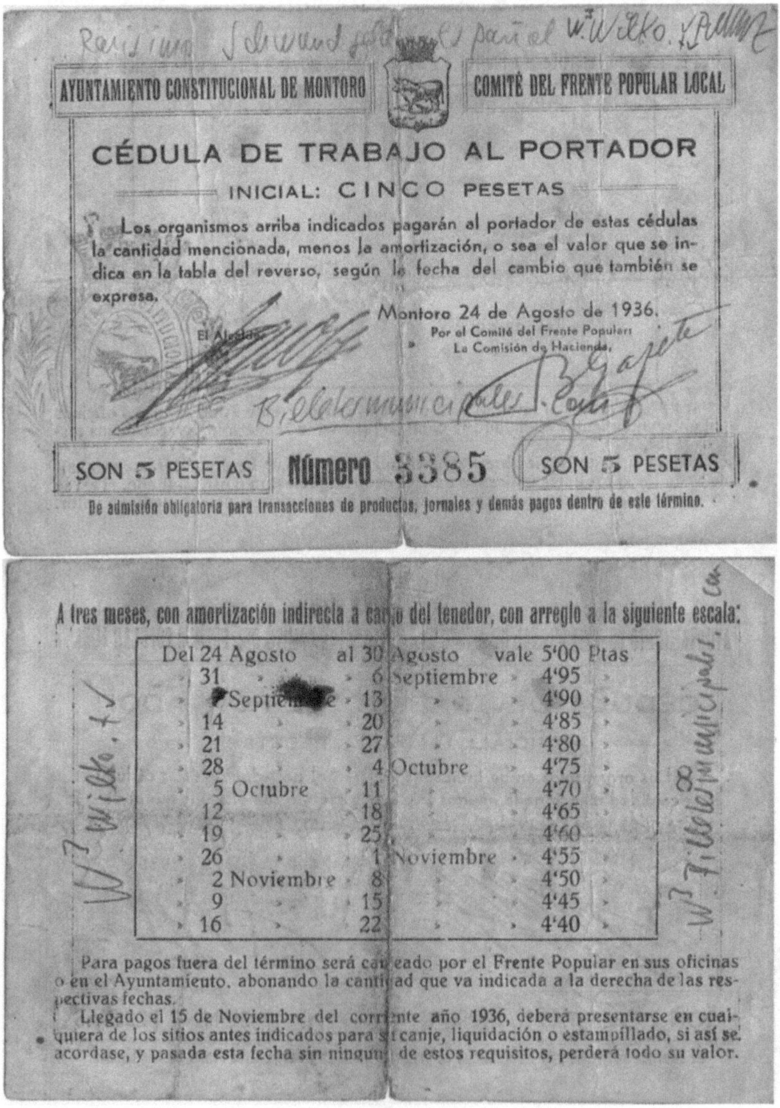

Figure 7.14 Emergency scrip with demurrage in Montoro, Spain

It is impossible to verify how many notes were issued and on what date they stopped circulating but a large collection is available on a website[1] and in Von Prittwitz (2014), *Schwundgeld Español*. The proliferation of municipal currencies followed the multiplication of individual and municipal responses to the ineffectiveness of the monetary authorities to alleviate the shortage of means of payment during the war, the fact that the population would keep gold and silver coins as reserve of value, and of course the war propaganda of numerous political fractions. At the end of the conflict, Franco's government decreed that all the municipal currencies issued by the winning national army could be exchanged at the Bank of Spain for the new Spanish currency (Order 5, Decree 27, August, 1938 published on 17 September, 1938). The republican money was confiscated and repudiated, and municipal coins and local banknotes were repressed. Franco's government created a new version of the peseta, the 'Peseta of the Spanish State', that circulated between 1937 and 1975. However, many complementary currencies continued to circulate among the population as medium of exchange in periods after the Spanish Civil War (1939–1949) and later after the Second World War (1945–1955), even if they were prohibited. Some notes were kept in secret and are still found today among collectors.

Many Spanish complementary currencies are unknown, perhaps due to the militarist oppression that followed in Spain for almost 40 years and its severe control of institutional and municipal authorities. The Second Republic basically closed the window of political opportunity that sustained monetary experimentation with the Popular Front and around the period of the conflict. Before the Civil War there were a large number of municipalities that reclaimed their right to issue money that related its value to labour and the reproduction of labour. Those complementary currencies derived from local aspirations to restructure the socio-economic system and to gain independence from the central bank and other monetary authorities. In comparison, the proliferation of municipal complementary currencies during the war sprang from the need to provide means of payment to distressed local economies, although even in those circumstances some groups and municipalities continued the monetary experimentation and issued depreciating currencies, for instance.

7.7 Conclusions

The period after the First World War in the German speaking countries in the 1920s, the Depression in Central Europe and in the United States in the 1930s, and the Spanish Civil War in the late 1930s have severe social and economic crisis in common. While sharply different in terms of causes, geography, duration and other characteristics, all four were episodes in which institutions broke down. The social structures that regulated how agents interacted with each other collapsed, together with the notions of what was socially acceptable and what was not. The money institutions were not an exception, as they ceased to be and do what was expected of them. So, who made money? The variety of places and actors that started complementary currency systems are as broad as the crises that embedded them and the aims they pursued. We tend to find that the agents in the field, such as municipal governments, citizens' organisations and business associations, venture into issuing complementary currencies to resolve immediate emergencies.

First and foremost, complementary currencies appeared as devices to resolve the needs for money in the local economies. In all four cases, there was evidence of hoarding metal bullion and other currencies perceived as more reliable. The retention of money as reserve of value quickly affected the availability of means of payment to perform trade. Stringent monetary policies to curb inflation and the need to use the metals for the war effort further dried the circulation of money. Demand rose significantly for small denomination notes that were most commonly used in daily transactions and by low income segments of the population. The function of money as means of payment hence collapsed, and the local solution of complementary currencies emerged as punctual, small scale and temporary solutions for daily transactions. Complementary currencies apparently emerge to fill in the gaps left by the regular monetary system in terms of smaller denomination notes, implying that local complementary currency systems are essentially low-denomination currencies. However, this proposition would require further research.

The sequence in these cases suggests that the four key functions of money do not necessarily fail at the same time. The function of unit of account apparently collapsed last, and complementary currencies indicated their value in the established unit of account (marks, pesetas, dollars, etc.). Only in the most extreme cases of the Spanish Civil War did some of notes refer to essential goods and not include a fixed value in a monetary unit of account; the local goods that sustained the reproduction of labour or the labour born to obtain the voucher were used as unit of account to value those notes. The sequence in which monetary plurality emerged and replaced the functions of money suggests that the role as unit of account is the ultimate or most essential function of money. In a discussion on John Maynard Keynes' *Treatise of Money* (1976 [1930]), Geoffrey Ingham (2004) identifies the unit of account as the primary and most basic function. In the cases referred to in this chapter, the replacement of an official unit of account for a local unit of account rarely happened. When it did, and if the monetary authorities had some capacity to react, the replacement of the unit of account at the local level was interpreted as a serious contestation to monetary sovereignty. At the same time, the issuers of the local currencies conceived their new units of account as the foundations to build a different socio-economic system that would free them from the central monetary authority.

While the widespread dissemination of complementary currencies can be seen as the result of the chaos that prevailed during hyperinflation and war, their origins were bottom-up efforts to recover economic order, or at least some sense of normality. The creation of local money centres on organising exchanges and can be analysed as an attempt to re-configure institutions to sustain circulation and production when these are interrupted (Pacione, 1999). Agents identify the need for tools of economic organisation and engage in the creation of institutions – monetary forms – that would perform that role. The background of chaos supports the emergence and acceptance of complementary currencies among groups that would normally not be open to such experimentation because weak money is perceived as a superior solution than no money. In political terms, the demise provided a window of opportunity to experiment and promote the restructuring of the social and economic system, although to different extents in the four cases. Experimentation with money has the political connotation of challenging the prevalent economic system that regular money serves. In post-war Germany and Austria, depreciating currencies were tied to Gesell's anarchist ideas about the 'natural order' in which money should be exposed to loss of value like in the case of agricultural products. In the case of the Spanish Civil War, the dissemination of political ideas of autonomy by the Popular Front was even more evident. It later translated into a competition between the two armies for the issuance of currencies such as currencies of the fascist and currencies of the communist armies, which defined the 'enemy's currencies' depending on the point of view of the users. Emergency notes are of great importance for local economies to climb out of social, political and economic demise. Like other issues in contexts of war and demise, who makes money becomes an area of contestation, because it denotes who enables economic life by organising exchanges and also who provides social order.

Note

1 www.billetesmunicipales.com

References

Blanc, J. 2012. 'Thirty Years of Community and Complementary Currencies: a Review of Impacts, Potential and Challenges', *International Journal Of Community Currency Research*, 16, 1–4.

Boyer-Xambeu, M. T., Deleplace, M. G. and Gillard, L. 1994. *Private Money and Public Currencies: The Sixteenth Century Challenge*, London: Sharpe.

Carothers, N. 1930. *Fractional Money*, New York: John Wiley & Sons, 1–90.

Cohen, B. K. 1999. 'The New Geography of Money', in E. Gilbert and E. Helleiner eds, *Nation-States and Money. The Past, Present and Future of National Currencies*, London, New York: Routledge, 121–138.

Cohrssen, H. 1932. 'Wara', *The New Republic*, 10th August.

Diessner, H. J. 2012. *Deutsches Notgeld 1914–1924*. Berlin: Gietl.

Fisher, I. 1933. *Stamp Scrip*, New York: Adelphi Co.

Fisher, I. 1934. *Mastering The Crisis – With Additional Chapters On Stamp Script*, London: Kimble And Bradford.

Gatch, L. 2009 'A Professor and a Paper Panacea: Irving Fisher and The Stamp Scrip Movement of 1932–1934', *Paper Money*, March-April, 125–142.

Gesell, S. 1958 *The Natural Economic Order*, London: Peter Owen, 6.

Gilbert, E. and Helleiner, E., eds. 1999. *Nation-States and Money. The Past, Present and Future of National Currencies*, London, New York: Routledge.

Graeber, K. 1978. *Paper Money of the 20th Century, V. 3. Local Paper Money Issued During the Spanish Civil War. International Bank Note Society.*

Greco, T. 2001. *Money: Understanding and Creating Alternatives to Legal Tender*, White River Junction, VT: Chelsea Green.

Ingham, G. 2002. 'New Monetary Spaces?' In OECD ed. *The Future of Money*. Paris: OECD.

Ingham, G. 2004. *The Nature of Money*, Cambridge, UK: Polity Press.

Keynes, J. M. 1976 [1930]. *A Treatise on Money*, New York: Harcourt, Brace and Co.

Kingdon, J. W. 2003. *Agendas, Alternatives, and Public Policies*, New York: Longman Classics.

Kuroda, A. 2007. 'The Maria Theresa Dollar in the Early Twentieth-Century Red Sea Region: A Complementary Interface Between Multiple Markets', *Financial History Review*, 14, 89–110.

Leyshon, A. and Thrift, N. 1996. *Money/Space*, London: Routledge.

Lindman, K. 2011. *Schwundgeld In Deutschland. Freigeld-Freiland-Frei Wirtschaft 1916–1952*. Gifhorn, Germany: Kolme-k Verlag.

López, I. and Lluch, A. 1983. *Les Monedes De Les Cooperatives Catalanes 1850–1950*. Departamento De Cultura De La Generalitat De Catalunya.

Miró Agulló, J. B. 2008. El sello moneda de la República, Alcoi. Scribd.

Offe, C. and Heinze, G. 1992. *Beyond Employment: Time, Work and the Informal Economy*, Cambridge, UK: Polity Press, 1–124.

Pacione, M. 1999. 'The Other Side of the Coin: Local Currency as a Response to the Globalisation of Capital', *Debates and Reviews, Regional Studies*, 33: 1, 63–72.

Pick, A. 1978. *Papiergeld Lexikon*. Ed. Mosaik, Munich, Germany: Verlagsgruppe Bertelsmann.

Proudhon, P. 1840. *Qu'est-Ce Que La Propriété?* Ed. Poche. Paris: Marcel Rivière.

Sánchez Asiaín, J. 2013. *La Financiación De La Guerra Civil Española*. Ed. Crítics. Barcelona: Crítica.

Schuldt, J. 1997 *Dineros Alternativos: Para El Desarrollo Local*, Lima: Universidad Del Pacífico.

Schwarz, F. 2006. *Das Experiment von Wörgle. Ein Weg Aus Der Wirtschaftskrise*, Madrid: Synergia Verlag.

Shafer, N. 1974. *Philippine Emergency and Guerrilla Currency of World War II*, with Special Support of Maurice M. Gould. Racine, WI: Western Pub. Co.

Tarrow, S. 1998. *Power in Movement: Social Movements and Contentious Politics*, Cambridge, UK: Cambridge University Press.

Tortella Casares, T. 2008. 'El Billete Español En La Edad Contemporánea, Mucho Más Que Un Medio De Pago', *VII Jornadas Científicas Sobre Documentación Contemporánea 1868–2008*. Madrid: Banco De España, 332–368.

Turró, I. and Martínez, A. 1982. 'El Paper Moneda Català 1936–1939 1982'; 'El Paper Moneda Al País Valencià 1936–1939 1995'; 'El Paper Moneda Catalá 1936–1939 1987'; 'El Paper Moneda Catalá A La Franja De Ponent 1936–1939'. Editorial Afers.

Von Muralt, A. 1934. 'The Woergl Experiment with Depreciating Money', *Annals of Public and Cooperative Economics*, 10, 48–57.

Von Prittwitz, W. 2014. *Schwundgeld Español*. AENP, Asociación Española De Numismáticos Profesionales.

8 Birth, life and death of a provincial complementary currency from Tucuman, Argentina (1985–2003)

Bruno Théret[1]

8.1 Introduction

This chapter discusses the complementary currency (CC), bocade, issued by the Argentinian province of Tucuman between 1985 and 2003. We shall first examine when, where and why this currency was issued, how it functioned initially and how it evolved. After this we shall give an evaluation of the bocade's economic efficiency and political viability. The questions we will tackle are: Has the bocade been useful and successful? Has its value maintained parity with the national unit of account? Did it favour growth at the provincial level? Did it reduce the provincial debt?

This CC is of interest for several reasons. First, it has been the longest lasting of the Argentinian provincial CCs of the third and fourth waves of issuances presented in Chapter 5. Second, a significant amount of money has been issued via this CC. Tucuman in 2002 was the fifth province in terms of amount of money issued, after Buenos Aires, Cordoba, Entre Rios and Corrientes (Schvarzer and Finkelstein 2003). Third, the bocade has left detailed quantitative traces allowing a scrutiny of its economic and financial impact, thanks notably to the presence of a numismatic association in the province which was concerned with the notes (Beckmann 1985, 2001, 2002, 2003; Hernandez Meson 2002). The fourth reason is that it was possible to get access to good quality oral and written documentation, notably a book of political memories of the founding father of the CC (Cirnigliaro 2004), as well as good parliamentary archives and a provincial newspaper (*La Gaceta*) covering day to day adventures of the bocade. Eventually, the heuristic interest of the Tucuman CC was outstanding since it is a province of small economic and demographic size that has played an important historic politico-symbolic role in Argentina. It has always been on the forefront of provincial paper money issuance. Tucuman is at the heart of the peripheral region of North West Argentina (NOA) where issuances of provincial money have been directly linked to regionalist and federalist stakes. This experiment, therefore, has not been completely conditioned by the provincial economic situation. The fact that it survived various economic and political crises on the federal level testifies that it was not completely conditioned by external factors either. For all these reasons the Tucuman bocade has been an exemplary manifestation of monetary federalism, and it is important to underpin this point.

8.2 Rebuilding the history of a long-lasting complementary fiscal currency

The bocade was issued for the first time in August 1985 for an amount of 10 million australes and it was totally redeemed in August 2003, after no less than 40 issues (26 in australes, and 14 in pesos).

Figures 8.1 and 8.2 give an overview of the amounts issued in nominal and deflated constant values.[2] Due to the estimation method, real circulation is probably between the two curves in Figure 8.2.[3]

8.2.1 Why was it issued?

The bocade was not different from other provincial tax-backed monies issued in response to local shortages of credit and currency. The Tucuman bocade is a typical example of currency finance, yet it is important to stress on two points. First, money shortage can result from not only a deflationist regime, as was the convertibility regime of the 1990s, but also from a high inflation regime as was the austral regime in the 1980s. Second, the political and symbolical dimensions of the emergence of the bocade seem important, as it is regarded as an instrument of autonomy of a province belonging to the North-West Region of Argentina. This dimension, combined with the fact that it has been significantly supported by the Tucuman business class, could explain its lasting character.

When it was implemented, the first purpose of the bocade was to stabilise political and social conflicts, notably between the government and civil servants (the local police was engaged in social unrest). It gave the provincial government

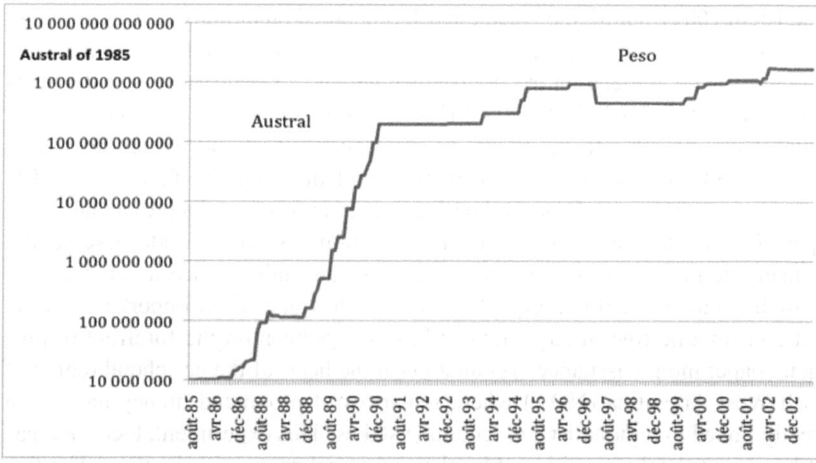

Figure 8.1 Evolution of the nominal value of the stock of bocades

Sources: Beckmann (1985, 2001, 2002, 2003); Cerro (1988, 2002); Cano et al. (1993); Hernandez Meson (2002); Licari et al. (2003); Direccion de estadistica de Tucuman (2006, 2007, 2008, 2009).

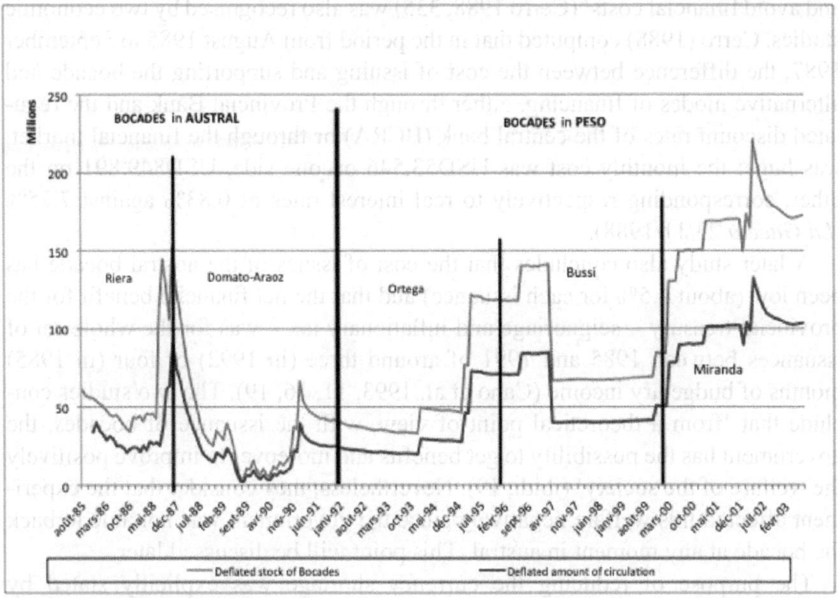

Figure 8.2 Stock and circulation of bocades

Sources: Beckmann (1985, 2001, 2002, 2003); Cerro (1988, 2002); Cano et al. (1993); Hernandez Meson (2002); Licari et al. (2003).

means to immediately pay public employees their wages which had been delayed by several months. The purpose of the bocade was also to improve the public finances of the province by reducing the public debt and its heavy burden on the budget. Rienzo Cirnigliaro, the Minister of Finance in charge of the implementation of the bocade, explains that:

> We had found an empty coffer, one month and a half of wages' debts, anticipated payments of revenue-sharing transfers, and moreover, late payments of wages with till 25 days of delay. There was a fall in federal transfers and provincial taxes to be levied and interests on the debts contracted.
>
> From August 1985, salaries were paid entirely, and the process of indebtedness due to belated payments of wages was stopped. The total debt was completely settled the 24th of December 1985. In five months we succeeded in paying the equivalent of six and a half months of public wages, in a critical and hard financial context. Till now the Bank of the Province of Tucuman was helping financially the State, some months by advances of 80% of the total spending for salaries. At the end of 1985, the balance of the account of the Province at the bank began to be positive.
>
> (Cirnigliaro 2004, 116–117)

The fact that 'the bocade was an excellent device for financing the fiscal deficit and avoid financial costs' (Cerro 1988, 335) was also recognised by two economic studies. Cerro (1988) computed that in the period from August 1985 to September 1987, the difference between the cost of issuing and supporting the bocade and alternative modes of financing, either through the Provincial Bank and the regulated discount rates of the central bank (BCRA) or through the financial market, was huge: the monthly cost was USD53.546 on one side, USD849.891 on the other, corresponding respectively to real interest rates of 0.83% against 7.25% (*La Gaceta* 23/11/1988).

A later study also concludes that the cost of issues of the austral bocade has been low (about 4.5% for each issuance) and that the net financial benefit for the provincial treasury – seignoriage and inflationary tax – was for the whole set of issuances between 1985 and 1991 of around three (in 1992) or four (in 1985) months of budgetary income (Cano et al. 1993, 11, 16, 19). The two studies conclude that 'from a theoretical point of view, with the issuance of bocade*s*, the government has the possibility to get benefits and moreover to improve positively the welfare of the society' (ibid., 19). Nevertheless, they consider that the experiment affected this welfare negatively since the government was not able to back the bocade at any moment in austral. This point will be discussed later.

The purpose of reducing the currency shortage was explicitly stated by Cirnigliaro, but he does not see the bocade as a simple currency, but rather 'an instrument of short-term credit', 'a loan from the People to the State, with an interest rate nil' (Cirnigliaro 2004, 123).

Eventually the bocade, for Cirnigliaro, was an 'instrument of provincial emancipation' from the outstanding invasive power of the central government or still 'a financial instrument of a monetary nature, but of a federal character' (ibid., 126). Cirnigliaro is, thus, not far from regarding the CC as a symbolic manifestation of monetary federalism. For him, it was a potential instrument of re-negotiation and adaptation of the federal monetary constitution, in order to take into account the detrimental effects on peripheral provinces of a centralised monetary policy. In this perspective, he recalls in his book that during his office as Minister of Economy, he had talks with his colleagues from the surrounding provinces of Jujuy, Salta, Catamarca and Santiago del Estero about a possible regionalisation of their respective bonds in order to guarantee their circulation at par in the whole NOA – a project in which the Banco de la Provincia de Tucuman would have possibly operated as a clearing house (ibid.). This project did not go further, but it was coherent and in line with the fact that Tucuman and La Rioja in 1985, as well as Jujuy in 1986, had implemented the same type of bonds as Salta, the first province to renew the issue of provincial currencies (Chapter 5).

These political and symbolic dimensions of the bocade that Cirnigliaro underlines are not the normative product of his imagination. They were shared by the Peronist Governor of the province, Riera, who had hired him as minister and signed the federalist sentence on the banner of the first series of bocade notes (Figure 8.3).

The federalist feelings of the Tucuman government echoed in the political pro-bocade attitude of the provincial business community. In the display advertisement

Figure 8.3 The first bocade of Tucumán issued in 1985

presented in Figure 8.4, this attitude is clearly asserted. This poster, published on the 20 November 2001, stresses the importance of the 'Tucuman Money' as a means of keeping alive provincial payments and trust. The significance of the bocade was appropriated by the business community, organised around the Tucuman Economic Federation (FET). Convertibility of the bocade in peso was threatened by huge national restrictions on the peso supply. Thus, the bocade was still strongly supported by local economic interests in 2001 not only as an economic instrument, but also as a representation of their mutual inter-dependencies and of their belonging to a territorial community of local development.

Nevertheless, Cirnigliaro was ambivalent, like the local business class supporting the bocade (*La Tarde* 17/02/1988; *La Gaceta* 03/03/1988). For instance, there is a paradox in Cirnigliaro's understanding of the status and future of the bocade. On one side, he considers it as a 'federal call' because its 'highest virtue' was to be 'an instrument of defence of the decision-making powers or sovereignty of the provincial states' (Cirnigliaro 2004, 125), that is, a way 'to reorganise the Nation' in order to tackle the fact that 'legally we are organised as a federal country, but in fact we constitute a unitary country' (ibid., 126). He also, however, speaks of it as a 'transitional instrument' (ibid., 122), and of the possibility and even the necessity to redeem it as soon as the provincial public finances were in order:

DEFENDER EL BOCADE ES DEFENDER A TUCUMAN

« STANDING UP FOR THE BOCADE IS STANDING UP FOR TUCUMAN. »

« The signing entities, concerned with provincial interests, support the bocade and the so called *Operatoria FET*. The Tucuman money above all, which during the 16 years of its existence allowed our companies, trades and industries to have at their disposal for their business a currency flow, is the bocade. The Tucuman *Bond* has allowed us to face successive national crises, hyperinflation, recession, adjustments in the National Economy, etc. Today newly the circonstancies make the bocade an essential device for the working of the economy of Tucuman. It is why we ask insistently the community in general to lend a hand all together, giving backing and a support which re-creates confidence in this Tucuman money. This trust in the BOCADE is also sustained by its convertibility in the legal tender currency, condition guaranteed by the sure device that has proved to be the *Operatoria FET*, and whose no other provincial currencies or bonds have. But all this backing must result from an effort shared by everybody, and there must be no exception in the acceptance of the bonds ; consequently we call all the utility companies to commit themselves, in an attitude of solidarity, to accept the bocades at their nominal value, besides an adequate treatment of the conversion of the *bonds* by the financial system. This way of acting and this solidarity will ensure the effectiveness and credibility of this provincial money which, in the present circonstancies of currency shortage, are necessary for us ».

Respaldando al BOCADE estaremos respaldando los intereses de la comunidad toda

FEDERACION ECONOMICA DE TUCUMAN (FET)
ASOCIACION DE PRODUCTORES DE PALTA (APROPAL)
HIPERMERCADO LIBERTAD S.A.
CAMARA DE SUPERMERCADOS Y AUTOSERVICIOS DE TUCUMAN
UNION DE TABACALEROS DE TUCUMAN (UTT)
CAMARA DE PRODUCTORES DE TABACO DE LA PROVINCIA DE TUCUMAN
ASOCIACION DE PRODUCTORES TABACALEROS DE TUCUMAN-LA COCHA
ASOCIACION DE PRODUCTORES DE PAPA-SEMILLA (APASE)
CAMARA ARGENTINA DE LA CONSTRUCCION-DELEGACION TUCUMAN
CONFEDERACION DE ASOCIACIONES RURALES DE TUCUMAN (CARTUC)
ASOCIACION DE PRODUCTORES DE PAPA PUCARA (APROPAP)
CENTRO DE AGRICULTORES CAÑEROS DE TUCUMAN (CACTU)
UNION CAÑEROS INDEPENDIENTES DE TUCUMAN (UCIT)
CENTRO AZUCARERO REGIONAL TUCUMAN (CART)
COOPERATIVAS DE TAMBEROS DE TUCUMAN Y TRANCAS
ASOCIACIÓN TUCUMANA DE CITRUS (ATC)
COLEGIO DE BIOQUIMICOS DE TUCUMAN
COORP. DEL MERCADO FRUTIHORTICOLA DE TUCUMAN (MERCOFRUT)

Figure 8.4 Tucuman's entrepreneurs supporting the bocade in 2001

If the governments that followed us would have stabilised public finances as we have done it, in rationalising public spending, in making efficient social spending, in increasing public investment and transforming the State into a promoter of economic development, the subnational bonds would not have had any motive to carry on during 18 years.

(ibid., 126–127)

But the politico-symbolic dimensions of the bocade seem to require its permanence, even if provincial finances are in order, once the structural reliance of provincial finances on federal financial and monetary policies are taken into account. Thus, the initiator of the CC balances between an instrumental and unitary view of money and a more sociological and pluralist one.

8.2.2 How did the bocade function at its outset and stabilise?

The bocade was issued and regulated by a legislative Act that shows how simple and short (only three pages were necessary in the original form) the juridical work to institute it was. Only eight articles of the Act 5728 (24/07/1985, Honorable Legislatura de Tucuman) concern the issue of the bocade and its regulation:

> Article 1 mainly defines the amount of issues authorised by the legislative power. It stipulates an important rule of possible adjustment of this amount by indexation on a local price index.
>
> Article 2 announces that the bocade is issued to the bearer, and that they have a limited life span fixed by law.
>
> Article 3 stipulates that it is state money, a medium of payment of debts, issued by the provincial treasury and rationed by the whole set of local State organisations who can use it also for intrastate transactions. It specifies that the redeeming power of the bocade is equal to its nominal value. It defines the use and holding of bocade as based on free acceptance, not on legal tender, and details that the CCs are accepted for taxes and other payments to the public sector.
>
> Article 4 states that the bocade is convertible at par with legal tender or federal money and exchangeable at the Bank of the Province instituted as a local currency board, leaving the definition of the methods of actual exchange (periods, places and schedule) to decrees of the executive power.
>
> Article 5 defines a possible use of the bocade for legal guarantees and deposits.
>
> Article 6 is relative to the possibility for bocade*s* to pay interests during the first three months of its circulation (which has not been actualised).
>
> Article 7 authorises the Executive to create lotteries and define the modes of their functioning.
>
> Article 8 suggests to municipalities to adopt similar norms concerning articles 3 and 5 of the Act.

Thus, it is defined a non-legal tender, tax anticipation scrip, a temporary bond of redemption of debts denominated in the federal unit of account, and a CC convertible into the legal tender currency at par, until its date of nullity and under specific conditions fixed by the provincial government.

This definition does not tell us how, beyond the apparent simplicity in legally defining it, this currency and its regime of convertibility concretely functioned at its outset in 1985 and adapted to changes in the economic and political environment. Before coming to that, we must specify that the bocade, under the form of notes of distinct small denominations (from 0.10 to 10 australes in the first issues), was introduced into the economic circuit through wages and payments of providers of the public sector.

It then came back into the public coffers through two main channels. The first channel was through payments of provincial taxes and other public fees. It was most comfortable for the province, since it did not imply any change of bocade for australes, but it was narrow because the autonomous revenue of the province in proportion to its total public spending was only 20%. To enlarge this channel, it would have been necessary to increase autonomous revenues, a difficult task. The second channel was through exchange in australes at the Provincial Bank. It was the most important to ensure the bocade's credibility and a testimony of circulation without discount in the market sphere. The aim was then to minimise the return of bocade to the treasury coffers. For this, lotteries were preferred to payments of interest and occurred weekly, and on exceptional occasions entailed four or five draws of the last numerals of the series' number on the notes. The People's Provincial Savings Bank was in charge of these lotteries and delivered weekly premiums of 20 times the value of the winning notes or, for exceptional draws, large cars or even houses.

The main means to extend use of the bocade in market exchanges was people'strust in the institution ensuring the parity between the bocade and the legal tender. Effective convertibility into the austral legal tender cash in a reasonable lapse of time was another means to extend its use, especially for payments outside of the province.

The Banco de la Provincia de Tucuman, as the financial agent of the provincial treasury, was playing the role of such currency board. People could change their bocade*s* at its branches and counters, in the People's Provincial Savings Bank, and also with a small discount in some other banks. There were, however, restrictions: the exchange was open only on working days during the 10 days between the 18th and the 28th of each month. These restrictions allowed the bocade to function as a pure short-term credit instrument, since even if all the bocades in circulation were presented for change every month, the device gave time to the provincial treasury, during the period of closure of the change, to collect australes and so avoid liquidity problems. This credit was almost free, so the province was able to reduce its floating debt.

Another effect was to allow the government to pay the monthly wages of public employees on time, and not late as had become usual. Thus, the bocade was also an instrument of social peace-keeping.

But it was financially much more interesting for the provincial government, as well as for the business community in some regards, that the bocade remained in circulation in the markets without being redeemed in austral every month. Only under these conditions could it be a device for reducing monetary and credit shortage and stimulating the local economy. Moreover, the fact that it stayed in circulation was proof of its credibility.

According to Cirnigliaro,

> The first month was the hardest (September 1985). The 18th of the month, a true avalanche occurred at the bank. We had 9 million of australes in cash for sustaining the change. The first day it was of nearly 7.5 million australes, while around one million were changed the second day. Afterwards, there were practically no exchanges. We paid that month the wages in time, and worked in order to gather the 10 million of australes we needed for the next change. This time, on the first day, the amount of exchanges has been less than 50% of our liquid assets at the Provincial Bank. In the subsequent months, at the end of the period of exchange at the Bank, the amount of bocades applying for change represented 70% of the total issued. It was a clear signal that the people had acquired the trust necessary for a short-term credit instrument functioning as a currency. The public held it, to the point that its acceptance was increasing.
>
> (Cirnigliaro 2004, 122–123)

Cerro (1988, 326–327) gives a similar description of the functioning of the bocade in its first two years and recognises that 'the Tucuman community was supporting, holding, and using the bocades'.

Nevertheless, both Cerro and Cirnigliaro agree on the bocade being mismanaged. According to Cirnigliaro (2004, 124), it was used 'as an inexhaustible resource to finance (government's) unbalances'. As for Cerro:

> The bocades were not accompanied by policies aimed at building credibility, supporting and trust. Lotteries were not promoted and were soon cancelled, the maximum amount of authorised issuance was not respected, and the exchange in australes was always risky for bocade's holders.
>
> (Cerro 1988, 333–334)

Neither of them is an objective observer. As we shall see, Cirnigliaro, a politician, extends the success of his own administration to all the 'federalist' years of the Riera government, and Cerro, an economist writing in a year when the bocade was suffering its first 'small crisis' (*La Gaceta* 06/02/1988), was projecting the situation of 1988 retrospectively on the two years of Cirnigliaro's administration. But to arrive at this interpretation, that is, to appreciate more objectively what has been the effective state of affairs, more issues need to be analysed.

8.3 How did the Bocade face the volatility of monetary policy and scarcity of legal tender?

Starting from a general description of the different periods of its life, we shall examine the successive national crises the bocade muddled through (1987–1988,

1990–1991, 1995–1996, 2001–2003). We first divide the bocade's life into three stages, concurrently with the national currencies of austral, dollarised peso and nationalised peso. Then we divide the first and second periods into sub-periods, while the third period is entirely one of crisis ending with the final redemption of the bocade and its extinction. Through such historical analysis, our aim is to understand how the same provincial CC has been able to function in the framework of monetary regimes as different as those of the austral, the dollarised and the nationalised pesos.

8.3.1 The austral bocade (1985–1991)

In the 'austral period', from 1985 to 1991, the bocade was denominated in australes, the national unit of account and means of payments that was created in June 1985 by the 'austral plan'. From August 1985 till June 1987, the bocade was successfully implemented and managed by R. Cirnigliaro who, with a moderate issue and benefiting from relatively decent national economic circumstances in 1986 (Table 8.1), achieved its good acceptance by the population as well as the support of the local business class.

Later on, money and credit shortages led to an over-issuing of bocade at the end of 1987, and then to a crisis of its convertibility at the start of 1988 (Table 8.2; Figure 8.5). This happened as the national macroeconomy was again deteriorating and the national monetary policy, through the Plan Primavera, was trying unsuccessfully to tackle a climbing inflation that would end in hyper-inflation in 1989.

The crisis was initiated by issuances starting in July 1987 after the departure of Cirnigliaro from the Ministry of Finance, issuances that greatly overcame the amount necessary to compensate inflation. His follower, Apaza, made five issuances between July and November 1987 that cannot be considered as simple adjustments to inflation and replacement of bocades out of circulation. The crisis of credibility of the bocade linked to its loss of convertibility started on 23 September when Apaza suspended the redemption of bocades in what was the usual period for that operation. The new governor, elected in December 1987, inherited this situation. In the first months of 1988, with fiscal revenues and federal transfers reduced by the recession (−3%), the government could not ensure the convertibility of bocades, now representing quite a large part of money in circulation.

Responsibilities were shared: the over-issuance resulted from a growing stagflation combined with the tightening of an already restrictive federal monetary policy, the provincial government was facing the quasi total closure of the discount window at the Central Bank of the Provincial Bank, which was simultaneously excluded by the BCRA from clearing (*La Gaceta* 06/02/1988). Unable to rediscount its credits, the Provincial Bank was lacking liquidity in australes. Consequently, the institutional device ensuring the convertibility of the bocade was momentarily interrupted, so credibility and confidence in the bocade were at stake. The market discount rate for changing bocade into australes increased strongly, reaching around 20% (*La Tarde* 30/10/1987).

Table 8.1 Growth and inflation between 1981 and 2006 in Argentina and Tucuman

Year	*Governor*	*Growth rate PIB*	*Growth rate PBG*	*Growth rate CPI % (dec/dec(t−1))*		*Growth rate CPI % (yearly mean/yearly mean(t−1))*	
		Argentina	*Tucuman*	*Argentina*	*Tucuman*	*Argentina*	*Tucuman*
1981		−7.0%	−5.7%	131.3	130.9	104.5	100.6
1982		−5.8%	1.8%	209.7	211.6	164.8	167.6
1983	Riera	2.6%	4.9%	433.7	443.2	343.8	362.1
1984		2.2%	1.6%	688.0	718.5	626.7	629.9
1985		−4.6%	−7.1%	385.0	345.8	672.2	620.1
1986		5.8%	2.1%	81.9	78.6	90.1	100.6
1987		1.8%	3.4%	174.8	184.7	131.3	133.2
1988	Domato	−3.0%	0.9%	387.7	391.6	343.0	350.3
1989		−7.2%	−15.2%	4923.6	5325.2	3079.5	3037.1
1990		−2.5%	0.3%	1343.9	960.0	2314.0	1939.2
1991	Arraoz	9.1%	10.5%	84.0	75.2	171.7	146.2
1992	Ortega	7.9%	2.5%	17.5	18.4	24.9	22.8
1993		8.2%	6.1%	7.4	8.9	10.6	12.1
1994		5.8%	4.4%	3.9	5.1	4.2	5.5
1995	Bussi	−2.8%	2.5%	1.6	5.0	3.4	5.9
1996		5.5%	1.0%	0.1	0.6	0.2	1.9
1997		8.1%	7.7%	0.3	−1.5	0.5	−0.8
1998		3.9%	5.5%	0.7	−0.2	0.9	−0.4
1999	Miranda	−3.4%	−3.8%	−1.8	−2.3	−1.2	−2.1
2000		−0.8%	1.5%	−0.7	−1.3	−0.9	−1.4
2001		−4.4%	−0.2%	−1.5	−0.5	−1.1	−0.8
2002		−10.9%	−8.0%	41.0	49.4	25.9	31.4
2003	Alperovitch	8.8%	6.1%	3.7	1.0	13.4	15.3
2004		9.00%	8.9%	6.1	6.5	4.4	2.8
2005		9.2%	10.8%	12.3	12.0	9.6	9.6
2006		8.7%	10.4%	9.8	11.3	8.8	12.1

Source: Guttierez et al. 2000a, 2000b.

Table 8.2 Issuances and redemptions of bocades under austral standard

Governor	*Year*	*Month*	*Issuances*	*Decree*	*Amount issued*	*Nominal stocks and bonds*
Fernardo Riera	1983/84					
	1985	August	1st issuance	12827/3	10,000,000	10,000,000
		November	2nd issuance	23885/3	188,000	10,188,000
	1986	June	3rd issuance	1126/3	721,000	10,909,000
		November	4th issuance	2808/3	3,500,000	14,409,000
	1987	January	5th issuance	98/3	1,975,000	16,384,000
		March			3,500,000	19,884,000
		April	6th issuance	766/3	800,000	20,684,000
		May			1,100,000	21,784,000
		July	7th, 8th and 9th issuances	1148–1733–1885/3	43,000,000	64,784,000
		August	10th and 11th issuances	2404/3 and 2944/3	27,000,000	91,784,000
		November	12th issuance	475/3	50,000,000	141,784,000
José Domato		December	Destruction (-)		21,784,000	120,000,000
	1988	March	Destruction (-)		5,400,000	114,600,000
		October	Destruction (-)		1,200,000	113,400,000
		December	13th issuance	307/3 or 27779/3	50,000,000	163,400,000
	1989	March	14th issuance	504/3	100,000,000	263,400,000
		April	15th issuance	850/3	76,100,000	339,500,000
		May	16th and 17th issuances	1111/3 1349/3	170,000,000	509,500,000
		September	18th issuance	1989/3	1,000,000,000	1,509,500,000
		October	Destruction (-)		7,700,000	1,501,800,000
		November	19th issuance	2704/3	1,000,000,000	2,501,800,000
	1990	February	20th issuance	505/3	5,000,000,000	7,501,800,000
		May	21st issuance	1135/3	10,000,000,000	17,501,800,000
		July	22nd issuance	1562/3	10,000,000,000	27,501,800,000
		September	23rd issuance	1951/3	10,000,000,000	37,501,800,000
		October	24th issuance	2101/3	10,000,000,000	47,501,800,000
		November	25th issuance	2781/3	50,000,000,000	97,501,800,000
Julio Araoz (interventor)		December				97,501,800,000
	1991	January	26th issuance	24/3	100,000,000,000	197,501,800,000

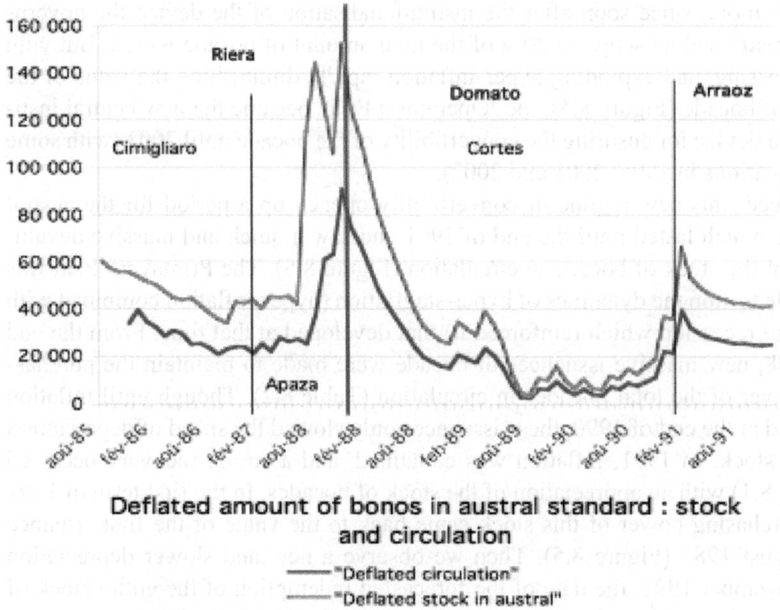

Figure 8.5 Deflated stock and amount in circulation of bocades issued between 1985 and 1991

We can now bring together the evaluations of the period by Cerro and Cirnigliaro, considering that both suffer from symmetrical memory lapses concerning the Riera period: Cirnigliaro forgets to speak of the over issuances of his surrogate in the Riera government, while Cerro forgets to speak of the careful policy of Cirnigliaro.

This crisis did not drive the experiment to an end, thanks to two innovations. First, in order to uphold the circulation of bocades and reduce the pressure on convertibility, a massive substitution of notes of 50 australes by small notes of 1 and 5 australes was operated (*La Tarde* 05/10/1987). Second, a new structural device for the management of convertibility was implemented at the initiative of the FET, the main business organisation of the province. From 17 February 1988 onwards, the convertibility of the bocade was managed in the new frame of the so-called 'Operatoria – FET' (*La Gaceta* 09/02/1988, 17/02/1988, 03/03/1988; *La Tarde* 17/02/1988).

This reform of the convertibility regime was negotiated between the government, business groups, the Provincial Bank and the regional leadership of the CGT (the Peronist Trade Union association). Holders were permitted to deposit their bocades any time to special accounts in the Provincial Bank. As soon as they were deposited, these bonds were usable at once by the treasury; meanwhile holders had to wait five working days before the treasury redeemed them daily in australes to cheque or time deposit accounts from 5% per working day up to 100% of the amount initially deposited.

The crisis was, however, not immediately resolved and lasted about two months more, since soon after the institutionalisation of the device the government restrained its scope to 20% of the total amount of bocade issued. But with time passing, and exploding hyper-inflation rapidly diminishing the value of the stock of bocade (Figure 8.5), the 'Operatoria FET' became the new central institutional device for ensuring the convertibility of the bocade until 2003 (with some modifications in 1995, 2001 and 2002).

Indeed, this new regime of convertibility opened up a period for the austral bocade which lasted until the end of 1991 and saw a quick and massive devaluation of the stock of bocade in circulation (Figure 8.5). The Primavera Plan was not able to stop the dynamics of hyper-stagflation (hyper-inflation combined with a strong recession which reinforced it) that developed at that time. From the end of 1988, new massive issuances of bocade were made to maintain the purchasing power of the total bocades in circulation (Table 8.2). Though until inflation reduced at the end of 1990, these issuances only slowed the speed of depreciation of the stock. In 1991, inflation was contained, and a strong recovery occurred (Table 8.1) with an appreciation of the stock of bocades. In the first term of 1991 the purchasing power of this stock came back to the value of the first issuance in August 1985 (Figure 8.5). Then we observe a new and slower depreciation till November 1991, the date of the forecasted redemption of the entire stock of bocade and its replacement by new ones denominated in dollarised pesos.

8.3.2 The dollarised peso bocade (1992–2001)

As already mentioned, the bocade did not disappear with the change from austral to the new dollarised peso at the federal level. After an extension of two years (until November 1993) in the redemption date of the last series of austral bocades, new issuances were made of bocades denominated in pesos, one peso being equivalent to 10,000 australes and immediately convertible at par with one US dollar. Thus, a new period in the life of the bocade started, the 'dollarised peso period', lasting from January 1992 to January 2002.

When the austral was destroyed by the hyper-inflationist process, the bocade tightly linked to it could have also disappeared, like in Salta. All the more so, since the circulating bocades were to lose their legal value at the end of November 1991. But the governor, contested inside his own Peronist Party, was replaced in January 1991 for the last year of his mandate by a federal 'interventor', Araoz, who declared that the bocade should carry on.

Thus, the dollarisation of the peso did not kill the Tucuman bocade. A rebirth Act – Act 6299 which simply modifies Article 2 of the Act 5728 of 1985 modified by the Act 5866 of 1987 – was prepared by the federal interventor and voted in by the legislative power of the province in October 1991. It authorised the issue of bocades in the new national money which was to be put into circulation at the start of 1992 (Figure 8.6). This Act allowed for new issuances of bocade, without changing their forms and the modalities of their conversion in pesos, considering that they were 'presently well accepted in the market' and only needed to be adapted 'to the new conditions established at the national level'.

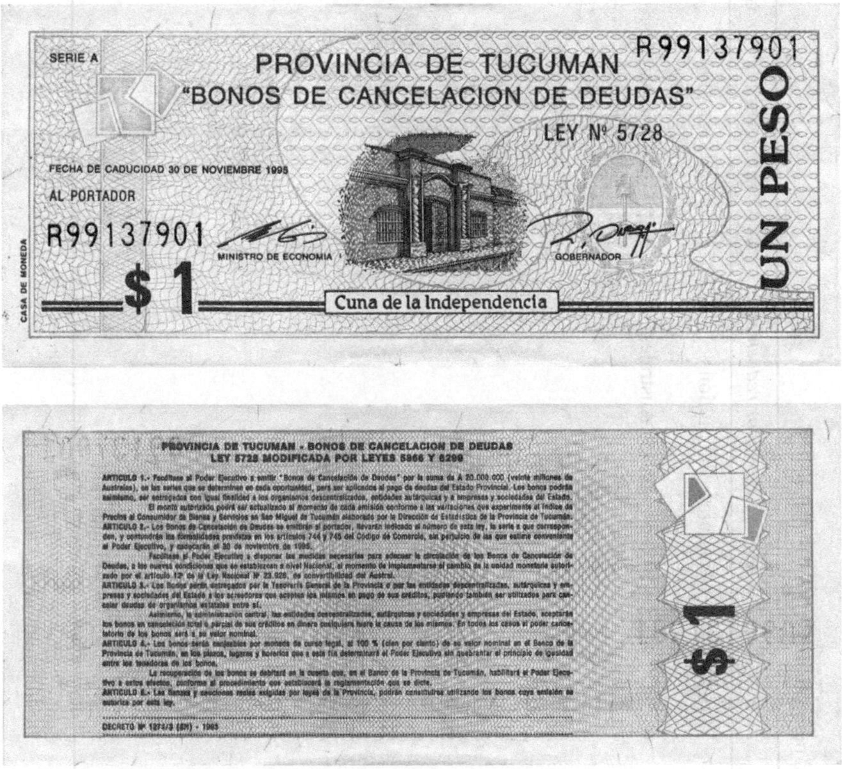

Figure 8.6 The bocade in peso issued in 1992

As shown in Figure 8.7, the monetary regime of the new bocade may be divided into four sub-periods that do not fit exactly with the timing of the three successive administrations of governors Ortega, Bussi and Miranda.

The first sub-period was one of transition and conversion from the austral to the peso bocade, with few new issuances. It lasted till the Tequila crisis at the end of 1994 under Ortega's government. Then in 1995, this crisis was the first challenge to the dollarised peso regime. The Tucuman government reacted to the monetary shortage by increasing strongly the amount of bocade in circulation (to be redeemed in 1999), thus avoiding recession: provincial GGP grew by 2.5% in 1995, meanwhile national GDP decreased by 2.8%, and for 1995 and 1996, total growth rates were 2.7% and 3.5% for Argentina and Tucuman respectively (see Table 8.1).

In this Tequila sub-period from January 1995 to December 1996, the massive increase in the stock of bocade from 30 to 80 million pesos (Table 8.3) did not threaten its credibility and convertibility at par into pesos. In fact, the financial and economic crises were more federal than provincial and the bocade did not suffer any discount vis-à-vis the peso. The North-American economist Harberger, who was observing on the spot and modelling the economy of the province at the moment, claimed in December 1996: 'Bocades circulate as if they were real

Table 8.3 Issuances and redemptions of bocades under the dollarised peso standard

Year and Governor	*Month*	*Issuance*	*Decree*	*Amounts issued or redeemed*	*Nominal stock of bonds*
1991	January	26th issuance	24/3	Australes: 100 million	197,501,800,000
Ramon Ortega	December				197,501,800,000
1992				1 Peso = 10,000 Australes	19,750,180
1993		27th issuance	1274/3	20,256,000	20,256,000
1994		28th issuance	3522/3	10,000,000	30,256,000
1995	February	29th issuance	1176/3	20,000,000	50,256,000
	April	30th issuance	2295/3	30,000,000	80,256,000
Antonio Bussi	December				80,256,000
1996	July	31st issuance	948/3	15,000,000	95,256,000
1997	April	Destruction		−50,000,000	45,256,000
1998					45,256,000
1999	Sept. Oct.	32nd issuance	20/3	30,000,000	45,256,000
		33rd issue	266/3	15,000,000	
		Destruction	212/3	−45,000,000	45,256,000
	November	34th issuance	1918/3	10,000,000	55,000,000
Julio Miranda	December				55,000,000
2000	February	35th issue	2767/3	30,000,000	85,000,000
	May	36th issue	750/3	12,000,000	97,000,000
2001	January	37th issue	7/3	12,000,000	109,000,000
	April	38th issue	1091/3	400,000	109,400,000
	November	Destruction		−400,000	109,000,000
	December	Destruction		−11,000,000	98,000,000

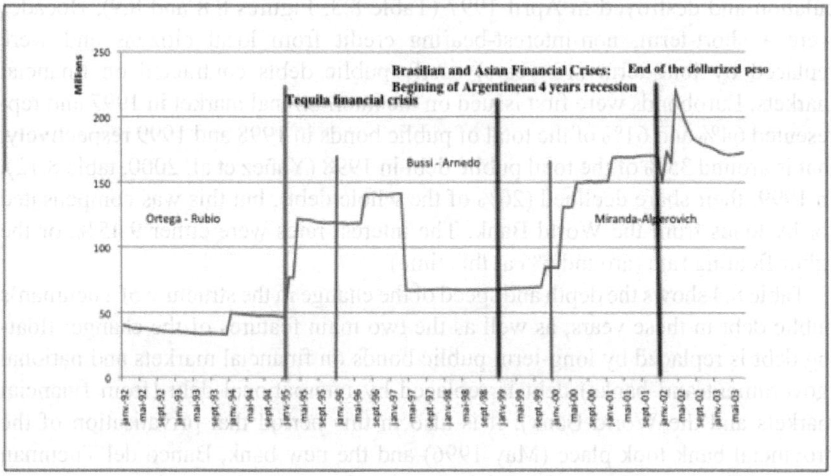

Figure 8.7 Deflated net stock of bocades issued between 1992 and 2003

money and are generally accepted at par within the province (though they are sold with discount outside). We do not observe any significant discount in the local market' (Harberger 1996, 154).

Newspaper articles also inform that the bocade was well accepted in local markets in 1995 (Heredia 1995). 'There is no problem with the circulation of bocades because the Bank of Tucuman redeems them as usual, in accordance to the law' (*La Gaceta* 24/11/1995). Only one article (*La Gaceta* 12/11/1995) suggests that the discount rates were 'between 1 and 10%' and that 'the situation became complicated in the last months as a result of doubts about the acceptance of the bocade for some payments'. In fact, the journalist describes a well organised and costless system. Despite 'Banco Nacion and branches of national private banks' not receiving bocades, at least three private and municipal banks 'implemented the immediate exchange in peso with a commission of 3%', or 'created custodian accounts for deposits in bocades'. Moreover, the Bank of Tucuman, beside the official system of Operatoria FET, received deposits of 50% in bocades that were 'credited in peso in 72 hours with a rebate of 1% for interest', and 'redeemed also the bocades of other banks, with a commission of 2% on the total amount'. Thus, rather than a situation of crises with large speculation this article shows a good integration of the bocade in the local economy. Another virtue is that convertibility of the bocade was a permanent constraint on the credibility of the provincial government, even if the bocade was well received in the local market. Lastly, it gives an evaluation of the costs of transaction of the bocade in the markets at around 3%.

Bussi's government followed the current path during its first year of administration (1996), but from December 1996, after the recovery from the Tequila crisis, he opened up a third period aiming at redeeming the entire stock of bocade and taking it out of circulation (Salvador 1997). Hence, this sub-period represents the first open political crisis of the bocade, questioning its existence through its replacement by a massive appeal to more costly public debt (Act 6796 enacted 02/12/1996).

Thus, 50 million bocade, nearly half the total stock, were withdrawn from circulation and destroyed in April 1997 (Table 8.3; Figures 8.8 and 8.9). Bocades were a short-term, non-interest-bearing credit from local citizens and were replaced by long-term (10 years) costly public debts contracted on financial markets. Eurobonds were first issued on the international market in 1997 and represented 64% and 61% of the total of public bonds in 1998 and 1999 respectively, that is around 35% of the total public debt in 1998 (Yañez et al. 2000, table 8.12). In 1999, their share declined (26% of the whole debt), but this was compensated for by loans from the World Bank. The interest rates were either 9.45%, or the Libor floating rate (around 6% at this time).

Table 8.4 shows the depth and speed of the change in the structure of Tucuman's public debt in these years, as well as the two main features of the change: floating debt is replaced by long-term public bonds on financial markets and national (government and banks) debt is replaced by international debt (from financial markets and the World Bank). It is also in this period that privatisation of the provincial bank took place (May 1996) and the new bank, Banco del Tucuman SA, acted as the exclusive financial agent for the provincial treasury (Clarke and Cull 1999).

Governor Bussi's attempt to get rid of the bocade fell short. In 1999, a new financial crisis occurred in East Asia, Russia and Brazil, depriving Latin American countries of external financing. The Argentinian monetary base was fully dependent on inflows of foreign capital under the convertibility regime, so a four-year long recession followed. Bussi was not able to find new funding and, as national government and banking funds shrunk, he had to return to the bocade. He issued 45 million bocades to redeem those whose redemption was due and added a net issuance of 10 million before leaving office (Act 6969 enacted on 29/11/1999).

The first two years of governor Miranda's government (2000 and 2001) form the last sub-period of the life of the dollarised bocade. As the recession deepened,

Table 8.4 Changes in the structure of the stock of Tucuman's public debt under the Bucci government

Types of borrowing (%)	*1996*	*1997*	*1998*
1 National government	6	5	3
2 Banco Provincia	6	2	2
3 Floating debt	26	23	17
4 Consolidated debt	1	2	1
(1+2+3+4)	39	32	23
5 Banking and financial institutions	32	5	9
6 Issuances of public bonds	18	54	51
(5+6)	50	59	60
7 International financial institutions	11	10	16
(5+6+7)	61	69	76
Total stock (millions of current $)	931	1,001	1,047

Source: Yañez et al. 2000, *cuadro 10* and *anexo estadistico.*

provoking the defeat of the Justicialist Party at the presidential federal election of 1999, the new provincial government, an alliance between Peronists and Radicals (UCR), carried on enlarging the quantity of circulating bocade. Legal authorisations for the issuance of 42 million in 2000 and 12 million more in January 2001 pushed the total stock up to 109 million, which is nearly twice the amount in January 2000 (Table 8.3; Figure 8.7). Nevertheless, the entire stock was not even immediately printed. In July 2001, it was estimated that only 70 million bocades were effectively circulating of a stock of around 79 million, an amount lower than the threshold of 80 million, which is 30% of the total amount of currencies in circulation. This was considered by local prominent economist, Victor Elias, as a limit not to exceed to avoid risking the credibility of the bocade (*La Gaceta* 11/07/2001). In September, there were still only 77 million bocades circulating and 10 million kept in reserve (*La Gaceta* 07/09/2001) but in November their amount reached $98 million (*La Gaceta* 16/11/2001; Beckmann 2002, 3). With the recession, the only way for the province not to go bankrupt was to issue more bocades. The expected difficulties of maintaining the convertibility of bocade at par with pesos, while increasing their amount in circulation, drove the provincial government to implement different measures at the end of July 2001.

Firstly, in parallel to the Operatoria FET, fixed term deposits in bocade (between 90 and 180 days) were introduced for large holders. By depositing bocades at the Banco del Tucuman, these holders could immediately receive cheques endorsable or usable to pay provincial taxes. On completing their terms, holders of the deferred cheques yielded an interest of maximum 12%, and bocades were changed in peso at par (*La Gaceta* 24/07/2001). Moreover, account holders were exempt of the stamp provincial tax. Due to the potential cost of the device, the government was willing to keep it under control by not fixing its different parameters like the minimum amount of deposit in the time accounts ($5000 at the outset), their duration in function of the province's available resources in pesos, and the minimum amount for the deferred cheques (of $500 at the outset) (*La Gaceta* 11/07/2001). By July, 25 million bocades were still, however, estimated to be waiting for conversion to national pesos, that is, 36% of the circulation and 32% of the stock (*La Gaceta* 29/07/2001).

In the second semester of 2001 the crisis of the national convertibility regime was worsening, and the federal government was reducing transfers. Pesos were becoming scarcer at the provincial level (Figure 8.8). Therefore, as seen in Chapter 5, a new wave of provincial quasi-monies spread throughout the whole country and even the national government issued its own CC, the lecop, in order to pay a large share of its transfers to provinces. In Tucuman, it mainly entailed immediate difficulties in the functioning of Operatoria FET (Cirnigliaro 2004, 268). Meanwhile, one of the largest monetary, economic, financial, political and social crises that Argentina has ever known was about to burst and the provincial government reacted with three measures.

On November 15th, the government abruptly increased the term for redeeming bocades to pesos from 35 to 60 days through the Operatoria FET (*La Gaceta* 15/11/2001). The outcome was that the market discount rate of the bocade, which had started to climb slightly above 4% in October (4.5%), jumped

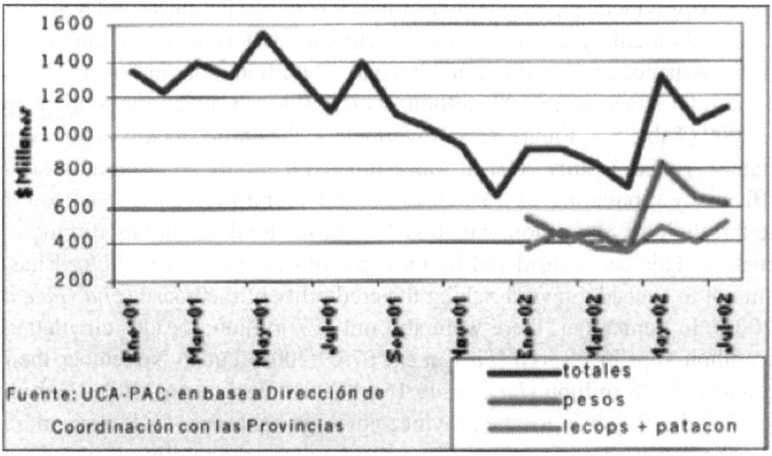

Figure 8.8 National transfers to provinces from January 2001 till July 2002

Source: Universidad Catolica Argentina (2002).

immediately to 7% in December (Figure 8.9) as soon as a preliminary discussion of extending this term to 45 days had been held (*La Gaceta* 15/11/2001). The measure, taken without any concertation, provoked a 'crack' since banks refused to receive bocades, and in the loan sharks' offices, the bocades were exchanged at a 10% discount. Nevertheless, 'entrepreneurs supported it cautiously, asking only for some adjustments and flexibility of application' (*La Gaceta* 16/11/2001, and Figure 8.4).

In December a decree instituted the 'Operatoria Paralela', allowing some companies holding deposits of more than 40,000 pesos to obtain lecops without the standard 'Operatoria FET' delay (Beckmann 2002, 2). Thus, 'between the 10th of December 2001 and the 8th of April 2002, the government changed $41 million in lecops to seven "privileged" firms' (Cirnigliaro 2004, 267–268). In December, confidence in the bocade was also weakened by suspicions about the issuance of counterfeited $20 notes in September (*La Gaceta* 07/09/2001); 11 million in bocades suspected of this forgery were destroyed. A legislative Act was also passed, stating that public and private firms delivering public services had to receive bocades and/or lecops at their nominal values without restrictions (Act 7171, enacted 13/12/2001). Ultimately, the delay of the Operatoria FET was reduced in January 2002 to 56 days (a return to the standard term of 35 days occurred in June 2002).

These measures may explain why until October 2001 the discount rate of the bocade stayed at 4% (or less), despite significant increases in the stock of bocades in 2000 and January 2001. On the contrary, the increases in December 2001 and March 2002 impacted immediately and cumulatively the discount rate till May 2002 (Figure 8.9). Due to massive social unrest, December 2001 was the culmination point of the crisis of the peso convertibility regime, which was abandoned on 11 January 2002. Then a new period was opened, the last in the life of the bocade.

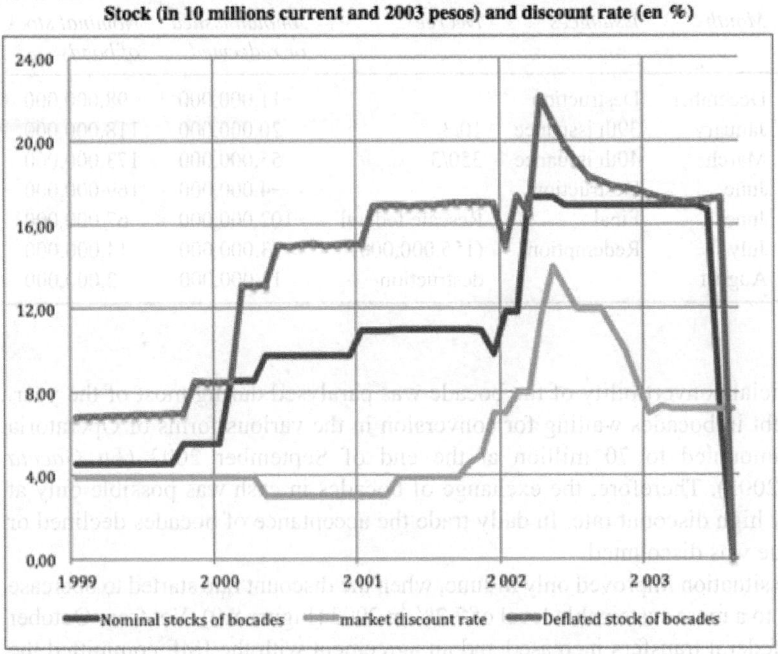

Figure 8.9 Tucuman bocades from January 1999 to May 2003
Source: BCRA 2003.

8.3.3 The nationalised peso bocade (2002–2003)

In January 2002, the currency board regime was broken down and Argentina returned to a nationalised peso and a so-called 'pesification' of debts. In 2002 Argentina was hit by an annual fall in the national GNP of about 11% and a strong devaluation of the peso against the dollar (Table 8.3), accompanied by widespread social unrest, political instability, poverty exceeding 50% of the population and deeply negative redistribution of wealth caused by the 'pesification' (Luzzi 2012). In Tucuman, the crisis was also deep and multidimensional, with an 8% fall in GDP and a 49.4% (Dec/Dec) inflation rate. Unlike the hyper-inflation crisis of 1989–1991, it brought about a crisis of confidence and shook the credibility of the bocade; its market discount rate reached 14% against the peso, a rate never observed before.

As shown in Table 8.5, the Miranda government proceeded between January and March 2002 to make large issuances of 20 and 50 million bocades respectively, which multiplied its nominal stock by 1.77 times, increasing the difficulties in securing its nominal value and convertibility at par. These issuances were justified by the state of emergency inherited from the Bussi government.

Table 8.5 Issuances and redemptions of bocades under the nationalised peso standard

Year	*Month*	*Issuances*	*Decree*	*Amount issued or redeemed*	*Nominal stock of bonds*
2001	December	Destruction		−11,000,000	98,000,000
2002	January	39th issuance	10/3	20,000,000	118,000,000
	March	40th issuance	350/3	55,000,000	173,000,000
	June	Destruction		−4,000,000	169,000,000
2003	June	Final	Rescate federal	−102,000,000	67,000,000
	July	Redemption	(155,000,000)	−53,000,000	14,000,000
	August		destruction	12,000,000	2,000,000

Official convertibility of the bocade was paralysed during most of the year. The debt in bocades waiting for conversion in the various forms of Operatoria FET amounted to 70 million at the end of September 2002 (*La Gaceta* 23/09/2003). Therefore, the exchange of bocades in cash was possible only at a fairly high discount rate. In daily trade the acceptance of bocades declined or its value was discounted.

The situation improved only in June, when the discount rate started to decrease slowly to a more sustainable level of 7.2% in 2003 (Figure 8.9). Yet from October 2002, federal transfers increased and an agreement with the IMF committed the national government to get rid of the provincial CCs. The bocade was now on the way to being killed, a death programmed for May 2003. So, the bocade ultimately did not survive the violent crisis of the currency board regime and its various consequences, but it was not because the device was inefficient and flawed in itself, as proven by its long-standing resilience and support by local entrepreneurs. The crisis of the peso bocade in 2002–2003 was very similar to that of 1987–1988 of the austral bocade. The bocade could have survived this crisis had it not been on the radar screen of the IMF.

As its founder recalls, 'The bocade disappeared at the expense of high provincial fiscal costs, at the requirement of the IMF to redeem these monies because they were ruining the business of the external and eternal debt' (Cirnigliaro 2004, 264).

8.4 Was the Bocade actually useful and successful?

The bocade was a successful device in the sense that it lasted in the long run and was supported by the provincial markets. We also noticed that at the time of monetary crises affecting the federal unit of account and legal tender, it had been mobilised efficiently, despite the weak autonomous tax capacity of the Province on which it was backed, and its correlative dependance on federal fiscal transfers, as an anti-cyclical device and a shock absorber, allowing the province to grow at a higher rate than the national economy. Eventually, we saw that the Tucuman CC regime was able to change through institutional innovations in order to maintain the convertibility of the bocade and therefore, its characteristics of a CC. These conclusions are not based on an extensive quantitative assessment, making them likely to be unacceptable by many economists. This section aims at substantiating our positive assessment.

Usually two indicators allow an evaluation of the quality of a monetary policy: the exchange rate of the national currency into an outside money considered as a stable standard of value, and the purchasing power measured by a consumer price index. In the case of regional monies that is also what has been used, for instance, by Grubb (2008 and 2012) in his studies of the monetary experiments in currency finance in the British colonies which became the United States of America. These indicators are important to appreciate the viability or the resilience of money. But, if we do not assume that money is neutral but impacts growth and debt regimes, the quality of a monetary regime cannot be reduced to the stability of these prices of money. Local fiscal CC are issued with a special purpose, to stimulate the local economy, including non-market production, and reduce the public debt. Their efficiency resides at this level. Therefore, to assess the viability and the efficiency of the Tucuman CC, we have to look into four dimensions.

One, was the bocade convertible at par into australes or pesos in the long run? Two, did the bocade add local inflation to the national one? Three, did the growth of the Tucuman Gross Provincial Product (GPP) improve while bocades were circulating? Four, did it reduce the provincial public debt?

Unfortunately, it is very difficult to answer these questions in a truly scientific way for three reasons. Firstly, provincial data is scarce and often not fully reliable. Secondly, it is impossible to use a contrafactual methodology to evaluate what the specific impact of the bocade on either inflation or growth would have been. Thirdly, many variables, exogenous and endogenous, other than the presence of a fiscal CC, impact the evolution of the quantitative indicators we need in order to answer the above four questions in a reliable way. A comparative approach based on studies of other provinces, those with or without the implementation of a fiscal CC, would be necessary for this. Since there are no such studies, the following evaluation must be seen as the first attempt to sift through the existing data.

8.4.1 Was the bocade at par with the austral and peso?

The discount rate on the local financial market of the bocade vis-à-vis the legal tender is surely a good indicator of its level of acceptance by the public and, theoretically, it is an observable variable. Unfortunately, we lack systematic data on this rate, especially for the austral period. Our guess, drawn from fragmented information in newspapers (*La Tarde, La Gaceta, La Nacion*, etc.), interviews and literature, is that the parity of the bocade with the austral as well as the dollarised peso was effectively maintained in the long run, which explains its resilience. As seen earlier, the discount rate of the bocade deteriorated and overtook the usual transaction costs only in 1988 and 2002–2003. These two crises of convertibility were caused by temporary over-issuance in stagflation contexts associated with stringent federal monetary policies. The discount functioned as a self-regulatory force in 1988 as well as 2002–2003, even if in the last case external actors blocked self-regulatory mechanisms. During the pesification crisis, despite Tucuman being in an unfavourable position as a poorer and less autonomous province than, for instance, Buenos Aires and Cordoba, the bocade did not depreciate as much as other CCs.

The bocade suffered exchange costs of between 1 to 10% in the informal economy, and probably around 3 to 4% in the private banking sector, as documented in 1995–1996. Whatever the exchange cost, it ought not to be taken as an indicator of depreciation of the bocade vis-à-vis the national all-purpose and all-province money. Present shopkeepers incur in transaction costs when they receive payments via different credit or payment cards. This fee is mainly a liquidity discount rate that all credit instruments suffer. Moreover, in the context of growing hyper-inflation in 1987–1989, a discount rate of 10% was less than the officially regulated Central Bank discount rate (Cerro 1988). The same is observed in the period 2001–2003 (Figure 8.10).

Many sources confirm that the public and businesses in Tucuman 'trusted the bocade as a financial device' (Salvador 1997), despite the discount to exchange the bocade into legal tender. As long as the bocade was backed by provincial taxes and convertibility at par, as guaranteed by the Operatoria FET, and with reasonable delay, the bocade was trusted. Thus, given the capacity of the Tucuman government supported by the local business community, the bocade's credibility could have been restored by adjusting its process of conversion at par and to reduce its market discount rate without having to redeem it in 2003.

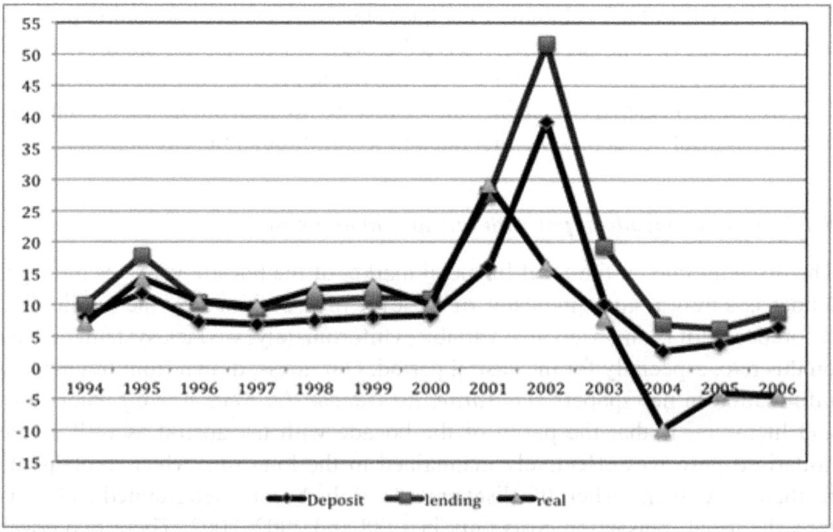

Figure 8.10 Interest rates (1994–2006): real, on deposit and on lending

8.4.2 Did the bocade accelerate local inflation?

For Thomas Greco, an early observer of monetary plurality in Argentina, the answer to this question is a logical 'No'. Inflation is the depreciation of legal tender, while the depreciation of a CC against legal tender takes the form of an increased discount rate. 'For this reason, a regional or provincial currency cannot cause inflation' (Greco 2001, 81). Inflation appears as a complex phenomenon, if we do not endorse the quantitative theory of money. A properly issued, not debased provincial CC may participate in local inflation by enlarging the provincial monetary base. Likewise, if a CC increases the velocity of the circulation of money, it can affect the local prices. Moreover, inflation is not equally distributed in time and space. Thus, the current monetarist discourse on the inflationist character of fiscal CC must also be addressed empirically. Do the theoretically higher transaction costs of monetary plurality really explain the higher price level in Tucuman, compared to the national level (*La Gaceta* 13/10/2001; Cerro 2002, 19)?

The local evolution of the purchasing power of the national unit of account is a complementary indicator of this efficiency. The problem with provincial CCs like the bocade is that inflation or deflation may be massively imported, which makes it difficult to isolate the imported inflation from the local one, possibly linked to local issuance.

For Tucuman, we can compare historical monthly series for the Consumer Price Index for Gran Tucuman (the capital and its agglomeration) with the equivalent series for Gran Buenos Aires, which is generally taken as representative of the consumer price level for all of Argentina. Both indexes are built on the same methodological bases, so we could *ceteris paribus* attribute differences between the two to the bocade.

Figure 8.11 displays the ratio of the two consumer price indexes (CPI), base 100 for both in 1985. We observe that inflation rates in Tucuman and Buenos Aires are generally close but always differ. Prices in Tucuman are lower than those in Buenos Aires after 1991, unlike ever before. Thus, the convertibility plan has had a huge impact on the hierarchy between the two price levels. Moreover, the ratio shows fluctuation margins of about 5%. It is difficult to observe any impact of the bocade on the Tucuman price level. During the bocade's lifetime, we find years when prices increased faster in Tucuman than in Buenos Aires, but also years when it was the opposite. We observe the same type of fluctuations in periods without the bocade. In fact, as shown in Figure 8.12 which displays the difference between the two indexes, the number of years in which price increases are higher in Tucuman is similar to the number of years when the opposite is true. Therefore, it is not possible to conclude a specific structural inflationist effect of the bocade on the price level in Tucuman.

However, it is necessary to consider short-term factors in Tucuman as well as in Buenos Aires that could explain the fluctuations in price indexes in both places. In Figure 8.11, the evidence is not only that deflation introduced by the national convertibility plan has been stronger in Tucuman than in Buenos Aires, but also that the relative price level in Tucuman compared to Buenos Aires

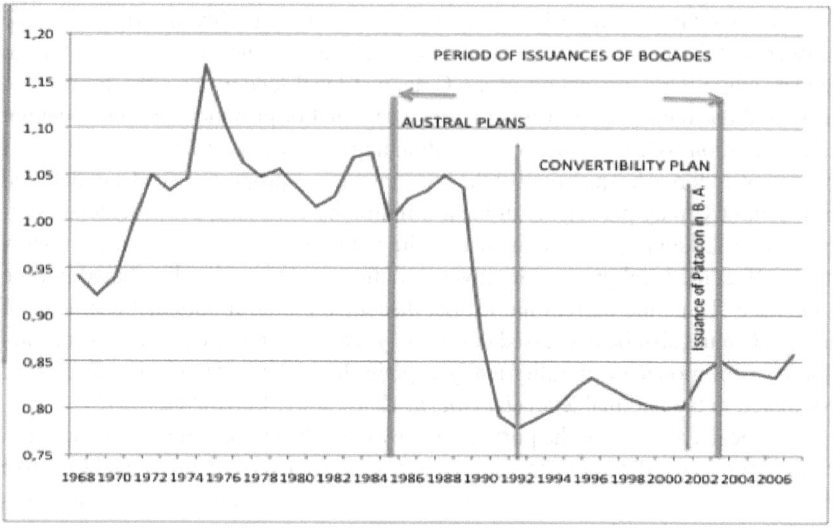

Figure 8.11 Relative level of Tucuman and Buenos Aires CPI

has increased during the three national crises of 1987–1988, 1995–1996, and 2002–2003. During these crises, the stock of bocades grew a lot and reached around half the value of the province's own resources and about 10% of its total expenditure (Figure 8.13).

As in two of these crises, the increase is coupled with the increasing discount rates of the bocade, and it could run contrary to Greco's theoretical reasoning that over-issuance of a CC only affects its discount rate in the market. But the evidence is also that these short-term periods of local overinflation are followed by periods of decrease in the relative price index, which means that the

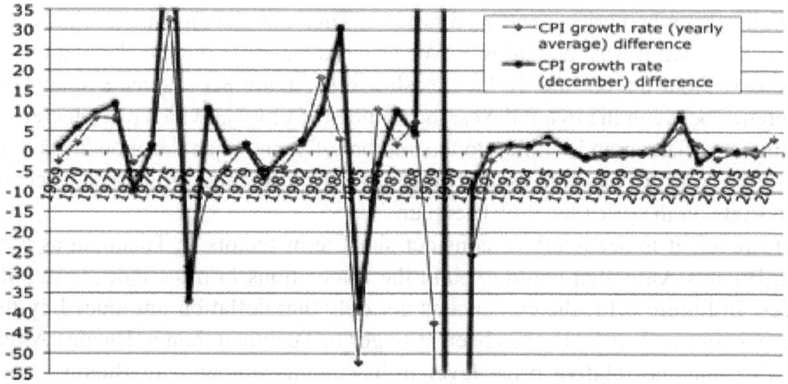

Figure 8.12 Differences between the annual rates of variation of CPI

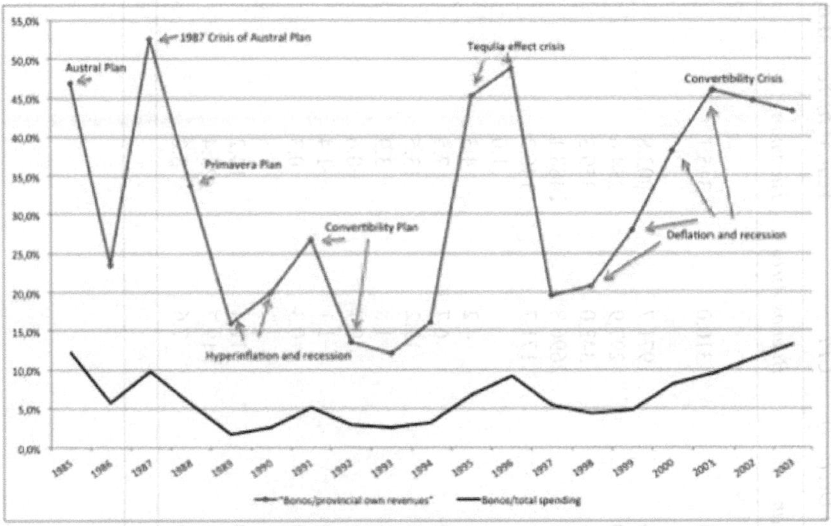

Figure 8.13 Stock of bocades related to provincial own resources and total expenses

bocade was not inflation prone per se. Moreover, the fact that the local response to the Tequila crisis was more inflation prone than in Buenos Aires, but did not threaten the confidence, credibility and trust in the local money, points out that inflation per se is not necessarily a criterion for inefficiency of a monetary policy. As Table 8.6 shows, either with a complementary provincial money (1985–2003) or without it (1980–1984 and 2004–2006), under a threshold more inflation means more growth through time as well as through space.

8.4.3 Did it improve provincial economic growth?

During the Tequila crisis, enlarging the bocade's circulation appeared successful for countering the credit crunch and curving the recession (Table 8.1). Similarly, from 1999 to 2002, the cumulated fall of GDP was 19.5% for all of Argentina, while it was only −13.5% for Tucuman's GPP. If we take only the last three years of the dollarised peso, 1999–2001, the data shows −8.6% and −2.5% for Argentina and Tucuman respectively. If we focus on the Miranda government's first two years (2000–2001), when there were still no tensions regarding the credibility of the bocade, we obtain −5.2% for Argentina and +1.3% for Tucuman. Thus, it seems that, at least for the dollarised peso period, the CC improved the provincial economic situation significantly in crucial times.

But Table 8.6 also exhibits periods with the circulating bocade when economic growth in the province was weaker than for the whole country. Thus, if we want to identify the conditions of a positive, nil or negative impact of the bocade on growth, we have to explain this impact in a more systematic way, despite the limitations in the availability and quality of data, for instance

Table 8.6 Average yearly growth rates of GNP–GPP and CPI by periods: Argentina and Tucuman compared

	GNP growth rate	*GPP growth rate*	*CPI*	*Dec (T)/Dec(t−1)*	*CPI*	*Year.M.(t)/Year.M.(t−1)*
	Argentine	*Tucuman*	*Buenos Aires*	*Tucuman*	*Buenos Aires*	*Tucuman*
Peso moneda nacional						
1981–1984	−2.00%	0.62%	365.7	376.0	310.0	315.1
Austral						
1985–1991	−0.09%	−0.71%	1054.4	1051.6	971.7	903.8
1985–1987	1.00%	−0.53	213.9	203.0	297.9	284.6
1988	−3.0%	0.9%	387.7	391.6	343.0	350.3
1988–1990	−4.85%	−7.42%	3133.8	3142.6	2696.8	2488.1
1991	9.1%	10.5%	84.0	75.2	171.7	146.2
Dolarised Peso						1.0
1992–2001	2.80%	2.72%	2.8	3.2	4.2	4.3
1992–2003	2.16%	2.11%	6.0	6.9	6.7	7.5
1992–1994	7.30%	4.33%	9.6	10.8	13.2	13.5
1995–1996	1.35%	1.75%	0.9	2.8	1.8	3.9
1997–1998	6.00%	6.60%	0.5	−0.9	0.7	−0.6
1999–2001	−2.87%	−0.83%	−1.3	−1.4	−1.1	−1.4
1995–2001	0.9%	2.0%	−0.2	0.0	0.3	0.3
Dedollarised Peso						
2002–2006	4.96%	5.64%	12.6	16.0	12.4	14.2
2002–2003	−1.05%	−0.95%	22.4	25.2	19.7	23.4
2004–2006	8.97%	10.03%	6.1	9.9	7.6	8.2

More inflation and more growth
Less inflation and less growth
Less inflation and more growth
More inflation and less growth

data relative to Tucuman's GPP and the fact that a contrafactual or comparative method is out of reach.

In spite of these limitations, the data comparing growth rates of Argentina and Tucuman allow for a first assessment of the impact of the bocade. In Figure 8.14 we see not only the volatility of the Argentinian macro-economy, but also important annual differences between the growth rate of Tucuman's GPP and the national GNP. As annual differences are either positive or negative, the differences in the medium and the long run are smaller, as shown in Table 8.6. Between 1981 and 2006 we count 14 years in which Tucuman grew faster than the national average, 8 slower and 4 at the same rhythm. With bocade the count is nine faster, eight slower, and two similar, a more balanced oscillation (Table 8.7).

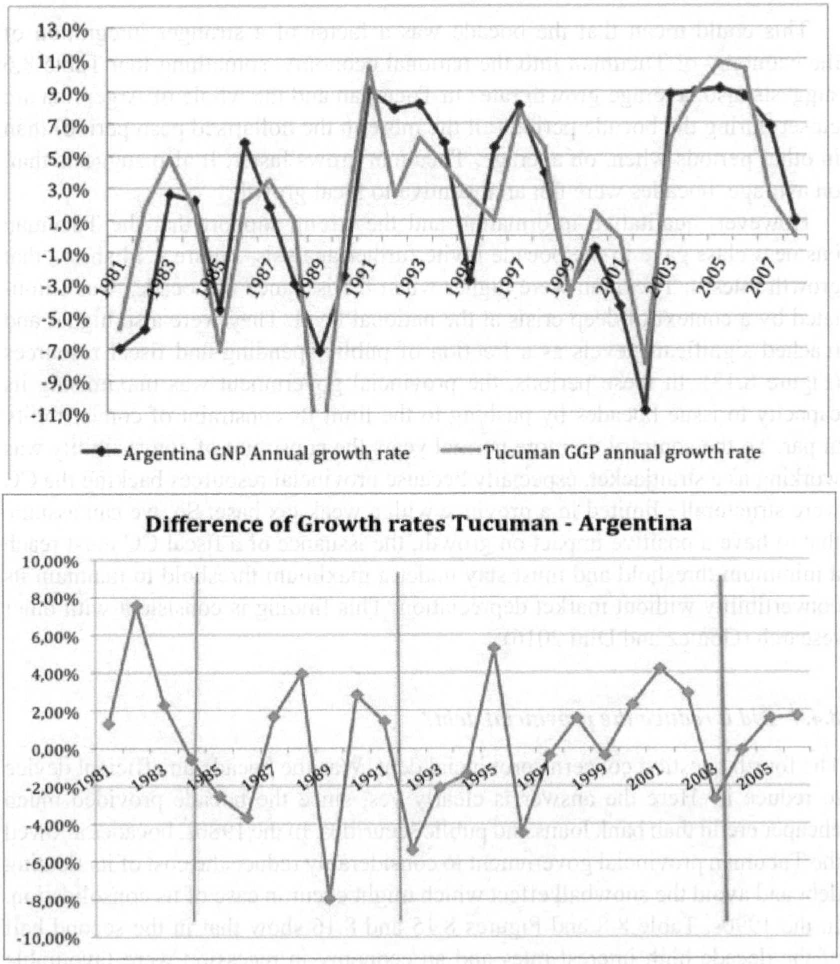

Figure 8.14 A comparison between Argentinian and Tucumani real growth rates

Source: Direccion de estadistica de Tucuman (2006, 2007, 2008, 2009).

Table 8.7 Number of years Tucuman grows faster or slower than Argentina as a whole

Periods	*Positive difference*	*No difference*	*Negative difference*
1981–2006	14	4	8
Periods without bocade:	5	2	0
1981–1984	3	1	0
2004–2006	2	1	0
Periods with bocade: 1985–2003	9	2	8
Austral bocade 1985–1991	4	0	3
Peso bocade 1992–2003	5	2	5

This could mean that the bocade was a factor of a stronger integration of the economy of Tucuman into the national economy, something that Table 8.6 suggests also: average growth rates in Tucuman and the whole of Argentina are closer during the bocade period (all the more in the dollarised peso period) than in other periods when, on average, Tucuman grows faster. It also suggests that, on average, bocades were not an incentive to local growth.

However, qualitative information and the strong support that the Tucuman business class gave to the bocade invite further analysis. Figure 8.14 shows that growth rates in Tucuman were higher when the issuance of bocades was stimulated by a context of deep crisis at the national level. They were also higher and reached significant levels as a fraction of public spending and fiscal resources (Figure 8.13). In these periods, the provincial government was maximising its capacity to issue bocades by pushing to the limit its constraint of convertibility at par. To the contrary, in more normal years the constraint of convertibility was working as a straitjacket, especially because provincial resources backing the CC were structurally limited in a province with a weak tax base. So, we can assume that to have a positive impact on growth, the issuance of a fiscal CC must reach a minimum threshold and must stay under a maximum threshold to maintain its convertibility without market depreciation. This finding is consistent with other research (Gómez and Dini 2016).

8.4.4 Did it reduce the provincial debt?

The fourth question concerns provincial debt. Was the bocade an efficient device to reduce it? Here the answer is clearly yes, since the bocade provided much cheaper credit than bank loans and public securities. In the 1980s, bocades allowed the Tucuman provincial government to considerably reduce the cost of its floating debt and avoid the snowball effect which might occur in case of its consolidation. In the 1990s, Table 8.8 and Figures 8.15 and 8.16 show that in the second half of the decade high interest rates and an economy in recession were favourable to snowball effects and accumulation of public debt. Bussi's policy of massive

Table 8.8 Tucuman stock of public debt (% of GPP)

1993	*1994*	*1995*	*1996*	*1997*	*1998*	*1999*	*2000*	*2001*
5.5	9.7	11.5	15.1	15.6	14.7	16.2	18.8	22.9

Source: Macian de Barbieri (2002), table 1.

public debt contracting, combined with a strong cut in the stock and circulation of bocades, were the cause of a strong increase in the stock and the burden of the Tucuman public debt (Yañez et al. 2000, 18–19). As costly 10-year term public bonds replaced a significant part of the bocades, these were not able to play the contra-cyclical role which they had during the Tequila crisis.

Moreover, in 2002, the major part of this debt contracted under the form of eurobonds was considerably increased by the strong devaluation of the peso vis-à-vis the dollar. Thus, Bussi public indebtedness pushed the deterioration of the provincial public finances in the following years, with payment of interests reaching 40% of provincial public spending (*La Gaceta* 07/09/2002) (Figure 8.15). This was what pushed the Miranda government in 2002 to issue more bocades than it was possible to back by federal legal tender (pesos and lecops) (*La Gaceta* 26/10/2002).

The capacity of quasi-monies to reduce provincial 'sovereign' debt is still displayed in this period, albeit in a negative way. A look at the 1988 and 1993 peaks of the debt burden in Figure 8.16 shows that these peaks occur in periods when there is a relative decrease in circulation of the bocade, which suggests the substitutability between allegedly inflationist quasi-money and public debt.

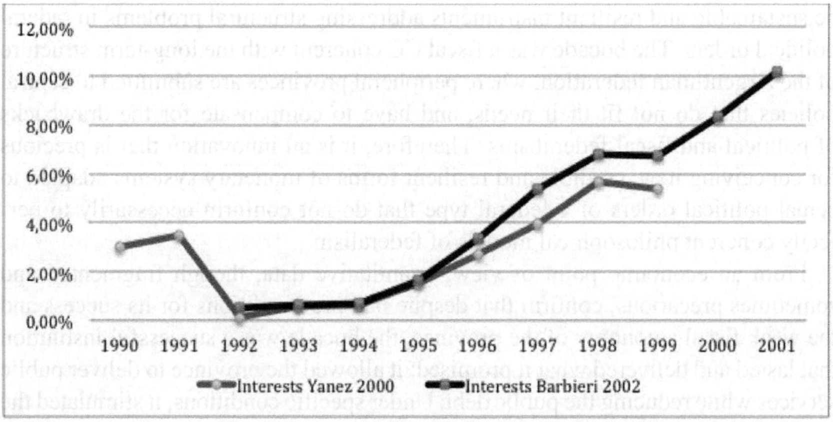

Figure 8.15 Share of provincial debt interests in the total provincial expenditures

Source: Macian de Barbieri (2002).

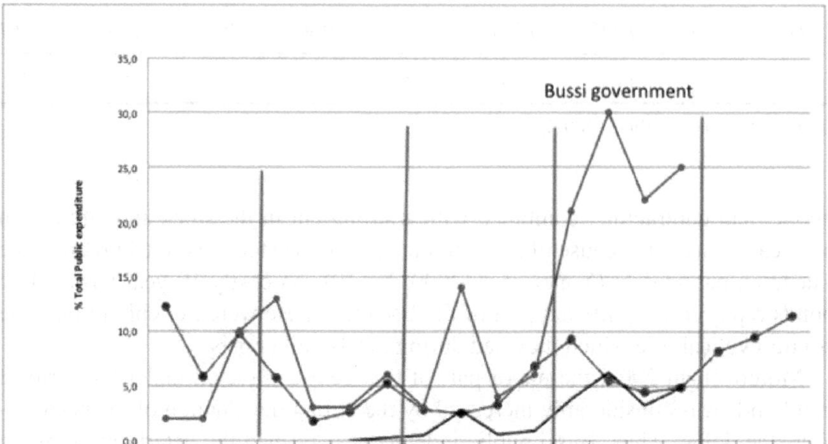

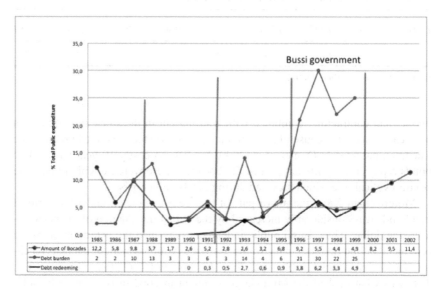

	1985	1986	1987	1988	1989	1990	1991	1992	1993	1994	1995	1996	1997	1998	1999	2000	2001	2002
Amount of Bocades	12,2	5,8	9,8	5,7	1,7	2,6	5,2	2,8	2,6	3,2	6,8	9,2	5,5	4,4	4,9	8,2	9,5	11,4
Debt burden	2	2	10	13	3	3	6	3	14	4	6	21	30	22	25			
Debt redeeming						0	0,3	0,5	2,7	0,6	0,9	3,8	6,2	3,3	4,9			

Figure 8.16 Provincial debt burden, debt redemption and amount of bocades

8.5 Conclusions

Compared to more well-known examples of provincial CCs such as the patacon, which emerged during the monetary crisis of 2001–2003, from a political point of view the Tucuman experiment was important for its permanence. It was not an emergency device and it shows that provincial CCs, under the form of tax anticipation scrips, are not only second best temporary innovations but can also be sustainable and resilient instruments addressing structural problems in federal political orders. The bocade was a fiscal CC coherent with the long-term structure of the Argentinian federation, where peripheral provinces are submitted to central policies that do not fit their needs, and have to compensate for the drawbacks of political and fiscal federalisms. Therefore, it is an innovation that is precious for conceiving new, credible and resilient forms of monetary systems adapted to actual political orders of a federal type that do not conform necessarily to perfectly coherent philosophical models of federalism.

From an economic point of view, quantitative data, though fragmented and sometimes precarious, confirm that despite bad pre-conditions for its success and the weak fiscal autonomy of the province, the bocade was a successful institution that lasted and delivered what it promised: it allowed the province to deliver public services while reducing the public debt. Under specific conditions, it stimulated the local economy without being inherently inflationist and/or depreciated. Moreover, being complementary and contra-cyclical, the bocade has been a factor of stabilisation. It was able to transform large national crises into smaller provincial crises: it reduced the consequences of national monetary turbulences at the local level.

Political resilience and economic efficiency are not inherent virtues to any CC. They depend on the fulfilment of several conditions. Resilience supposes a capacity of the provincial government to build confidence, credibility and trust in the local money, a capacity to forge social commitments, to regulate social and territorial conflicts, and to mobilise historical regional identities as well as to put in action politicians and civil servants (Théret and Zanabria 2007). The long-run resilience, through evolution of the Operatoria FET, illustrates the existence of such capacity in Tucuman. Efficiency in reducing the public debt and stimulating the local economy also supposes conditions more or less hard to fulfil. As we have seen, the impact of the bocade on provincial growth seems to have been limited in time (1995–1996 and 2000–2001), and this limitation was likely the outcome of a 'hard convertibility constraint' combined with a weak autonomous tax capacity of the province.

As suggested by L. Gatch (2012, 22–23) in relation to the tax anticipation scrips issued by US cities in the 1930s, the level of a CC circulation must be maintained between two thresholds, a minimum under which there is no local effect on growth, and a maximum above which the CC is no longer sustainable. Thus, to be perfectly efficient is to be able to reduce public debt without inflation and promote a local economy less dependent on external fluctuations. Federal monetary policy with a local fiscal CC hence requires a minimum mastery of its tax base by the local public power.

Notes

1 The author warmly thanks Alexandre Roig and Miguel Zanabria, the former among other things for alerting him to the Tucuman bocade as a long-run monetary experiment, the latter for nice and fruitful discussions, and for his crucial help in collecting data and building the field research. The author thanks also Guillermo Perez-Sosto and the Casa de la Provincia de Tucuman in Buenos Aires for recurrent support to the field research in San Miguel de Tucuman, as well as all his informants from Tucuman – political actors, civil servants, economists and others – who have helped him to rebuild this tentative history of the bocade.

2 The sources for the data are Beckmann (1985, 2001, 2002, 2003), Cerro (1988, 2002), Cano et al. (1993), Hernandez Meson (2002), Licari et al. (2003).

3 As only a part of the entire stock of bocade was circulating, we estimated the part in circulation from Cerro (1988) for the period 09/1985–09/1987 and by extrapolation for the period 10/1987–11/1991 (using the means ratio on the period covered by Cerro: 60%). Fragments of information in newspapers were also helpful to fix this ratio at 60%. For the period of the dollarised peso bocade we applied this ratio of 60%, which is supported by information from the Central Bank (BCRA 2002, 43). It is likely to be a minimum rate, especially in periods of national monetary shortage, as during 2001–2003.

References

BCRA. 2002. *Boletin monetario y financiero. Edicion anual*. Buenos Aires: Banco Central de la Republica Argentina.

BCRA. 2003. *Informe monetario mensual*. Buenos Aires: Banco Central de la Republica Argentina. Febrero.

Beckmann, G. A. 1985, 2001, 2002, 2003. *Boletin 1, 2, 3, 4 et 5*, San Miguel de Tucuman, Argentina: Centro Numismatico de Tucuman.

Cano, S. C., Druck, P. and Flaja, J. L. 1993. 'Una evaluacion economica de los 'bonos de cancelacion de deudas'. El caso de Tucuman', *La Economia del Tucuman 9*. San Miguel del Tucuman, Argentina: Fundacion del Tucuman.

Cerro, A. M. 2002. 'De la Anarquia Monetaria al Crecimiento', *Indicadores economicos y sociales* 1: 11, 18–19, 31–32. Universidad Nacional de Tucuman.

Cerro, E. R. 1988. 'Estudio Financiero del bono emitido por el Gobierno de la Provincia de Tucuman'. In *Anales de la Asociacion de Economia Politica XXIII Reunion Anual*. La Plata.

Cirnigliaro, R. 2004. *Tucuman– Argentina*. El festin de los caranchos, San Miguel de Tucuman, Argentina: Editorial Kerigma.

Clarke, G. R. G. and Cull, R. 1999. 'Provincial bank privatization in Argentina: the why, the how, and the so what', *Policy Research Working Paper 2159*, Washington, D.C.: World Bank.

Direccion de estadistica de Tucuman 2006, 2007, 2008, 2009. 'Evolucion del Producto Bruto Geografico de la Provincia de Tucuman', *Informe PBG* 2005, 2006, 2007 and 2008.

Gatch, L. 2012. 'Tax anticipation scrip as a form of local currency in the USA during the 1930s', *International Journal of Community Currency Research* 16: 22–35.

Gómez, G. M. and Dini, P. 2016. 'Making sense of a crank case: monetary diversity in Argentina (1999–2003)', *Cambridge Journal of Economics* 40.5: 1421–37.

Greco, T. H., Jr. 2001. *Money. Understanding and Creating Alternatives to Legal Tender*. White River, VT: Chelsea Green Publishing Company.

Grubb, F. 2008. 'Testing for the economic impact of the U.S. Constitution: purchasing power parity across the colonies versus across the States, 1748–1811', *NBER* Working Paper 13836. www.nber.org/papers/w13836

Grubb, F. 2012. 'Is paper money just paper money? Experimentation and local variation in the fiat paper monies issued by the colonial governments of British North America, 1690–1775', *NBER* Working Paper 17997. www.nber.org/papers/w17997.pdf

Guttierez, J. I., Cerisola, J. A., Yañez, D. E, Lopez Cleip de Sosa, A. and Amoroso de Maza, M. T. 2000a. 'Exportaciones y Desarollo Economico Regional. Tucuman (1983–1999)', *Informe Estadistico 20*. Universidad Nacional de Tucuman. November.

Guttierez, J. I., Cerisola, J. A., Yañez, D. E. and Rollan, P. 2000b. 'Nivel de Actividad y Ocupacion. Tucuman (1990–1999)', *Informe Estadistico 23, Serie Investigaciones*. Universidad Nacional de Tucuman. November.

Harberger, A. C. 1996. 'Una vision de la economia de Tucuman'. In *La economia de Tucuman*, edited by V. Elias, 147–192, San Miguel de Tucuman, Argentina: Fundacion de Tucuman.

Heredia, R. 1995. 'Donde reciben los bonos'. *La Gaceta* July 27.

Hernandez Meson, A. 2002. Bonos de cancelacion de deudas de la Provincia de Tucuman. *Catalogacion General*. San Miguel de Tucuman, Argentina: Centro Numismatico de Tucuman.

Honorable Legislatura de Tucuman. Digesto Juridico. Acts between 29/07/1985 and 04/02/2003. www.hlt.gov.ar/digest_main.html.

La Gaceta. 1984–2003. *Articles about the bocade*. San Miguel de Tucuman, Argentina.

La Tarde. 1984–2003. Various articles about the bocade. Buenos Aires.

Licari, J. M., Calgagno, J. C., Oviedo, J. M. and Pellegrini, S. 2003. 'Cuasimonedas provinciales. Medición absoluta y comparada'. Documento del Observatorio de la Economia. Universidad Nacional de Córdoba.

Luzzi, M. 2012. La monnaie en question. Pratiques et conflits à propos de l'argent lors de la crise de 2001 en Argentine, PhD. diss., Paris: Ecole des Hautes études en sciences sociales.

Macian de Barbieri, L. A. 2002. 'Diez años en las Finanzas Publicas de la Provincia de Tucuman, Presupuesto, Gastos y Rendimentos, 1992–2001', Documento de trabajo. San Miguel del Tucuman, Argentina: Fundacion del Tucuman. Agosto.

Salvador, D. 1997. 'Panorama Tucumano. Adios a los bonos. El rescate no admite improvisaciones', *La Gaceta* January 9.

Schvarzer, J. and Finkelstein, H. 2003. 'Bonos, cuasi monedas y política económica', *Realidad Económica* 193: 79–95.

Théret, B. and Zanabria, M. 2007. 'Sur la pluralité des monnaies publiques dans les fédérations. Une approche de ses conditions de viabilitéà partir de l'expérience argentine récente', *Economie et Institutions* 10–11: 9–65.

Universidad Catolica Argentina. 2002. Informe semanal de coyuntura economica 7, August 14.

Yañez, D. E., Cerisola, J. A, Guttierez, J. I., Kreisel de Ruiz, L. and Lopez de Corbalan, F. M. 2000. 'Analisis de las Finanzas del Sector Publico de Tucuman. 1977–1999)'. Informe Estadistico 21, Noviembre. San Miguel de Tucuman, Argentina: Universidad Nacional de Tucuman.

9 Community currency and sustainable development in hilly and mountainous areas

A case study of forest volunteer activities in Japan

Yoshihisa Miyazaki and Ken-ichi Kurita[1]

9.1 Introduction

Since the Great East Japan Earthquake of 11 March 2011 and the resulting Fukushima Daiichi nuclear disaster, the Japanese have become more interested in self-sufficient local energy. Many local governments have focused on the diffusion and development of renewable energy – such as solar, wind and biomass energy – as well as the formation of intra-regional economic circulation. Such efforts were possible only because of a sharp decline in nuclear power dependence and regeneration of sustainable local communities in accordance with the living environment of local residents. Community designs, thus, focus on intra-regional economic development and social ties, while taking advantage of natural resources. The increase in activity at the local community level can generate a multitude of benefits, such as an increase in employment opportunities and non-resident population. In addition, community currencies (CCs) have attracted attention as a tool to support community development projects (CDPs) at the local level. Some places have redistributed revenue from natural energy electricity sales as CCs or have distributed CCs to reward environmental conservation activities. In this way, there is an increase in the momentum of CC circulation among local and intra-regional residents.

However, there has not been sufficient research into the role of CCs and their impacts on CDPs. This study aims to clarify the characteristics of intra-regional circulation systems using CCs. We use a case study on forest volunteering activities to analyse the perceptions and behaviour of both volunteers and CC users. Studying people's perceptions regarding life satisfaction and reward mentality is important because different mentalities have different effects on the sustainability of CC circulation. Based on these findings, we discuss CC's role in CDPs that use forest resources as well as the problems and prospects that accompany sustainable local community development.

The subject of our study is the non-profit organisation Tosa-no-Mori Kyūentai (hereinafter referred to as Kyūentai) based in Kochi Prefecture and the CC issued by Kyūentai called 'Mori-ken' (hereinafter referred to as MK). Our analysis of the CC system consists of interview results and other primary or secondary data in order to assess forest volunteers' perceptions. From 24–26 August 2011, we polled Kyūentai, local shopkeepers and a local bank. We distributed the questionnaire to forest volunteers and local residents between 27 August and 24 October 2011. At that time, we adopted the snowball sampling approach, which is a research method where study subjects recruit future subjects from among their personal acquaintances. The questionnaire has 54 questions on three topics: community living, volunteering activities and community currency. We received 49 responses from 176 people (response rate: 28%. The attributes of the respondents are indicated in an endnote). In addition, data were analysed using SPSS 21.0. Based on these findings, this study attempts to provide a multi-dimensional evaluation of MK circulation, and of the perceptions and behaviour of volunteers and CC users.

The case study analysis proceeds as follows. In Section 9.2, we summarise the current situation, issues and solutions of the hilly and mountainous areas, and also review previous relevant research. Based on the summary, we describe why CCs are needed for sustainable development of these areas. In Section 9.3, we account for Kyūentai's activities and the CC circulation scheme based on previous research and existing literature. We also clarify the significance and features of CCs according to our survey findings. The impact on local residents and the effects of introducing CCs cannot be understood merely by observing CC systems. Therefore, using the findings of our questionnaire survey, we analyse the forest volunteers' perceptions and behaviour in Section 9.4. Lastly, Section 9.5 offers a summary of the results and concluding remarks.

9.2 Circumstances and issues of the hilly and mountainous areas of Japan

A 'hilly and mountainous area', which is the focus of this study, includes flatlands comparatively far from urban areas and inter-mountain zones; in addition, the percentage of forest area and the gradient ratio of land are both high. In Japan, hilly and mountainous areas constitute approximately 65% of the total land area and about 13.6% of the population resides there. These areas constitute about 80% of Japan's forest and approximately 43% of them are used for cultivation, having relatively abundant natural resources compared to other areas (Ministry of Agriculture Rural Development Bureau 2009, p.1). Since Japan's forests account for such a huge percentage of the land, sustainable development in hilly and mountainous areas is a highly important subject in Japan.

Previous research shows three perspectives on the value of hilly and mountainous areas (Niigata Prefecture Nagaoka City 2006; Teranishi, Yamakawa, Fujitani and Fujii 2010; Ohnishi, Odagiri, Nakamura, Ando, and Fujiyama 2011). First, the natural resource based industries rely on land, forests, water and minerals of the hilly and mountainous areas. Therefore, areas abundant in natural resources are crucial to agriculture and forestry. Second, these areas not only produce crops and wood, but also conserve land, protect source water and preserve the natural environment (Science Council of Japan 2001). Third, these areas promote the co-existence of humans and nature. Beyond their specific value, they provide natural resources to urban communities. Therefore, it is important for Japan to sustain the multiple values of its hilly and mountainous areas, which consist of the provision of local foods and natural resources, conservation or reproduction of natural environment and diversity of local culture and tradition.

As these areas face challenges, significant effort and funding are required to sustain them. In particular, the areas' aging demographics and depopulation mean there are fewer forestry workers and volunteers to contribute to forest management, resulting in a decline in forests and community degradation. Under current conditions, the multi-functionality of the hilly and mountainous forest is not being sufficiently managed, resulting in grave impacts on the global environment with regard to CO_2. In addition, it is increasingly difficult to sustain the lives of local residents and community functions. Some researchers have coined the phrase 'marginal hamlet' (Ohno 2005), which refers to local societies where 'hollowing out of population, land, and hamlet' refers to the process they have undergone (Odagiri 2009 and Odagiri 2012). Thus, people are turning toward sustainable CDPs to resolve these issues.

As local residents proceed with the sustainable CDPs, they are obliged to work on problem solving initiatives and alter the flow of human resources, natural resources and money. In particular, they need to think about how they can discover the potential of local resources in order to foster and use them. In this regard, a community needs sufficient funding or money flow to manage human and natural resources in the sub-region. However, owing to the stagnation of money flows, local economies and communities are quite challenged. Therefore, businesses and/or communication must be revitalised and new intra-regional circulation systems built for linking human resources, natural resources and money. For example, 'the intra-regional reinvestment power' as advocated by Okada (2005) has great potential as a policy for changing intra-regional money flow.

It should be noted that CCs have the potential for new intra-regional circulation. Community currencies are defined as a supplement to conventional money not only for exchange, but also for expression of gratitude for volunteering activities, mutual aid or regional contributions within a community. By combining economic and social transactions, community agents create new relationships among local residents and alter perceptions regarding such actions. Considered an intra-regional circulation medium, CCs may promote the circulation of human resources, natural resources, money and information.

In Japan, CCs are distributed as a reward for volunteering and environmental conservation activities and can be used for shopping in local stores (Kurita, Miyazaki and Nishibe 2013). Through the use of CCs by CDPs, local residents show their preference for revitalising shopping districts and supporting volunteering activities. However, it is very difficult to design sustainable intra-regional circulation systems and many areas face challenges in terms of CC circulation flows. In Japan, the first CCs could only be used in volunteering activities related to social welfare and mutual aid (for example, Fureaikippu, Eco-money, etc.). As Nishibe (2006a) has pointed out, this type of CC is strongly dependent on the community and presents its challenges such as shortage of CC circulation flow or community participation. Subsequently, CC coupons have also appeared which could be used in commercial transactions but as Yamazaki (2013) pointed out, this type of CC flows mostly into commercial transactions and may not lead to rebuilding relationships in the community. Under these circumstances, our case study, Kyūentai, has been active for more than ten years promoting the sustainable intra-regional circulation model it designed using CCs in the hilly and mountainous areas of Japan.

As previously mentioned, Kyūentai considers the role that CCs play in achieving sustainable CDPs. This study focuses particularly on how CCs are positioned within CDPs, how intra-regional circulation is designed and how the introduction of CCs changes the perceptions and behaviour of participants in CDPs such as forest volunteers and CC users. By looking at the existing state of these aspects, we can discuss how CDPs use CCs for sustainable development of hilly and mountainous areas and the sustainability of intra-regional circulation systems. In the next section, we provide an overview of Kyūentai's activities and clarify the significance of intra-regional circulation systems that use forest resources and CCs.

9.3 The forest volunteer activities of Tosa-no-Mori Kyūentai

9.3.1 Background on the establishment of Kyūentai

The Kochi Prefecture land area (710,000 km^2) is covered with lush forests: the greatest forest coverage (approximately 84%) in Japan. In all, 57% of privately owned artificial plantations require thinning. However, due to the aging of private forest owners, it is very difficult to sustain forest management. In order to correctly use lumber resources and sustain the multi-functional role of the forest (such as preservation of national land, water resources, natural environment, public health, prevention of global warming) and supply of forest products, woodlands must be continuously managed in an appropriate way (Forest Development and Environment Department 2012, p.1). Despite the abundant natural resources, tertiary sector industry, such as retail and service, is the backbone of the Kochi Prefecture economy. Just 12.7% of all available employees work in this sector. As a result, forest management is neglected. In order to solve this problem, many forest volunteer associations have been established and even the former governor of the Kochi Prefecture has said that volunteers are needed to solve the problems resulting from an emigrating workforce. Thanks to this declaration, the Prefecture staff was able to establish forest volunteer associations. One such association, Kyūentai, was approved as a non-profit organisation in 2003. It had 64 members on 1 April 2013, and its main purpose is to support forest management practices.

The members of Kyūentai have extensive knowledge and experience because they draw on the expertise of professional foresters and the local residents. In addition, supporting members such as local shops, agricultural farms and fruit gardens also assist the organisation. Kyūentai collaborates with forest volunteer associations in Kochi, private firms (Shikoku Bank, Ltd, Mitsui & Co., Ltd, ToTo, etc.), local governments (Ino Town, Niyodo Town, Kochi City, Kochi Prefecture, etc.) and other organisations (National Land Afforestation Promotion Organisation and the New Energy and Industrial Technology Development Organisation). It supports a wide range of activities such as offering technical guidance, financial support and knowledge. Thus, local governments, private firms and NPOs take on forest projects based on the cooperation of labour in Kochi.

9.3.2 An outline of Kyūentai's activities

Kyūentai seeks to manage natural resources properly and to make the community liveable. Its three main activities are: (i) maintaining and conserving the forest, (ii) training volunteers and promoting environmental education, and (iii) managing the forest. In these activities, Kyūentai seeks bottom-up public participation, partly through the aforementioned educational programs and partly through renewing traditions, such as self-cutting and small-scale forestry, thus striving to restore forests and rural areas.

Forest volunteers build strip roads, thin trees and carry the thinned wood. These activities are not only major tasks of the traditional forest industry, but are now also regarded as having multi-functional purposes including protecting watersheds, biodiversity, traditional culture, etc. The Tosa-no-Mori model, which is at the core of the organisation's activities, has three aspects. First, forest volunteers work cooperatively toward forestry preservation, helping forest owners, who very often comprise single-person or aged households. Volunteers effectively thin the forest and carry the wood using light cables and other tools. In addition, the thinned wood is classified as for sale in the market. What cannot be sold is used as firewood, chips and pellets. After necessary expenses are covered, the profit from the sales is distributed among forest owners and volunteers using money or CCs.

Second, people with little or no experience can learn about the significance and methods of forest activities through research, symposiums and green tourism. Kyūentai aims to spread knowledge and skills through training and environmental education. In the past, conventional forestry has been entirely left to specialised workers, such as those in the forestry business or forestry cooperatives. However, non-specialised individuals such as volunteers, supporting businesses and so on now participate in these activities. Kyūentai removes the entry barriers to forestry, thus augmenting the workforce available for maintaining the woodlands. It promotes interaction between volunteers and outside participants through events and visits. The organisation also undertakes projects such as running forest volunteer associations in other prefectures and offers technical support to newly established groups.

Third, Kyūentai has constructed a regional self-sufficient energy system for creating sustainable energy using local resources, such as the lumber from thinning.

Through the effective use of local resources, the environmental burden can be lessened. As a part of this system, Kyūentai established the Tosa-no-Mori Firewood Club in November 2010. In this club, volunteers cut thinned wood to a practical size for household use in stoves or bathtubs. Kyūentai uses these activities to support the reconstruction of regions affected by the Tohoku earthquake and the tsunami of 11 March 2011.

In sum, Kyūentai's approach to forest maintenance is of great significance but their measures are not sufficient to ensure the sustainability and regeneration of hilly and mountainous areas. Therefore, we should note the existence of MK, which is given in return for forest volunteering activities and which links human resources, natural resources and money donated by some local organisations or volunteers, and aids in the sustainable development of hilly and mountainous areas. In the next section, we describe the intra-regional circulation system that uses MK.

9.3.3 Various circulation schemes of the Mori-ken

The key to the success of Kyūentai's activities is a paper type CC known as MK. The design is shown in Figure 9.1. Kyūentai gives MK to volunteers as an expression of gratitude. It consists of coupons given to people who have taken part in activities to maintain the forest (either by donating labour or money). MK rewards both direct and indirect participation that supports Kyūentai's activities. These coupons are designed to encourage cooperation in the revitalisation of hilly and mountainous areas.

The following is an overview of the specific MK circulation scheme (Figure 9.2), which is issued mainly on the basis of funds received as investments and donations from individual members and companies. Giving CC as a token of gratitude for volunteering carries the expectation that it will promote the exchange of local goods and intra-regional economic development. Kyūentai issues them freely

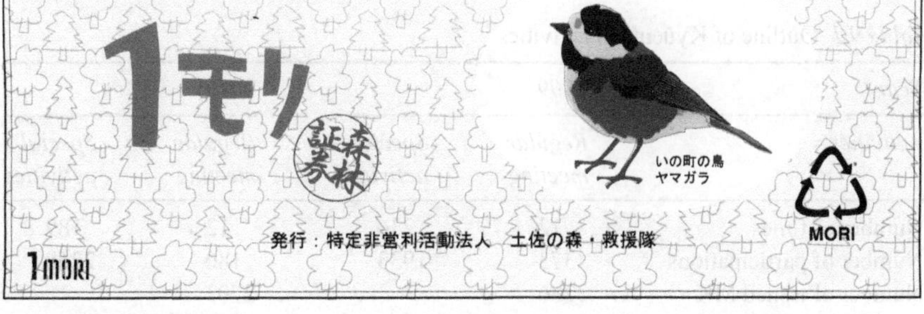

Figure 9.1 Mori-ken

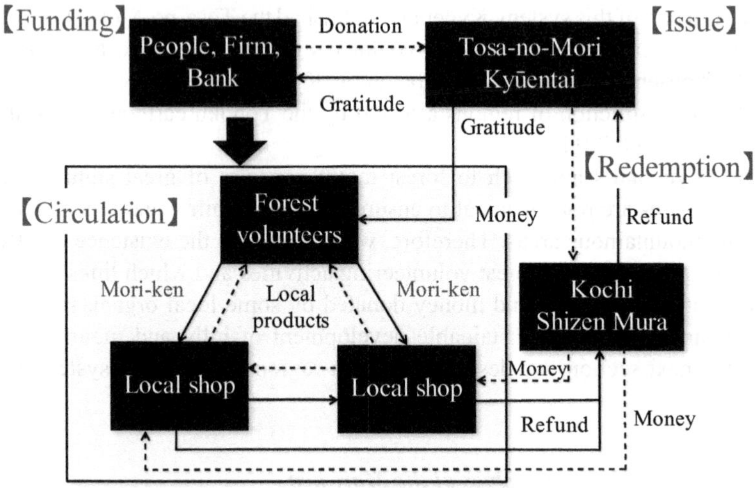

Figure 9.2 Circulation flow of MK

within the limits of these received funds. On an average, 2,500 to 3,000 coupons are distributed every year, with 3,286 coupons issued in 2009 and 2,703 in 2010 (Table 9.1). The unit of MK is 'mori' and users can not only express gratitude, but also exchange one mori for a local product (made and sold in the activity area) priced at or under 1,000 JPY.

There are three ways to obtain MKs: (i) taking part in the forest maintenance of Kyūentai, (ii) taking part in preparing firewood with the Firewood Club, and (iii) funding Kyūentai. MK serves as a proof that people have participated as forest volunteers. In addition, special MKs (coloured MKs), which are issued to those who take part in special activities, can be used at specific gas stations. Forest volunteers can exchange MKs for local products multiple times until the executive office pays them off. Therefore, MKs can be used in transactions among local shops, possibly helping the revitalisation of economic activities of the area, just like CC coupons.

Table 9.1 Outline of Kyūentai's activities

Year	*2009*		*2010*	
Activities	*Regular meeting*	*Special activities*	*Regular meeting*	*Special activities*
Number of times	12	236	12	189
Number of participations	373	1933	180	2268
Number of issued MK	3286		2703	

Source: NPO Tosa-no-Mori Kyūentai 'Financial Statement'.

Ultimately, supporting shops will give MK back to Kochi Shizen Mura (a voluntary association for the adjustment of MKs) or the MK fund and they will receive the same amount of JPY in return. By using MK, users can support local shops, promote local product exchange and reduce the outflow of money to areas outside the region. For example, when a volunteer exchanges MK for a local product that costs 700 JPY, the sellers will receive 700 JPY from the Kochi Shizen Mura when MK is returned. MKs will be given back to Kyūentai through the MK fund. Subsequently, 1,000 JPY per MK will devolve from Kyūentai to the MK fund. As a result, the difference between 1,000 JPY and the price of the local product is kept as a donation to the MK fund, which can be used for issuing new MKs.

Thus, MK is slightly different from CCs or local coupons (gift certificates) and it is recognised as an exchange coupon for local products. This type of CC supports many activities in hilly and mountainous areas through multiple circulation flows. Kyūentai circulates MKs as a way of thanking forest volunteers or the companies, banks and others who support it. Then, the participants exchange their MKs for local products or put them toward local consumption. Kyūentai has taken over the knowledge and skills of the traditional forest industry through these practices. Moreover, it has sustained forest conservation activities, thanks to the interaction and cooperation within and outside the area and has encouraged intra-regional circulation by involving local stores. This circulation is important for the regeneration of hilly and mountainous areas. At the same time, the CC has acted as a medium to connect humans, materials and money.

9.4 Perceptions and behaviour of the participants in Kyūentai activities

9.4.1 Participants' perceptions of forest volunteering activities

In order to analyse the perceptions of forest volunteers (Table 9.2), we looked at life satisfaction, community perceptions and reward perceptions. To assess the status of the forest volunteers, we presented the following question: 'Did you participate in volunteering work?' Individuals answered this question on a five-point scale (5: monthly; 4: once every couple of months; 3: once or twice a year; 2: once a year; 1: never). Overall, 66.7% of the participants were then divided into two groups consisting of those who volunteered frequently or rarely (monthly and less than monthly), and those who never volunteered. In the first group, 45.8% volunteered frequently, 20.9% rarely and the second group consisted of 33.3% who never volunteered. Life satisfaction was measured with a single item question on an 11-point scale: 'How satisfied are you with your life, all things considered?' Responses ranged on a scale from 0, completely dissatisfied to 10, completely satisfied.

Figure 9.3 presents the correlation between the frequency of volunteering and life satisfaction. The descriptive statistics show a positive relationship between the two factors. On an average, people who never volunteer reported the lowest life

Table 9.2 Profile of the respondents

Items		*N (ratio)*
Sex	Male	35 (74.5%)
(N=47)	Female	12 (25.5%)
Age	39 years and below	8 (19.9%)
(N=44)	40 years and over	36 (6.2%)
Occupation	Agriculture workers	4 (9.5%)
(N=42)	Self-employed	6 (14.3%)
	Local government employees	9 (21.4%)
	Company workers	5 (11.9%)
	Unemployment	8 (19.0%)
	Others	10 (23.3%)
Place of residence	Hilly and mountainous areas	17 (37%)
(N=46)	Urban areas	20 (43.5%)
	Other areas	9 (19.6%)

satisfaction scores (mean of 5.8 points), whereas people who volunteer frequently or rarely reported high scores (7.0 points, or 1.2 points higher). The difference is sizeable and highly significant statistically. This analysis is consistent with that by Meier and Stutzer (2008).

Next, we determined the differences in community perception among volunteer activists. Community perception was captured by the following question: 'What is your perception of your community?' Seven responses were possible: 1) A tie exists in the community; 2) Cooperation exists among organisations; 3) Local residents aid each other; 4) Affection exists in the community; 5) It is necessary to activate people; 6) I would like to continue to live in this community; and 7) I would like to contribute something. The responses were rated on a scale of 1 (low) to 5 (high). Table 9.3 presents the correlation between forest volunteering and community perception. On an average, people who volunteered frequently

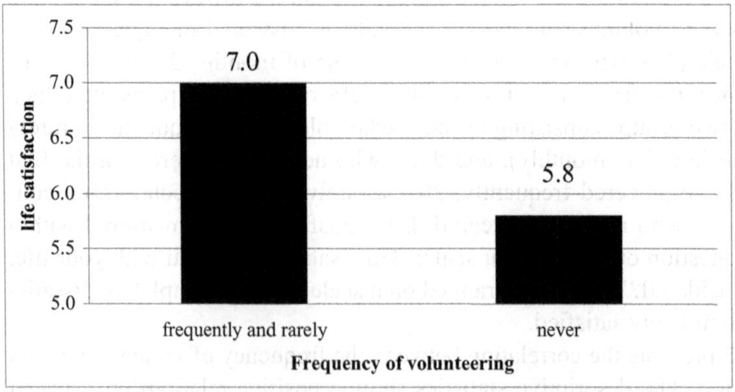

Figure 9.3 Frequency of forest volunteering and life satisfaction (p-value=.054*)

Table 9.3 Frequency of forest volunteering and community perceptions

	Frequently and rarely	*Never*	*Difference*	*p-value*
1 A tie exists among people in the community	3.81	3.57	0.24	.503
2 Cooperation exists among organisations	3.23	3.43	−0.2	.541
3 Local residents aid each other	3.68	3.43	0.25	.495
4 Affection exists in the community	4.16	3.57	0.59	.095*
5 It is necessary to activate the community	3.94	3.93	0.01	.983
6 I would like to continue to live in this community	3.97	3.71	0.26	.487
7 I would like to contribute something.	4.26	3.57	0.69	.008**
N	31	14		

Note: **p-value<.0.5; *p-value<.10, two-tailed test.

or rarely reported high scores on responses 4 and 7, which concern community affection and the wish to contribute. The mean for community perceptions of those who never volunteered was 3.57 points for responses 4 and 7. For those who volunteered frequently or rarely, the mean for response 4 was 4.16 points (0.59 points higher) and 4.26 points for response 7 (0.69 points higher). The differences are sizeable and statistically highly significant. Thus, forest volunteers have high levels of positive community perceptions and involvement.

Finally, we considered the relation between volunteering and reward perceptions. This relation was captured by the question ‘Do you need a reward for regular or forest volunteering?’ Figure 9.4 shows the descriptive statistics. Of those questioned, 46.9% felt that regular volunteering required a reward and 67.7% felt that forest volunteering also required rewarding. In contrast, 21.9%

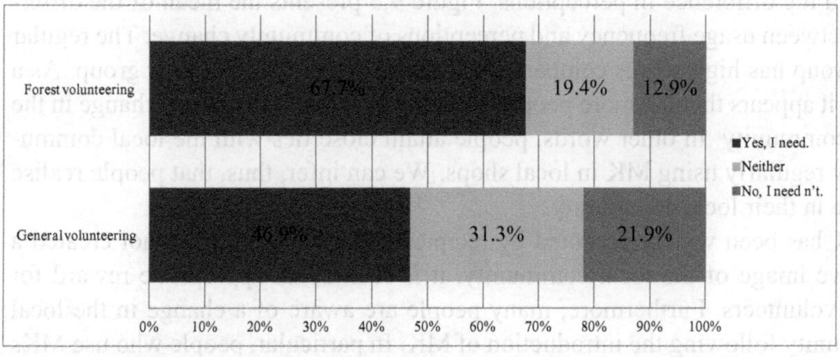

Figure 9.4 Volunteering and necessity of reward

did not believe that the former activity should be rewarded while only 12.9% for the latter activity. Thus, the perceived necessity of reward differed according to the type of volunteering. The time and labour required for forest volunteering are both greater than those for regular volunteering. Therefore, those who engaged in forest volunteering were seen as needing some sort of reward. For this reason, we argue that volunteers need special skills and knowledge to develop the forest.

9.4.2 Perceptions of the Mori-ken User

How do forest volunteers feel about MK? Most respondents answered, 'I would like to participate in forest volunteering more and obtain MKs'. The second most frequent response was, 'I would like to exchange many goods and services for MKs'. In contrast, only one person answered, 'Obtaining and using MKs is troublesome, honestly'. Other research indicates that people have negative impressions of CCs (Nishibe 2006b, p.29). In our study, forest volunteers freely accepted MK. Although it is not necessary to compare these findings, it is important to know if CCs circulate smoothly.

We also obtained MK user responses to the question, 'Did you feel a change after MK was introduced into the community?' The impact was that 45.2% of people answered either, 'Yes, I feel a big change', or, 'Yes, I feel a little change'; and only 16.1% reported, 'No, I feel little change', or, 'No, I do not feel any change at all'. The results show that many people feel that something has changed. However, we couldn't understand the contents of change because we didn't include a question that would provide us with this information. We interpret this finding to indicate that MK support to forest volunteers enhances participation motivation and revitalises some activities, such as natural environmental conservation and regional economic development. Consequently, MK does affect the local community.

Is there a difference between usage frequency and perceptions? People who use MK frequently may have a positive view of its community impact. Therefore, we separated the regular user group (almost every day, several times a week and a few times a month) from the irregular user group (a few times a year or never) and verified the difference in perceptions. Figure 9.5 presents the mean of the difference between usage frequency and perceptions of community change. The regular user group has high scores compared with those of the irregular user group. As a result, it appears that the more people use MK, the more they realise change in the local community. In other words, people attain close ties with the local community by regularly using MK in local shops. We can infer, thus, that people realise change in their local community.

MK has been widely accepted by recipients and because it has not created a negative image of the local community, it is seen as an appropriate reward for forest volunteers. Furthermore, many people are aware of a change in the local community following the introduction of MK. In particular, people who use MKs regularly realise this change. The key to regeneration and sustainable development of hilly and mountainous areas is the amount of MK used in the local community.

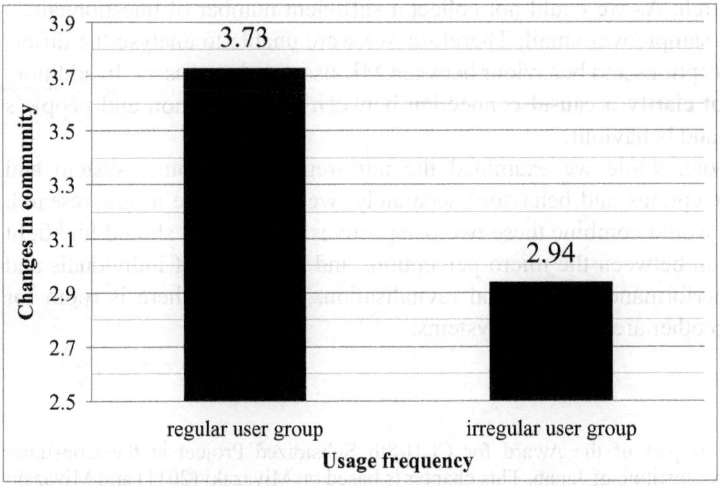

Figure 9.5 Usage frequency and community changes(p-value=.024*)
*p-value<.05, two-tailed test

9.5 Concluding remarks

Thus far, our findings can be summarised with two general conclusions. The first is regarding the importance of the activities of Kyūetntai and the significance of MK. Traditional forestry and forest conservation have focused on how to achieve efficiency in tree thinning and timber production. However, using CCs in hilly and mountainous areas can provide local residents with an opportunity to focus not only on forests, but also on the entire local community. It gives a chance to consider the intra-regional economy and social connections. In that sense, CCs hold great significance. From this research, we have shown that Kyūentai's forest volunteer activities and the circulation of MK mutually promote forest maintenance and community development. One of the outcomes of this research is the discovery of the possibilities of an intra-regional economic system that uses natural resources and CCs.

The second aspect that we have clarified refers to forest volunteers' and CC users' perceptions and behaviour. From an analysis of the questionnaire survey, we have shown three things: (i) forest volunteers have a high degree of life satisfaction; (ii) forest volunteers have a stronger degree of attachment to the community and are more willing to make a contribution to the community than non-volunteers; and (iii) depending on the type of volunteering activities, the need for reward is different. We were unable to clarify the primary factors behind these features in this research. However, as evidenced by previous research, there are differences in perceptions and behaviour between proactive volunteers or CC users and those who are not. Therefore, it is just as conceivable that there is a causal relationship between the degree of perception towards the community, degree of life satisfaction, view of rewards and CC circulation.

The findings show that we need to overcome a variety of challenges to conduct further research. As we could not collect a sufficient number of questionnaires, the research sample was small. Therefore, we were unable to analyse the differences in perceptions and behaviour between MK users and non-users. In addition, we could not clarify a causal connection between CC circulation and people's perceptions and behaviour.

Furthermore, while we examined the intra-regional economic system and people's perceptions and behaviour separately, we now require a new research method that would combine these two perspectives. Finally, we should highlight the interaction between the micro perceptions and behaviour of individuals and the macro performance of regional revitalisation. Moreover, there is room for research into other areas and CC systems.

Note

1 This study is part of the Award for CCIJ-8th Subsidized Project at the Consumer Co-operative Institute of Japan. This chapter is based on Miyazaki (2011) and Miyazaki and Kurita (2012). We would like to thank the Consumer Co-operative Institute of Japan for the grant that allowed us to conduct this CC research. For our field research, we wish to thank the NPO Tosa-no-Mori Kyūentai, local shops and a local bank. Masayuki Yoshida, Associate Professor at the Joetsu University of Education, gave us a chance to do this study. We received polite opinions and kind advice from Masahiro Mikami, Senior Assistant Professor at the School of Business Administration, Meiji University. We wish to express our thanks to everyone.

References

Forest Development and Environment Department, 2012. *Forestry, and Wood Industry*. Kochi Prefecture, Japan.

Kurita, K., Miyazaki, M. and Nishibe, M. 2013. 'CC Coupon Circulation and Shopkeepers' Behaviour: A Case Study of the City of Musashino, Tokyo, Japan', *International Journal of Community Currency Research*, 16, 136–145.

Meier, S and Stutzer, A. 2008. 'Is Volunteering Rewarding in Itself?' *Economica* 75: 39–59.

Ministry of Agriculture Rural Development Bureau, Direct Payments for Hilly and Mountainous Areas. 2009. *Final Report*. Japan: Ministry of Agriculture, Forestry, and Fisheries.

Miyazaki, Y. 2011 'The Vitalization of Hilly and Mountainous Areas and Community Currency – Focusing on the Activities of Non-Profit-Organization Tosa-no-Mori Kyūentai in the Town of Ino Kochi', *A Study of Regional Vitalization* 2: 177–184.

Miyazaki, Y. and Kurita, K. 2012. 'A Study on the Way to Utilize Community Currency Toward the Vitalization of Hilly and Mountainous Areas', *Consumer Co-operative Institute of Japan Research Awards collected paper* 8: 92–111.

Nagaoka City. 2006. *Hilly and Mountainous Area Community Development Promotion Report* by a Collaboration of Various Organizations in the Disaster Area, National land policy emergent survey 2005.

Nishibe, M. 2006a. 'Chiiki Tuka no Seisakushiso', *Shinka Keizaigaku Ronsyu* 10: 337–346.

Nishibe, M. ed. 2006b. *A Report on the Experimental Circulation Project of Tomamae-cho's Community Currency*, Tomamae-cho Society of Commerce and Industry.

Odagiri, T. 2009. *Rural Regeneration*. Tokyo: Iwanami booklet.

Odagiri, T. 2012. 'Rural Regeneration in Japan', *Centre for Rural Economy Research Report, University of Newcastle upon Tyne*, UK: Centre for Rural Economy.

Ohnishi, T., Odagiri, T., Takamura, R., Ando, H. and Fujiyama, H. 2011. *Consent in This! Hamlet Regeneration*. Tokyo: Gyosei.

Ohno, A. 2005. *Introduction to Environmental Sociology on Mountain Areas*. Tokyo: Nosangyoosonbunka-kyokai.

Okada, T. 2005. *Introduction to Economics for Regional Regeneration*. Tokyo: Jititai Kenkyusha.

Science Council of Japan. 2001. *Evaluation of Multifunctionality of Forest and Agriculture Related to the Global Environment and Human Life*.

Teranishi, S. Yamakawa, T., Fujitani, T. and Fujii, K. 2010. 'Natural Resource-Based Economies and Rural Sustainability', *Journal of Rural Planning* 29 no.1: 29–35.

Yamazaki, S. 2013. *Community Currency as a Tool of Regional Revitalization*. Osaka, Japan: Osaka Municipal University Press.

URLs (All accessed June 14, 2013)

Tosa-no-Mori Kyūentai: http://mori100s.exblog.jp/.

Digi-Mori.com: www.digi-mori.com/.

ShimantoTsusin: http://kawauso100.exblog.jp/.

Satoyama's Bar: http://washinosat.exblog.jp/.

Ministry of Agriculture, Forestry, and Fisheries: www.maff.go.jp/.

10 Sustainable territorial development and monetary subsidiarity

Marie Fare

10.1 Introduction

Since 1992, the local dimension of sustainable development has featured in the different versions of Agenda 21 calling for local governments to implement projects based on the principles of sustainable development using participatory process (Report of the United Nations Conference on Environment and Development, 1992). Such actions are materialised, for example, in development of public transport, building of energy-saving homes, inclusion of social and environmental criteria in government procurement, education on sustainable development, advances in environmentally friendly means of transport, etc. Alongside this, citizens' initiatives seek to address the issues of sustainable development through economic and social changes at local level. 'Transition Towns' (Hopkins, 2008) implement concrete initiatives to meet the challenges of climate change and peak oil by improving the resilience of local communities. Resilience is an area's capacity to cope with and respond to outside shocks. The concept was popularised by Rob Hopkins (2008) and is widely used by the Transition Towns movement as a basis for its actions (Folke et al., 2002; Olsson, 2003; Walker et al., 2004). Part of these emerging local initiatives involves complementary or community currencies (CCs) since they try to provide a local basis for socio-economic activities by developing social interactions among members through the activation of various forms of proximity. The territorial optic of sustainable development underscores the capacity of local actors to impel a dynamic endogenous sustainable development as part of a bottom-up approach.

These currencies are intended to provide the requisite framework for developing the exchange of services, goods or knowledge. These frameworks are organised by and for communities through an ad hoc currency scheme, for which accounts can be maintained and settlements made using an internal currency (Blanc, 2006). From this perspective, money is understood as a fundamental social institution of any society, not just the markets (Aglietta and Orléan, 1982, 1995 and 1998; Blanc, 2000; Théret, 2007).

The approach taken here is a crosswise one, that is, instead of using the standard three-way (economic, social and environmental) division of sustainable development, the three shall be interwoven so that the potential of the various CC schemes can be studied in terms of sustainable development around three analytical criteria: territorialisation of activities, stimulation of exchange and transformation of practices and social representations. Money seldom figures among the transition tools or projects for economic reform that can promote more sustainable development. In what circumstances can CCs advance the transition towards sustainable territorial development? It is assumed that this implies determining the conditions of their insertion in territorial projects and their articulation with other tools and mechanisms of transition, on the one hand, and their scale of action and the way they are established on the other hand. In this article we will concentrate on the second point which will lead us to develop a monetary scheme grounded in monetary subsidiarity. In this perspective, each currency circulating as a complementary currency on an infra-national scale involves a monetary use and level of circulation that are socio-economically and geographically defined, or in other words, a spatio-socio-economic sphere of use. Subsidiary currencies attempt to democratically implement a special-purpose currency at each relevant level and at the best decision-making level at which to achieve the objectives ascribed to them.

First, we develop the three potentials of CCs which we have identified with respect to the challenges of sustainable territorial development and the findings of empirical surveys conducted using a socio-economic approach (part 1). Then we show that deploying these currencies might activate their monetary complementarity by mobilising the principle of monetary subsidiarity (part 2). Finally we propose a subsidiary monetary scheme for increasing the capacity of CCs to promote the transition towards sustainable territorial development by focusing on two territorial scales of action: the local (urban districts or rural localities) and the bioregional scales (part 3).

10.2 CCs' potential with respect to the challenges of transition to sustainability in contemporary societies

In order to evaluate the potential and the impact of CC schemes, we have constructed a framework for evaluation combining sustainable development and territorial economies. This evaluative framework, which is constructed from field surveys of the SOL and the Accorderie schemes, covers three potentialities of CCs with respect to the challenges of sustainable territorial development: territorialisation of economic, social and political activities; stimulation of exchange; and transformation of social practices and representations (Fare, 2011a). These three potentialities are developed next and then we present the main results of the empirical surveys conducted.

10.2.1 The territorial challenges of CCs

Territorialisation of activities

By creating a community based on the use of the currency, some CCs schemes trigger spatial and socio-economic proximities (Pecqueur and Zimmermann,

2004; Bouba-Olga and Grossetti, 2008), which generate cooperation processes. In these cases, the networking of actors via a bottom-up approach promotes the emergence of a community of solidarity potentially able to generate a programming process for sustainable territorial development. Indeed, the monetary design, selected through collective decision making, depends on the development jointly defined and adopted by the community to meet the identified needs. In this regard, the territorialisation of activities is a process that stems from the active construction by the territory's actors.

Furthermore, when CCs facilitate social inclusion, via the active participation of their members and the implementation of participatory practices, they help to promote governance that is both collective and territorial. By affecting learning and strengthening citizenship, they are thought to contribute to developing the appropriation of the territory by citizens. The positive externalities involve promoting the development of territorial governance based on a common project: sustainable territorial development. The CCs schemes are thereby thought to lay the foundations for territorial governance, renewed by the existence of a 'spillover effect' (Colletis et al., 2005) of the systems towards territories through the contributions they make to territorial dynamics.

Finally, as their use is confined to a space for circulation, CCs promote the territorialisation of economic activities and therefore endogenous territorial development. The use of CCs is geographically limited, increasing consumption inside the neighbourhood and therefore circulates at the local level, creating resources in the community.

Stimulation of exchange

The second objective of CCs regarding sustainable territorial development is to stimulate exchange. The territorialisation of activities should mechanically lead to more dynamic exchange within the CC scheme. Restricting the use of internal money to territorial level, internal exchange should increase in volume and so generate increased internal activity by multiplier effect. However, the outcome is not necessarily an overall increase in exchange, since internal exchange may simply substitute for external exchange. Various factors that stimulate exchange can be identified. First of all, stimulation varies with the scope of the scheme, which is dependent on the diversity of the stakeholders in the scheme and also on the diversity of transactions. Indeed, the more actors there are in the scheme and the more varied they are, the more likely it is that there will be a high and strong level of exchange. There are size effects (minimum and maximum) and effects from the diversity of actors, which depend on the type of scheme.

Secondly, the implementation of mechanisms to promote monetary circulation (automatic open access to credit or solidarity microcredit) or discouraging asset money (demurrage) is intended to stimulate local exchange. Credit allocated for the creation of local activities allows local circuits to be created. Exchange can also be stimulated by reinforcing social inclusion by proposing additional means of solvency to individuals through microcredit or mutual credit.

Transformation of practices, lifestyles and social representations

The third potentiality of CCs in terms of sustainable development relates to the change in practices, lifestyles and social representations. The creation of a CC is said to bring about new practices by transforming values and representations as well as orienting lifestyles and forms of consumption and production in a more sustainable direction. These practices, in this context, supposedly become vehicles of transformation or even of complete breaks with the growth model. Sustainable development requires changes in both daily practices and social representations. The Brundtland Report emphasises the need for 'changes in attitudes, in social values, and in aspirations' (WCED, 1987).

By de-constructing social representations, by heightening awareness of the challenges of sustainable development, and by setting up new socio-economic relations and new consumer practices, CCs might have a direct impact on the emergence of a form of ecological citizenship. Here we shall question their capacity to bring about the emergence of a new paradigm of sustainable development and therefore their capacity to affect broader changes through innovative solutions.

10.2.2 Findings of empirical studies of the Accorderie and the SOL Alpin schemes

In the late 1990s in Quebec, two organisations, the Caisse d'économie solidaire Desjardins and the Fondation St-Roch de Québec, began thinking about the fight against poverty and exclusion, leading to the creation of the Accorderie in the autumn of 2001. The Accorderie combines a time-based system of exchange in services, a social lending scheme and a centralised buying organisation (Fare, 2009–2010). It is intended to forge ties within the community and to allow people on low incomes to better their socio-economic lot by promoting new forms of social cohesion. It has opted for scriptural mutual credit money. Each participant or Accordeur has a 'time account' to keep track of outgoings (services received) and income (services rendered). The aggregate balance of all accounts is always zero. The currency does not exist before exchange but it is consubstantial with it.

The SOL was tried out from 2005 onwards in three regions of France (Ile de France, Nord-Pas-de-Calais and Bretagne) broken down into experimental areas and then in five regions (by adding Alsace and Rhône-Alpes). The experimental version of the SOL (Fare, 2011b) has three aspects: the eco SOL, time SOL and dedicated SOL. The eco SOL is similar to standard loyalty card systems but is aimed at organisations that share ecological and social values with respect to sustainable development. 'Consum-actors' collect SOL on their electronic cards when they make purchases in shops that have joined the SOL circuit or when they engage in collective or responsible actions. These points are then used for future purchases from the same outlets, which accept SOL in full or part payment of their goods or services. The two lesser developed aspects of SOL in the area of experiment are time (SOL is designed essentially to develop and enhance the exchange of time among participants) and dedicated SOL (which is the SOL distributed by local authorities, work committees, local social action centres called Centres Communaux d'Action Sociale, CCAS, or any other organisation as part of social policies aligned with the SOL project objectives). The SOL studied in the 2010–2011 survey is in the area of Grenoble, known as the SOL Alpin. Since 2011, the SOL has grown in scope with the development of what might be characterised as a 'neo-SOL' scheme the earliest example of which is the SOL Violette developed in Toulouse after a long preparatory participatory process initiated by the city council and non-profit organisations.

Territorialisation of activities, stimulation of exchange, transformation of social practices and representations: these three dimensions also contain the seeds of a project for social change. CCs bring together local actors and invite users to own economic, social, political and environmental issues. The subject of study was constructed first of all by collecting empirical data. This major empirical input is essential to an understanding of social reality in a socio-economic perspective. The choices imply taking a comprehensive approach by starting from observable monetary practices and by using empirical evidence to formulate and enhance theoretical concepts. The empirical corpus is made of practical observations, a documentary study, semi-directed interviews of the actors involved and questionnaire results. Our surveys (Fare, 2011a; 2012) reveal that the Accorderie has created a local community based on reciprocity and giving, with the use of a common currency as its medium. The working rules of the group (charter, code of ethics) allow exchange regulation. Individual behaviour should be adapted to the established guiding principles; the economy is submitted to reciprocity. In this way, a gift does not necessarily mean an absence of interest, on condition that it does not conflict with the collective, the community (Mauss, 1993). Solidarity development represents the most popular reason to join the Accorderie (94.8% of interviewees) while 93.5% of people believed that it provides an alternative to the notion of profit. Hence, the Accorderie would allow strengthening local solidarities by building a socio-economic solidarity network.

This community fights against exclusion and poverty by providing additional means of solvency for its members, not just through access to mutual and free credit but also through interdependent credit. Indeed, 41.8% of interviewees used to pay someone in order to obtain the service before joining the Accorderie. Thanks to the Accorderie, they save money (for 81.1% of interviewees) and gain purchasing power (69.5% obtain services that they couldn't afford to buy). It is a locus for integration and socialisation but also for personal value enhancement. The Accorderie also promotes more sustainable ways of life and 'ecological citizenship' by promoting the sharing of goods and sustainable consumption. In this way, 88% of interviewed people consider that the Accorderie encourages recycling and sharing of goods and 87.9% believe that the Accorderie guides to more sustainable consumption and production modes. If 86.7% of those interviewed believe that the Accorderie enhances a more environment respectful society, it is thanks to the fact that it organises awareness raising events around social or environmental topics (screening of films on MGO, environment, food, currency, etc; workshops on responsible consumption, recycling, compost, seed production, etc). 62.1% of Accordeurs consider that the Accorderie has given them access to higher quality nutrition and 74.2% believe that they consume in the most environmentally respectful way or consume less (56.6%). It transforms social representations by enhancing individual skills through the introduction of egalitarian principles, which makes the principle of intra-generational and inter-generational equity at the core of sustainable development easier to understand. First, the Accorderie accounting in hours allows the instauration of new practices by changing conventional economy rules. This allows the development of ethical values such as equality and solidarity as well as the reconsideration of the value of work and wealth.

The Accorderie provides visibility to activities and competences not accounted for in conventional economy such as household activities or voluntary work. It imposes a strict equality principle, that is, an hour equals an hour independent of the activity or social status of the person. This is a fundamental value of the Accorderie which has a totally inflexible position on the negotiation of currency value. This principle, aiming to recognise the social contribution capacities of everyone, is generally well seen by members of the Accorderie. In this way 96.4% of interviewed people consider that the Accorderie recognises everyone's capacities; 91.9% say that it fosters other values such as equality and solidarity; 79.6% think that it values competences and knowhow, which are ignored by the real economy.

The SOL Alpin has potential with respect to the territorialisation of activities, the stimulation of commerce and the transformation of practices, but its limited scope is a considerable handicap. Although it has promoted sustainable consumption by rewarding consumers for going to shops which abide by sustainable criteria, it has failed to extend beyond niche actors who were already aware of the issues of sustainable development and social economy, therefore failing to increase trade within its sphere. Furthermore, 60.8% of interviewed SOL members consider that their exchanges within the network have substituted a purchase to a national or international enterprise. Hence, there would be a clear effect of re-orientation towards the local economy. 92.5% believe that they contribute to the re-localisation of economy thanks to SOL while 92.3% say that SOL enhances short chains. If these effects, in terms of perception, seem to meaningfully affect localised exchanges, the weakness of SOL exchanges limits their scope notably due to the lack of partner structures. Consequently, there has been seen to be an absence of any dynamic collective appropriation and a genuinely interdependent community. It was more of a market instrument where the commitment was materialised in individual consumption. The act of buying embodies the engagement.

In fact, 89.9% of SOL members view themselves as consumer-actors ('consom-acteur' in French). They do not see themselves necessarily as partners of the SOL network construction, but their engagement is essentially framed by their consumption. From a quantitative point of view, almost half of the interviewees (45.6%) use their SOL card to buy only a few times during the year and 27.8% never. Two explanations seem to be behind this weak use. Firstly, some people join the network due to cognitive proximity (affinity) and then because of different reasons, which can be linked to a geographic distance to businesses in the network, they will rarely or never use their card. Secondly, the lack of supply inside the network seems to be an important explanation for the weakness in exchange. In fact, the SOL Alpin counts 620 SOL active members (i.e. possessing an active card) for 1000 distributed cards and 22 suppliers. For the 91.7% of those interviewed, the product range is too limited and 98.9% wish that the network develops. This is confirmed by the amount of exchanges in SOL of which 76.6% are lower than 100 euros a year and 58.5% lower than 30 euros a year. Total expenses in SOL are insignificant. One way to boost its impact would be to develop the dedicated SOL and time SOL aspects so as to facilitate relations among members, to foster a greater diversity of stakeholders and to develop its collective dimensions (governance, community, etc).

The deconstruction of representation is rooted first in better visibility of the Social and Solidarity Economy (SSE) and sustainable development practices. Indeed, the items aiming to change representations and global society are the best motivation to join the network: 92.5% of members interviewed think that SOL enhances another vision of development, 90.9% consider that it puts into practice an ideal based on values different from the capitalist market economy and 81.8% believe SOL is a label for the SSE and sustainable development. For businesses, this should help them to gain client loyalty. Nevertheless, this loyalty effect remains marginal given the few number of structures and members as well as the lack of legibility of the SOL. The SOL has probably suffered from a lack of local appropriation related to centralised governance in the experimental phase and the lack of diversity of organisations has failed to help members make a habit of using the card. It did, however, highlight alternative economic options and positively impact social representations. The new perspectives opened up by the introduction of the SOL Violette in Toulouse with the development of a paper SOL (voucher), a far higher number of service providers and local participatory governance of the SOL heralds a new dynamic.

Through the analysis of the different examples of CCs and their potentialities, we think they can be tools for sustainable development provided that the relevant conditions for their implementation and scale of action are determined. The diversity of schemes makes it possible to think about the possible complementarity of currencies so as to satisfy the objectives of sustainable territorial development. They seem to contain the seeds of societal change by proposing to re-think the economic system bottom-up.

10.3 Activating monetary complementarity through monetary subsidiarity

The findings of empirical studies and the review of literature underscore the need to understand a multiple monetary scheme given that CCs each promote one or more objectives and do not come into play at the same level (various degrees of local scales). It is possible to achieve specific objectives set by stakeholders through mobilising appropriate organisational choices and monetary forms

(Blanc, 2009b). We propose leads in terms of monetary plurality and even monetary subsidiarity (Fare, 2011a). This section therefore seeks to be prospective and will try to determine the currency arrangement capable of serving the transition towards a new paradigm, that of sustainable territorial development.

While beginning with an approach addressing monetary complementarity developed by Blanc (2008; 2009a), we shall try to go beyond it to pave the way for an approach in terms of monetary subsidiarity (Fare, 2011a) by which the scale of implementation and the objectives assigned to CCs can be brought together.

In orthodox approaches, money is a generalised means of payment. Supposedly money is homogeneous. It does not have individual signs for distinguishing between two assets in the same money which are therefore taken to be perfectly interchangeable. But monetary practices invalidate this assumption on the strength of two qualitative criteria: i) the differentiation among monetary assets and ii) their convertibility (Blanc, 2008 and 2009a).

The qualitative dimensions of money underscore the absence of a purely fungible character of money. Monetary assets are not perfectly undifferentiated or convertible and so they are not fully fungible (Blanc, 2008). They cannot be depicted exclusively through quantitative criteria; their qualitative characteristics must be taken into account. These cover three dimensions (Blanc, 2008): the monetary form of the various monetary instruments that can be used as means of payment (metallic coins, paper money or electronic forms of money), the symbolic universe of which they are part and which rests on a set of values and norms illustrating membership of the payment community and conveying socio-economic earmarking that guides its uses (means of subjective differentiation rooted in cognitive factors and moral standards).

The observation of daily practices in the real world invites us to, therefore, temper the fungible character of money. For example, Zelizer (2005 [1994]) emphasises the compartmentalisation and assignment of income by the 'housewife' (school money, rent money, coal money, funeral insurance money, etc) and the conflicts that may arise within households over these different attributions. Individuals mark money psychologically or materially by assigning it through the use of envelopes (see also Weber, 2006 and 2009) or boxes to specific expenditure. Moreover, the existence of the varied forms and moneys such as CCs further underscores the non-fungible character of money.

This absence of pure fungibility (absence of pure convertibility and principle of differentiation of monetary assets) suggests the necessary articulation between moneys which presupposes a conversion process precisely because they are not wholly fungible. Blanc uses four criteria to determine the forms of monetary articulation: i) commensurability (the possibility of obtaining a common evaluation between two moneys from a given rate), ii) convertibility (or the transformation of the money's characteristics so that all its qualities (or part of them) are transformed symbolic universe or monetary form), iii) co-use (or the simultaneous use of means of payment of different forms or sorts), and iv) coincidence of spheres of uses (various money assets are usable in the same socio-economic spheres). These different qualitative and quantitative criteria provide an understanding of the modes of articulation between moneys. Blanc (2009c) identified four ideal types of articulation among moneys: competition, simultaneousness, supplementarity and autonomy. The last three forms of articulation characterise the principle of monetary complementarity and make it possible to go beyond the traditional approach to monetary competition. They underscore the diversity of uses (Zelizer, 2005 [1994]) and diversity of monetary forms by emphasising the qualities of money. It is because the postulate of fully fungible money is not observed that monetary plurality co-exists and the competitive mode of articulation is not exclusive. To go further in determining the monetary conditions of sustainable territorial development, we wish to mark out an approach in terms of monetary subsidiarity.

The aim is ultimately to propose a subsidiary monetary scheme that is appropriate for the various levels of economic and social organisations. This makes it possible to couple the approach of monetary complementarity with a territorial approach defining relevant levels of action that results from the capacity of each level to come up with suitable solutions. In other words, the principle of subsidiarity enables us to activate possible complementarities for a specific purpose. That purpose here is sustainable territorial development. In this way, subsidiary moneys are rolled out at the lowest relevant level for them to make an optimal impact.

The principle of monetary subsidiarity proposes that currencie should fulfil objectives or uses that are not fulfilled by the official currency, at least in a relevant way. They perform in a complementary mode rather than as monetary competition. However, this complementarity is framed as subsidiarity, that is, every subsidiary currency comes from a deployment level dependent on the objectives defined by the monetary community. Every territorial level or scale is characterised by a governance space as well. Sustainable development normatively includes a subsidiarity principle to the extent that it is developed in a participative framework at the lowest possible level. It is up to local governments, socio-economic actors and citizens to 'execute democratically and at the appropriate levels [. . .] integral policies allowing a sustainable development' (Theys, 2002, p. 9). Subsidiarity currencies are part of this framework since they aim to execute in a democratic way a specific currency, in every level and at the best decision-making level in order to achieve the given objectives that respond to sustainable development issues. Subsidiarity currencies do not conflict with the official currency given that they imply different uses at different scales mediated by different qualitative signifiers. They are deployed in socio-economic spaces separated and differentiated. This principle of monetary or economic subsidiarity comes from the premise that every scale of action needs to respond to an identified sustainable development objective by using its own resources and means. Monetary subsidiarity is then characterised by the execution of devices at the lowest appropriate level, that is, where results are optimal according to the wished objectives.

The aim is ultimately to propose a subsidiary monetary arrangement appropriate for the different levels of economic and social organisations. This allows the combination of an approach of complementary currency to a territorial one that delimits the levels of appropriate action and, as a result, also limits the capacity of every level to create adequate solutions. In other words, the principle of subsidiarity allows us to activate the possible complementarities for a specific aim, which here is local sustainable development. In that way, subsidiarity currencies are deployed at the lowest pertinent level enabling the achievement of optimal results.

If we take up the modes of articulation defined by Blanc (2010), CCs have all of the characteristics of complementarity (supplementarity and/or autonomy and/or simultaneousness) and of subsidiarity as they seek to meet needs identified at their level of action through stakeholder rationale depending on the objectives pursued while being adapted to the context. This might however be termed weak subsidiarity (Figure 10.1). From the perspective of strong monetary subsidiarity, currencies would not have characteristics of either simultaneousness or supplementarity, that is, neither would their usages be joint nor their spheres of use overlap. Their monetary qualities would also greatly limit their convertibility. In other words, each currency circulating on an infra-national scale in complementary mode would circulate at a relevant level which is defined socio-economically and territorially (or within a sphere of socio-economic and territorial use) and would be characterised by a stakeholder and democratic mode of governance developed on the scale on which the currency was deployed. Each territorial scale corresponds with a specific monetary use but with possibilities for conversion, except for the autonomous mode. In the context of transition to sustainable territorial development, the principle of subsidiarity means giving precedence to the use of the corresponding currency, wherever possible on each territorial scale.

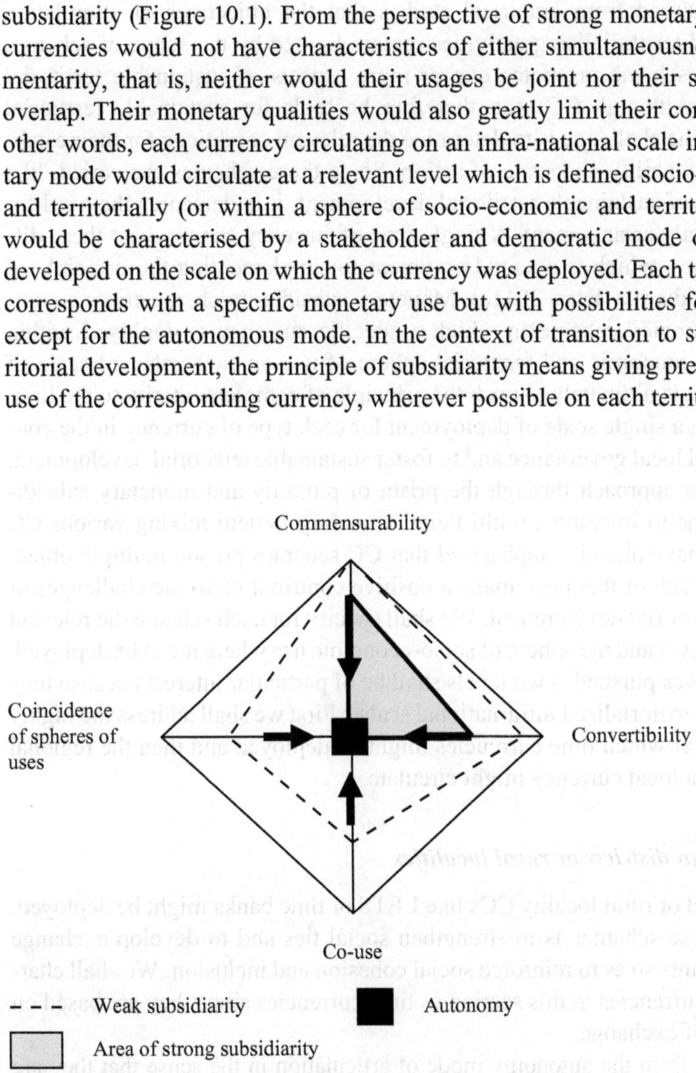

Figure 10.1 The subsidiary modes of monetary articulations

The arrows in the diagram show what the subsidiary currencies should tend towards, that is, the transition from weak to strong subsidiarity which is intended to increase the autonomy of each scheme. The tips of the diamond indicate the maximum degree for the four criteria, tending towards an absence in the centre (e.g. the absence of commensurability is in the centre of the diamond and full commensurability at the tip).

10.4 Implementing the principle of monetary subsidiarity to promote sustainable territorial development

It can be observed from empirical studies that the objectives of stimulation exchanges and territorialising activities remain limited by the scope of schemes and that each scheme promotes one or more aspects of sustainable territorial development. Although CCs can therefore be tools for sustainable territorial development, the challenge is to determine the relevant conditions for their establishment, acceptability and scale of action. Since these schemes are varied, like the challenges of sustainable territorial development, it underscores the need for a plural monetary arrangement. A single type of currency cannot meet these different objectives, which is a sound argument for implementing the principle of monetary subsidiarity (Fare, 2011a). Monetary subsidiarity characterises a complementary currency scheme in which a specific currency is deployed within a single socio-economic and territorial sphere of use on each relevant scale of action. The aim is ultimately to push the principle of complementarity to the limit by determining a single scale of deployment for each type of currency in the context of renewed local governance and to foster sustainable territorial development.

Adopting an approach through the prism of plurality and monetary subsidiarity invites one to imagine a multi-tiered monetary system mixing various CC schemes. We have already emphasised that CC schemes pursue multiple objectives and that each of them can make a positive contribution to the challenges of sustainable territorial development. We shall specify for each scheme the relevant geographical level and the sphere of socio-economic use where it can be deployed, and the objectives pursued. Two levels shall be of particular interest because they correspond to territorialised infra-national scales. First we shall address the highly localised level at which time currencies might be deployed and then the regional level at which a local currency might circulate.

10.4.1 In urban districts or rural localities

In urban district or rural locality CCs like LETS or time banks might be deployed. The aim of these schemes is to strengthen social ties and to develop exchange among inhabitants so as to reinforce social cohesion and inclusion. We shall characterise these currencies in this section as time currencies since they are based on time as a unit of exchange.

They derive from the autonomy mode of articulation in the sense that they are neither commensurable (hence not convertible) nor usable in other socio-economic spheres. They are not articulated with any other currency, whether subsidiary or the national currency (cf. Figure 10.2).

As a locus of socialisation, they can activate social cohesion through the creation of a network of mutual aid and inclusion in local life. They forge relations among members of a community by promoting equity and solidarity. Being based on the concept of symmetry (Polanyi, 1983 [1944]), reciprocity places individuals in a position of interdependence and complementarity, both with respect to each other and the environment. This develops the feeling of belonging to a social unit. These schemes promote social and economic inclusion of all members of the community by enhancing skills all around. The implemented egalitarian principles develop the feeling of social justice leading to a better grasp of the principle of intra and inter-generational equity which is at the heart of sustainable development (Jany-Catrice, 2011, p. 63).

This emphasis on other economic rationales such as social inclusiveness and reciprocity signals that human behaviour cannot be reduced to the maximisation of individual interest. The establishment of sustainable exchange relations among members means that those relations can be extended over time. The interpersonal relations foster the establishment of relations of solidarity and reciprocity in return. Moreover, the implementation of monetary and institutional schemes keeps out exchange in terms of purely market relations. These schemes have to seek to create a specific 'symbolic universe' established on social and environmental ethics to escape from the purely market rationale (or commodification). Thus the services exchanged in this context sometimes extend beyond the market rationale (especially for personal services) and move into the rationale of de-commodification, that is, 'the transition from market exchange to a generalised social exchange which includes various forms of monetary and non-monetary transactions, including symbolic transactions' (Perret, 2011, p. 216). This alteration of logic of 'need satisfaction' is essential in decoupling improved well-being

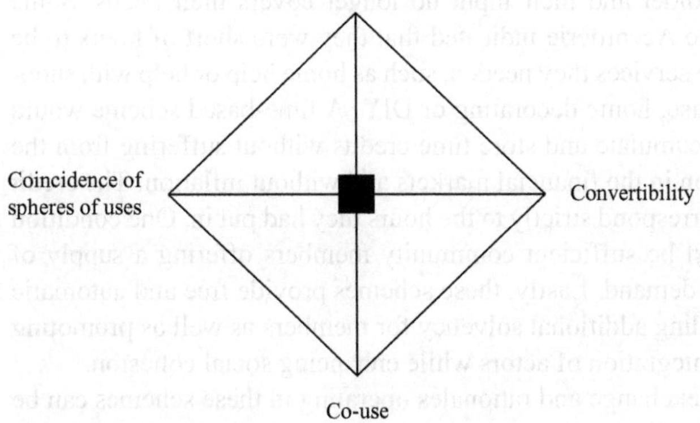

Figure 10.2 The subsidiary mode of articulation of time-based currencies: autonomy

and consumption (Max-Neef, 1992), which impacts social representations. It is part of assessing the labour value and enhancing of non-labour activities.

Money is a social bond (Aglietta et al., 1998; Théret, 2007), and tends to be understood in western societies as 'money that separates' rather than 'money that joins'. Here the establishment of sustainable exchange relationships is a vehicle of social cohesion. Exchange is inserted into human relations or logic of 'esteem' of the other rather than of market prices (Servet, ed, 1999). Services rendered cannot readily be dissociated from the personal relations that the exchangers create.

Next, these schemes make it possible to develop property sharing which can limit material individual consumption by enhancing the pooling of resources and 'the invention of new co-operative social relations' (Gleizes, 2011, p. 81) while contributing to 'disconnecting well-being from material abundance' (Perret, 2011, p. 215). This may involve tool sharing, car-pooling, loans of cultural property, and so on. This limits not just material output, but also waste. A sharing economy is developing and it is more important to have use of property than to own it. This mutualisation is embodied by the creation of collective services which can be offered within the scheme: central purchasing possibly coupled with grocery, library, laundrette, car rental, digital service area and so on. Access to all of these collective services can be had in exchange for hours or time. These collective services seek to meet both individual and collective needs by moving away from a rationale of market consumption. Some of the principles can be seen in the Accorderie.

Moreover, time-based schemes are suitable for certain matters associated with retirement and support for the elderly. First of all they promote inter-generational equity by developing relations of solidarity among members of a community as a vehicle of social cohesion. They can be used in supporting the elderly which is one of the major societal concerns for the ageing western societies. This support emphasises once again the interdependence of people and the need to rebuild inter and intra-generational bonds.

Next, people of working age may find a way of capitalising their resources in this type of scheme. Anyone can store up hours to be used at a later date, especially when they are older and their input no longer covers their needs. Some elderly members of the Accorderie indicated that they were short of hours to be able to secure all of the services they needed, such as home help or help with shopping trips, moving house, home decorating or DIY. A time-based scheme would make it possible to accumulate and store time credits without suffering from the speculation that goes on in the financial markets and without inflation. The credit accumulated would correspond strictly to the hours they had put in. One condition is essential: there must be sufficient community members offering a supply of services that can meet demand. Lastly, these schemes provide free and automatic access to credit, providing additional solvency for members as well as promoting social and economic integration of actors while enhancing social cohesion.

This conception of exchange and rationales operating in these schemes can be used to counter individualism and promote new values at the heart of sustainable development, especially solidarity and equality through the recognition of each and every member. The reciprocity promoted through these schemes highlight interdependence among individuals which is a vehicle of equity. Re-assessing the value of labour and the nature of work, measuring wealth differently, meeting needs through other means than market integration, generating well-being on something other than 'having' through 'being', 'doing' or 'interacting' (Max-Neef, 1992) are ways to transform social representations which can lead to sustainable development. The ultimate aim is to create 'new relational rationales which produce non-market social bonding' (Arnsperger, 2010, p. 11). This develops relations among people who have a sense of a common interest and leads to the moral obligation of not doing disservice to others and to the environment.

Such experiences in cooperation must have positive repercussions fostering civic involvement in the challenges of sustainable territorial development. This strengthening of citizenship can lead to a renewal of different forms of public action and governance and build the foundation of local participation. CCs involve 'civic governance' which is 'initiated and taken forward by non-institutional players' (Petrella and Richez-Battesti, 2010, p. 66). Activating bonds of solidarity and proximity can develop relational proximity and create a public space of proximity, which itself must facilitate learning of the different forms of citizenship, given that citizenship is multidimensional (economic, social, political and cultural) (Fotopoulos, 2002). This public space of proximity favours interaction among members inducing 'collective creativity' (Laville, 2011). In this way, learning through the establishment of specific, participative and democratic rules within these schemes may create a positive 'spill-over effect' (Colletis et al., 2005, p. 16) throughout the locality.

10.4.2 The bio-regional level

At the regional level, the objective is to promote endogenous sustainable development based on the resources and potential at that level. Development is a process of 'revelation of resources of all kinds' (Courlet, 2008, p. 11) knowing that these resources may be latent, hidden and/or to be constructed (Gumuchian and Pecqueur, 2007). This scale may be clarified by the concept of the bio-region (Berg and Dasmann, 1977; Sale, 1985; Aberley, 1999; McGinnis, 1999), eco-region (Bailly, 2005a; 2005b) and 'bio-anthropo-region' (Arnsperger, 2010). The term 'bio-anthropo-region' denotes a space that is mid-way between what in France are regional and departmental administrative levels and is suitable for taking into consideration the natural characteristics of the area while ensuring the satisfaction of the local needs of the population. To determine the relevant size of this space, geographical surveys are required to study monetary circuits, the food sovereignty index, local dependence on outside resources, potential for intra-territorial exchange, means to develop these features and the local ecological footprint. This territorial review will highlight the degree of dependence of the territory on outside resources and energy. This will also provide a clearer collective understanding of the challenges in the purpose of building collective solutions through a participatory approach.

The objective is to construct an economy of proximities (Pecqueur and Zimmermann, 2004) which is resilient and able to meet the needs of the local populations, that is, ultimately 'an ecosytem endowed with an effective agro-immunity apparatus, reforming its forces within its regional space' (Bailly, 2005b, p. 15). Its principles can be found at the heart of 'Transition Towns' (Ryan-Collins, 2011). This regional level can be used to apprehend, at the meso-economic level, a complex socio-economic system where places of production and consumption need to be 're-associated'.

Constructing this bio-anthropo-regional territory is part of a progressive approach and process:

> Development is by its nature a gradual process arising from the establishment and structuring of partial subsystems [. . .]. In this process, the territory can play a major part. It is the meeting point between development actors. It is also the place where forms of cooperation among firms, individuals and activities are deliberately or spontaneously organised. Ultimately, it is the junction between market forms and forms of social regulation.
>
> (Courlet, 2007, p. 44)

On this scale, the aim is to develop a currency to foster territorial sustainable development associated with a charter of responsibility with selection criteria for professionals in the exchange network (Blanc and Fare, 2016), incentivising individuals and businesses to produce and consume in a more sustainable manner while promoting the territorialisation and stimulation of exchange and activities.

The involvement of government through the introduction of assigned money might promote access to sustainable consumption for all. Here we find certain operating principles of third or fourth generation currencies like the SOL (in its operating principles, even if we have discussed its limitations above), Brazilian community development banks or local currencies of Transition Towns or German Regiogeld.

Regional money circulates in the territorial sphere among the socio-economic actors of the area. Its use is reserved to this spatio-economic sphere. It is commensurable but its convertibility is limited by its monetary qualities which make it special-purpose money (Figure 10.3). It is nonetheless convertible into another regional or national currency on certain conditions. In a perspective of strong subsidiarity and with regard to the challenges of transition towards sustainable territorial development, the objective is to reinforce the territory's autonomy to create a sphere of spatio-socio-economic use overlapping, as little as possible, with that of the national currency through the construction of a meaningful symbolic universe.

A regional currency must be based on 'multi-lateral or stakeholder governance', which implies 'a variety of public and private players involved in designing and implementing local public policies' and which allows 'the co-construction of the general interest based on the range of interests present' (Petrella and Richez-Battesti, 2010, p. 56–60). This joint construction must be performed within a

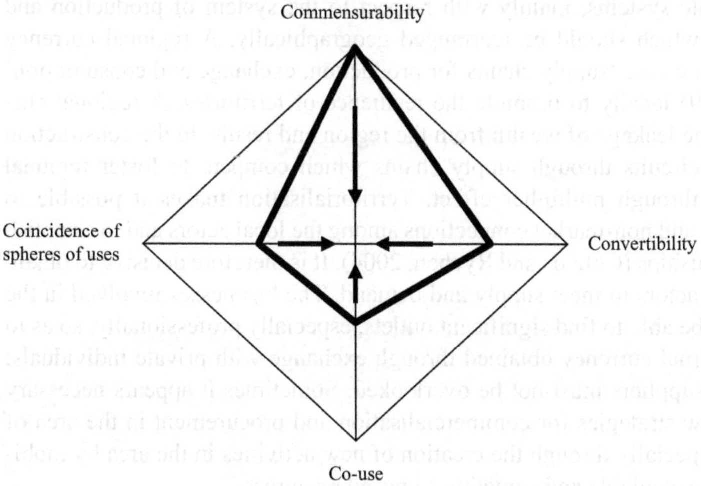

Figure 10.3 Subsidiary mode of articulation of bio-regional currencies: towards strong subsidiarity

geographical area of deliberation so as to determine 'the framework and institutional arrangement for decision making about the form of territorial development through public debate, public action and more specifically through public policy making' (Demoustier and Richez-Battesti, 2010, p. 8). The creation of a regional currency must arise from these various partnerships without being disconnected from the appropriation of money by citizens. From 'these situated modes of coordination of the players among themselves' (Pecqueur, 2009, p. 60), there must arise the pursuit of a territorial project reconciling individual interests and being shaped by a common interest – sustainable territorial development, through the implementation of a collective tool – a regional currency. This 'theory of territorial economics' can be used to integrate 'the specific features of places and the ties of the players not just among themselves but with their geographical environment' (Pecqueur, 2009, p. 61). The challenge is to develop a process of territorialisation centred on sustainable development.

The introduction of this type of currency would make it possible to create local exchange circuits and hence territorialise activities and study interactions among the different actors at regional levels. An absence of diversity observed through insufficient monetary circulation or the lack of outlets in internal currency should lead to decisions being taken about certain sectors and/or business locations in the area. The study of interactions and monetary circulation schemes will make it possible to highlight (or not) shortcomings at regional levels, say related to procurement for businesses, and then develop them especially through social lending. Money can thus be used as a tool for tracing circuits of consumption and production that can lead to a territorial appraisal.

This scale of action can be used to adopt a global approach in terms of complex socio-economic systems, mainly with respect to the system of production and consumption which should be rearranged geographically. A regional currency can be used to create 'supply chains for production, exchange and consumption' (Calame, 2009) locally to promote the resilience of territories. A regional currency limits the leakage of wealth from the region and results in the construction of economic circuits through supply chains which compete to foster regional development through multiplier effect. Territorialisation makes it possible to weave market and non-market connections among the local actors and to establish lasting relationships (Colletis and Rychen, 2004). It is therefore decisive to obtain a diversity of actors to meet supply and demand. The businesses involved in the scheme must be able to find significant outlets, especially professionally, so as to move the internal currency obtained through exchange with private individuals; raw material suppliers must not be overlooked. Sometimes it appears necessary to develop new strategies for commercialisation and procurement in the area of circulation, especially through the creation of new activities in the area by mobilising all of the available and sometimes unused resources.

It is a matter of constructing a supply chain with production and consumption circuits through the 'combination of a close-knit institutional tie between key actors of different types, both private and public, and different standings, including players from the non-profit and cooperative realms' (Colletis et al., 2005, p. 13) from which to obtain as autonomous an area as possible with an objective of resilience around the use of an internal currency. The fabric of territorial economic life will be reinforced by the use of bio-regional currency for bringing together all of these flows.

Figure 10.4 summarises the levels of action in terms of the use of each currency. We reconcile monetary complementarity and monetary subsidiarity in terms of the objective of sustainable territorial development and of varying degrees of local intervention. However, this monetary arrangement is only viable if subsidiary currencies are deployed on different scales of action. Our focus on

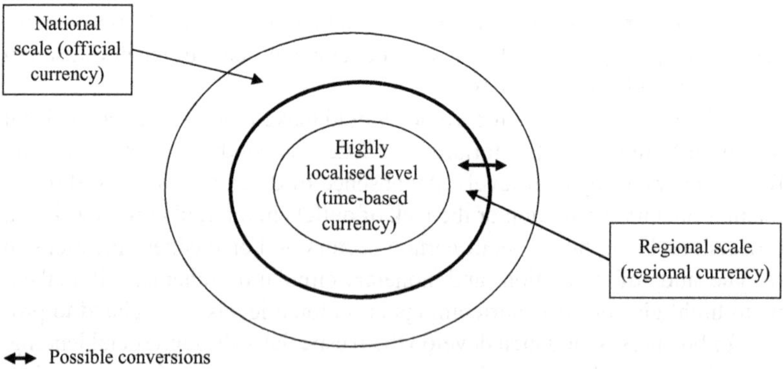

Figure 10.4 Application of the principle of monetary subsidiarity

local dimension should not mask the interdependence among different scales and also within those scales: local, national and international (Galtung, 1986; Dally and Cobb, 1989; Nijkamp et al., 1991). It should also not preclude one from thinking about their complementarity on different scales.

10.5 Conclusion

The results we have obtained from field surveys of the SOL and the Accorderie have enabled us to discuss both the potential of CCs and the limits upon them in three dimensions: territorialisation of activities, stimulation of exchange and the transformation of practices, ways of life and social representations. CCs may be tools for sustainable territorial development, provided that one can determine the relevant conditions for establishing them and their scale of action. The diversity of schemes makes it possible to think of possible complementarity between these currencies so as to satisfy the objectives of sustainable territorial development.

Starting from these lessons, we have proposed a monetary scheme which seems best able to support sustainable territorial development. This scheme is based on the principle of monetary subsidiarity which characterises the implementation of schemes at the lowest relevant level, that is, where their effects seem to be optimal given the objectives. Subsidiary currencies thus seek to democratically implement a specific currency at each relevant level as well as the best decision-making level for achieving the objectives assigned to them with the perspective of answering the challenges of sustainable territorial development. The principle of subsidiarity then makes it possible to activate potential monetary complementarities. In this sense, each currency circulating in complementary mode on the infra-national scale specifically has a defined socio-economic and territorial monetary use and a level of circulation, or in other words a spatio-socio-economic sphere of use. Each territorial level at which money is deployed is also characterised by stakeholder and democratic governance exercised at the lowest relevant level.

In this way, time-based currencies might be developed at highly localised levels (districts, localities). They make it possible to activate social ties and develop a rationale of social inclusiveness and reciprocity as well as to contribute to the de-commodification of needs by highlighting alternative means of meeting needs other than through material consumption. Time-based currencies promote mutual help, reciprocity and solidarity and they help to change social representations. Regionally, one might see the development of a currency of the same name, making it possible to territorialise and stimulate exchange by promoting networking among firms in a supply chain rationale on the basis of needs expressed at the local level. The development of a currency scheme of this kind thus presents real potential in the face of the challenges of sustainable development. The implementation and the principles guiding all of these schemes should be part of renewed, democratic and civic governance.

The implementation of subsidiary currencies may bring about the emergence of bottom-up development. By connecting up the actors in the area, it could activate forms of proximity and make it possible to synergise them around a common objective. Nonetheless, one should not ignore the questions of time related to the process of monetary mobilisation and appropriation. As a lever for change, currencies can neither impose themselves nor their uses be decreed but they are constructed in partnership with many actors in an area, that is, ultimately in the context of renewed stakeholder governance. This new form of governance is part of active participation by citizens and all socio-economic and public actors in the area at the heart of the process of defining a territorial project for sustainable development.

The role of government in this process needs to be discussed (see Blanc and Fare, 2013). Locally the authorities may promote and support the deployment of these schemes as part of a rationale of subsidiarity and they may actively participate in schemes by accepting and using the currencies as means of payment. Nationally, it is urgent to provide them with a clear legal framework to bring them out of the grey area and facilitate intervention by different players. Thinking along these lines is under way in Latin America, especially in Brazil, and might lead to an integrated monetary organisation based on monetary subsidiarity (Fare et al., 2015).

Lastly, we do not claim that the implementation of subsidiary currencies is the exclusive remedy, or a sufficient one, to lead to sustainable territorial development but rather that subsidiary currencies might be part of a whole raft of structural and global reforms. For example, based on the development of a local appraisal and mapping of exchanges, subsidiary currencies can be dove-tailed with local planning and development schemes so as to fit in with an overall programme for transition. It might be relevant to include a monetary policy within territorial policies so as to enhance the autonomy, self-sustainability and resilience of local areas. It is therefore a question of studying the conditions of their insertion in territorial projects and their articulation with other tools and mechanisms of transition (Fare, 2016). This, however, cannot be separated from more comprehensive thinking about the relevant size of areas, their autonomy and their democratic functioning, thus highlighting the need for local and fiscal reform.

More generally, CCs are recent schemes compared to the length of time needed for monetary appropriation. Appraisals must still be made, especially of those schemes that are moving towards a relevant size and visible socio-economic impact such as the Chiemgauer or the community development bank of Fortaleza. In this sense, our framework of analysis might be applied to these schemes to validate or invalidate our findings.

References

Aberley, D. 1999. 'Interpreting bioregionalism. A story from many voices'. In: Mcginnis, M. V. (ed.) *Bioregionalism*. London: Routledge.

Aglietta, M., Andreau, J., Anspach, M., Birouste, J., Cartelier, J., Coppet, D. de, Malamoud, C., Orléan, A., Servet, J.-M., Théret, B. and Thiveaud, J.-M. 1998. 'Introduction collective'. In: Aglietta, M. and Orléan, A. (eds) *La monnaie souveraine*. Paris: Odile Jacob, pp. 9–31.

Aglietta, M. and Orléan, A. 1982. *La violence de la monnaie*. Paris: PUF.

Aglietta, M. and Orléan, A. (eds) 1995. *Souveraineté, légitimité et confiance*. Paris: AEF/CREA.

Aglietta, M. and Orléan, A. (eds) 1998. *La monnaie souveraine*. Paris: Odile Jacob.

Arnsperger, C. 2010. 'Transition écologique et transition économique: quels fondements pour la pensée? Quelle stâches pour l'action?' www.philosophie-management.com/docs/2010/Arnsperger-1.TRANSITION.12.02.2010.pdf.

Bailly, E. 2005a. 'L'écorégion', *Actes des Assises du Limousin, ENSIL, Limoges, Ecorégionalité et souveraineté alimentaire*. www.docplayer.fr/32947932-Actes-des-1ieres-assises-du-limousin.html.

Bailly, E. 2005b. 'Vers une demarche écorégionale. . . Le concept de l'écorégion' ou 'comment restaurer le système immunitaire des régions', *Rapport de l'étude pour intelligence verte*.

Berg, P. and Dasmann, R. 1977. 'Reinhabiting California', *The Ecologist*, 10 (7): 399–401.

Blanc, J, 2000. *Les monnaies parallèles. Unité et diversité du fait monétaire*. Paris: L'Harmattan.

Blanc, J. 2006. 'Introduction générale. Les monnaiessociales: un outil et seslimites'. In: Blanc, J. (ed.) *Exclusion et liens financiers: monnaies sociales, rapport 2005–2006*. Paris: Economica.

Blanc, J. 2008. 'Fongibilités et cloisonnements de la monnaie'. In: Baumann, E., Bazin, L., Ould-Ahmed, P., Phélinas, P., Selim, M. and Sobel, R. (eds) *L'argent des anthropologues, la monnaie des économistes*. Paris: L'Harmattan.

Blanc J. 2009a. 'Usages de l'argent et pratiquesmonétaires'. In: Steiner, P. and Vatin, F. (eds) *Traité de sociologie économique*. Paris: PUF (Quadrige).

Blanc, J. 2009b. 'Contraintes et choix organisationnels dans les dispositifs de monnaies sociales', *Annals of Public and Cooperative Economics*, 80 (4): 547–577.

Blanc, J. 2009c. 'Beyond the competition approach to money: a conceptual framework applied to the early modern France', *Asymmetric Monies: Revisiting Global Monetary History from the Viewpoints of Complementarity and Viscosity*, University of Tokyo Symposium, March.

Blanc, J. 2010. 'Converting money. On articulation modes of money'. In: Ponsotet, J.-F. and Rochon, L.-P. (eds) *What is the Nature of Money? A Pluridisciplinary Approach*. Chelthenham, UK: Edward Elgar.

Blanc, J. and Fare, M. 2013. 'Understanding the role of governments and administrations in the implementation of community and complementary currencies', *Annals of Public and Cooperative Economics*, 84 (1): 63–81.

Blanc, J. and Fare, M. 2016. 'Turning values concrete: the role and ways of business selection in local currency schemes', *Review of Social Economy*, 74 (3): 298–319.

Bouba-Olga, O. and Grossetti, M. 2008. 'Socio-économie de proximité', *Revue d'Économie Régionale et Urbaine*, 3: 311–328.

Calame, P. 2009. *Essai sur l'oeconomie*. Paris: Ed. Charles Léopold Meyer.

Colletis, G., Gianfaldoni, P. and Richez-Battesti, N. 2005. 'Economie sociale et solidaire, territoires et gouvernance', *RECMA – Revue internationale de l'économie sociale*, 296: 8–25.

Colletis, G. and Rychen, F. 2004. 'Entreprises et territoires: proximités et développement local'. In: Pecqueur, B. and Zimmermann, J.-B. (eds) *Economie de proximités*. Paris: Lavoisier.

Courlet, C. 2007. 'Du développement économique situé'. In: Gumuchian, H. and Pecqueur, B. (eds), *La resource territoriale*. Paris: Économica et Anthropos.

Courlet, C. 2008. *L'économie territoriale*, Grenoble, France: PUG.

Daly, H. E. and Cobb, J. B. 1994 [1989]. *For the Common Good. Redirecting the Economy toward Community, the Environment, and a Sustainable Future.* Boston, MA: Beacon Press.

Demoustier, D. and Richez-Battesti. N. 2010. 'Introduction. Les organisations de l'Économiesociale et solidaire: gouvernance, régulation et territoire', *Géographie, Économie, Société*, 12 (1): 5–14.

Fare, M. 2009–2010. 'L'Accorderie (Québec): un dispositif de monnaie sociale singulier?' *Économie et Solidarités*, 40 (1–2): 2–16.

Fare, M. 2011a. *Les conditions monétaires d'un développement local soutenable: des systems d'échange complémentaire aux monnaies subsidiaires*, Thèse de doctorat en sciences économiques, Université Lumière Lyon 2, Lyon.

Fare, M. 2011b. 'The SOL: A Complementary Currency for the Social Economy and Sustainable Development', International Journal of Complementary Currency Research, 15: 57–60.

Fare, M. 2012. 'Les apports de deux dispositifs de monnaies sociales, le SOL et l'Accorderie, au regard des enjeux du développement local soutenable', *RECMA – Revue internationale de l'économie sociale*, 324: 53–69.

Fare, M. 2016. *Repenser la monnaie, transformer les territoires, faire société.* Paris: Editions Charles Léopold Mayer.

Fare, M., Meyer, C. and de Freitas, C. 2015. 'Community currencies in Brazilian community development banks: the symbolic meaning of the Palmas currency', *International Journal of Community Currency Research*, 19 (D): 6–17.

Folke, C., Carpenter, S., Elmqvist, T., Gunderson, L., Holling, C. S. and Walker, B. 2002. 'Resilience and sustainable development: building adaptative capacity in a world of transformations', *Ambio*, 31 (5): 437–440.

Fotopoulos, T. 2002 [1997]. *Vers une démocratie générale, une démocratie directe, économique, écologique et sociale.* Paris: Seuil.

Galtung, J. 1986. 'Towards a new economics: on the theory and practice of self-reliance'. In Ekins P. (ed.) *The Living Economy: A New Economics in the Making.* London and New York: Routledge.

Gleizes, J. 2011. 'La croissance verte est-elle possible?' In: Coutrot, T., Flacher, D. and Méda, D. (eds) *Les chemins de la transition, pour en finir avec cevieux monde.* Paris: Editions Utopia.

Gumuchian, H. and Pecqueur, B. (eds) 2007. *La resource territoriale.* Paris: Économica et Anthropos.

Hopkins, R. 2008. *The Transition Handbook: From Oil Dependency to Local Resilience.* Dartington, UK: Green Books.

Jany-Catrice, F. 2011. 'Nouveaux indicateurs et nouvelles pratiques sociales'. In: Coutrot, T., Flacher, D. and Méda, D. (eds) *Les chemins de la transition, pour en finir avec cevieux monde.* Paris: Editions Utopia.

Laville, J.-L. 2011. *Agir à gauche, l'économie sociale et solidaire.* Paris: Desclée de Brouwer.

Mauss, M. 1993 [1950]. *Sociologie et anthropologie.* Paris: PUF.

Max-Neef, A. 1992. 'Development and human needs'. In: Ekins, P. and Max-Neef, M. A. (eds) *Real-Life Economics: Understanding Wealth Creation.* London: Routledge.

Mcginnis, M. V. (ed.) 1999. *Bioregionalism.* London: Routledge.

Nijkamp, P., Laschuit, P. and Soeteman, F. 1991. 'Sustainable development in a regional system', Serie Research Memoranda from VU University Amsterdam, Faculty of Economics, Business Administration and Econometrics, no. 93.

Olsson, P. 2003. *Building Capacity for Resilience in Social-Ecological Systems*. Doctoral Dissertation, Department of Systems Ecology, Stockholm University.

Pecqueur, B. 2000. *Le développement local. Pour uneéconomie des territoires*. Paris: La Découverte et Syros (2nd edition).

Pecqueur, B. 2009. 'De l'exténuation à la sublimation: la notion de territoire est-elle encore utile?' *Géographie, économie, société*, 11 (1): 55–62.

Pecqueur, B. and Zimmermann, J.-B., (eds) 2004. *Economie de proximités*. Paris: Hermès-Lavoisier.

Perret, B. 2011. *Pour une raison écologique*. Paris: Flammarion.

Petrella, F. and Richez-Battesti, N. 2010. 'Gouvernance et proximité: des formes de participation et de cooperation renouvelées? Une observation sur l'accueil des jeunes enfants en France', *Géographie, Économie, Société*, 12 (1): 53–70.

Polanyi, K. 1983 [1944]. *La grande transformation. Aux origins politiques et économiques de notre temps*. Paris: Gallimard.

Ryan-Collins, J. 2011. 'Building local resilience: the emergence of the UK Transition Currencies', *International Journal of Community Currency Research*, 15 (Special issue): 61–67.

Sale, K. 1985. *Dwellers in the Land: The Bioregional Vision*. San Francisco, CA: Sierra Club Books.

Servet, J.-M. (ed.) 1999. *Une économie sans argent. Les systems d'échange local*. Paris: Seuil.

Théret, B. (ed.) 2007. *La monnaie dé voilée par ses crises. Crises monétaires d'hier et d'aujour d'hui*. Paris: Editions de l'EHESS.

Theys, J. 2002. 'L'approche territoriale du 'développement durable', condition d'une prise en compte de sa dimension sociale', *Développement durable et territoires. Dossier 1. Approches territoriales du Développement Durable*.

Walker, B., Hollinger, C. S., Carpenter, S. R. and Kinzig, A. 2004. 'Resilience, adaptability and transformability in social-ecological systems', *Ecology and Society*, 9 (2): article 5.

Weber, F. 2006. 'Séparation des scenes sociales et pratiques ordinaires du calcul. À la recherche des raisonnements indigènes'. In: Coquery, N., Menant, F. and Weber, F. (eds) *Ecrire, compter, mesurer*, vol. 2.

Weber, F. 2009. 'Le calcul économique ordinaire'. In: Steiner, P. and Vatin, F. (eds) *Traité de sociologie économique*. Paris: PUF.

World Commission for Environment and Development (WCED). 1987. *Our Common Future*. Oxford, UK: Oxford University Press.

Zelizer, V. 2005 [1994]. *The Social Meaning of Money*. Princeton, NJ: Princeton University Press.

11 Relationship between people's money consciousness and circulation of community currency

Shigeto Kobayashi, Takashi Hashimoto, Ken-ichi Kurita and Makoto Nishibe

11.1 Introduction

Complementary Currencies (CCs) are institutions at the social level (outer institutions) that can only exist and function when inner institutions (people's money consciousness) act as their individual foundations. Inner institutions support CCs by spreading their acceptance to a significant number of individuals and organisations at the micro level. When CCs grow in membership, every participant has more choice of types and volumes of goods and services within the CC system. At the macro level we observe a certain economic order or pattern, which relies on a shared money consciousness at the meso level and individual transactions as underpinnings at the micro level. In turn, the emerging institutional order at the social level affects individual cognition, decision and behaviour through money consciousness. This chapter aims at clarifying how money consciousness as an internal institution sustains CC systems as external institutions.

Section 11.2 provides the theoretical basis and methodology of the study. Two results of the questionnaire survey analysis are explained in Section 11.3: (i) the difference of money consciousness between community currency participants and financial organisation participants, and (ii) the difference of money consciousness in various currency systems. Section 11.4 discusses these differences from the viewpoint of the micro-meso-macro loop in the circulation of community currencies.

11.2 Micro-meso-macro loop and money consciousness

Only a few CCs have successfully stayed in high circulation and maintained a certain economic scale over a long period, although there have been 3,418 local projects for community currencies in 23 countries across six continents (Seyfang and Longhurst, 2013). We postulate two types of rules, external and internal. The external rules are exemplified by laws, norms and codes; the internal rules include cognitive frames, awareness and habits. Institutions are formed by socially common rules shared by many individuals in a group or society. We call shared external and internal rules outer and inner institutions respectively.[1] Inner institutions are important underpinning structures or foundations of outer institutions in currency systems.

Systematic design for circulating CCs as shared external rules, even if predetermined, do not necessarily function well. People's shared awareness and values regarding money should also be considered for CCs to be beneficial and meaningful. We assume that people's money consciousness must actually exist, forming not only standards for decision making in a given currency system, but also value judgments for multiple alternatives or complementary currency systems.

We consider that the evolution (i.e. emergence, growth, change and extinction) of social institutions including CCs are described by interacting loops among the micro, meso and macro levels (Figure 11.1). The micro level consists of individual cognition, decision and behaviour that are based on internal rules and are constrained by external rules. The macro level comprises performance, order and pattern shown in a social consequence as a collection of individual cognition, decision and behaviour on the micro level.

Both outer and inner institutions are supposed to lie at the meso level, between the micro and macro levels, constantly mediating interactions between the two levels. They are maintained, differentiated and dissolved depending on the variable distribution of individual cognition, decision and behaviour on the micro level. The outer and inner institutions indicate an emergent property which enables the possible ways to restrict or constrain an individual's cognition, decision and behaviour on the micro level. They do not, however, necessarily determine performance, order or pattern shown in social consequences on the macro level.

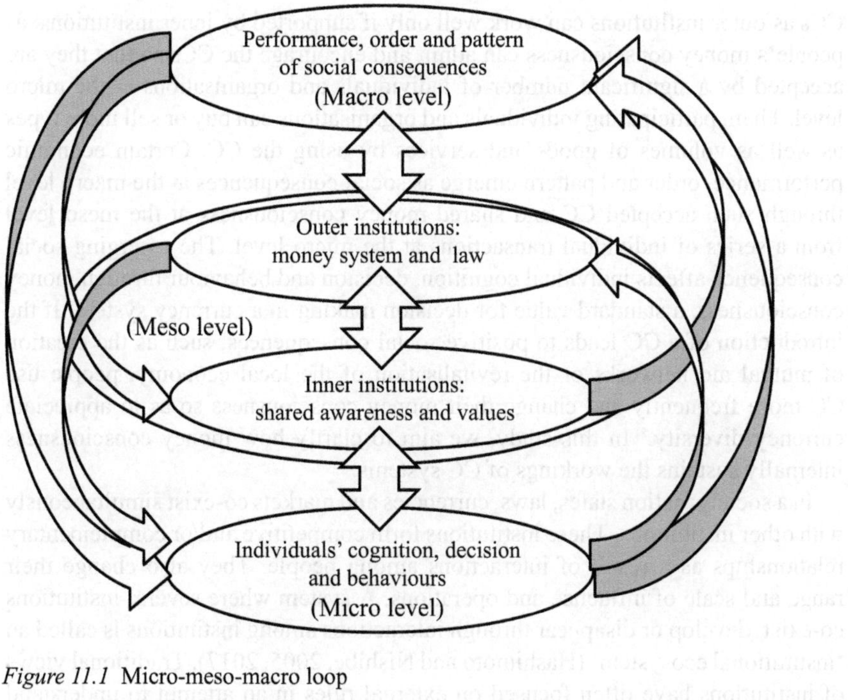

Figure 11.1 Micro-meso-macro loop

Furthermore, certain performances, orders and patterns of social consequences on the macro level affect both currency systems as the outer institutions and money consciousness as the inner institutions, that is, shared awareness and values of the outer institutions on the meso level.

Three different types of mutually determining loops exist: (i) between the micro and macro level, (ii) between the micro and meso level, and (iii) between the meso and macro level. We call such multi-levelled bi-directional interactions the 'micro-meso-macro loop' as a whole (Nishibe, 2012).

Outer and inner institutions form another loop to strengthen each other through interactions between the micro individuals and the meso institutions. When a particular value consciousness is common in a society, it is an institution. Although people's consciousness involving their awareness and values is neither an explicit law nor a norm, it governs people's thoughts and behaviour. Therefore, value consciousness is thought to belong to the meso level indirectly, mutually influencing the external rules at the meso level and consequences at the macro level, which govern the cognition and behaviour of the micro actors. This complex interaction of the micro-meso-macro loop is schematically shown in Figure 11.1. As long as individuals follow the outer and inner institutions on the meso level, they are each free to possess different internal rules, such as their own routines and habits, at the micro level.

11.3 Roles of inner and outer institution in CC circulation

CCs as outer institutions can work well only if supported by inner institutions, as people's money consciousness can admit and encourage the CCs so that they are accepted by a significant number of individuals and organisations at the micro level. Then, participating individuals and organisations can buy or sell more types as well as volumes of goods and services by using the CC. Certain economic performance, order and pattern emerge as social consequences at the macro level through such accepted CC and shared money consciousness at the meso level from a series of individual transactions at the micro level. The emerging social consequence affects individual cognition, decision and behaviour through money consciousness, a standard value for decision making in a currency system. If the introduction of a CC leads to positive social consequences, such as the creation of mutual aid networks or the revitalisation of the local economy, people use CC more frequently and change their money consciousness so as to appreciate currency diversity.[2] In this study, we aim to clarify how money consciousness internally sustains the workings of CC systems.

In a society, nation states, laws, currencies and markets co-exist simultaneously with other institutions. These institutions form competitive and/or complementary relationships as a result of interactions among people. They also change their range and scale of influence and operations. A system where several institutions co-exist, develop or disappear through interactions among institutions is called an 'institutional ecosystem' (Hashimoto and Nishibe, 2005, 2017). Traditional views of institutions have often focused on external rules in an attempt to understand institutions, which has led to ignoring the existence and roles of internal rules. However, as previously stated, understanding the interactional dynamics between external and internal rules within the conceptualisation of the micro-meso-macro loop is critical. Many external rules (e.g. laws and regulations) and internal rules (e.g. customs, practices and values) are shared among a relatively large part of society. In an institutional ecosystem, the relative frequency of people's value consciousness produces diversity at the institutional level. The two types of institutions, which interact within and between each type, mutually support and induce changes in each other.

Formation of CCs must be based on a variety of values and norms. In reference to the Argentine case, Kobayashi et al. (2010) explained that the currency system can be considered an institutional ecosystem. In 2001, the Argentine peso collapsed because the government defaulted. As a result, people's value consciousness regarding the credit of the currency system rapidly changed. A great shortage in the Argentine national currency peso resulted in three large shifts in relation to different currencies:

- Argentine peso → US dollar (the key currency);
- Argentine peso → Patacón or LECOP (bonds issued by the central or provincial governments); and
- Argentine peso → Crédito (a community currency issued by the Redes de Trueque, such as the Red Global de Trueque (RGT))

After the default on the Argentine debt, alternative currencies to the Argentine peso developed for several years. Four different currencies (global key, national, bond, and community currencies) circulated in Argentina concurrently. Once an ecosystem of mutually complementary currencies had developed, the network externalities of the single currency system did not work, and the transaction costs increased as a result of using different currencies in the same market. Such a situation in which multiple currencies co-existed cannot be explained using the concepts of economic rationality such as convenience and efficiency. Assuming that a currency system reflects people's diverse values, the concept of consciousness is more appropriate.

In actual societies, institutional diversity corresponding to value consciousness diversity does not always exist. Kobayashi et al. (2010) proposed the following three reasons for the lack of such a variety of social institutions:

- a society is locked in dominant economic efficiency, although most people are aware of the diversity of value consciousness;
- most people are not entirely conscious of the diversity of their own values; and,
- there is no diversity of values.

Thus, establishing a social institution implies that a particular value consciousness is shared by most of the people and is taken for granted in the society. In understanding the institutional formation and change, we should consider the relationships among the micro and macro levels as well as shared value consciousness at the meso level; it is not enough to analyse the relationships between the micro individual values and economic consequences at the macro level. We need to consider the latter relationship when we review the sustainability and evolution of CC systems.

11.4 Our study

We investigated the correlations between the circulation of a community currency and the money consciousness among participants of the community currency. We developed a new questionnaire on people's attitudes toward money and used it in areas where community currencies were introduced. Existing money attitude scales were developed to mainly examine people's attitudes toward the intended use of money (Yamauchi and Templer, 1982; Furnham, 1984). Our questionnaire consisted of 27 questions and asked broad and latent value consciousness questions, such as criteria for selecting an institution from multiple currency systems, purposes and current status of issuing, steering and distributing currency, and uses for money (questionnaire in Appendix). Our questionnaire was scored using a five-point Likert scale. We conducted the questionnaire survey in Japan, Argentina, Canada, Brazil and Italy by snowball sampling method and over 500 people responded. Survey questionnaires that were conducted outside Japan were translated from Japanese into Spanish, English, Portuguese and Italian, respectively.

We tested two hypotheses:

There is a difference in money consciousness between participants in CCs and non-participants.

There is a correlation between citizens' money consciousness and the circulation status of a CC.

11.4.1 Survey respondents

To test the first hypothesis, we investigated the correlations between social activities and money consciousness in participants of CCs and members of financial organisations. We focused on these two types of people because the participants of a CC belong to a reciprocal community where they develop collaborative relationships. In contrast, members of financial organisations belong to communities that pursue daily interests in a competitive environment.

The questionnaire surveys in Argentina and Canada were conducted in December 2006 while the survey in Japan was conducted from April 2007 to March 2008 using a paper-based or web-based questionnaire. In our survey 76.9% of community currency participants were in Buenos Aires, Argentina. They were users or operators of 'crédito', the community currency in Buenos Aires. Almost all financial organisation members were Japanese and worked at a domestic commercial bank or a foreign security firm.[3] Characteristics of the sample are reported in Table 11.1. In the group of 'workers' we selected non-students and citizens who were not active in either CCs or financial organisations. We categorized those who were not active in CCs, were not members of financial organizations, and were not students as 'workers' because they worked for various companies.

To test the second hypothesis, we examined the difference of money consciousness in various currency systems in the three countries of Japan, Brazil and Italy. Table 11.2 shows the survey respondents per research area. The first group included citizens in the Musashino-chuo area, Tokyo, Japan (n = 85), where the community currency 'Mu-chu' was issued as a social experiment.[4] This community currency was mainly used for compensating paid volunteers. The area is a wealthy quarter in Japan and the average income of the citizens is approximately $50,000 (at the time of the survey). The 'Mu-chu' circulation experiment was conducted for nine months from July 2008 to March 2009 and the questionnaire survey was applied twice to the same people, before and after the circulation experiment.

The second group included users and operators of Banco Palmas[5] in Palmeira, Fortaleza, Brazil (n = 32). We collected data in February 2011 in face to face interviews. Banco Palmas operates a microcredit system through its community currency 'Palma', which has been used to purchase commodities in Palmeira.

The third group comprised people who lived in Turin or Milan, Italy (n = 28). Paper-based questionnaires were distributed to them in October 2011. Italy is a euro zone nation, and the respondents were not familiar with community currencies. The samples in the two tests were independent.

Table 11.1 Occupational breakdown of the sample

Group	*Sex*			*Sum*
	Male	*Female*	*No response*	
Working people	17	11	0	28
CC participants	18	7	1	26
Members of financial organisations	12	14	1	27
Undergraduate students	34	5	0	39
Graduate students	22	12	0	34
Sum	103	49	2	154

Table 11.2 Geographical distribution of the samples in the three areas

Area	*Sex*			*Sum*
	Male	*Female*	*No response*	
Musashino-chuo	15	67	3	85
Palmeira	13	18	1	32
North Italy	10	16	2	28
Sum	38	101	6	145

11.5 Results

11.5.1 CC participants versus financial organisations' professionals

A factor analysis was performed on the 27 question items (variables). The scree plot suggested a three-factor solution, included 18 items and explained 45.5% of the variance in the data with eigenvalues greater than 1.0 and factor loadings greater than 0.35. A three-factor solution was attempted using Promax rotation. The first factor had an eigenvalue of 3.72, accounting for 23.2% of the variance and consisting of eight items. The second factor had an eigenvalue of 1.91, accounting for 12.0% of the variance and comprising seven items. The third factor had an eigenvalue of 1.75, accounting for 10.9% of the variance and consisting of three items.

The factor pattern after the Promax rotation is reported in Table 11.3. Items with a high loading on the first, second and third factors represent people's demand for diversity of money, equitable distribution of money and pursuit of money, respectively. The three factors were currency diversity (F1), fairness (F2) and profit orientation (F3). A reliability analysis was conducted to test the reliability and internal consistency of each factor. The results showed that the Alpha coefficients of F1 and F2 were 0.80 and 0.67, respectively. This is well above the minimum value of 0.50 which is considered an acceptable indication of reliability for basic research. However, the Alpha coefficient of F3 was 0.47, which indicated low internal consistency.

Table 11.4 shows the correlation among the three factors. The results indicated a significant correlation between only F1 and F2 ($r=.30$, $p< .01$). Table 11.5 indicates the correlation among the three subscale scores with CC and financial organisation participants. The scores of the CC participants indicated a significant inverse correlation between F1 and F3 ($r=-.53$, $p< .01$), whereas those of the members of the financial organisations showed a significant direct correlation between F1 and F3 ($r=.40$, $p< .05$). That means that participants of the CC considered currency diversity and profit orientation to be opposites, whereas the members of financial organisations thought currency diversity and profit orientation were closely related. Both apparently see little connection between currency diversity and fairness.

We classified the samples into three groups based on affiliation (participants of the CC, members of financial organisations and others). An analysis of variance (ANOVA) was conducted for the dependent variables (the scores of the three factors). The number of CC participants, members of financial organisations and others were 26, 27 and 101, respectively. Table 11.6 presents significant differences in currency diversity and fairness among the three groups ($F(2, 150) = 22.49$, $p<.01$; $F(2, 150) = 34.23$, $p<.01$). Differences in the scores of the three factors were determined using Tukey's test because the ANOVA was significant. Significant differences between all groups in currency diversity and fairness were identified.

Table 11.6 shows that the participants of community currency tended to place more importance on currency diversity than the members of financial organisations did. Furthermore, the former were likely to consider that government and

Table 11.3 Factor analysis of money consciousness (factor pattern after Promax rotation)

	Fl	*F2*	*F3*
22) Do you think it is good that we have different moneys from national currencies to live with?	**.72**	−.05	.04
4) Do you think it is good that money can be created or issued freely by people?	**.71**	.11	.00
25) Do you think it is good that money can be issued or created not only by the central bank or commercial banks, but also by people or communities?	**.67**	.12	−.11
23) Do you think it is good for money to be single?	**−.64**	.40	.14
8) Do you think it is good that money can be issued or created not only by the central bank or commercial banks, but also by the government?	**.54**	.14	.14
11) Do you think it is good that money can be something that mutually connects people?	**.51**	.02	.26
17) Do you think it is good that we can choose favourite ones out of different moneys?	**.48**	.17	.20
2) Do you think it is natural for money to be interest-bearing?	**−.40**	−.17	.24
10) Do you think the government should provide every adult beyond a certain age with basic income for their minimum standard of living?	.14	**.60**	−.05
19) Do you think it is good that we accommodate each other with money?	.15	**.53**	.02
13) Do you think moneylenders should not be in such financial institutions as commercial banks, but the government?	.10	**.49**	−.17
18) Do you think money should not concentrate in a tiny fraction of people, but disperse among them?	.05	**.47**	−.22
27) Do you think it is good for money to be able to be passable at any place and area?	−.05	**.45**	.43
21) Do you think it is good for money to be stable in its value?	−.21	**.42**	.01
20) Do you think it is good to lend your friend your money when they are in a financial need?	−.03	**.39**	−.06
7) Do you think it's good for the money to be able to buy anything you want?	.07	−.15	**.63**
12) Do you think it is good that money can be created or issued for the purpose of profit?	.26	−.19	**.48**
15) Do you think it is better to earn more money?	−.03	.00	**.42**

Table 11.4 Factor correlation, mean and deviation of subscale scores

	Currency diversity	*Fairness*	*Profit orientation*	*Mean*	*SD*
Currency diversity	—	.30**	−.02	2.78	.83
Fairness		—	−.09	3.47	.69
Profit orientation			—	2.91	.90

Table 11.5 Breakdown of factor correlation of subscale scores (CC participants and members of financial organisations)

	Currency Diversity	*Fairness*	*Profit orientation*
	CC Participants (n = 26)		
Currency diversity	—	−.08	−.53**
Fairness		—	−.31
Profit orientaion			—
	Members of financial organisations (n = 27)		
Currency diversity	—	.02	.40*
Fairness		—	−.15
Profit orientaion			—

** $p<.01$ * $p<.05$

Table 11.6 ANOVA table of subscale scores for the three groups

	CC Participants	*Members of financial organisations*	*Others*	*p - value*
Currency diversity	3.41 (1.15)	2.14 (.50)	2.76 (.57)	.00
Fairness	4.28 (.45)	3.06 (.58)	3.37 (.60)	.00
Profit orientaion	2.72 (1.14)	2.80 (.82)	2.98 (.84)	.33

Mean(SD)

peers should ensure stable livelihoods for poor people as they had high fairness value. These three groups did not seem to place value on profit orientation because each average subscale score of profit orientation was less than the average of 3.0.

11.5.2 Differences in money consciousness among currency systems

An ANOVA was conducted using three factors as dependent variables found from the previous analysis (Table 11.7). The results showed significant differences in all factors and in the three areas where we conducted research.

Table 11.8 indicates the average scores of items belonging to currency diversity per study area. As the first question, 'Do you think it is good to have a single

Table 11.7 ANOVA table of subscale scores in the three areas

	Musashino-chuo	*Palmeira*	*North Italy*	*p - value*
Currency diversity	2.53 (.54)	3.26 (.55)	2.65 (.63)	.00
Fairness	3.10 (.55)	3.91 (.60)	3.86 (.58)	.00
Profit orientaion	2.41 (.72)	3.45 (1.03)	2.45 (.98)	.00

Mean (SD)

Table 11.8 Average scores for the questions on 'currency diversity'

	Musashino-chuo	*Palmeira*	*North Italy*
Do you think it is good for money to be single?	3.26	2.78	4.11
Do you think it is good that money can be issued or created not only by the central bank or commercial banks, but also by people or communities?	2.14	4.00	1.89
Do you think it is good that we have different moneys from national currencies to live with?	2.76	3.38	2.29
Do you think it is good that we can choose favourite ones out of different moneys?	2.3	3.28	2.61

Table 11.9 Average scores of the questions on 'fairness'

	Musashino-chuo	*Palmeira*	*North Italy*
Do you think the government should provide welfare payment for poverty class?	3.39	4.09	4.46
Do you think money should not concentrate in a tiny fraction of people, but disperse?	3.42	4.41	4.61

money?', is an inverse question for currency diversity, a higher score in this question item means that currency diversity is less appreciated. Most citizens in the Musashino-chuo area did not want to use a currency other than the Yen because scores in this category, except for first question, were lower than 3.0. The question items on denationalisation of money scored higher in Palmeira than in other areas. Conversely, people in Northern Italy did not appreciate currency issuance by community organisations and approved of a single currency in the area.

Table 11.9 shows the average scores of the group of questions on fairness, per study area. Most mean scores on fairness were higher than 3.0 in the three areas and the fairness scores in Palmeira were higher than those in both the Musashino-chuo area and Northern Italy. Palmeira had a high fairness score mainly because Banco Palmas had conducted a microcredit programme using CC in order to develop a solidarity economy.

11.6 Discussion

The results supported our hypotheses that currency diversity was appreciated by people engaging in activities related to the management of CC (Table 11.6), whereas citizens of areas where CCs were introduced did not necessarily appreciate such currency diversity (Tables 11.7 and 11.8). We believe that the degree of currency diversity may differ based on people's concerns with CCs. The understanding of CC is key to enhancing currency diversity. If a CC circulates effectively in an area or if citizens have better understanding of CC, it is possible that people's consciousness regarding currency diversity is improved. The understanding of CC then helps to circulate it effectively. To confirm this hypothesis, we must establish a causal relationship between citizens' money consciousness and the circulation status of CC.

11.6.1 Change of people's money consciousness through CC circulation experiment

How does money consciousness change by introducing a new currency system? To examine the effect of money consciousness at the meso level on an individual's cognition at the micro level, we conducted a questionnaire survey before and after a CC circulation experiment in the Musashino-chuo area in Tokyo, Japan. Differences in the scores of the three factors before and after the experiment were tested using paired t-tests (Table 11.10). Differences having $p < 0.05$ were considered not significant in all cases: currency diversity ($t(73) = -6.51$, n.s.: not significant), fairness ($t(73) = -0.34$, n.s.), and profit orientation ($t(75) = 1.07$, n.s.). We could not confirm significant differences in money consciousness before or after the circulation experiment.

We then sought to determine the relationship between money consciousness and the understanding of CC. People's money consciousness may change if they understand the purpose and basic philosophy of CC. Table 11.11 shows the degree of citizens' understanding of CC before and after the experiment. To examine the change in understanding of CC, the statistical difference was determined using McNemar's test ($\chi^2(5) = 22.60$, $p < .001$). Citizens' understanding of CC increased after the experiment. Many people answered 'I have heard about community currency, but I have little understanding of it' before the experiment, but after the experiment they changed their response to 'I understand a little about community currency' or 'I understand community currency well'. In total, 85% of respondents answered 'I understand a little' or 'I understand well' after the experiment (Table 11.12). The results indicate that the degree of understanding of CC was improved and many respondents understood CC well through the experiment.

Table 11.10 Subscale scores on money consciousness before-and-after experiment

	Before-experiment		*After-experiment*		
	Mean	*SD*	*Mean*	*SD*	*t - value*
Currency diversity	2.53	.54	2.58	.55	−6.51
Fairness	3.10	.55	3.10	.57	−0.34
Profit orientation	2.41	.72	2.32	.67	1.07

Table 11.11 Understanding of CC before-and-after the experiment

	Degree of understanding about CC after the experiment				*McNemar test*
Degree of understanding about CC before the experiment	*I do not understand CC at all.*	*I have heard of CC, but I do not understand it well.*	*I understand CC a little.*	*I understand CC well.*	*p – value*
I do not understand CC at all.	1	3	3	0	
I have heard of CC, but I do not understand it.	0	4	14	2	.00
I understand CC a little.	0	5	30	13	
I understand CC well.	0	0	1	8	

n=84

The respondents were grouped into 'not improved' and 'improved' according to their understanding of CC before and after the experiment (Table 11.11). The former, inside the solid line in Table 11.11, represents people whose answers were unchanged before and after the experiment (n = 43). The latter, indicated inside the dashed line boxes, shows people who improved their understanding of CC through the experiment (n = 35).[6] There were significant differences between the two groups.

We focused on further analysing these differences. Table 11.13 shows changes in the subscale scores of the two groups across the three factors. The scores for fairness and profit orientation did not differ significantly between the two groups. However, the score of the improved group for currency diversity was significantly higher than the not improved one (t (31) = −2.01, p <.1).

Table 11.12 Degree of understanding CC after the experiment

	Distribution of degree of understanding about CC after the experiment					
	I do not understand CC at all.	*I have heard of CC, but I understand it.*	*I understand CC a little.*	*I understand CC well.*	χ^2 *(df=3)*	*p – value*
Frequency (proportion)	1(1%)	12(14%)	49(58%)	23(27%)	59.71*	0.00

n=85* *p*<.001

Table 11.13 Subscale scores on understanding CC before-and-after the experiment

	Degree of understanding about CC	*Before-experiment*	*After-experiment*	*Deviation*	*p-value*
		Mean	*Mean*		
Currency diversity	Not improved group (*n* = 37)	2.68	2.6	−0.08	.37
	Improved group (*n* = 31)	2.34	2.56	0.22	.05*
Fairness	Not improved group (*n* = 37)	3.18	3.18	0	1.00
	Improved group (*n* = 32)	2.9	2.92	0.02	.78
Profit orientaion	Not improved group (*n* = 37)	2.36	2.36	0	1.00
	Improved group (*n* = 33)	2.42	2.29	−0.13	.30

**p*<.1

11.6.2 Flow of the micro-meso-macro loop in the circulation test of CC

We apply the flow of the micro-meso-macro loop discussed in the theoretical section (section 11.2) to the results of our investigations (Figure 11.2). The introduction of CC at the meso level ([1] in Figure 11.2) improved the understanding of CC at the micro level ([2] in Figure 11.2). This change strengthened the tendency to approve of currency diversity by recognising the significance and implications of CC ([3] in Figure 11.2). Thus far, the process has been proven by our investigation (Table 11.13). Once currency diversity is accepted, the consciousness of currency diversity may be transmitted in a society ([4] in Figure 11.2). The interactions [3] and [4] may act as a positive feedback loop between the meso and micro levels, causing shared consciousness and encouraging reviews of the CC system ([5] in Figure 11.2). Moreover, actions from the micro or meso levels to the macro level may occur. If we observe these flows, we can show that the micro-meso-macro loop functions in socio-economic regions.

We think that the micro-meso-macro loop framework is useful in designing a CC system that includes changes in people's consciousness, although only the relationship between the micro and meso levels is shown in Figure 11.2 due to the lack of investigation on how the introduction of CC affects the macro level (e.g. economic revitalisation). The usefulness comes from the fact that the framework makes it possible to consider the types of effects that the introduction of CC has on each level in the community. In fact, the analysis, based on the framework about several instances of CC, brought about the claim that increasing citizens' understanding of CC is critical in maintaining its circulation. In order for the framework to be more efficient, circulation experiments with longer periods and large-scale investigation should be conducted to clarify how CC affects the macro level.

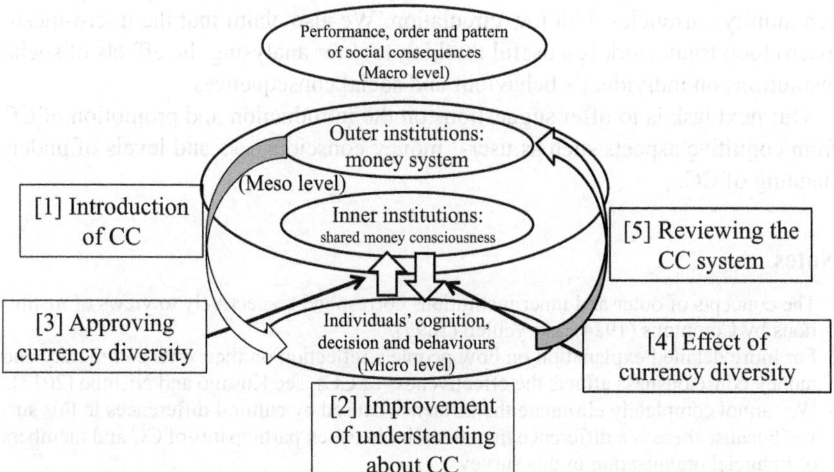

Figure 11.2 Flow of micro-meso-macro loop in the circulation experiment of CC

11.7 Conclusion

In this study, we considered how shared money consciousness at the meso level affects the micro or macro levels and how it changes through the use of CC based on the micro-meso-macro loop. By analysing responses to questionnaires on money consciousness in the areas of Japan, Brazil and Italy, we positively prove our two hypotheses: (i) there is a difference in money consciousness between participants of community currency and others, and (ii) there is a correlation between citizens' money consciousness and the circulation status of CC.

First, the operators and users of CCs tended to place more importance on currency diversity and fairness than others (currency diversity: 3.41 vs. 2.76; fairness: 4.28 vs. 3.37). Their money consciousness was in significant contrast to that of members of financial organisations who placed less significance on currency diversity and fairness than 'others' (currency diversity: 2.14 vs. 2.76; fairness: 3.06 vs. 3.37).

Second, the users of a CC with a high circulation (e.g. Palmas) had higher currency diversity and fairness than those (e.g. Japan) using one with a low circulation (currency diversity: 3.26 vs. 2.53; fairness: 3.91 vs. 3.01). Thus, the introduction of CC at the meso level enhanced the currency diversity and fairness of users at the micro level according to CC circulation status.

In an experiment of community currency circulation conducted in the Musashino-chuo area of Japan, no significant differences were found in the three factors before and after the circulation experiment. However, the users with a better understanding of community currency placed a high value on currency diversity, indicating that implementing activities to enhance citizens' understanding of community currency may develop their tolerance for currency diversity.

By analysing shared money consciousness regarding the three factors, we conclude that participants in CCs with high circulation have money consciousness characteristics of higher currency diversity and fairness, unlike participants in community currencies with low circulation. We also claim that the micro-meso-macro loop framework is a useful thinking tool for analysing the effects of social institutions on individual's behaviour and social consequences.

Our next task is to offer suggestions on the introduction and promotion of CC from cognitive aspects such as users' money consciousness and levels of understanding of CC.

Notes

1 The concepts of outer and inner institutions correspond respectively to views of institutions by Commons (1924) and Veblen (1899).
2 For more detailed explanation on how people's reflection on their own community and money consciousness affects the effectiveness of CCs, see Kusago and Nishibe (2017).
3 We cannot completely eliminate the influence caused by cultural differences in this survey because there is a difference in nationality between participants of CC and members of financial organisation in this survey.
4 For further details on 'Mu-chu', refer to Kurita et al. (2012).
5 For further details on 'Banco Palmas', refer to Jayo et al. (2009).
6 The number of samples in Tables 11.11 and 11.13 differs because respondents who did not answer all the questions on money consciousness were removed from the analysis in Table 11.13.

References

Commons, J. R. 1924. *Legal Foundations of Capitalism.* New York: The Macmillan Company.

Furnham, A. 1984. 'Many Sides of the Coin: The Psychology of Money Usage', *Personality and Individual Differences* 5, no. 5: 501–509.

Hashimoto, T. and M. Nishibe. 2005. 'Rule Ecology Dynamics for Studying Dynamical and Interactional Nature of Social Institutions', in *Proceedings of the 10th International Symposium on Artificial Life and Robotics*, CD-ROM.

Hashimoto, T. and M. Nishibe. 2017. 'Theoretical Model of Institutional Ecosystems and Its Economic Implications', *Evolutionary and Institutional Economics Review* 14, no. 1: 1–27.

Jayo, M., M. Pozzebon and E. H. Diniz. 2009. 'Microcredit and Innovative Local Development in Fortaleza, Brazil: The Case of Banco Palmas', *Canadian Journal of Regional Science* 16, no. 1: 115.

Kobayashi, S.*, M. Nishibe*, K. Kurita. and T. Hashimoto. 2010. 'Difference of Money Consciousness by Social Activities: Community Currency Participants VS Financial Organization Participants', (in Japanese) *Chuo Business Review* 17: 73–91. (*equal contribution)

Kurita, K., Y. Miyazaki. and M. Nishibe. 2012. 'CC Coupon Circulation and Shopkeepers' Behavior: A Case Study of the City of Musashino, Tokyo, Japan', *International Journal of Community Currency Research* 16: 136–145.

Kusago, T.* and M. Nishibe.* 2017. 'Community Dock: A New Policy Approach for Altering Institutions', *in this volume. (*equal contribution)*

Nishibe, M. 2012. 'Community Currencies as Integrative Communication Media for Evolutionist Institutional Design', *International Journal of Community Currency Research* 16.D: 36–48.

Seyfang, G. and N. Longhurst. 2013. 'Growing Green Money? Mapping Community Currencies for Sustainable Development', *Ecological Economics* 86: 65–77.

Veblen, T. 1899. *The Theory of the Leisure Class: An Economic Study in the Evolution of Institutions.* New York: Macmillan.

Yamauchi, K. T. and D. J. Templer. 1982. 'The Development of a Money Attitude Scale', *Journal of Personality Assessment* 46, no. 5: 522–528.

Appendix: survey questionnaire for money consciousness

Please answer the following questions by choosing and circling one of the five options intuitively without thinking too much or taking too long (within 20 seconds). The questions should be answered in the same order as presented below.

1) Do you think the government should provide welfare payment for the poverty class?

   a) Strongly agree, b) Weakly agree, c) Neutral, d) Weakly disagree, e) Strongly disagree

2) Do you think it is natural for money to be interest-bearing?

   a) Strongly agree, b) Weakly agree, c) Neutral, d) Weakly disagree, e) Strongly disagree

3) Do you think it is good that we have free time even without a lot of money?

   a) Strongly agree, b) Weakly agree, c) Neutral, d) Weakly disagree, e) Strongly disagree

4) Do you think it is good that money can be created or issued freely by people?

   a) Strongly agree, b) Weakly agree, c) Neutral, d) Weakly disagree, e) Strongly disagree

5) Do you think it is good for money to be created or issued by a credible group or organisation?

   a) Strongly agree, b) Weakly agree, c) Neutral, d) Weakly disagree, e) Strongly disagree

6) Do you think money is not as important as health?

   a) Strongly agree, b) Weakly agree, c) Neutral, d) Weakly disagree, e) Strongly disagree

7) Do you think it's good for money to be able to buy anything you want?

   a) Strongly agree, b) Weakly agree, c) Neutral, d) Weakly disagree, e) Strongly disagree

8) Do you think it is good that money can be issued or created not only by the central bank or commercial banks, but also by the government?

   a) Strongly agree, b) Weakly agree, c) Neutral, d) Weakly disagree, e) Strongly disagree

9) Do you think money can't buy love and friendship?

   a) Strongly agree, b) Weakly agree, c) Neutral, d) Weakly disagree, e) Strongly disagree

10) Do you think the government should provide every adult beyond a certain age with basic income for their minimum standard of living?

   a) Strongly agree, b) Weakly agree, c) Neutral, d) Weakly disagree, e) Strongly disagree

11) Do you think it is good that money can be something that mutually connects people?

   a) Strongly agree, b) Weakly agree, c) Neutral, d) Weakly disagree, e) Strongly disagree

12) Do you think it is good that money can be created or issued for the purpose of profit?
    a) Strongly agree, b) Weakly agree, c) Neutral, d) Weakly disagree, e) Strongly disagree

13) Do you think moneylenders should not be in such financial institutions as commercial banks, but the government?
    a) Strongly agree, b) Weakly agree, c) Neutral, d) Weakly disagree, e) Strongly disagree

14) Do you think we do not need extra money while we can get along?
    a) Strongly agree, b) Weakly agree, c) Neutral, d) Weakly disagree, e) Strongly disagree

15) Do you think it is better to earn increasingly more money?
    a) Strongly agree, b) Weakly agree, c) Neutral, d) Weakly disagree, e) Strongly disagree

16) Do you think it is good to do volunteer work or make donations without compensation?
    a) Strongly agree, b) Weakly agree, c) Neutral, d) Weakly disagree, e) Strongly disagree

17) Do you think it is good that we can choose favourite ones out of different moneys?
    a) Strongly agree, b) Weakly agree, c) Neutral, d) Weakly disagree, e) Strongly disagree

18) Do you think money should not concentrate in a tiny fraction of people, but disperse among all?
    a) Strongly agree, b) Weakly agree, c) Neutral, d) Weakly disagree, e) Strongly disagree

19) Do you think it is good that we accommodate each other with money?
    a) Strongly agree, b) Weakly agree, c) Neutral, d) Weakly disagree, e) Strongly disagree

20) Do you think it is good to lend money to your friend when they are in a financial need?
    a) Strongly agree, b) Weakly agree, c) Neutral, d) Weakly disagree, e) Strongly disagree

21) Do you think it is good for money to be stable in its value?

    a) Strongly agree, b) Weakly agree, c) Neutral, d) Weakly disagree, e) Strongly disagree

22) Do you think it is good that we have different moneys other than national currency to live with?

    a) Strongly agree, b) Weakly agree, c) Neutral, d) Weakly disagree, e) Strongly disagree

23) Do you think it is good to have single money?

    a) Strongly agree, b) Weakly agree, c) Neutral, d) Weakly disagree, e) Strongly disagree

24) Do you think it is good that we have special money for paying for volunteer work?

    a) Strongly agree, b) Weakly agree, c) Neutral, d) Weakly disagree, e) Strongly disagree

25) Do you think it is good that money can be issued or created not only by the central bank or commercial banks, but also by people or communities?

    a) Strongly agree, b) Weakly agree, c) Neutral, d) Weakly disagree, e) Strongly disagree

26) Do you think money transactions should be anonymous?

    a) Strongly agree, b) Weakly agree, c) Neutral, d) Weakly disagree, e) Strongly disagree

27) Do you think it is good for money to be able to be passable at any place and area?

    a) Strongly agree, b) Weakly agree, c) Neutral, d) Weakly disagree, e) Strongly disagree

12 Gaming simulation using electronic community currencies

Behavioural analysis of self-versus-community consciousness

Masahiro Mikami and Makoto Nishibe

12.1 Introduction

In terms of their issuance and circulation, traditional community currencies (CCs) are classified into three types: paper money CCs (centrally issued, physically circulating), draft CCs (dispersedly issued, physically circulating) and account CCs (dispersedly issued, mutually paid) (Nishibe 2002, 36–43).[1] Recent ICT advancements have not only made these three types of CCs electronic, but also facilitated a fourth type, namely centrally issued, mutually paid CCs.[2] For example, CCs that use media such as smartcards are centrally issued but owned by each user in a decentralised way. However, owing to existing networking technology and networking devices and lines, it is now possible to make payments through mutual value transfers on remote servers.[3] Although such payment technology is typically used for business-to-consumer commercial transactions, CCs that deal with non-commercial transactions (volunteering) and electronic money that deals with commercial transactions (business) could merge further in the future.

Centrally issued, mutually paid electronic CCs improve the convenience and efficiency of individual payments by using electronic recording and calculation processes. Moreover, they can change the operation of CCs in two main ways. First, they make it possible to create several complicated media designs (institutional currency designs) and can incorporate more than one currency in each medium. Furthermore, during the introduction, or circulation period, one can change such parameters as the premium rate (the rate of the bonus added to the value of the CC during the conversion of the legal tender to the CC), the redemption fee rate (the rate of the discount reduced from the value of the CC during the conversion of the CC to the legal tender), the depreciation rate (the negative interest rate to devaluate the CC over time), upper-lower balance limits and points or fees per transaction.[4] Second, the traceability of transactional data has improved, making it possible to analyse in real time records on individual transactions, issued balances, transaction amounts, circulation velocity, circulation route and circulation network.[5] Such information could be used to select a suitable media design that could meet issuers' objectives and disclose information on CCs to participants.

Such changes in the operation of CCs could alter the type of information possessed by participants on CCs and their communities, thus affecting the participant's subsequent knowledge and behaviour. The participants' understanding of the communities and the CCs would enhance if the aggregate information of circulation amount, CC transactions and activities are provided along with various CC parameters. Keeping this in mind, in the present study we have built a contactless card payment system and a virtual community of local shops, local non-profit organisations (NPOs), local consumers and national chain stores to examine how electronic CCs work. We then perform an experiment using a gaming simulation and an ex post questionnaire to examine participants' behaviour patterns. Such patterns can change depending on (i) the premium rates of CCs, (ii) participants' consciousness about self and community, and (iii) the availability of aggregate information on the transactions and activities in the community.

The rest of this chapter is organised as follows. In the next section we explain the method of experiment for this study using gaming simulation, including the subjects of the experiment, structure of the virtual community using CCs and the game conditions. Section 12.3 considers results of the experiment and questionnaire in terms of the circulation of currencies (Section 12.3.1), activities of the subjects (Section 12.3.2), their behavioural objectives and community consciousness (Section 12.3.3), and the effects of providing aggregate information (Section 12.3.4). Section 12.4 is the conclusion.

12.2 Method of the experiment

In this study of a contactless card payment system, we recruited 12 subjects (undergraduate and graduate students) and carried out an experiment using a gaming simulation.[6] In the computer room we set up a virtual community composed of two local shops, two local NPOs, two chain stores and 12 local citizens (consumers). Each player used an electronic card to record the values of the legal currency, Yen, and the fabricated CC, Clark.[7] Using their own computers, consumers could perform a number of actions: exchange Clark for Yen (thereby the CC goes into circulation), inquire about their balances or confirm their transaction histories. Consumers could also carry out 'transactions' in local shops, local NPOs or chain stores by choosing to buy goods and services, donating, volunteering or working part-time. However, consumers could pay by using either Clark or Yen (or both) in local shops that could convert Clark into Yen, whereas NPOs accepted only Clark and chain stores (located outside the community) accepted only Yen (Figure 12.1).

As this experiment aimed to observe economic behaviour with respect to the CCs investigated here, we abstracted irrelevant factors to smoothen the progress of the game. For example, to carry out actual market transactions it would be necessary to discover the parties with whom we would be dealing with, to know what we were dealing with and on what terms, to conduct negotiations, to draw up the contract, to confirm that the terms of the contract were being observed and so on. The transaction costs of these activities might then condition the manner in which these transactions are conducted and even the establishment of the transactions

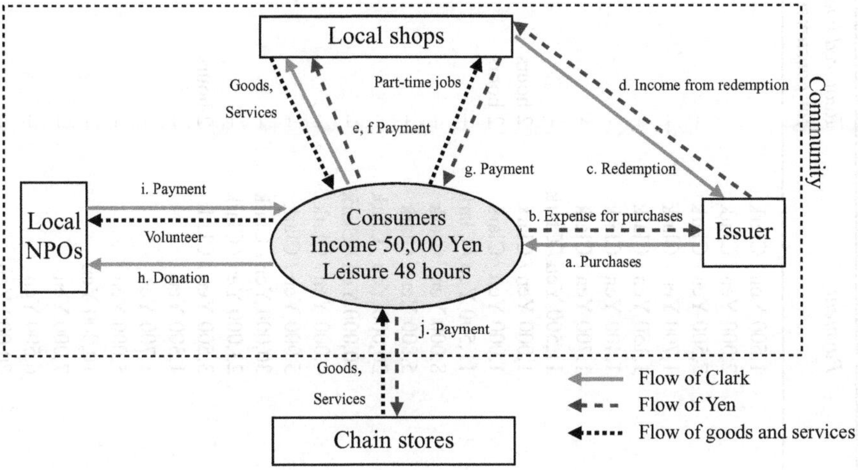

Figure 12.1 Flows of Clark and Yen

themselves (Coase 1937, 1960). This fact might be essential in the case of transaction of CCs as well. However, we removed any transaction costs that were not specific to the use of CCs in order for players to focus their attention on the choice between CCs and legal currencies. Further, to prevent the games from becoming only a problem of price negotiation and supply-and-demand matching (which are irrelevant to the characteristics of the currencies used) the types and prices of the goods and services provided by players were defined in advance (Table 12.1). It was also assumed that their stock was unlimited.

In this experiment, for simplification, we focused on consumers' behaviour towards CCs and assumed that all shops and NPOs play only passive roles. In other words, the roles of the local shops, local NPOs and chain stores were played by assistants (not by the experiment's subjects). Specifically, these assistants sold goods and services to (and received Clark or Yen from) consumers, accepted part-time workers from (and paid Yen to) consumers, accepted volunteers from (and paid Clark to) consumers and accepted donations (in Clark) from consumers under the allocated budgets. By contrast, within their income of 50,000 Yen and leisure time of 48 hours per game, consumers could buy the necessary amount of Clark and choose freely from the various uses of their Clark or Yen amounts. At the beginning of each game, subjects were required to choose 'self' or 'community' as their behavioural priority, write down their choice on the reverse of their currency cards and follow their behavioural priority in each game.[8]

Each game lasted 20 minutes and we played five games under different conditions. These game conditions included the media design of the CC and the method of providing feedback about the transaction data to the subjects as aggregate information (Table 12.2). For the parameters concerning the media design of the CC, we set the premium rate (10%, 15% and 20%) in each game. However, we did not

Table 12.1 Menu of goods and services provided

Seller	*Buyer*	*Name of goods and services*	*Payment*	*Required hours for consumers*
Local shop A	Consumers	1 Side dishes, lunch	1,500 Yen / Clark	–
		2 Alcohol	2,000 Yen / Clark	–
		3 Kitchen items	7,500 Yen / Clark	–
		4 Stationery	1,700 Yen / Clark	–
		5 Books	1,150 Yen / Clark	–
		6 Music CDs	1,400 Yen / Clark	–
		7 Movie DVDs	1,700 Yen / Clark	–
		8 Game software	11,500 Yen / Clark	–
		9 Tearoom	1,000 Yen / Clark	2 hours
		10 Cheap restaurant	1,000 Yen / Clark	2 hours
Local shop B	Consumers	1 Bags	11,500 Yen / Clark	–
		2 Clothes	8,000 Yen / Clark	–
		3 Shoes	5,800 Yen / Clark	–
		4 Sporting goods	20,000 Yen / Clark	–
		5 Tools	10,000 Yen / Clark	–
		6 Gardening supplies	4,000 Yen / Clark	–
		7 Pet products	5,000 Yen / Clark	–
		8 Camping equipment	30,000 Yen / Clark	–
		9 Bicycles	23,000 Yen / Clark	–
		10 Karaoke	3,500 Yen / Clark	2 hours
Chain store A	Consumers	1 Side dishes, lunch	1,300 Yen	–
		2 Alcohol	1,700 Yen	–
		3 Shoes	5,000 Yen	–
		4 Bags	10,000 Yen	–
		5 Clothes	7,000 Yen	–
		6 Kitchen items	6,500 Yen	–
		7 Interior accessories	20,000 Yen	–

		8 Stationery	1,500 Yen	–
		9 Café	2,000 Yen	2 hours
		10 Restaurant	5,000 Yen	2 hours
Chain store B	Consumers	1 Books	1,000 Yen	–
		2 Music CDs	1,200 Yen	–
		3 Movie DVDs	1,500 Yen	–
		4 Game software	10,000 Yen	–
		5 Bicycles	20,000 Yen	–
		6 PCs	50,000 Yen	–
		7 Karaoke	3,000 Yen	2 hours
		8 Bowling	2,000 Yen	1 hour
		9 Movie theater	1,800 Yen	2 hours
		10 Domestic travel	70,000 Yen	24 hours
Consumers	Local NPO A[1]	1 Educational activity for the youth (assistance for camping)	1,000 Clark	24 hours
		2 Assistance for festivals and events	200 Clark	3 hours
		3 Patrol for the safety of children and road users	100 Clark	1 hour
		4 Cleaning and gardening activity in the community	150 Clark	1 hour
		5 Teaching at a free school	450 Clark	3 hours
		6 Donation	1,000 Clark	–
	Local NPO B[2]	1 Support for child care (temporary day care)	500 Clark	5 hours
		2 Support for the elderly (shopping and so on)	300 Clark	2 hours
		3 Nursing care for the elderly (personal care)	800 Clark	8 hours
		4 Assistance for neighbours (yard maintenance and pet care)	300 Clark	3 hours
		5 Crop work in the neighborhood	600 Clark	6 hours
		6 Donation	1,000 Clark	–
	Local shop A	Part-time job	1,000 Yen	1 hour
	Local shop B	Part-time job	1,000 Yen	1 hour

* Shaded goods and services can be replaced by those with the same name.

[1] Volunteer work at NPO A concerns the events and activities held in the local community

[2] Volunteer work at NPO B concerns care for individuals in the local community

introduce a depreciation rate, upper balance limit and points or fees per transaction. The lower balance limit was fixed at zero. The redemption fee rate was the same as the premium rate because local shops in this experiment that would pay the redemption fee had no option to join or leave the CC, nor could they decide on the prices of their merchandise. To give feedback and information on the aggregate data we prepared three modes (non-display, bar chart and line chart) and the selected mode was altered between different games or in the middle of the game (ten minutes after the game had started). The information used in this experiment was composed of 11 types of aggregate information based on the quantity of the various transactions and activities in terms of Clark and Yen (Table 12.3).

The game design discussed above is based on the following hypotheses: first, for the premium rate, we made the hypothesis that the higher the premium rate at which the subjects buy Clark for Yen, the more Clark they purchase. Consumers compare inside and outside prices in real terms (with the premium rate considered) and consume either in local shops or in chain stores depending on those prices. In this experiment, we offered some goods and services with the same name in both local shops and chain stores. The prices of this merchandise were fixed so that the 10% premium rate made inside prices higher than outside prices,

Table 12.2 Changes in the conditions between the games

Game progress	*Premium and redemption fee rates*	*Feedback method (arrows show a change after 10 minutes)*
Game I	both 10%	non-display -> bar chart
Game II	both 10%	non-display -> line chart
Game III	both 20%	non-display -> bar chart
Game IV	both 20%	non-display -> line chart
Game V	both 15%	bar chart -> line chart

Table 12.3 Information displayed in the games

a	Cumulative total purchases of Clark by consumers (in Clark)
b	Cumulative total expenses for purchases of Clark by consumers (in Yen)
c	Cumulative total redemption of Clark by local shops (in Clark)
d	Cumulative total income of local shops from redemption of Clark (in Yen)
e	Cumulative total consumption in Clark in local shops (in Clark)
f	Cumulative total consumption in Yen in local shops (in Yen)
e&f	Cumulative total consumption in local shops (in Clark and Yen) (=*e*+*f*)
g	Cumulative total payment for part-time jobs in local shops (in Yen)
h	Cumulative total donations to local NPOs (in Clark)
i	Cumulative total payment for volunteering in local NPOs (in Clark)
j	Cumulative total consumption in chain stores (in Yen)

* The letters in Table 12.3 correspond to the flows of Clark and Yen in Figure 12.1.

the 20% premium rate made outside prices higher than inside prices and the 15% premium rate made either price higher depending on the type of merchandise.

Second, for the methods of displaying information, we hypothesised that if the subjects could see that information they would know other people's behaviour and thus alter their behaviour by using Yen and Clark. Furthermore, different ways of displaying information would bring about different influences. For example, bar charts (which show information at a specific point in time) would be less useful than line charts (which show information changing over time) for grasping the overall trends in the community. The changes in these conditions such as the premium rate and methods of displaying information were not told to the subjects before each game.

Lastly, for the knowledge and behaviour of the subjects, we made the hypothesis that each player's consciousness of self and community would determine his or her behaviour and the activity of the community. To test this hypothesis, we asked the subjects to choose their behavioural priority (self or community) at the beginning of each game to compare this ex ante priority with the ex post priority in their actual behaviour. In this way, we aimed to examine how such a simple behavioural priority might lead to particular behaviour under the particular institutional structures including the CC.[9]

12.3 Experiment results, questionnaire results and implications

12.3.1 Amounts of currencies and their circulation velocity

In general, the circulating conditions of CCs can be estimated by using the amount of currency issued, amount redeemed, outstanding issued amount and aggregate amounts of the various transactions using those currencies.[10] Furthermore, based on those aggregate amounts, we can calculate their circulation velocity as their degree of contribution to the activeness of communities, which we can compare with that of legal currencies. Under the experimental framework, we can calculate the amount of Clark issued (a), amount of Clark redeemed (c), outstanding issue of Clark (a-c), amount of transactions using Clark (e+h+i), local inflow of Yen (e.g. if the income is Yen 50,000, then 12 consumers earn Yen 600,000), local outflow of Yen (j), local circulating balance of Yen (600,000–j), and local amount of transactions using Yen (f+g). For each of the five games, Table 12.4 shows the results obtained by calculating these indexes. The velocities of circulation of Clark and Yen can be calculated with the following formulae, respectively.

The circulation velocity of Clark

$$= \frac{\textit{The amount of transactions using Clark from the game start to the game end } (e+h+i)}{\textit{The outstanding issue of Clark at the game end } (a-c)}$$

Table 12.4 The amounts and the circulation velocity during each game[11]

Game progress	*The amount of transactions using Clark*	*The amount of Clark issued*	*The amount of Clark redeemed*	*The outstanding issue of Clark*	*The circulation velocity of Clark*	*The amount of transactions using Yen*	*The local inflow of Yen*	*The local outflow of Yen*	*The local circulating balance of Yen*	*The circulation velocity of Yen*
Game I	270,000	306,658	217,350	89,308	3.02	218,700	600,000	298,900	301,100	0.73
Game II	476,750	476,740	312,400	164,340	2.90	209,900	600,000	185,400	414,600	0.51
Game III	479,300	473,334	269,600	203,734	2.35	202,000	600,000	289,800	310,200	0.65
Game IV	641,500	657,737	349,500	308,237	2.08	231,400	600,000	156,800	443,200	0.52
Game V	482,500	562,806	328,500	234,306	2.06	248,000	600,000	190,500	409,500	0.61

$$\textit{The velocity of circulation of Yen} = \frac{\textit{The amount of transactions using Yen from game start to the game end } (f+g)}{\textit{The outstanding issue of Yen at the game end } (600{,}000 - j)}$$

Table 12.4 shows that the circulation velocity of Clark is three to six times higher than that of Yen as a result of the institutional structure of the local CC used in this experiment. The flows of Clark and Yen (Figure 12.1) show that Yen obtained as income or earnings for part-time work by consumers must be used (when used within the community) in local shops or converted into Clark (i.e. excluding chain stores). By contrast, although Clark obtained in exchange for Yen or volunteer work can be used in local shops or local NPOs, consumers cannot exchange Clark into Yen. This shows that Clark, which has several usages or several circulation routes, is therefore structurally easy to circulate, and thus contributes to the transaction activity and has a significantly higher circulation velocity than the Yen.

In addition, the per-minute circulation velocity of Clark and Yen are calculated by using the following formulae, respectively:

$$\textit{The per-minute circulation velocity of Clark from } t \textit{ to } t+1 \textit{ minutes after game start} = \frac{\textit{The amount of transactions using Clark from } t \textit{ to } t+1 \textit{ minutes after game start}}{\textit{The outstanding issue of Clark at } t+1 \textit{ minutes after game start}}$$

$$\textit{The per-minute velocity of circulation of Yen} = \frac{\textit{The amount of transactions using Yen from } t \textit{ to } t+1 \textit{ minutes after game start}}{\textit{The outstanding issue of Yen at } t+1 \textit{ minutes after game start}}$$

By using these formulae, the development of the circulation velocity in each game is shown in Figures 12.2 to 12.6.

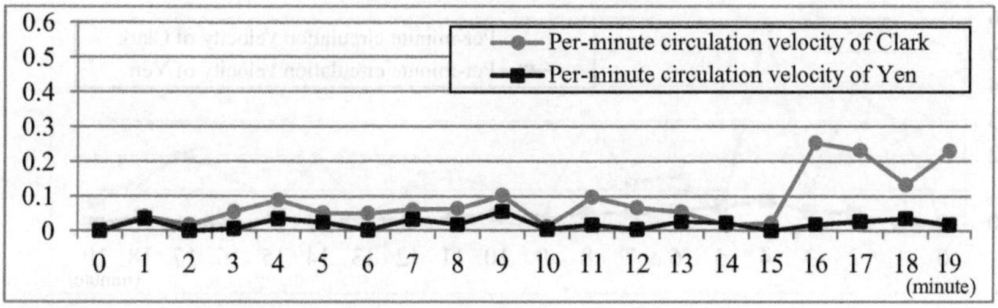

Figure 12.2 The development of circulation velocity in Game I

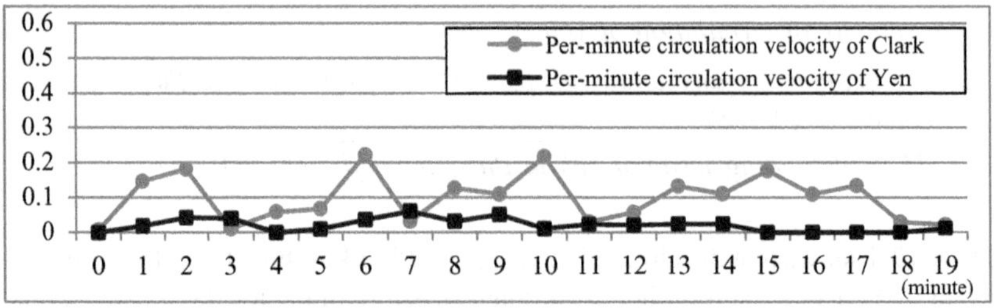

Figure 12.3 The development of circulation velocity in Game II

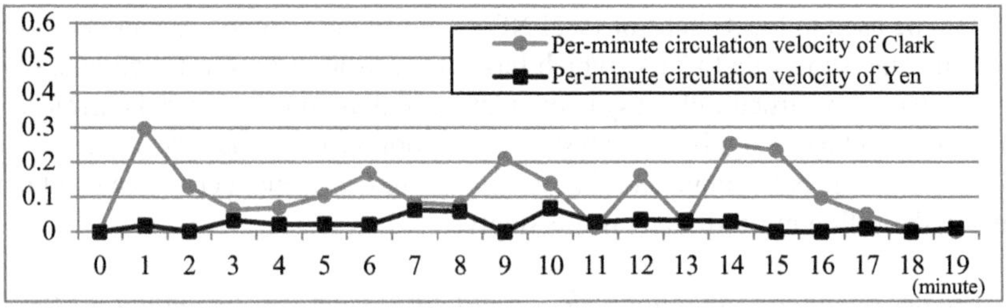

Figure 12.4 The development of circulation velocity in Game III

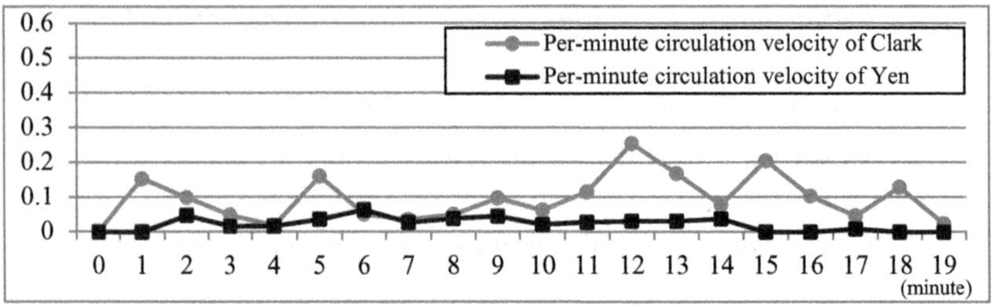

Figure 12.5 The development of circulation velocity in Game IV

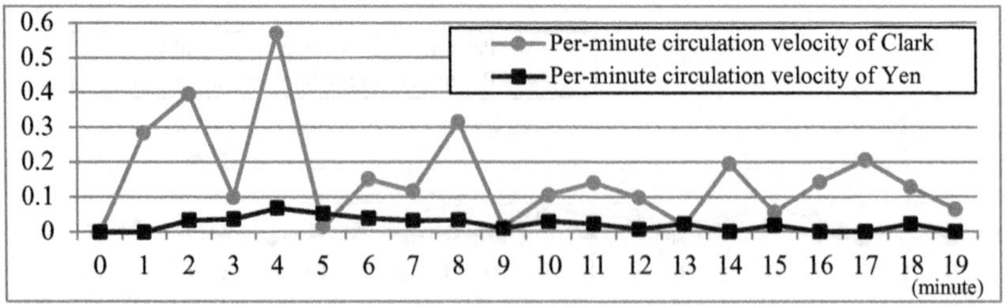

Figure 12.6 The development of circulation velocity in Game V

The causes behind the changes in circulation velocity are identified by using the development of the subject's activities, which in turn are related to the alterations in game conditions (e.g. increase and decrease in the premium rate) as well as methods of displaying aggregate amounts and also to the subject's behavioural objectives. In Section 12.3.2, we first confirm the attributes of the subjects that could condition the game, the quantitative development of the subject's behaviour and the influence of the different premium rates on those behaviours. We then examine the relationship between the subjects' behaviour and their behavioural objectives in Section 12.3.3 and the relationship between the subjects' behaviour and the graphs of aggregate amounts in Section 12.3.4.

12.3.2 Attributes of the subjects, the premium rate and the amount of activities

According to the results of the ex post questionnaire, the majority of the subjects had little prior knowledge or experience in CCs. Regarding the question, 'Do you know about community currencies?', two subjects answered, 'I know them well', nine answered, 'I don't know them well but I have heard about them', and one answered, 'I know nothing about them'.[12] To the question, 'Have you ever used community currencies?', two subjects (i.e. those that were knowledgeable in the previous question) answered, 'I have used community currencies' and ten answered, 'I've never received or used community currencies'. Therefore, the majority of the subjects had to learn the role of CCs, especially the meaning and function of the electronic CC used in the virtual community set-up in this experiment. Although the subjects were provided with a map of the virtual community in the room and the flowchart of currencies (Figure 12.1), they might have understood the structure of the games only after they actually experienced them.

We then attempted to understand the factors that determined the amount purchased and amount of the various Clark transactions in each game. According to our hypothesis proposed in Section 12.2, one of those factors might be the premium rate. However, the relationship between the premium rate and all consumers' amounts of the various activities in each game in Table 12.5 showed no statistically significant correlation.

Table 12.6 shows the correlation coefficients between the premium rates and amount of the various activities in Games I–V per consumer. Only two of the 12 subjects (i.e. Consumers A and C) took action to increase their consumption in local shops when the premium rate rose, which increased the amount purchased. For Consumer A, when the premium rate rose, he or she increased his or her part-time job (receiving more Yen to purchase more Clark), increased his or her donation to local NPOs (using more leftover Clark), used no Yen in local shops and decreased his or her consumption in chain stores (buying relatively inexpensive items in local shops). Two other consumers (i.e. Consumers B and G) reduced their volunteering work in local NPOs when the premium rate rose (because the purchase from Yen was a more advantageous method for obtaining Yen than payment for volunteering was). Thus, while the response of the subjects

Table 12.5 Correlations between the premium rates and the amount of activities in each game

Game Progress	*Premium rate*	*Cumulative total purchases of Clark by consumer (in Clark)*	*Cumulative total expenses for purchases of Clark by consumer (in Yen)*	*Cumulative total consumption in local shops (in Clark and Yen)*	*Cumulative total consumption in Clark in local shops (in Clark)*	*Cumulative total consumption in Yen in local shops (in Yen)*	*Cumulative total payment for part-time jobs in local shops (in Yen)*	*Cumulative total donations to local NPOs (in Clark)*	*Cumulative total payment for volunteering in local NPOs (in Clark)*	*Cumulative total consumption in chain stores (in Yen)*	*Consumption in local shops / Consumption in chain stores*	*Payment for volunteering / Payment for part-time jobs*
Game I	10	306,658	278,780	279,550	237,850	41,700	177,000	21,000	11,150	298,900	0.935	0.062
Game II	10	476,740	433,400	391,800	354,900	36,900	173,000	105,000	16,850	185,400	2.113	0.097
Game III	20	473,334	394,445	411,400	392,400	19,000	183,000	73,000	13,900	289,800	1.419	0.076
Game IV	20	657,737	548,114	553,700	541,300	12,400	219,000	86,000	14,200	156,800	3.531	0.065
Game V	15	562,806	489,388	441,600	397,600	44,000	204,000	74,000	10,900	190,500	2.318	0.053
Correlation coefficient with the premium rate		0.670	0.565	0.745	0.785	−0.830	0.663	0.265	0.010	−0.144	0.481	−0.291
p-value		0.216	0.321	0.148	0.116	0.082	0.222	0.667	0.987	0.817	0.411	0.634

to the premium rate varied, on average the effect of the premium rate was small in this experiment.

This analysis was based on the *behaviour* of the subjects. Next, we include their *motives* in our analysis.

12.3.3 The subjects' behavioural objectives and self-versus-community consciousness

In this experiment, the subjects were given the following three instructions for their behaviour:

- Choose and mark 'self' or 'community' on the reverse of your currency card and follow that behavioural priority.
- It is up to you how to use or save the given income and leisure time.
- Do not touch other people's currency cards or PCs and avoid looking at their PCs.

Before each game started the subjects were asked, 'In this game, will you prioritise self or community?' and were required to choose between the two. After all the five games, they were asked in the questionnaire, 'What was your actual weight on self and community in game . . .?' and were required to choose the self to community ratio that matched their actual feelings on a scale of 10:0 to 0:10. That is, the rationality or internal consistency required to be followed by the subjects would not be their constant pursuit of self-interest but the consistency in their weight placed on self or community.[13]

Table 12.7 shows the ex ante behavioural priorities that the subject chose before each game started and their counts by game and by person. As there was no constraint on how many times the subject could choose self or community in the five games, self was selected 37 times and community was selected 23 times if counted for all the games. If counted for each game, Game I had 11 self-oriented participants and only one community-oriented participant, whereas the rest of the games had five or seven self-oriented participants and the remainder were community-oriented, which shows no particular tendency across games.

We then attempted to examine the specific behavioural objectives of self-oriented and community-oriented subjects. In the ex post questionnaire, we asked about their behavioural objectives in each half of each game (up to three answers per person). The result shown in Figure 12.7 highlights that many self-oriented subjects choose 'to earn as much Yen as possible', 'to consume as much as possible' and 'to do as much part-time work in local shops as possible'. On the contrary, many community-oriented subjects chose 'to consume as much as possible in local shops', 'to do as much volunteering as possible in local NPOs' and 'to make as much donations as possible to local NPOs'.

Grouped by their ex ante behavioural priorities, experimental subjects showed the following patterns in their amount of activities in Games I–V. First, all self-oriented consumers followed this pattern: *Consumption in chain stores* >

Table 12.6 Correlations between the premium rate and the amount of activities across all games

Correlation coefficient with the premium rate in Games I–V	*Cumulative total purchases of Clark by consumers (in Clark)*	*Cumulative total expenses for purchases of Clark by consumers (in Yen)*	*Cumulative total consumption in local shops (in Clark and Yen)*	*Cumulative total consumption in Clark in local shops (in Clark)*	*Cumulative total consumption in Yen in local shops (in Yen)*	*Cumulative total payment for part-time jobs in local shops (in Yen)*	*Cumulative total donations to local NPOs (in Clark)*	*Cumulative total payment for volunteering in local NPOs (in Clark)*	*Cumulative total consumption in chain stores (in Yen)*
Consumer A	0.940*	0.939*	0.937*	0.937*	–	0.896*	0.913*	−0.559	−0.892*
Consumer B	0.108	0.060	0.044	0.074	−0.140	0.824	0.502	−0.907*	0.192
Consumer C	0.910*	0.898*	0.932*	0.932*	–	–	0.792	−0.265	−0.165
Consumer D	0.554	0.518	0.869	0.751	0.180	−0.066	−0.456	0.208	−0.559
Consumer E	−0.244	0.310	−0.193	−0.197	0.020	0.591	−0.280	−0.434	0.388
Consumer F	−0.842	−0.890*	−0.475	−0.475	–	–	−0.280	0.770	0.242
Consumer G	−0.187	−0.247	−0.183	0.292	−0.559	0.749	−0.563	−0.906*	0.754
Consumer H	−0.496	−0.542	−0.783	−0.711	−0.908*	−0.498	0.273	0.326	0.544
Consumer I	0.829	0.727	0.375	0.375	–	0.688	−0.144	−0.205	−0.493
Consumer J	0.553	0.644	0.201	0.201	–	−0.494	0.570	0.400	−0.662
Consumer K	0.669	0.609	0.755	0.753	−0.559	−0.227	0.354	0.407	−0.521
Consumer L	0.018	−0.034	−0.051	0.023	−0.559	−0.030	0.157	−0.028	0.303

- not applicable * Statistically significant at 5% significance level

Table 12.7 Behavioural priorities chosen ex ante by the subjects

	Game I	*Game II*	*Game III*	*Game IV*	*Game V*	*Self-oriented*	*Community-oriented*
Consumer A	Self	Self	Community	Self	Self	4 games	1 game
Consumer B	Self	Community	Self	Community	Community	2 games	3 games
Consumer C	Self	Community	Self	Self	Self	4 games	1 game
Consumer D	Self	Community	Community	Self	Community	2 games	3 games
Consumer E	Self	Community	Self	Self	Community	3 games	2 games
Consumer F	Self	Self	Community	Self	Self	4 games	1 game
Consumer G	Self	Community	Self	Self	Self	4 games	1 games
Consumer H	Self	Self	Self	Community	Community	3 games	2 games
Consumer I	Self	Community	Self	Community	Self	3 games	2 games
Consumer J	Self	Self	Community	Self	Community	3 games	2 games
Consumer K	Community	Self	Community	Community	Self	2 games	3 games
Consumer L	Self	Community	Self	Community	Self	3 games	2 games
Self-oriented	11 persons	5 persons	7 persons	7 persons	7 persons	37 games	23 games
Community-oriented	1 person	7 persons	5 persons	5 persons	5 persons		

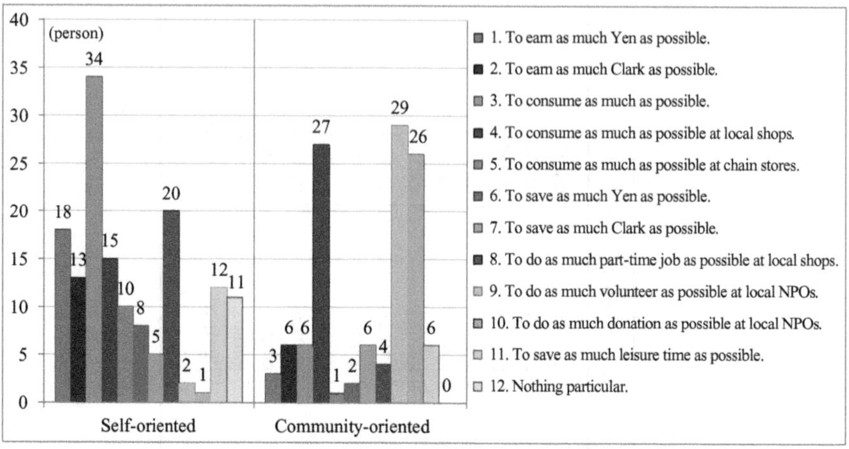

Figure 12.7 Experiment subjects' behavioural objectives through all the games

Consumption in local shops and *Part-time jobs* > *Volunteering*, while community-oriented consumers followed: *Consumption in chain stores* < *Consumption in local shops* and *Part-time jobs* < *Volunteering.*

Second, the following characteristics of the two groups were noted:

- *Consumption in chain stores by self-oriented consumers* > *Consumption in chain stores by community-oriented consumers*
- *Consumption in local shops by self-oriented consumers* > *Consumption in local shops by community-oriented consumers*
- *Part-time job by self-oriented consumers* > *Part-time job by community-oriented consumers* *
- *Volunteering by self-oriented consumers* > *Volunteering by community-oriented consumers* *
- *Donation by self-oriented consumers* < *Donation by community-oriented consumers*

(* Valid in terms of both monetary amount and number of hours)

Thus, we observe clear differences in the amount of activities between the self-oriented and community-oriented groups. Further, for Games I–IV, we find an additional pattern, namely *Clark purchased by self-oriented consumers* < *Clark purchased by community-oriented consumers*, which did not apply for Game V.

The analysis above was based on the subjects' self-determined behavioural priorities (self-oriented or community-oriented) at the beginning of each game. Next we examine whether the rules of such behavioural priorities were actually followed in the games. The subjects may not have necessarily always followed their own choice of behavioural priority. Indeed, in the process of experiencing electronic CCs, behavioural priorities could change from the subject's ex ante choices. Figures 12.8 to 12.12 show their ex post weights on self and community in each group.

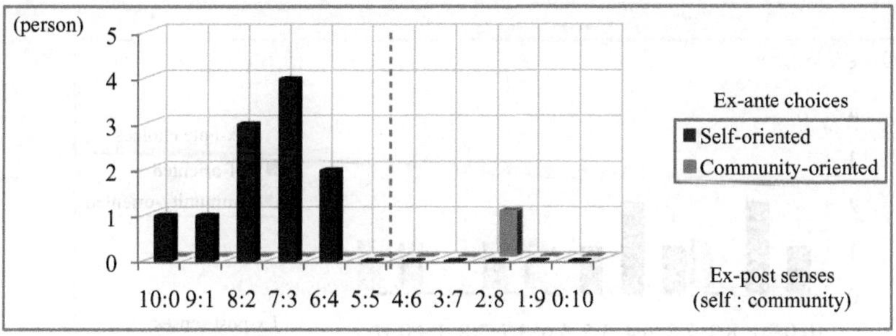

Figure 12.8 Ex ante choices and ex post senses of subjects' behavioural priorities (Game I)

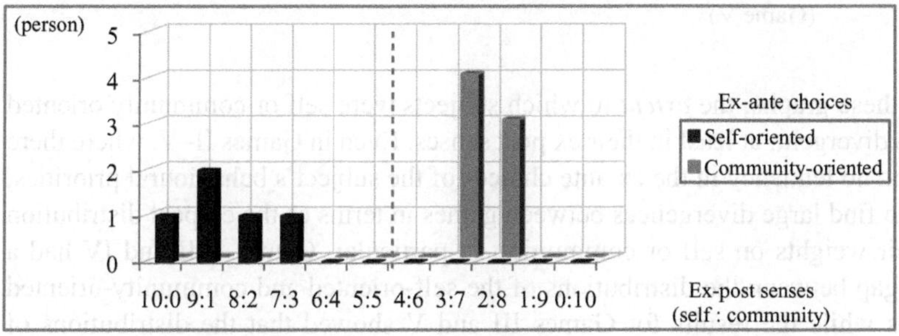

Figure 12.9 Ex ante choices and ex post senses of subjects' behavioural priorities (Game II)

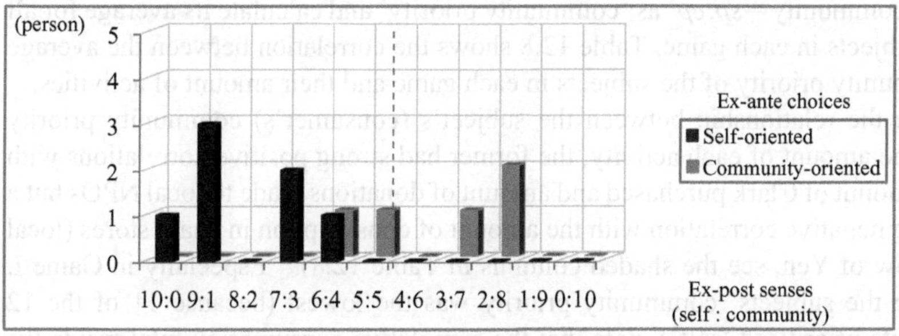

Figure 12.10 Ex ante choices and ex post senses of subjects' behavioural priorities (Game III)

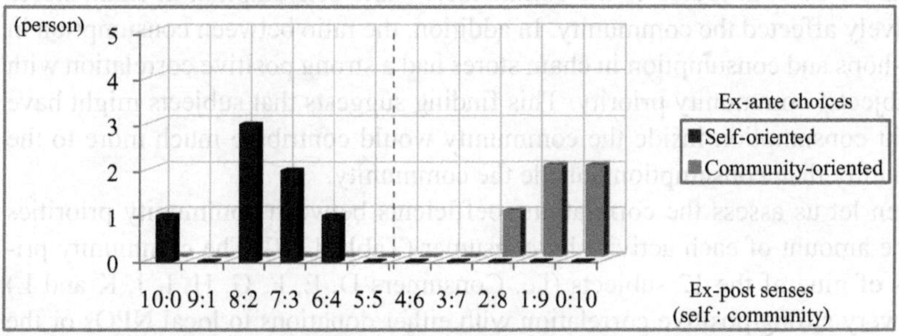

Figure 12.11 Ex ante choices and ex post senses of subjects' behavioural priorities (Game IV)

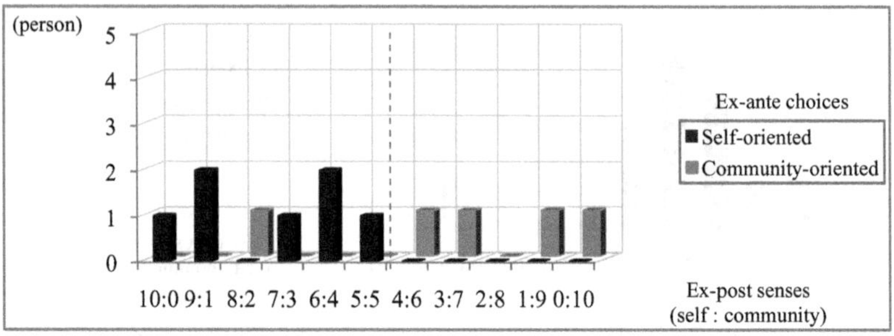

Figure 12.12 Ex ante choices and ex post senses of subjects' behavioural priorities (Game V)

In these graphs, the *extent* to which subjects were self or community oriented seems divergent, at least in their ex post senses. Even in Games II–V, where there seemed no tendency in the ex ante choices of the subject's behavioural priorities, we can find large divergences between games in terms of the ex post distribution of their weights on self or community. In particular, Games I, II and IV had a large gap between the distributions of the self-oriented and community-oriented groups while the results for Games III and V showed that the distributions of both groups overlapped.[14] Furthermore, the distribution in Game V was uniformly scattered and flat. To quantify this point, let us define *cp* ($0<=cp<=10$) when 'self:community = *sp:cp*' as 'community priority' and calculate its average for all the subjects in each game. Table 12.8 shows the correlation between the average community priority of the subjects in each game and their amount of activities.

On the relationship between the subject's (consumer's) community priority and the amount of each activity, the former had strong positive correlations with the amount of Clark purchased and amount of donations made to local NPOs but a strong negative correlation with the amount of consumption in chain stores (local outflow of Yen, see the shaded columns in Table 12.8).[15] Especially in Game I, where the subjects' community priority was the lowest (because 11 of the 12 subjects prioritised 'self'), note that the cumulative consumption total inside the community fell below that of the total outside the community. The subjects thus seem to have understood that the purchases (charges) of CCs or donations of CCs to local NPOs contributed to the community, while consumption in chain stores negatively affected the community. In addition, the ratio between consumption in local shops and consumption in chain stores had a strong positive correlation with the subjects' community priority. This finding suggests that subjects might have thought consumption inside the community would contribute much more to the community than consumption outside the community.

Then let us assess the correlation coefficients between community priorities and the amount of each activity by consumer (Table 12.9). The community priorities of nine of the 12 subjects (i.e. Consumers D, E, F, G, H, I, J, K and L) had a very strong positive correlation with either donations to local NPOs or the

Table 12.8 Correlations between community priority and the amounts of activities in each game

Game Progress	*Average of community priority*	*Cumulative total purchases of Clark by consumers (in Clark)*	*Cumulative total expenses for purchases of Clark by consumers (in Yen)*	*Cumulative total consumption in local shops (in Clark and Yen)*	*Cumulative total consumption in Clark in local shops (in Clark)*	*Cumulative total consumption in Yen in local shops (in Yen)*	*Cumulative total payment for part-time jobs in local shops (in Yen)*	*Cumulative total donations to local NPOs (in Clark)*	*Cumulative total payment for volunteering in local NPOs (in Clark)*	*Cumulative total consumption in chain stores (in Yen)*	*Consumption in local shops / Consumption in chain stores*	*Payment for volunteering / Payment for part-time jobs*
Game I	2.92	306,658	278,780	279,550	237,850	41,700	177,000	21,000	11,150	298,900	0.070	0.063
Game II	4.92	476,740	433,400	391,800	354,900	36,900	173,000	105,000	16,850	185,400	0.566	0.097
Game III	3.75	473,334	394,445	411,400	392,400	19,000	183,000	73,000	13,900	289,800	0.251	0.076
Game IV	5.17	657,737	548,114	553,700	541,300	12,400	219,000	86,000	14,200	156,800	0.548	0.065
Game V	4.33	562,806	489,388	441,600	397,600	44,000	204,000	74,000	10,900	190,500	0.388	0.053
Correlation coefficient with 'community priority'		0.856	0.900*	0.825	0.800	–0.394	0.524	0.902*	0.625	–0.937*	0.992**	–0.291
p-value		0.064	0.037	0.085	0.104	0.512	0.365	0.036	0.259	0.019	0.001	0.635

* Statistically significant at 5% significance level.

** Statistically significant at 1% significance level.

payment for volunteering in local NPOs. When participants placed more weight on the community, they donated more and carried out more volunteering tasks. The community priorities of two of the 12 subjects (i.e. Consumers B and K) had a very strong negative correlation with consumption in chain stores, which means that if their community priorities rose, their consumption outside the community would decrease. In particular, Consumer B had such a large correlation that his or her amount of Clark purchased and consumption in Clark within the community increased at the same time as his or her community priority increased. In this manner, the sense of 'community-oriented' differed from subject to subject.

Note here that two participants showed no correlation between their community priority and amount of activities (i.e. Consumers A and C). These participants were the same as those who had strong correlations between the premium rates and amount of activities in all games (see Table 12.6). That is, the behaviour of Consumer A and C were mainly determined by the changes in premium rates, while the remaining ten subjects were influenced by their community priorities. As an overall tendency in these games, the amounts of each activity were dominated by the community priority. In other words, the dominant factor in this experiment was the community priority.

In the next section we assess the relationship between the methods of displaying aggregate information and behaviour of the subjects.

12.3.4 Methods of displaying aggregate amount and the subjects' behaviour

In this section, we examine whether the methods of displaying the aggregate amounts (see Table 12.3) affect the subject's behaviour. We calculate how many times they referred to the graphs of aggregate amounts in each game (i.e. how many times they switched their window to display the aggregate amounts on their computer monitors).

Although the method of displaying the graphs changed ten minutes after the start of each game, this seemed to have no effect on the amount of the various activities. There was no statistically significant correlation between the access counts of the graphs of aggregate amounts and the amount of the various activities. There was little correlation even by subject. Only one of the 12 consumers (i.e. Consumer A) showed a correlation between the access counts of the graphs of aggregate amounts and the amount of the various activities. The *frequency* of the subject looking at the aggregate amounts might be one thing, while the *extent* to which they understand and pay attention to the aggregate amounts is another. Mechanical counts of views might thus be inadequate for the latter criterion.

In the ex post questionnaire, we asked participants their top three reasons for looking at the bar charts of aggregate amounts (in Games I, III and V) and the line charts of aggregate amounts (in Games II, IV and V). According to the results, the most popular reason for focusing on these charts was 'because they reflect other participants' behaviour'. Also, more people chose this reason for line charts than for bar charts. The subjects might therefore have considered line charts over bar

Table 12.9 The correlations between community priority and the amounts of activities through all games

Correlation coefficient with 'community priority' through Games I–V	*Cumulative total purchases of Clark by consumers (in Clark)*	*Cumulative total expenses for purchases of Clark by consumers (in Yen)*	*Cumulative total consumption in local shops (in Clark and Yen)*	*Cumulative total consumption in Clark in local shops (in Clark)*	*Cumulative total consumption in Yen in local shops (in Yen)*	*Cumulative total payment for part-time jobs in local shops (in Yen)*	*Cumulative total donations to local NPOs (in Clark)*	*Cumulative total payment for volunteering in local NPOs (in Clark)*	*Cumulative total consumption in chain stores (in Yen)*
Consumer A	0.314	0.319	0.307	0.307	–	0.683	0.748	−0.250	−0.18
Consumer B	0.994**	0.997**	0.993**	0.997**	0.526	0.548	0.782	−0.147	−0.976**
Consumer C	−0.465	−0.439	−0.596	−0.596	–	–	−0.588	0.749	−0.272
Consumer D	−0.759	−0.768	0.219	−0.672	0.946*	−0.904*	0.553	0.919*	0.431
Consumer E	0.291	0.330	0.510	0.137	0.655	0.655	0.935*	0.764	0.677
Consumer F	−0.875	−0.868	−0.714	−0.714	–	–	0.161	0.982**	0.420
Consumer G	0.803	0.842	0.107	0.317	−0.281	−0.038	0.989**	0.407	−0.706
Consumer H	0.357	0.303	−0.293	−0.262	−0.354	−0.473	0.938*	0.923*	−0.382
Consumer I	−0.177	−0.289	−0.718	−0.718	–	−0.349	0.915*	0.845	−0.727
Consumer J	0.059	−0.012	−0.517	−0.517	–	−0.871	0.924*	0.869	−0.468
Consumer K	0.685	0.676	0.418	0.422	−0.610	−0.858	0.951*	0.976**	−0.974**
Consumer L	0.603	0.594	0.538	0.545	0.299	−0.396	0.993**	0.994**	−0.689

- Not applicable
* Statistically significant at 5% significance level,
** Statistically significant at 1% significance level

charts to be more suitable for observing the *tendency* of other participants because the former show diachronic changes, while the latter only show temporal information on the situation in the community.

Lastly, we assessed the relationship between participant's ex ante chosen behavioural objectives and the aggregate amounts, especially the aggregate amount on which the subjects focused in each game. The number of participants who answered 'nothing particular' was much larger in the self-oriented group than in the community-oriented group. Therefore, the 11 types of aggregate amounts may have been more useful for community-oriented participants than self-oriented participants. In addition, self-oriented participants evenly focused on various aggregate amounts, while more than ten community-oriented participants especially focused on several aggregate amounts such as 'cumulative total donations to local NPOs' and 'cumulative total payment for volunteering in local NPOs'. These two aggregate amounts correspond to the popular behavioural objectives seen in community-oriented participants, that is, 'To make as many donations as possible to local NPOs' and 'To do as much volunteer work in local NPOs as possible' (Figure 12.4). Moreover, throughout all the games compared to community-oriented participants, self-oriented participants focused more intensively on 'My balance of Yen', 'My balance of Clark' and 'My hours of leisure time'. This finding suggests that they were more interested in their own status than that of the entire community. This result concurs with the analysis above.

12.4 Conclusion

In this study, we examined the premium rates of CCs, participants' behavioural priorities (self or community) and access counts of the graph of aggregate amounts. The most influential factor determining the extent of activities was the participants' priority (community or self-interest) rather than the premium rates of CCs or access to aggregate information. In this regard, participants' specific activities induced by those factors showed several patterns, while activities of two of the 12 participants were dominated by the premium rates of the CCs rather than the priority they placed on community. As for access to aggregate information, only one of the 12 participants showed a correlation between his or her activities and his or her access to graphs of aggregate amounts; indeed, the relevant factor in this regard was the specific information on which the participants focused.

Under the specific institutional structure of a virtual CC community, participants that display such a simple behavioural priority (self or community) could exhibit certain suitable behaviour to meet their objectives. The ex post questionnaire results revealed that aggregate information on activities was relatively useful for community-oriented participants. However, our set-up for this experiment was only able to demonstrate the correspondent relations between aggregate amounts and participants' behavioural objectives, not the causal relations between the display/non-display of the aggregate amounts and participants' consciousness and behaviour.[16]

These results indicate that the effect of increasing premium rates is limited for CC users balancing between self and community. As participants differ in the extent of their priority to giving to community, it is important to invite various actors to join the community as well as to provide extensive information on the activities within the community, thereby facilitating various channels of distribution for CCs and allowing them to contribute to the community in various ways. In doing so, aggregate information (which expresses the institutional contexts of CCs) would help participants understand the structure of communities, focus their attention on other participants and foster the transactions between them.

Despite these findings and implications, this study has some limitations. First, 12 subjects recruited from the same university are insufficient for confirming the generality of the results. With more subjects instead of assistants, we could give active roles to local shops, local NPOs, chain stores and the issuer. This would endogenise their activities as the primary determinants, comparable to those of the consumers. Second, some initial values in the experiment (e.g. consumers' income and leisure time, the menu of goods and services) are pre-determined exogenously, and therefore, leave arbitrariness in the study. Finally, we could provide the subjects with more types and forms of aggregate information on CCs and their community. These tasks remain for future research to tackle.

References

Coase, R. H. 1937. 'The Nature of the Firm'. *Economica* 4(16): 386–405.

Coase, R. H. 1960. 'The Problem of Social Cost'. *Journal of Law and Economics* 3: 1–44.

Kichiji, N. and Nishibe, M. 2007. 'Characteristic Comparison between Dispersive and Concentrated Money Creation – Random Network Simulation of Local Exchange Trading System (LETS) [in Japanese]'. *Keizaigaku Kenkyu*, University of Hokkaido 57(2): 1–14.

Kichiji, N. and Nishibe, M. 2008. 'Network Analyses of the Circulation Flow of Community Currency'. *Evolutionary and Institutional Economics Review* 4(2): 267–300.

Kichiji, N. and Nishibe, M. 2012. 'A Comparison in Transaction Efficiency between Dispersive and Concentrated Money Creation'. *International Journal of Community Currency Research* 16, 49–57.

Kurita, K., Miyazaki, Y. and Nishibe, M. 2012. 'CC Coupon Circulation and Shopkeepers' Behaviour: A Case Study of the City of Musashino, Tokyo, Japan'. *International Journal of Community Currency Research* 16, 136–145.

Mikami, M. and Nishibe, M. 2012. 'The Application of Electronic Community Currency for Media Design and Community Dock [in Japanese]'. *Discussion Paper Series B* (The Graduate School of Economics and Business Administration, Hokkaido University) 103: 1–24.

Nishibe, M. 2002. *Let's Learn about Local Currencies [in Japanese]*. Tokyo: Iwanami Shoten Publishers.

Nishibe, M. 2012a. 'Community Currencies as Integrative Communication Media for Evolutionist Institutional Design'. *International Journal of Community Currency Research* 16: 36–48.

Nishibe, M. 2012b. 'The Present Problem of the Hokkaido Regional Economy and a Remedy: A Reform Plan of the Institution of Money and Finance by Using Hokkaido Community Currency'. *Evolutionary and Institutional Economics Review* 9(Suppl.): 113–133.

Nishibe, M. 2016. The Enigma of Money: Gold, Central Banknotes, and Bitcoin. Heidelberg, Germany: Springer.

Notes

1 For a comparison of the transaction efficiency between dispersed and concentrated money creation, see Kichiji and Nishibe (2012). For the full simulational and mathematical analysis of the same topic, see Kichiji and Nishibe (2007). For the history and development of CCs in Japan, with a case study of the city of Musashino, see Kurita et al. (2012).

2 Electronic CCs enable the flexible media design of currencies and facilitate bottom-up policy implementation (Mikami and Nishibe 2012). See also Nishibe (2012a, 2012b) for the framework of evolutionist institutional design including media design and community dock.

3 Although such CCs are similar to account CCs (dispersedly issued, mutually paid), they are different in that they have such media as smartcards and are issued centrally. For example, WIR in Switzerland, Community Hero Card in the United States and the Community Currency Model System in Japan are classified into this type. On the other hand, the recent development of Bitcoin using block-chain technology suggests the scalability of electronic account CCs. For the implications of the worldwide diffusion of Bitcoin and similar cryptocurrencies on the modern capitalist market economy based on national currencies, see Nishibe (2016, 37–58). A fifth type of CC (dispersedly issued, mutually paid) has become possible as such monetary innovations as block-chain and proof of work that Bitcoin initially introduced are now available to build various virtual CCs.

4 To make traditional paper money CCs depreciate over time, a complicated procedure is necessary, such as putting stamps on CCs periodically to keep their value.

5 To trace traditional paper money CCs, issuers have to ask users to write their names on the back of the CCs in every transaction and withdraw all the CCs after the period of redemption. For an example of calculating the circulation velocity of CCs, see Kichiji and Nishibe (2008).

6 The experiment was held at Hokkaido University on 31 July 2012. The time required for the experiment was three hours, for which we provided participants with book vouchers worth 2,000 Yen (about 20 euros at the exchange rate at the time).

7 This was named after William Smith Clark, a prominent adviser for Sapporo Agricultural College, now Hokkaido University, where the experiment was conducted.

8 In addition, we asked the subjects about their ex post weight for self and community (on a scale of 10:0 to 0:11) in their actual behaviour in each game. Although we cannot completely control for experimental subjects' behaviour, we can secure the reproducibility and analysability of the experiment by making them choose their behavioural tendencies alone and quantifying those tendencies by using such a scale.

9 In this respect, this experiment is different from laboratory experiments that produce a completely controlled environment. This experiment rather aims to provide the subjects with social contexts that are free to some extent and to reconstruct realities for them.

10 For the detailed data of the game, see Appendix. Figure 12.13 to 12.17 respectively show the development of aggregate amounts in each game, while Tables 12.10.1 to 12.10.5 respectively show the agents' balances and cumulative transactions at the end of each game.

11 Only local shops can transfer Clark into Yen. Because redemption is performed as needed at the experiment assistants' discretion, some Clark are left in local shops at the end of the game. Therefore, to remove such arbitrariness in the calculation of the circulation velocity, we assume that all Clark in local shops are redeemed. Then, the recalculated circulation velocity of Clark in Games I–V are 3.92, 3.91, 5.92, 5.51 and 3.57, respectively, even higher than those of Yen.

12 To the question 'What image do you have about community currencies?', 11 of the 12 subjects chose 'Vitalisation of local areas' (1 of the 12 provided an invalid answer) from the alternatives of 'Volunteer', 'Vitalisation of local areas', 'Ecology', 'Connection of people' and 'I'm not sure'.

13 Therefore, in this experiment, we did not use such a method to motivate the subjects to participate by promising monetary rewards (cash) linked to the result of the game. Payment for the subjects' participation was provided in a non-cash form (i.e. book vouchers).

14 Especially in Games III and IV, one subject who chose community before the relevant game started answered, in the ex post questionnaire, that he or she actually placed more weight on self than community.

15 One of the two amounts of activities concerning Clark purchases, namely 'Cumulative total purchases of Clark by consumers (in Clark)' did not have any correlation with the community priority. However, this does not necessarily negate the correlation between purchases of CCs and the community priority because the amount purchased was determined by both Yen expenses and premium rates, the latter of which were different game by game.

16 One reason might be that subjects made their consumption decisions at the start of the game; if so, even if we had changed the method of displaying the aggregate amounts ten minutes after the game had started and they had adequately recognised the change, it would hardly have affected their consumption behaviour in the last half of the game.

Appendix

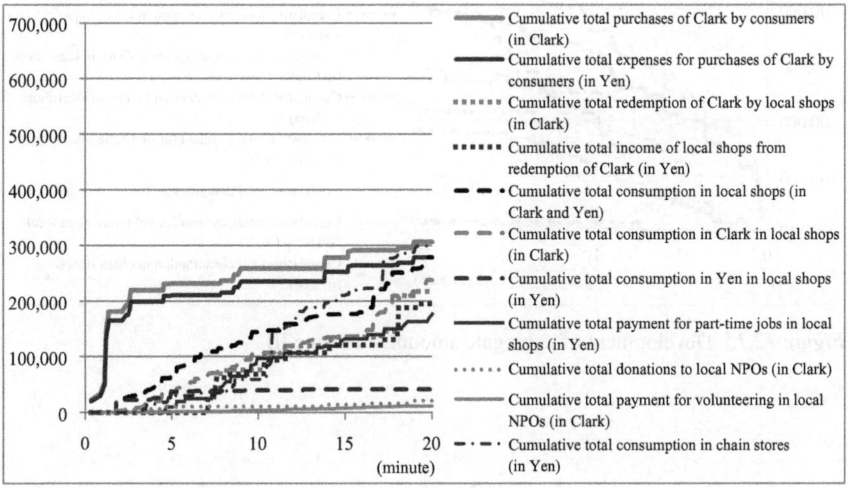

Figure 12.13 Development of aggregate amounts in Game I

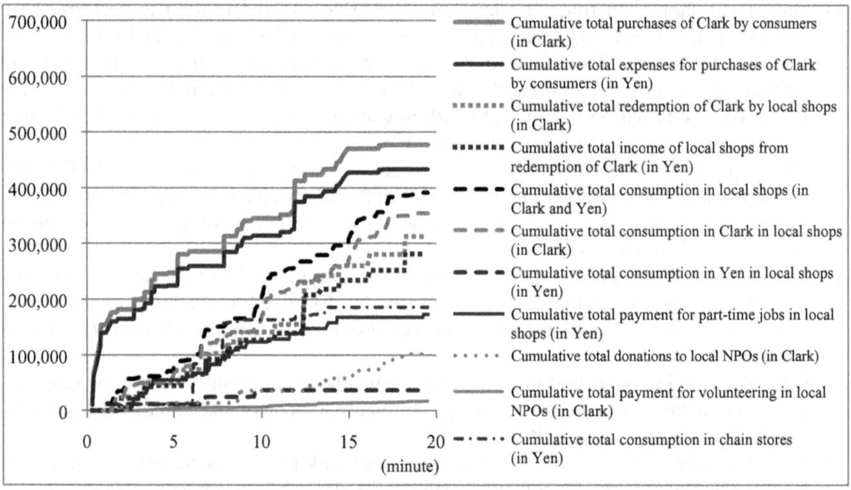

Figure 12.14 Development of aggregate amounts in Game II

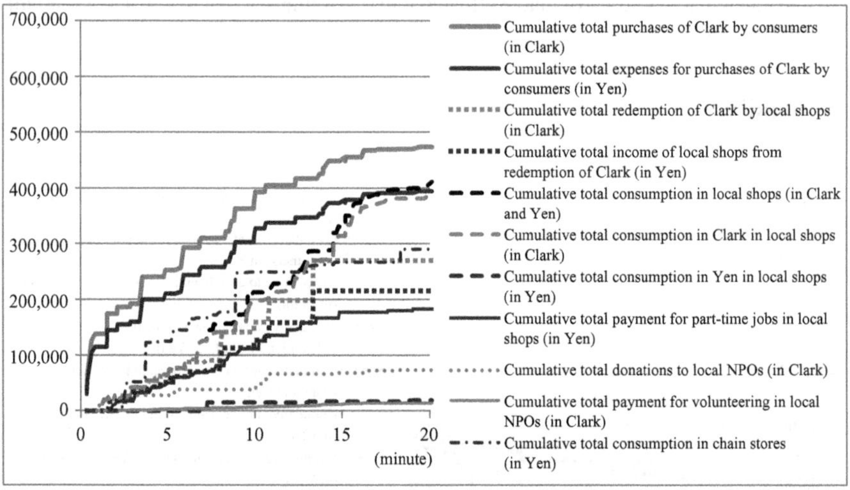

Figure 12.15 Development of aggregate amounts in Game III

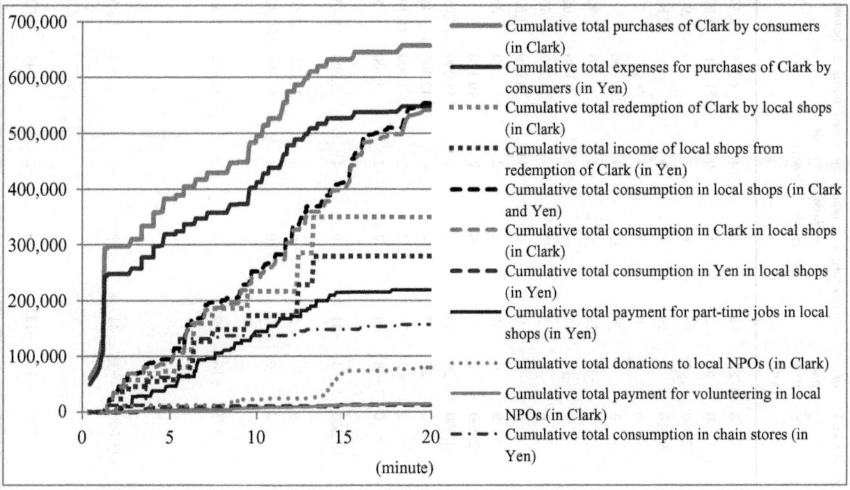

Figure 12.16 Development of aggregate amounts in Game IV

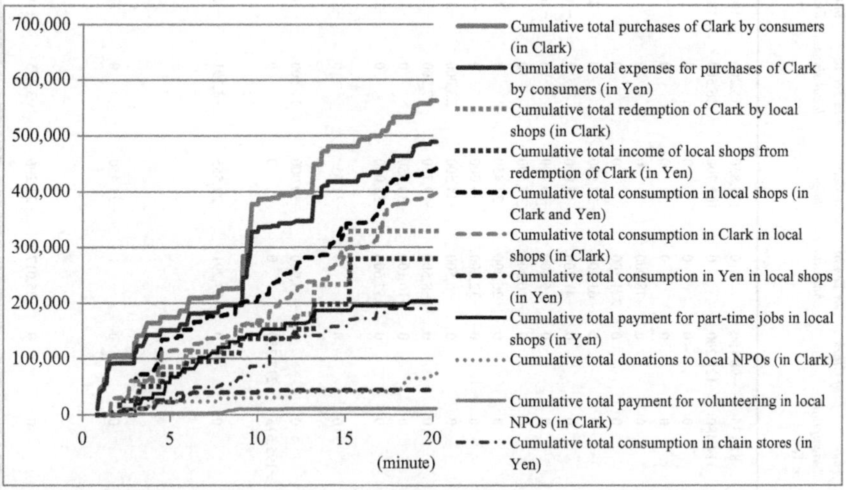

Figure 12.17 Development of aggregate amounts in Game V

Table 12.10.1 Agents' balances and cumulative transactions at the end of Game I

Player Name	*Income in Yen*	*Leisure time in hours*	*Expenses for purchases of Clark in Yen*	*Purchases of Clark*	*Income from Redemption in Yen*	*Redemption of Clark*	*Consumption in Yen in chain stores*	*Consumption in local shops*	*Consumption in Yen in local shops*	*Consumption in Clark in local shops*	*Payment for part-time jobs in Yen*	*Payment for volunteering in Clark*	*Donations in Clark*	*Hours of part-time jobs*	*Hours of volunteering*	*Hours consumed in chain stores*	*Hours consumed in local shops*	*Yen balance*	*Clark balance*	*Time balance*
Local shop A	0	0	0	0	81,135	−90,150	0	117,850	15,200	102,650	−88,000	0	0	88	0	0	14	8,335	12,500	102
Local shop B	0	0	0	0	114,480	−127,200	0	161,700	26,500	135,200	−89,000	0	0	89	0	0	10	51,980	8,000	99
Local NPO A	0	0	0	0	0	0	0	0	0	0	0	−5,100	12,000	0	86	0	0	0	6,900	86
Local NPO B	0	0	0	0	0	0	0	0	0	0	0	−6,200	9,000	0	59	0	0	0	2,800	59
Chain store A	0	0	0	0	0	0	78,900	0	0	0	0	0	0	0	0	8	0	78,900	0	8
Chain store B	0	0	0	0	0	0	221,300	0	0	0	0	0	0	0	0	22	0	221,300	0	22
Consumer A	50,000	48	−20,200	22,220	0	0	−61,800	−22,500	0	−22,500	32,000	1,200	0	−32	−12	−2	−2	0	920	0
Consumer B	50,000	48	−15,000	16,500	0	0	−41,200	−16,000	0	−16,000	10,000	500	0	−10	−5	−7	0	3,800	1,000	26
Consumer C	50,000	48	−20,000	22,000	0	0	−6,800	−10,700	0	−10,700	0	450	0	0	−3	−2	0	23,200	11,750	43
Consumer D	50,000	48	−10,000	11,000	0	0	−20,000	−7,500	0	−7,500	8,000	0	0	−8	0	0	0	28,000	3,500	40
Consumer E	50,000	48	−23,800	26,180	0	0	−26,200	−27,450	0	−27,450	0	1,600	0	0	−30	−2	−2	0	330	14
Consumer F	50,000	48	−7,280	8,008	0	0	−32,600	−6,000	0	−6,000	0	0	−2,000	0	0	−4	−2	10,120	8	42
Consumer G	50,000	48	−22,500	24,750	0	0	−6,500	−44,500	−23,000	−21,500	20,000	1,800	−1,000	−20	−14	−1	0	18,000	4,050	13
Consumer H	50,000	48	−20,000	22,000	0	0	−8,500	−19,750	−7,200	−12,550	28,000	0	0	−28	0	−4	−6	42,300	9,450	10
Consumer I	50,000	48	−40,000	44,000	0	0	−10,100	−30,650	0	−30,650	2,000	1,750	0	−2	−30	−2	−2	1,900	15,100	12
Consumer J	50,000	48	−30,000	33,000	0	0	−52,600	−33,050	0	−33,050	38,000	800	0	−38	−8	0	−2	5,400	750	0
Consumer K	50,000	48	−50,000	55,000	0	0	0	−31,450	0	−31,450	3,000	2,900	−18,000	−3	−41	0	−4	3,000	8,450	0
Consumer L	50,000	48	−20,000	22,000	0	0	−33,900	−30,000	−11,500	−18,500	36,000	300	0	−36	−2	−6	−4	20,600	3,800	0
Issuer	0	0	278,780	−306,658	−195,615	217,350	0	0	0	0	0	0	0	0	0	0	0	83,165	−89,308	0
Average of self–oriented consumers	50,000	48	−20,798	22,878	0	0	−27,291	−22,555	−3,791	−18,764	15,818	764	−273	−16	−9	−3	−2	13,938	4,605	18
Average of community-oriented consumers	50,000	48	−50,000	55,000	0	0	0	−31,450	0	−31,450	3,000	2,900	−18,000	−3	−41	0	−4	3,000	8,450	0
Average of all consumers	50,000	17	−23,232	25,555	0	0	−25,017	−23,296	−3,475	−19,821	14,750	942	−1,750	−15	−12	−3	−2	48	13,027	4,926

* Shaded consumers are 'community-oriented'

Player Name	Income in Yen	Leisure time in hours	Expenses for purchases of Clark in Yen	Purchases of Clark	Income from Redemption in Yen	Redemption of Clark	Consumption in Yen in chain stores	Consumption in local shops	Consumption in Yen in local shops	Consumption in Clark in local shops	Payment for part-time jobs in Yen	Payment for volunteering in Clark	Donations in Clark	Hours of part-time jobs	Hours of volunteering	Hours consumed in chain stores	Hours consumed in local shops	Yen balance	Clark balance	Time balance
Local shop A	0	0	0	0	143,100	−159,000	0	189,400	25,400	164,000	−58,000	0	0	58	0	0	16	110,500	5,000	74
Local shop B	0	0	0	0	138,060	−153,400	0	202,400	11,500	190,900	−115,000	0	0	115	0	0	8	34,560	37,500	123
Local NPO A	0	0	0	0	0	0	0	0	0	0	0	−8,050	50,000	0	128	0	0	0	41,950	128
Local NPO B	0	0	0	0	0	0	0	0	0	0	0	−8,800	55,000	0	84	0	0	0	46,200	84
Chain store A	0	0	0	0	0	0	25,600	0	0	0	0	0	0	0	0	0	0	25,600	0	0
Chain store B	0	0	0	0	0	0	159,800	0	0	0	0	0	0	0	0	55	0	159,800	0	55
Consumer A	50,000	48	−4,000	4,400	0	0	−70,000	−4,400	0	−4,400	24,000	0	0	−24	0	−24	0	0	0	0
Consumer B	50,000	48	−53,100	58,410	0	0	0	−68,000	−12,900	−55,100	16,000	600	0	−16	−6	0	−4	0	3,910	22
Consumer C	50,000	48	−25,000	27,500	0	0	−3,000	−7,500	0	−7,500	0	1,600	−3,000	0	−30	0	0	22,000	18,600	18
Consumer D	50,000	48	−2,100	2,310	0	0	0	−13,000	−11,500	−1,500	0	1,850	−2,000	0	−17	0	0	36,400	660	31
Consumer E	50,000	48	−46,200	50,820	0	0	−3,800	−48,500	0	−48,500	0	2,900	−5,000	0	−41	−3	−4	0	220	0
Consumer F	50,000	48	−7,000	7,700	0	0	−32,600	−8,000	0	−8,000	0	300	0	0	−3	−2	−6	10,400	0	37
Consumer G	50,000	48	−85,000	93,500	0	0	0	−41,500	0	−41,500	35,000	1,500	−50,000	−35	−12	0	0	0	3,500	1
Consumer H	50,000	48	−50,000	55,000	0	0	0	−47,000	−11,500	−35,500	32,000	1,700	−20,000	−32	−14	0	−2	20,500	1,200	0
Consumer I	50,000	48	−27,000	29,700	0	0	0	−11,850	0	−11,850	0	2,750	−18,000	0	−41	0	−4	23,000	2,600	3
Consumer J	50,000	48	−64,000	70,400	0	0	−6,000	−69,300	0	−69,300	25,000	1,600	0	−25	−17	−2	−4	5,000	2,700	0
Consumer K	50,000	48	0	0	0	0	−70,000	−1,150	−1,000	−150	21,000	450	0	−21	−3	−24	0	0	300	0
Consumer L	50,000	48	−70,000	77,000	0	0	0	−71,600	0	−71,600	20,000	1,600	−7,000	−20	−28	0	0	0	0	0
Issuer	0	0	433,400	−476,740	−281,160	312,400	0	0	0	0	0	0	0	0	0	0	0	152,240	−164,340	0
Average of self–oriented consumers	50,000	48	−25,000	27,500	0	0	−35,720	−25,970	−2,500	−23,470	20,400	810	−4,000	−20	−7	−10	−2	7,180	840	7
Average of community-oriented consumers	50,000	48	−44,057	48,463	0	0	−971	−37,421	−3,486	−33,936	10,143	1,829	−12,143	−10	−25	0	−2	11,629	4,213	11
Average of all consumers	50,000	48	−36,117	39,728	0	0	−15,450	−32,650	−3,075	−29,575	14,417	1,404	−8,750	−14	−18	−5	−2	9,775	2,808	9

* Shaded consumers are ‘community-oriented’

Table 12.10.3 Agents' balances and cumulative transactions at the end of Game III

Player Name	*Income in Yen*	*Leisure time in hours*	*Expenses for purchases of Clark in Yen*	*Purchases of Clark*	*Income from Redemption in Yen*	*Redemption of Clark*	*Consumption in Yen in chain stores*	*Consumption in local shops*	*Consumption in Yen in local shops*	*Consumption in Clark in local shops*	*Payment for part-time jobs in Yen*	*Payment for volunteering in Clark*	*Donations in Clark*	*Hours of part-time jobs*	*Hours of volunteering*	*Hours consumed in chain stores*	*Hours consumed in local shops*	*Yen balance*	*Clark balance*	*Time balance*
Local shop A	0	0	0	0	76,080	−95,100	0	127,400	4,000	123,400	−63,000	0	0	63	0	0	14	17,080	28,300	77
Local shop B	0	0	0	0	139,600	−174,500	0	284,000	15,000	269,000	−120,000	0	0	120	0	0	0	34,600	94,500	120
Local NPO A	0	0	0	0	0	0	0	0	0	0	0	−5,700	43,000	0	109	0	0	0	37,300	109
Local NPO B	0	0	0	0	0	0	0	0	0	0	0	−8,200	30,000	0	81	0	0	0	21,800	81
Chain store A	0	0	0	0	0	0	48,900	0	0	0	0	0	0	0	0	6	0	48,900	0	6
Chain store B	0	0	0	0	0	0	240,900	0	0	0	0	0	0	0	0	52	0	240,900	0	52
Consumer A	50,000	48	−72,700	87,240	0	0	−21,300	−86,150	0	−86,150	44,000	0	−1,000	−44	0	0	−4	0	90	0
Consumer B	50,000	48	−5,800	6,960	0	0	−64,200	−4,450	0	−4,450	20,000	0	0	−20	0	−2	−2	0	2,510	24
Consumer C	50,000	48	−47,000	56,400	0	0	−2,700	−43,000	0	−43,000	0	800	−10,000	0	−8	0	0	300	4,200	40
Consumer D	50,000	48	−6,600	7,920	0	0	0	−27,000	−17,000	−10,000	0	2,100	0	0	−35	0	0	26,400	20	13
Consumer E	50,000	48	−46,000	55,200	0	0	−5,000	−57,600	0	−57,600	1,000	2,400	0	−1	−38	−2	−2	0	0	5
Consumer F	50,000	48	−3,834	4,601	0	0	−34,800	−5,000	0	−5,000	0	2,200	−1,000	0	−19	−4	0	11,366	801	25
Consumer G	50,000	48	−55,011	66,013	0	0	−20,000	−53,000	0	−53,000	48,000	0	−3,000	−48	0	0	0	22,989	10,013	0
Consumer H	50,000	48	0	0	0	0	−70,000	−2,000	−2,000	0	24,000	0	0	−24	0	−24	0	2,000	0	0
Consumer I	50,000	48	−43,500	52,200	0	0	−1,800	−49,300	0	−49,300	12,000	750	0	−12	−6	−2	−4	16,700	3,650	24
Consumer J	50,000	48	−60,000	72,000	0	0	0	−34,100	0	−34,100	10,000	2,550	−40,000	−10	−38	0	0	0	450	0
Consumer K	50,000	48	−50,000	60,000	0	0	0	−45,000	0	−45,000	0	3,100	−18,000	0	−46	0	−2	0	100	0
Consumer L	50,000	48	−4,000	4,800	0	0	−70,000	−4,800	0	−4,800	24,000	0	0	−24	0	−24	0	0	0	0
Issuer	0	0	394,445	−473,334	−215,680	269,600	0	0	0	0	0	0	0	0	0	0	0	178,765	−203,734	0
Average of self-oriented consumers	50,000	48	−28,759	34,510	0	0	−33,386	−30,593	−286	−30,307	18,429	564	−1,857	−18	−7	−8	−1	5,998	2,910	13
Average of community-oriented consumers	50,000	48	−38,627	46,352	0	0	−11,220	−39,450	−3,400	−36,050	10,800	1,990	−12,000	−11	−28	−1	−1	7,553	292	8
Average of all consumers	50,000	48	−32,870	39,445	0	0	−24,150	−34,283	−1,583	−32,700	15,250	1,158	−6,083	−15	−16	−5	−1	6,646	1,820	11

… community-oriented'

Table 12.10.4 Agents' balances and cumulative transactions at the end of Game IV

Player Name	Income in Yen	Leisure time in hours	Expenses for purchases of Clark in Yen	Purchases of Clark	Income from Redemption in Yen	Redemption of Clark	Consumption in Yen in chain stores	Consumption in local shops	Consumption in Yen in local shops	Consumption in Clark in local shops	Payment for part-time jobs in Yen	Payment for volunteering in Clark	Donations in Clark	Hours of part-time jobs	Hours of volunteering	Hours consumed in chain stores	Hours consumed in local shops	Yen balance	Clark balance	Time balance
Local shop A	0	0	0	0	126,960	−158,700	0	267,900	12,400	255,500	−99,000	0	0	99	0	0	10	40,360	96,800	109
Local shop B	0	0	0	0	152,640	−190,800	0	285,800	0	285,800	−120,000	0	0	120	0	0	6	32,640	95,000	126
Local NPO A	0	0	0	0	0	0	0	0	0	0	0	−6,500	52,000	0	101	0	0	0	45,500	101
Local NPO B	0	0	0	0	0	0	0	0	0	0	0	−7,700	34,000	0	72	0	0	0	26,300	72
Chain store A	0	0	0	0	0	0	30,800	0	0	0	0	0	0	0	0	10	0	30,800	0	10
Chain store B	0	0	0	0	0	0	126,000	0	0	0	0	0	0	0	0	27	0	126,000	0	27
Consumer A	50,000	48	−98,000	117,600	0	0	0	−116,200	0	−116,200	48,000	0	−1,000	−48	0	0	0	0	400	0
Consumer B	50,000	48	−69,600	83,520	0	0	0	−86,100	−9,400	−76,700	29,000	0	−5,000	−29	0	0	−4	0	1,820	15
Consumer C	50,000	48	−50,000	60,000	0	0	0	−41,500	0	−41,500	0	800	−7,000	0	−8	0	0	0	12,300	40
Consumer D	50,000	48	−20,000	24,000	0	0	0	−23,000	0	−23,000	7,000	500	0	−7	−6	0	−2	37,000	1,500	33
Consumer E	50,000	48	0	0	0	0	−71,000	−1,000	−1,000	0	22,000	0	0	−22	0	−24	−2	0	0	0
Consumer F	50,000	48	−4,504	5,405	0	0	−31,800	−6,000	0	−6,000	0	750	0	0	−5	−10	−2	13,696	155	31
Consumer G	50,000	48	−22,010	26,412	0	0	−50,000	−25,000	0	−25,000	37,000	0	0	−37	0	0	0	14,990	1,412	11
Consumer H	50,000	48	−30,000	36,000	0	0	−4,000	−4,500	−2,000	−2,500	9,000	3,750	−37,000	−9	−34	−3	−2	23,000	250	0
Consumer I	50,000	48	−43,000	51,600	0	0	0	−15,400	0	−15,400	6,000	2,950	−13,000	−6	−39	0	−2	13,000	26,150	1
Consumer J	50,000	48	−74,000	88,800	0	0	0	−89,500	0	−89,500	24,000	1,000	0	−24	−24	0	0	0	300	0
Consumer K	50,000	48	−56,000	67,200	0	0	0	−56,500	0	−56,500	6,000	2,650	−13,000	−6	−40	0	−2	0	350	0
Consumer L	50,000	48	−81,000	97,200	0	0	0	−89,000	0	−89,000	31,000	1,800	−10,000	−31	−17	0	0	0	0	0
Issuer	0	0	548,114	−657,737	−279,600	349,500	0	0	0	0	0	0	0	0	0	0	0	268,514	−308,237	0
Average of self-oriented consumers	50,000	48	−38,359	46,031	0	0	−21,829	−43,171	−143	−43,029	19,714	436	−1,143	−20	−6	−5	−1	9,384	2,295	16
Average of community-oriented consumers	50,000	48	−55,920	67,104	0	0	−800	−50,300	−2,280	−48,020	16,200	2,230	−15,600	−16	−26	−1	−2	7,200	5,714	3
Average of all consumers	50,000	48	−45,676	54,811	0	0	−13,067	−46,142	−1,033	−45,108	18,250	1,183	−7,167	−18	−14	−3	−1	8,474	3,720	11

* Shaded consumers are 'community-oriented'.

Table 12.10.5 Agents' balances and cumulative transactions at the end of Game V

Player Name	Income in Yen	Leisure time in hours	Expenses for purchases of Clark in Yen	Purchases of Clark	Income from Redemption in Yen	Redemption of Clark	Consumption in Yen in chain stores	Consumption in local shops	Consumption in Yen in local shops	Consumption in Clark in local shops	Payment for part-time jobs in Yen	Payment for volunteering in Clark	Donations in Clark	Hours of part-time jobs	Hours of volunteering	Hours consumed in chain stores	Hours consumed in local shops	Yen balance	Clark balance	Time balance
Local shop A	0	0	0	0	76,415	−89,900	0	200,000	29,000	171,000	−58,000	0	0	58	0	0	20	47,415	81,100	78
Local shop B	0	0	0	0	202,810	−238,600	0	271,600	15,000	256,600	−146,000	0	0	146	0	0	4	71,810	18,000	150
Local NPO A	0	0	0	0	0	0	0	0	0	0	0	−7,800	20,000	0	175	0	0	0	12,200	175
Local NPO B	0	0	0	0	0	0	0	0	0	0	0	−3,100	54,000	0	29	0	0	0	50,900	29
Chain store A	0	0	0	0	0	0	81,300	0	0	0	0	0	0	0	0	6	0	81,300	0	6
Chain store B	0	0	0	0	0	0	115,700	0	0	0	0	0	0	0	0	12	0	115,700	0	12
Consumer A	50,000	48	−30,200	34,730	0	0	−63,800	−33,400	0	−33,400	44,000	0	−1,000	−44	0	0	−4	0	330	0
Consumer B	50,000	48	−71,000	81,650	0	0	0	−76,800	0	−76,800	21,000	0	−4,000	−21	0	0	0	0	850	27
Consumer C	50,000	48	−22,000	25,300	0	0	−26,500	−11,500	0	−11,500	0	1,000	−10,000	0	−24	0	0	1,500	4,800	24
Consumer D	50,000	48	−15,000	17,250	0	0	0	−25,300	−11,500	−13,800	5,000	1,500	−2,000	−5	−29	0	0	28,500	2,950	14
Consumer E	50,000	48	−21,500	24,725	0	0	0	−45,900	−28,500	−17,400	0	2,850	−10,000	0	−40	0	−8	0	175	0
Consumer F	50,000	48	−7,261	8,351	0	0	−35,000	−8,800	0	−8,800	0	450	0	0	−4	−8	−2	7,739	1	34
Consumer G	50,000	48	−82,690	95,103	0	0	0	−31,850	0	−31,850	33,000	0	−20,000	−33	0	0	−4	310	43,253	11
Consumer H	50,000	48	−33,921	39,011	0	0	0	−34,000	−4,000	−30,000	0	2,000	−11,000	0	−48	0	0	12,079	11	0
Consumer I	50,000	48	−38,000	43,700	0	0	−1,800	−25,050	0	−25,050	13,000	1,100	0	−13	−11	−2	−6	23,200	19,750	16
Consumer J	50,000	48	−40,000	46,000	0	0	−10,000	−32,000	0	−32,000	0	2,000	−16,000	0	−48	0	0	0	0	0
Consumer K	50,000	48	−47,826	55,000	0	0	−50,000	−55,000	0	−55,000	48,000	0	0	−48	0	0	0	174	0	0
Consumer L	50,000	48	−80,000	92,000	0	0	−9,900	−92,000	0	−92,000	40,000	0	0	−40	0	−8	0	100	0	0
Issuer	0	0	489,398	−562,820	−279,225	328,500	0	0	0	0	0	0	0	0	0	0	0	210,173	−234,320	0
Average of self-oriented consumers	50,000	48	−43,997	50,598	0	0	−26,714	−36,800	0	−36,800	25,429	364	−4,429	−25	−6	−3	−2	4,718	9,733	12
Average of community-oriented consumers	50,000	48	−36,284	41,727	0	0	−2,000	−42,800	−8,800	−34,000	5,200	1,670	−8,600	−5	−33	0	−2	8,116	797	8
Average of all consumers	45,455	44	9,200	−10,580	−25,384	29,864	−12,109	−32,855	−4,000	−28,855	12,636	991	−6,273	−13	−19	−2	−2	25,798	−14,853	9

13 For the policy maker

When and how is monetary plurality an option?

Georgina M. Gómez

13.1 Introduction

There is little doubt that monetary plurality has been prevalent throughout history and that monetary singularity is characteristic only of the last century of humankind. We find numerous periods and areas of monetary plurality across the world, in developed as well as developing countries, from the distant past to our present days. Despite this ubiquitousness, the idea of monetary plurality in our times is seen as a signal of monetary failure or malfunction due to extraordinary circumstances such as war and hyperinflation. Political proposals to deploy complementary currencies within a regular monetary system are quickly disregarded without sufficient discussion to determine how and when these initiatives could make sense to support economic activity. This is a sign that monetary singularity is installed around the globe, even if it is far from unchallenged, but it does not mean that it has been proven as the superior option.

Aware that an informed debate requires reliable data and research, this book aimed at contributing to the public discussion on how, when and where monetary plurality is a viable alternative. The different chapters tackled various aspects of monetary plurality, its characteristics, the ways in which it works in theory and in practice, and the variety of forms it adopts. This chapter is not meant for the convinced practitioner, but for a regular policy maker who has not yet decided on whether monetary plurality makes any sense. It explores the origin of the reasoning for monetary singularity. So, the issue is approached from more mainstream angles and in dialogue with more orthodox sources. Matthew Forstater (2015: 198) notes that complementary currency experts have not engaged sufficiently with modern monetary theorists. Taking up that challenge, this chapter offers some policy reflections on monetary plurality. Under what circumstances does it emerge? What are its potentials and pitfalls as a policy tool? These reflections seek to guide the analysis without proposing a specific design for complementary currencies, because monetary plurality by definition implies diversity and adaptation to space, time and context.

13.2 Monetary plurality: a black hole of habit?

It is puzzling that the existence of monetary plurality is almost ignored by many economists. As a matter of fact, most students of economics do not know that monetary singularity need not be the rule and that its superiority as a monetary solution is debatable. A publication by the Institute of Economic Affairs (Schwartz et al., 2013) characterises the lack of public and academic debate on monetary plurality as an intellectual loss for the discipline. Why is this?

The lack of understanding of how monetary plurality works prevents economists and policy makers from considering it as a policy option that may be worth discussing. Marie Fare and Pepita Ould-Ahmed (2017) dive into the reasons behind this black hole in the discipline, and attribute it to the methodological and normative concepts in economics that are designed to capture macro phenomena with large amounts of data but are ill-suited to study small economic systems at the local level. While there are 3,500 to 4,500 complementary currencies around the world (Blanc, 2012; Seyfang and Longhurst, 2013), each one is relatively small and rarely engages more than a few hundred participants. In turn, the epistemological foundations of economics point in the direction that can safely ignore these small-scale phenomena because they would not affect the larger picture – that is, a macro economic system that works on the basis of one official currency per country.

Once the narrative is repeated ad infinitum, the existence of monetary plurality is established as a 'habit of thought' (Veblen, 2004 [1899]) that prevents human beings from considering other options. The invisibility of other, smaller and alternative schemes contributes to making monetary singularity a social fact (Searle, 1995, 2005) that is too obvious to need proof or reconsideration. The separation of the four monetary functions in different types of money, for example, appears in the literature only rarely because it is assumed that all four functions are to be performed by one type of money, the superior one. Money is defined as all-purpose money and other monetary expressions are discarded as primitive, small, and generally not worth considering as an object of enquiry.

Against the negative perception of monetary plurality, various groups across the political spectrum, and in different countries, have never stopped flirting with the idea of complementary or parallel currencies. A myriad of time banks exists across continents, often with the approval of the local governments and sometimes with their financial support in cash or kind (Gregory, 2014). Complementary currencies based on voucher systems are used in several European countries to induce environmentally sustainable behaviour, such as recycling and caring for public spaces. The best-known variation of community currencies are the Local Exchange and Trading Systems (LETS), that work as mutual exchange systems often tied up to official currencies (North, 2007; Williams et al., 2001). These complementary currencies often seek the promotion of one or more dimensions of economic development at the local and regional level (Gómez and Dini, 2016; Gómez and Helmsing, 2008).

At the same time, the possibility of introducing monetary plurality at the national or multiregional scale has been considered in countries as diverse as Greece, Italy and Ecuador (Lynn, 2017). In Greece it was considered more than once (2010, 2012 and 2015), each time the country ran out of euros to serve the debt and seemed on the verge of default. *The Economist* (25 April 2015; 2016) characterised the introduction of a Greek currency, parallel to the euro, as a 'monetary trick' sometimes used in emergencies. Bruno Théret and others (Kalinowski et al., 2015) called the policy instrument a 'monetary lifeline' in an article in the French magazine, *Libération*. At that time, it seemed plausible that Greece would face an emergency situation if it was expelled from the Eurozone in chaotic circumstances and was forced to readopt an unbacked Greek currency. The introduction of monetary plurality appeared as an intermediate way between that catastrophic scenario and the continuation in the Eurozone, in which euros need to be extracted as taxes to serve the interests on the debt. A parallel national currency represented a way of keeping the euro while the government could regain some flexibility with its own complementary currency. The Greek currency could be used, in principle, only as means of payment for local and national exchanges. With regular changes of ministers and governments, the proposal never made significant progress.

Another European country where there is some public debate on the use of a complementary currency is Italy, similarly proposing to keep the euro but introducing an Italian currency at the same time (Bossone et al., 2015). Although for different reasons, political groups from both left and right refer to monetary plurality as a way to reactivate the economy, create jobs and bring the public debt under control. From the left, the proposal of the Sylos Labini Institute, for example, underlines the positive effects of adding flexibility to the rigid monetary singularity of the Eurozone (2015). At the other end of the political spectrum, Silvio Berlusconi proposed an Italian currency as a symbol of national sovereignty in relation to the euro and the European Union (Montalto Monella, 2017). The discussion is ongoing, and it has had periods in which it resurfaces and then recedes, until it builds up again.

Ecuador is in a different continent and context but faces a related problem. The country adopted the US dollar as legal tender in the crisis of 1999. Once the economy was stabilised, subsequent governments found that the dollarisation of their economy was often a straightjacket for economic growth, considering its dependency on oil prices, and its sovereign decision-making powers. There have been repeated discussions on reforming the monetary system back to having an Ecuadorian currency, but the responses of economic agents have been invariably negative. Since then, the discussion on how to exit dollarisation is paralysed by the fear that reintroducing a national currency would cause massive crisis. The implementation of a complementary currency was considered as an intermediate solution that would not require abandoning the dollar but would give the Ecuadorian government its own monetary system again. The debate in Ecuador is also hungry for reliable data and research that would inform such a critical decision.

The implementation of monetary plurality in all three countries, like others where the interest in the issue is less notorious, has met sharp scepticism. The introduction of complementary currencies is perceived as an untidy solution and is associated with governments that lack fiscal discipline; hence it may put banks and the entire financial system at risk (Schwartz et al., 2013). More importantly, such a solution has rarely been tried and that generates, quite understandably, all sorts of fears. The debate has not been mainstreamed around specific and clear lines of discussion, often mixing arguments and experiences of local, community and national complementary currencies. Besides confusing levels of implementation, the criticism refers to proposals that vary and show that there is limited understanding of the implications of monetary plurality in theory as in practice.

13.3 Good currency versus bad currency

A clear argument for monetary singularity refers to Gresham's Law. Almost 500 years ago, British banker Thomas Gresham observed that if a country has more than one currency, the one that is perceived as more valuable would be stored and the one that is considered less valuable would be used for circulation. Eventually, the 'bad' currency loses its value because nobody wants to hold it and, ultimately, will not accept it any more. Gresham's postulation is often invoked to explain why 'good' currency disappears through exporting or hoarding while 'bad' currency is used in exchange, hence prevailing over the 'good' currency. The time frame, within which the bad currency is rejected by users, remains undetermined in the statement, but it can be inferred that in the medium run, monetary singularity will prevail.

The aim of this section is to better understand how the claim that 'bad money drives out good money' still dominates the current thinking against monetary plurality among economists. It does not seek to discuss the details of the postulation itself, which has been covered by others (Fetter, 1932; Greenfield and Rockoff, 1995; Rolnick and Weber, 1986; Selgin, 1996). Before that, it is essential to contextualise that Gresham lived in times when commodity money was the norm. In his day, 'currency' necessarily meant metals such as gold and silver, which were too valuable for the vast majority of the population of the 16th century, who were mainly engaged in farming. Discussions about gold coinage were detached from the daily lives of the majority who did not use metallic money, but mainly concerned the courts, merchants and other elites.

There is significant confusion regarding Gresham and his actual publications. As noted by Fetter (1932), Gresham was neither Minister of Finance nor Director of the Mint, as cited by several sources (for a list, see Fetter, 1932: 481). Gresham was a merchant, ambassador, financial representative of the British crown in Antwerp, founder of the London Royal Exchange and, upon his death, donor of the Gresham College in London. Burgon (1839) published a detailed bibliographic study based mainly on Gresham's correspondence, and there are no records that the banker ever postulated the statement known as 'Gresham's Law'. Instead, Gresham observed that the exchange rate of the English currency dropped in relation to other currencies in Flanders, where he was posted, after King Henry VIII debased English silver coinage. In 1558, Gresham explained this relationship in his correspondence with the newly crowned young Queen Elizabeth I, who reacted with a currency reform and recoinage within a few years.

Before the reform became effective, the queen issued a proclamation on 27 September 1560 in which she announced the value at which the old coins would be accepted by the public offices and referred to their devaluation as a 'crying down' of value. In the proclamation two days later on 29 September, she explained that 'divers subtle people have changed' the coins and have 'transported and carried out the same gold and silver' to locations where thc metal content in these coins was valued more (letter in Ruding, 1840: 334–336, quoted in Fetter, 1932). In the same document, Elizabeth I laments that great quantities of gold and silver used in her new coins had left her kingdom, so 'no part thereof is seen commonly current' while part still circulated and another part 'percace by the wiser sort of people kept in store, as it were to be wished that the whole were'. The Queen hence distinguished between the coins that were in circulation and coins that disappeared by hoarding or had left the kingdom because of their metal content. She implemented the currency reform according to what she understood of what Gresham was reporting from abroad on the disappearance or hoarding of British coins that contained more valuable metal than their face value.

About three centuries after Elizabeth's reign ended, Henry Dunning MacLeod stated that 'good money and bad money cannot circulate together'. MacLeod was a key scholar on monetary thought at a time when modern single-currency systems were being established (Skaggs, 1997). During these debates, he resurfaced Gresham's name as the inspirer of his own reflections on why good and bad money cannot circulate together and concluded that 'we may call it Gresham's law of the currency' (MacLeod, 2007 [1858]: 478). Jevons (1875) also mentioned Gresham as initiator of the statement that 'light' and 'good' currency could not circulate together and added that the 'law' on bimetallism applied to paper money, too. Fetter (1932: 484), hence, attributed to MacLeod what became known as Gresham's Law.

However, in the fourth edition of *The Theory and Practice of Banking*, MacLeod (1884) elaborated on his previous versions of Gresham's Law and admitted that bimetallism was possible if the currencies were given different monetary valuations by legal tender laws. He referred to a multiple monetary system in terms of 'light' and 'good' coins and claimed there would be two possibilities:

> [e]ither those persons who have commodities to sell will make a difference in their nominal price according as they are paid in good or in light coin; that is, the light coin will be at a discount as compared with the good coins: or if there be a law to prevent this, and to make both to pass at the same nominal value, every one will endeavour to discharge his debt at the least possible expense.
>
> (MacLeod, 1884, quoted in Fetter, 1932: 488)

In other words, MacLeod suggested that monetary plurality was possible, and several currencies could circulate together as long as the nominal valuation represented their metallic value. That is how the claim that 'bad money drives out good money' became established, in a context in which what qualified money as 'good' or 'bad' was the veracity of its metallic content.

The confusion around who actually postulated Gresham's Law is less important than exploring why it still dominates monetary thinking in current days. When the US economy was in free fall during the Great Depression and the principle of the gold standard was being questioned, Fetter (1932: 492) elaborated that the favour for a single currency system was ultimately one of 'familiarity' and Gresham's Law was used as a 'catchword' to support monetary singularity. The belief that monetary singularity is a superior monetary solution resonates with the discussion on 'habits of thought' in this volume, a concept coined by Veblen that helps us understand the limitations of some economists, policy makers and so on to revisit the convenience of monetary plurality. Five centuries of repeating Gresham's Law seem to have made it what Searle terms 'an institutional fact' (Searle, 1995) and the statement that 'bad money drives out good money' easily resists scrutiny against substantial empirical evidence that monetary plurality has been and continues to be pervasive. The implication is that monetary singularity has the undeniable advantage that the public feels generally comfortable with it. So, the transition to a different multiple currency system would not happen unless there were undeniably significant advantages and an institutional framework which enables multiple currencies to coexist.

13.4 Modern version of good versus bad money

Finding no trace of Thomas Gresham in Gresham's Law is not sufficient cause to dismiss it as an institutional fact that shapes modern perceptions that money is intrinsically valuable because it is scarce. Gresham and other scholars who constructed the statement that bad money drives out good money framed their thoughts in a world of metallic currencies, reasoning that the difference between the metallic content of money and their legal tender value was the cause for money being 'light' or 'bad'. Currently, almost all money worldwide is fiat money, which is ruled by legal tender laws and normally bears no relation to physical collateral. In other words, money is a layering of credit-debt relations embodied in paper notes and coins, and presently often circulating as electronic and digital transactions via financial institutions. In modern days, Friedman (1990) hence suggested that Gresham's Law needs to be specified more precisely. There have been various attempts to make it more precise, although some authors argued that it should be entirely dismissed. For example, Rolnick and Weber (1986) declared it a 'fallacy', while Velde, Weber and Wright (1999: 1) considered that its 'empirical validity is questionable, or at least seems to depend on circumstances'. This section will look into the modern versions of Gresham's Law in which money is fiat money.

A way to adapt Gresham's Law refers to the 'market value' of money (Selgin, 1996; White, 2000) or to international comparisons between currencies in terms of trust or acceptance, however these are defined. Sometimes the geographical dissemination of a currency in international trade is taken as key indicator of 'good' money. For instance, Hogan (2011) refers to the intrinsic or international value of currencies, in reference to currencies circulating in larger economies that present themselves as more stable in international trade, but which do not have any intrinsic value either. With some rephrasing, Gresham's Law hence results in 'bad or legally overvalued money drives good or legally undervalued money out of circulation' (Hogan, 2011: 2). So, the key issue in the preference for currencies is the difference between the market value (in goods or foreign currency) and the legal value of the notes. If there were no legal tender laws setting a fixed exchange rate between currencies, they would always have equal market value because their values would adjust (White, 2000).

Other authors have considered that Gresham's statement bares little ground, anyway. Rolnick and Weber (1986) showed that there have been multiple cases in history in which 'good' and 'bad' monies circulated together, at the same time and within the same territory. The authors also suggested a further specification for the relation between good and bad money and proposed instead that a multiple currency system is possible when the transaction costs of using more than one currency are similar.

Selgin (1996) built on that version and claimed that the modern version of Gresham's Law is verified in some situations, but a multiple monetary system is possible when there is no loss or gain to be made from the choice of the currency. The relation between currencies depends on the legal tender laws that affect the transaction costs of using various currencies. Selgin (1996) reasoned that monetary plurality creates a Prisoners' dilemma in which domestic transactions emerge as a non-cooperative equilibrium, but legal tender laws can offset that situation and solve or affect the dilemma. That is, Selgin brought back the state as key actor that can affect the fate of currencies in a multiple monetary system. The presence of the state is frequently ignored in discussions about 'good' and 'bad' money under conditions of monetary plurality. The conclusion can also be interpreted as a call to consider the institutional framework around monetary plurality, in contrast to looking at money alone as a reified instrument.

13.5 Institutional frameworks of monetary plurality

The re-introduction of the state as the key actor that affects the value of currencies under conditions of monetary plurality indicates a different direction for the modern version of Gresham's Law and the possibility of monetary plurality. Good and bad money can circulate together provided that legal tender laws equal the transaction costs of the two currencies. In this version, the emphasis is on the state and the institutional framework at national or regional level to define legal tender laws within its territory in such a way that the transaction costs would not create a gain or loss. The last sentence in Selgin's article (1996: 648) addresses precisely that point: 'just how strict legal tender laws must be to give effect to Gresham's law remains an open question'.

On that key issue, several contributions in this volume added information and reflected on the institutional frameworks that enable monetary plurality. Théret's chapters on fiscal federalism are particularly enlightening. If legal tender is a debt that the state has with its citizens, then it can be paid back with a debt that citizens have with the state. The debt with the state is cancelled as tax revenue and it is certain in terms of payment dates and amounts. The state indicates what legal tender it will accept as tax collection, so it can also choose to accept instruments that are not the main currency. An example is the tax anticipation scrip which is not a legal tender, but a voucher or bond accepted in payment for goods and services under specific conditions (for example, during a certain period of time) and that eventually 'dies' when it returns to the state to cancel tax payments. So, its nominal value is pegged to its ultimate fiscal value to repay debts. It was used all over the USA at the local level during the 1930s (Gatch, 2008, 2012).

Forstater (2015) proposes this kind of instrument be issued by local and regional governments to promote their economies and to finance public works. Their taxes act as guarantee of what these vouchers will be worth at the end of their circulation. When recession and unemployment are widespread in a locality, money becomes scarce while labour and resources do not move (Lerner, 1951). Such vouchers can help to increase the mobility of labour and resources. In current days, state agencies have laws that determine what legal tender is, but they do not always have provisions to specify what means of payment are accepted in contracts or to cancel tax debts. The amount of taxes to be paid are indicated in the unit of account enforced in the country, but it is not the same as declaring that the taxes have to be paid with the medium that corresponds to the national unit of account.

California used this system of scrip in 2009. Théret (Chapter 8, this volume) has extensively researched the example of Argentina where badly hit regional economies got a boost and provincial public services were improved when local governments circulated local currencies backed by local taxes. Fiscal federalism is centred on the design of specific local monetary systems that accommodate the interests and needs of subnational entities. It is a middle path for areas that cannot or do not want to leave a national currency area although they need some extra flexibility to manage their finances. It is what Fare (Chapter 10, this volume) refers to as the principle of monetary subsidiarity.

Local tax anticipation scrip is an intermediate solution with a few points of concern. During the Great Depression, when hundreds of local scrips flourished in the USA, Fetter (1932) underlined that the unit of account in which amounts are nominated signals the preference for a currency and indicates it as 'good' money. The unit of account reflects an institutional framework in which all other currencies are to be seen as 'light' currencies: acceptable as long as they can be returned to tax collection offices or converted into 'good' money with transaction costs. This consideration implies that legal tender laws are not enough to defend 'bad' currency and that a closed circular flow, a la Schumpeter (2014 [1970]), is needed to keep a sustainable currency circuit. This point is discussed in the last section of this chapter.

The second point of concern is the scale of the issuance. Again, Fetter (1932: 487) gave a hint that monetary plurality at the local level is possible as long as there is 'not too much of the "bad" money'. *The Economist* presented a similar position when it discussed the example of Greece and concluded that the country could alleviate its shortage of cash by issuing such tax anticipation vouchers, but this solution would only help for a while. The time span hence seems an issue of concern, but the length of this time span is actually unknown. Théret (Chapter 8, this volume) researched the case of the small Argentine province of Tucuman, which used regional scrips for over two decades with the support of the local government and its business elites.

Apart from the role of the subnational state in creating monetary plurality, there is another scenario in which bad money need not drive out good money. It refers to circumstances in which agents may not be able to determine which one is the 'good' and which one is the 'bad' money for them. Fetter (1932) referred to situations in which the public did not care to use some monies because of custom, prejudice or appearance. Accepting any currency is a matter of choice exercised by the seller or the creditor and this choice may be biased by different groups' perceptions, information at the time of defining the transaction costs of the currencies, and a number of non-economic considerations.

In this scenario, the four functions of money become fragmented and performed by different currencies. While the function of reserve of value may best be served by one currency and not others, it is generally of little relevance for the segments of the public that do not save. Agents that use all their income immediately to satisfy basic needs may not have any preference for reserving value but will certainly have a preference for currencies that are easier to obtain and can be used as media of exchange. Examples of this scenario are the *Redes de Trueque* in Argentina, the Community Banks in Brazil and other cases of monetary plurality widespread among the poor in developing countries. These experiences are essentially contextualised and engage specific groups of agents and their circumstances. In this volume, several authors discussed such cases of complementary currencies even when legal tender laws operate. Gómez (Chapter 4, this volume) and Kuroda (Chapter 6, this volume) referred to periods in which multiple currencies performed different functions. Miyazaki and Kurita (Chapter 9, this volume) researched the use of complementary currencies to motivate volunteers. Kobayashi, Hashimoto, Kurita, and Nishibe (Chapter 11, this volume) presented it as a matter of ideological values and perceptions. The difficulties in defining individual preferences are related to one or a combination of reasons: geography, ideology, convenience, accessibility, or function. Again, we reach a discussion on institutions and how they define transaction costs in general, and those of currencies in particular.

There is a third and final scenario in which monetary plurality is possible and which follows Gresham's Law. Once the good money has disappeared, agents continue to exist and need money to sustain their daily economic activities. This scenario relates to situations of crisis in which all the higher quality money has been hoarded or exported from the territory and bad money or no money is left. The reasoning is that the transaction costs of having no media of exchange are infinite, so any currency of whatever quality is better than no currency at all. In situations of extreme economic downturns, such as the Great Depression, the World Wars, the crisis of the Millennium in Argentina and other similarly dramatic events, the good currency is exported or disappears from circulation. These situations confirm the so-called Gresham's Law in the way that MacLeod and Jevons stated it, and they also fit in what Kuroda (Chapter 6, this volume) calls 'famines of cash'. However, that is only one side of the story. Unlike the authors that contributed to phrasing Gresham's Law, Kuroda addressed what happened in various historical moments in reaction to famines of cash. Once the good money is gone, other monies appear and bad money – the only money – becomes 'good enough' money. Elites, local businesses and other groups use the authority they have left to take action to create new local currency. Gómez and von Prittwitz (Chapter 7, this volume) discuss several such historical cases.

So, while Gresham's Law has been historically applied to repeated occasions, there have been many exceptions because it only tells part of the story. Creative agents followed suit to offset the effects of scarce good money. They established new currencies with new units of account or means of payment and media of exchange tied to the disappeared unit of account. The immediate effect was that trade and economic production resurged in the short term, because economic relations got reconnected. For a while at least, monetary plurality has provided suitable though temporary solutions to local economies. In these cases, complementary currencies are no indication of malfunction of the economy but a creative reaction to a crisis that helps in re-establishing some sense of normality in the economy.

13.6 Design principles of monetary plurality

This chapter sought to take a more orthodox monetary approach and follow the established thought on multiple currency systems along the lines of competition between them and the so-called Gresham's Law that would eventually drive the system to monetary singularity. Gresham's Law, however, is not a law and Gresham has barely been involved in it. The statement that bad money drives out good money was accepted as an institutional fact in Searle's sense (1995), which means that it counts as social reality because it relies on the attitudes of mutually independent participants and leads to the subsequent reproduction of attitudes under similar circumstances. At the same time, the chapter adhered to the principle that there is more than one way of organising monetary systems, as repeated by various scholars (Dodd, 2014; Gómez and Dini, 2016; Redish, 2016). It concludes by elaborating on a few principles of complementary currency systems that were discussed in the chapter.

The first design principle has to do with legal tender laws and institutional framework. This presents a triple challenge. First, if a complementary currency has to depend on legal tender laws to make it acceptable, these regulations need to be formal, simple and transparent to secure its stability and confidence. The participation of the state at any level of governance assures the legitimacy and institutionalisation of complementary currencies (Blanc and Fare, 2013). Second, they must be consistent with the national or supranational legal tender laws, which sometimes prohibit the creation of other legal tenders. However, a complementary currency is not necessarily a legal tender but a payment voucher with different attributes. It need not fully qualify as money in terms of the four functions of legal tender laws and other monetary regulations. It ought to be different in terms of its usage or geographical coverage to develop its own appeal to users. This is the third point: it should provide a clear benefit to the networks of users or local economy by promoting income generation, supporting vulnerable groups, disseminating environmentally friendly behaviour, increasing local production and trade, reconnecting economic activities, facilitating access to local services, or any other similar benefits that would make the currency attractive. Considering all the limits and challenges on legal tender regulation, the implementation of a complementary currency would not make sense if the aims or expected outcomes are not substantial and clear to everyone who is supposed to accept it. Théret zooms in on the case of Tucuman with its tax backed currency as a scheme that found an intermediate solution to these three restrictions. Tax anticipation scrips in the USA (Gatch, 2008, 2012) and the vouchers for volunteers in Japan (Miyazaki and Kurita, Chapter 9, this volume) are examples that present similarly intermediate solutions: consistent with the national legal tender laws, easy to defend and use, and with clear expected benefits. In these cases, legal tender laws balanced transaction costs, a requirement of modern versions of Gresham's Law.

The second design principle relates to the conditions of public commitment at the time of introducing the complementary currency. This refers to the insight among the public and media that monetary plurality is a solution to a social problem or, more modestly, at least a tool to alleviate a perceived common difficulty. A complementary currency that most people do not see the need for will probably not become popular once it is launched. Théret (Chapters 5 and 8, this volume) and Gómez (Chapter 4, this volume) emphasise the consensus around some of the provincial currencies in Argentina: the agreement of a series of governors, the local business elites and several groups in the population on creating and sustaining subnational currencies, at least for a period of time. Their circulation increased their acceptance and created a local virtuous circle, but there was significant support or need when they started. Those conditions enabled Tucuman (Chapter 8, this volume) to sustain the Bocade scrip as a structural effort to create a long-term device to gain local autonomy, strengthen the provincial fiscal accounts, increase resilience and promote regional economic development. Gatch (2012) and Blanc (Chapter 3, this volume) similarly underline the importance of public support to accept that the short-term transaction costs may be offset and become a benefit in the longer term.

The third principle is relatively less understood and relates to the separation and completeness of the currency circuits. If multiple currencies do the same in terms of function, time, space, goods and services to trade, actors, and other characteristics, then the currencies will compete in such a way that there will be a distinction between 'good' and 'bad' money. This point was already raised above in connection with legal tender laws. Monetary plurality depends on currency circuits not being competitive but complementary, as shown by Gómez (Chapter 4, this volume), and this has two implications. The first corollary is that multiple currencies should not perform the exact same functions. Each type of money should do something that others do not, which means a supplementary relationship. Kuroda (2008) and Gómez (Chapter 4, this volume) further introduce the idea of 'couples' in reference to the connections between currency, function, and agent. Each currency should be preferred for a specific use or group of users, or characteristic.

A second implication of the completeness of a currency circuit draws on the monetary circuit theory (see, for example, Graziani, 2003; Parguez and Seccareccia, 2000; Realfonzo, 2006; Rochon and Rossi, 2003; Sardoni, 2017) and the Schumpeterian monetary conception (see, for example, Ingham, 2004; Lakomski-Laguerre, 2016; Schumpeter, 1961 [1934], 2014 [1970]). When a currency is introduced, it should subsequently circulate to create a circuit that binds the exchange of a myriad of independent transactions and agents. By definition, a circuit has no start and no end, and this point should be contemplated at the design stage. What are the uses that will support the circulation of the currency with no additional transaction costs? The issuer needs to contemplate both the introduction of the parallel currency and its permanent re-entrance in the circuit, so that the transaction costs would stay the same as those of the currency that serves as unit of account. Again, the tax anticipation scrip is an example. The provincial currencies in Argentina, introduced by partial payment of the wages of public servants, further circulated among independent economic agents such as supermarkets and utilities providers, and were eventually used to pay local taxes at their face value from which they were re-introduced as public wages (Gómez and Dini, 2016). If the currency circuit is not designed as a complete circle (entrance and re-entrance) the transaction costs will be higher than the currency that serves as unit of account. Additional ways of securing its acceptability are access to a common public service (e.g. public transport, tolls and parking), utilities or a key good that most of the public consumes (e.g. petrol, and fresh farm products).

A fourth principle addresses the dimensions of context and purpose and relates to the case of an accomplished Gresham's Law situation in which money has disappeared. In the case of crisis and demise of the financing infrastructure, there would be no 'good' currency as reference, so the principle of comparing preferences and transaction costs would not apply in the same way. Choices are constrained by dire need of media of exchange. Alternatively, there may be a strong shared ideology that creates a similar perception among a group of the population, creating the inclination to favour complementary currencies among a certain public. Blanc (Chapter 3, this volume) refers to them as social currencies, when there is a strong ideology to empower a social group to take back issuing powers from the banks, promote local economies and subnational finances, regenerate social ties, or encourage desirable behaviour such as volunteering and environmental sustainability (examples by Fare, Chapter 10, this volume, and Miyazaki and Kurita, Chapter 9, this volume). Along the same vein, complementary currencies may be specifically targeted at groups that earn irregular or low income.

These four design principles of a multiple money system are based on empirical historical data and several theoretical considerations presented in this volume. The final implication is that in the same way as monetary plurality has been pervasive along the history of human kind, it can also serve as a policy tool. Like all tools, complementary currencies will serve their purpose within specific limits and the appropriate alignment between design and purposes.

References

Blanc J. 2012. Thirty years of community and complementary currencies: a review of impacts, potential and challenges. *International Journal of Community Currency Research* 16(D):1–4.

Blanc J. and Fare M. 2013. Understanding the role of governments and administrations in the implementation of community and complementary currencies. *Annals of Public and Cooperative Economics* 84(1):63–81.

Bossone B., Cattaneo M., Grazzini E. and Labini, S.S. 2015. *Per una moneta fiscale gratuita. Come uscire dall'austerità senza saccare l'euro*. Rome: MicroMega.

Burgon J.W. 1839. *The Life and Times of Sir Thomas Gresham*. https://archive.org/details/in.ernet.dli.2015.40825. London: Effingham Wilson, Royal Exchange London.

Dodd N. 2014. *The Social Life of Money*. Princeton, NJ: Princeton University Press.

The Economist, 25 April 2015. Scrip tease. *The Economist*.

Fare M. and Ould-Ahmed P. 2017. *Why are Complementary Currency Systems difficult to grasp within conventional economics?* Papers in Political Economy, special issue Dialogues et controverses sur la nature sociale du rapport monétaire. Revue Interventions économiques/Papers in Political Economy, no 59. https://journals.openedition.org/interventionseconomiques/3960.

Fetter F.W. 1932. Some neglected aspects of Gresham's Law. *The Quarterly Journal of Economics* 46(3):480–495.

Forstater M. 2015. Complementary currencies, communities, cooperation: the local job guarantee in the Eurozone. In: Bitzenis A., Karagiannis N. and Marangos J., eds., *Europe in Crisis: Problems, Challenges, and Alternative Perspectives*. New York: Palgrave Macmillan. 195–204.

Friedman M. 1990. The crime of 1873. *Journal of Political Economy* 98(6):1159–1194.

Gatch L. 2008. Local money in the United States during the Great Depression. *Essays in Economic and Business History: The Journal of the Economic and Business Historical Society* 26:47–63.

Gatch L. 2012. Tax anticipation scrip as a form of local currency in the USA during the 1930s. *International Journal of Community Currency Research* 16(D):22–35.

Gómez G.M. and Dini P. 2016. Making sense of a crank case: monetary diversity in Argentina (1999–2003). *Cambridge Journal of Economics* 40(5):1421–1437.

Gómez G.M. and Helmsing A.H.J. 2008. Selective spatial closure and local economic development: what do we learn from the Argentine local currency systems? *World Development* 36(11):2489–2511.

Graziani A. 2003. *The Monetary Theory of Production*. Cambridge, UK: Cambridge University Press.

Greenfield R.L. and Rockoff H. 1995. Gresham's Law in nineteenth-century America. *Journal of Money, Credit and Banking* 27(4):1086–1098.

Gregory L. 2014. Resilience or resistance? Time banking in the age of austerity. *Journal of Contemporary European Studies* 22(2):171–183.

Hogan T.L. 2011. Gresham's Law revisited. In: Hogan T.L., ed., *Essays on Money, Banking, and Finance*. Fairfax, VA: George Mason University. 1–24.

Ingham G. 2004. *The Nature of Money*. Cambridge, UK: Polity Press.
Jevons W.S. 1875. *Money and the Mechanism of Exchange* (2001 ed.). London: Elibron Classics.
Kalinowski W., Théret B. and Coutrot T. 2015. Th Veblen Institute, The Euro-Drachma, a Monetary Lifeline for Greece, 16 March 2015. www.veblen-institute.org/The-Euro-Drachma-a-Monetary-Lifeline-for-Greece.html.
Kuroda A. 2008. What is the complementarity among monies? An introductory note. *Financial History Review* 15(1):7–15.
Lakomski-Laguerre O. 2016. Joseph Schumpeter's credit view of money: a contribution to a 'monetary analysis' of capitalism. *History of Political Economy* 48(3):489–514.
Lerner A. 1951. *Economics of Employment*. New York: McGraw Hill.
Lynn, M. 2017. Opinion: Italy's economy could soar with a parallel currency. *MarketWatch*, Vol. Nov 2017. www.marketwatch.com/story/italys-economy-could-soar-with-a-parallel-currency-2017-08-23.
MacLeod H.D. 1884. *The Theory and Practice of Banking*, 4 ed., Vol. 1. London: Longmans, Green, Reader, and Dyer.
MacLeod H.D. 2007 [1858]. *The Elements of Political Economy*. New York: Cosimo Classics.
Montalto Monella L. 2017. Doppia valuta in Italia: primo passo per l'abbandono dell'euro o per il suo rilancio? euronews.com, Vol. Nov 2017. http://it.euronews.com/2017/09/22/doppia-valuta-italia-minibot-borghi-aquilini-dacrema-euro.
North P. 2007. *Money and Liberation. The Micropolitics of Alternative Currency Movements*. Minneapolis, MN and London: University of Minnesota Press.
Parguez A. and Seccareccia M. 2000. The credit theory of money: the monetary circuit approach. In: Smithin J., ed., *What is Money?* London: Routledge. 101–123.
Realfonzo R. 2006. The Italian circuitist approach. In: Arestis P. and Sawyer M., eds., *A Handbook of Alternative Monetary Economics*. Cheltenham, UK: Edward Elgar Publishing. 105–120.
Redish A. 2016. Monetary systems. In: Cassis Y., Grossman R.S. and Schenk C.R., eds., *The Oxford Handbook of Banking and Financial History*. Oxford, UK: Oxford University Press. 321–340.
Rochon L.P. and Rossi S. 2003. *Modern Theories of Money: The Nature and Role of Money in Capitalist Economies*. Cheltenham, UK: Edward Elgar.
Rolnick A.J. and Weber W.E. 1986. Gresham's Law or Gresham's fallacy? *Journal of Political Economy* 94(1):185–199.
Ruding R. 1840. *Annals of the Coinage of Great Britain and its Dependencies: From the Earliest Period of Authentic History of the Reign of Victoria*. London: Hearne.
Sardoni C. 2017. Circuitist and Keynesian approaches to money: a reconciliation? *Metroeconomica* 68(2):205–227.
Schumpeter J.A. 1961 [1934]. *The Theory of Economic Development: An Inquiry into Profits, Capital, Credit, Interest, and the Business Cycle*. New York: Oxford University Press.
Schumpeter J.A. 2014 [1970]. *Treatise on Money*. Aalten, Netherlands: Wordbridge Publishing.
Schwartz P., Cabrillo F. and Castaneda J.E. 2013. Saving monetary union? A market solution for the orderly suspension of Greece. In: Booth P., Rodríguez F.C., Castaneda J.E., Chown J., Dannhauser J., Dowd K., Hengstermann K., Herzog B., Lilico A., Minford P., Record N. and Schwartz P., eds., *The Euro – The Beginning, the Middle . . . and the End?* London: Institute of Economic Affairs. 123–146.

Searle J.R. 1995. *The Construction of Social Reality*. New York: Simon and Schuster.
Searle J.R. 2005. What is an institution? Journal of Institutional Economics 1(1):1–22.
Selgin G. 1996. Salvaging Gresham's Law: the good, the bad and the illegal. *Journal of Money, Credit and Banking* 28(4):637–649.
Seyfang G. and Longhurst N. 2013. Growing green money? Mapping community currencies for sustainable development. *Ecological Economics* 86:65–77.
Skaggs N.T. 1997. Henry Dunning Macleod and the credit theory of money. In: Cohen A.J., Hagemann H. and Smithin J., eds., *Money, Financial Institutions and Macroeconomics*. Dordrecht, Netherlands: Springer. 109–123.
Veblen T. 2004 [1899]. *Theory of the Leisure Class*. Whitefish, MT: Kessinger Publishing.
Velde F.R., Weber W.E. and Wright R. 1999. A model of commodity money, with applications to Gresham's Law and the debasement puzzle. *Review of Economic Dynamics* 2(1):291–323.
White L.H. 2000. *The History of Gold and Silver*. London: Pickering and Chatto.
Williams C., Aldridge T., Lee R., Leyshon A., Thrift N. and Tooke J. 2001. Bridges into work: an evaluation of local exchange trading schemes. *Policy Studies* 22(2):119–132.

Index